973.7
DEN

Denney, Robert E.

THE CIVIL WAR YEARS.

DISCARDED

$29.95

DATE			

THE
CIVIL WAR
YEARS

THE
CIVIL WAR
YEARS

AN ILLUSTRATED CHRONICLE OF THE LIFE OF A NATION

ROBERT E. DENNEY

Foreword by
Gregory J. W. Urwin

Sterling Signature
NEW YORK

Sterling Signature
NEW YORK

An Imprint of Sterling Publishing
387 Park Avenue South
New York, NY 10016

Library of Congress Cataloging-in-Publication Data is available.

10 9 8 7 6 5 4 3 2 1

© 2011 by Robert E. Denney
Distributed in Canada by Sterling Publishing
c/o Canadian Manda Group, 165 Dufferin Street,
Toronto, Ontario, Canada M6K 3H6
Distributed in the United Kingdom by GMC Distribution Services
Castle Place, 166 High Street, Lewes, East Sussex, England BN7 1XU
Distributed in Australia by Capricorn Link (Australia) Pty. Ltd.
P.O. Box 704, Windsor, NSW 2756, Australia

The text featured in this edition is abridged from *The Civil War Years: A Day-by-Day of the Life of a Nation*
originally published by Sterling Publishing Co., Inc., in 1992.

Page ii: Union flag (top), Confederate flag (bottom)
Facing page: The Battle of Nashville, December 16, 1864
Page vi: United States map c. 1860s

Cover design: Kimberly Glyder
Interior design: Oxygen Design/Sherry Williams

ISBN: 978-1-4027-7866-7
ISBN: 978-1-4027-8970-0 (book club)

For information about custom editions, special sales, premium
and corporate purchases, please contact Sterling Special Sales
Department at 800-805-5489 or specialsales@sterlingpublishing.com.

CONTENTS

"This country will be drenched in blood. God only knows how it will end. Perhaps the liberties of the whole country, of every section and every man will be destroyed. . . ."

—**William T. Sherman, December 1860**

"This is no time for man to war against man. The forces of Heaven are loose and in all their fury, the wind howls, the sea rages, the eternal is here in all his majesty. . . ."

—**Private Day, off Cape Hatteras, N.C., January 1862**

" . . . [B]ut just then a white flag was seen to flutter from the rebel works, which proclaimed that the finale had been reached. Then one long, joyous shout echoed and re-echoed along our lines. Its cadence rang long and deep over hill and valley until we caught the glad anthem and swelled the chorus with our voices in one glad shout of joy. It was a glorious opening for the Fourth of July. . . ."

—**Corporal Barber, at the surrender of Vicksburg, July 1863**

EXPLANATION OF THE COLOURS.

Free States and Territories coloured Green.
  The dark Green shows the Free settled States,
  and the light Green the Territories.

Slave-holding States coloured Red.
  The dark Red shows the Slave importing,
  and the light Red the Slave exporting States.

Boundary of the Seceding States, coloured thus ....

Scale of English Miles.

Longitude West of Greenwich.

POPULATION IN 1856.	
FREE STATES.	SLAVE STATES.
California. 335.000	Alabama. 835.192
Connecticut. 401.292	Arkansas. 253.117
Illinois. 1.242.917	Delaware. 97.295
Indiana. 1.149.606	Florida. 110.725
Iowa. 325.014	Georgia. 935.090
Maine. 623.862	Kentucky. 1.086.587
Massachusetts 1.133.123	Louisiana. 600.387
Michigan. 509.374	Maryland. 639.580
New Hampsh. 324.701	Mississippi. 671.649
New York. 3.470.059	Missouri. 831.215
New Jersey. 569.499	N. Carolina. 927.852
Ohio. 2.215.750	S. Carolina. 705.661
Pennsylvania 2.542.960	Tennessee 1.092.970
Rhode Island. 166.927	Texas. 500.000
Vermont. 325.206	Virginia. 1.512.583
Wisconsin. 552.109	10.793.413
15.887.399	

GENERAL MAP OF THE
UNITED STATES
Showing the area and extent of the
FREE & SLAVE-HOLDING STATES,
and the Territories of the
UNION.
also the
Boundary of the Seceding States.

"*... the country mourned the loss of one of its more illustrious defenders, the brave and noble McPherson. When his death became known to the army that he commanded, many brave and war-worn heroes wept like children. ... It is said that Gen. Grant wept when he heard of his death. ...*"

—**Corporal Barber, outside Atlanta,
July 1864**

"*... [I] regard it as my duty to shift from myself the responsibility of any further effusion of blood, by asking of you the surrender of that portion of the C. S. Army known as the Army of Northern Virginia. ...*"

—**Gen. U. S. Grant to Gen. Robert E. Lee,
April 7, 1865**

FOREWORD

✦ ✦ ✦

—

GREGORY J. W. URWIN

THE CIVIL WAR CLAIMED MORE AMERICAN LIVES than any other war in history. It is also the most written-about of America's wars. Though the Confederacy fell nearly [150] years ago, interest in the conflict that swept away the Old South remains high. The best-selling status achieved by such titles as *Battle Cry of Freedom* by James M. McPherson and *The Civil War* by Geoffrey Ward, Ric Burns, and Ken Burns attests to the public's enduring fascination with a period in which the United States nearly destroyed herself.

The elements that account for the Civil War's undying appeal are the same that go into the making of great drama. What other era in American history is so teeming with noble heroes and outright villains, military geniuses and bunglers, unspotted idealism and base corruption, miraculous battlefield victories and tragic defeats? And what single event so changed the nature of this nation or molded the character of her people? Anyone who wishes to understand what the United States is today cannot afford to ignore the Civil War.

In *The Civil War Years*, Robert E. Denney has prepared a rare treat for devotees of what the Lincoln Administration called the War of Rebellion. More than an authoritative reference tool, this is a book to be read from cover to cover, for it allows the reader to experience the Civil War as that struggle unfolded to the people caught up in it. Unlike E. B. Long's straightforward chronology, *The Civil War Day by Day*, Denney augments his daily entries with generous doses of eyewitness testimony. Here are the words of the soldiers, sailors, and civilians of the North and South, woven together in a narrative that is both moving and informative.

Perhaps the two most praiseworthy features of *The Civil War Years* are its comprehensiveness and balance. Far too many overviews of the Civil War are written by authors infatuated with Robert E. Lee and his brilliant exploits in the Eastern Theater. Instead of giving proper coverage to the campaigns waged in Western Theater, where hard-marching Union armies under Grant, Sherman, and Thomas scored the breakthroughs that actually decided the conflict, acolytes of the "Lee Cult" devote a disproportionate amount of their attention to the seesaw struggle in northern Virginia. Consequently, too many Americans still tend to view Johnny Reb as a superman and find it difficult to understand how he lost the war. Furthermore, Denney does not neglect the North's massive naval effort, which turned the South's navigable rivers into invasion routes and steadily inhibited the Confederacy's attempts to sustain her outnumbered armies.

Finally, Denney avoids the common pitfall of depicting the Civil War as some intricate chess game played by politicians and generals. It was a people's contest, demanding an unprecedented level of sacrifice from the opposing masses. It was the people of the North and South, black and white alike, who shaped the war's outcome as much as their leaders. To his credit, Denney lets the men in the ranks tell much of the story. These were the men who did the killing and the dying, the men who upheld the causes defined by the politicians and carried out the decisions made by the generals, and their accounts lead us to an intimate familiarity with the real Civil War.

Denney acquired his sympathy for the lowly GIs of the Civil War—the Billy Yanks and the Johnny Rebs—through hard experience. A decorated combat veteran who saw action both in Korea and Vietnam, he served for three years in the U.S. Marine Corps, followed by seventeen years in the Army. He understands what truly matters to the men who fight wars, which is readily apparent on every page of *The Civil War Years*. He has assembled a haunting chorus of soldier voices to guide us on an unforgettable journey through four years of nightmare and glory.

The Civil War Years possesses a timeless quality, which makes it a worthy addition to our long canon of distinguished Civil War literature. A work of this size and scope demands a considerable amount of a reader's time, but those who make that investment will reap tremendous dividends in both entertainment and increased insight.

PROLOGUE

THE AMERICAN CIVIL WAR has probably been written about more than any other war in history. During the actual conflict, many writers, diarists, and magazines contributed millions of words (representing many man-hours of effort) to the description of people, places, and events. Today, countless scholars and buffs write articles, pamphlets, and books explaining the most minute events of the war. During the centennial celebration, a great surge of literature was published and this flood has scarcely abated.

This book doesn't attempt to prove a point, or establish guilt (or innocence) for any action, political or military, that occurred during that period. It uses actual diaries and books of soldiers who participated in the conflict and records their daily lives. No attempt is made to analyze strategy, tactics, or troop movements.

The characters described within this book are real. Every attempt has been made to breathe life into their stories by providing a perspective of the overall event—the war.

THE MILITARY FORCES AT THE BEGINNING OF THE WAR

At the beginning of 1861, the United States Army and Navy were small indeed for so vast a country. The Army consisted of less than 16,000 officers and men. These were scattered over the entire country, with most of them in the west guarding settlers against Indians.

General Winfield Scott, a native Virginian, the senior officer in the service, was born in 1786. He was 75 at the beginning of the war. A veteran of every war since 1812, he had never commanded more than a few thousand troops in a single mass. Before the war, he was partial to the enlistment of Southern "gentlemen" into the Army, and took great pains to groom them for command. He would eventually be replaced by Major General George B. McClellan (whose ego was larger than Scott's own) and fade from public view. He refused an offer to head the Confederate Army, and chose instead to stay with the Union he had served for more than 40 years.

At the outset of the war there were 1,108 officers in the Army, counting all grades and ranks. Of these, 387 either resigned to join the Confederacy or were dismissed for sympathy with the South. The place of birth wasn't always a factor in where the individual officer placed his loyalty. Many Northerners went with the Confederacy, many Southern-born officers stayed with the North. There were 162 officers of slave-state origin who stayed with the Union. Of the 308 Army officers who listed their birthplaces within the 11 Confederate states, not counting the border states, 222 resigned in 1861, the remaining 86 staying with the Union. Eighty-one Virginia-born officers resigned, 47 remained; from Tennessee, 18 resigned, 7 remained; 24 sons of North Carolina resigned while 8 stayed with the Union; and 6 of 34 South Carolinians fought in Union blue.

Within the United States Navy, in December 1860, there were 1,554 officers present for duty. Of these, 373 "went South"; 157 of that number were dismissed for Southern sympathies.

Much has been made of the resignation of the officers and little is heard of the common soldier or sailor and his beliefs. In the service of 1861 there was little room for regional preferences among the enlisted personnel. They did not have the option of resigning, as did the officers. If they left their duty station to go to the South, they were classed as deserters, and subject to execution if caught. In addition, the army of that day consisted mostly of the dregs of society—

General Winfield Scott (1786–1866), a native Virginian, was in command of the U.S. Army at the onset of the Civil War.

Major General George B. McClellan (1826–85) took control over the Union Army upon Winfield Scott's resignation in November 1861.

After turning down Lincoln's request to head the Union Army in early 1861, Robert E. Lee (1807–70) served as a military advisor to Confederate President Jefferson Davis, eventually taking command of the Army of Northern Virginia.

Joseph E. Johnston (1807–91) was the highest-ranking U.S. Army officer to resign his post to join and lead the Confederate forces.

foreigners, misfits, malcontents, romantics, illiterates, wanderers, and adventurers. Few had regional ties to family or group. Life was hard on the frontier for the common soldier. He could hope for little more than long treks in pursuit of Indians, sleeping on the ground in all kinds of weather and a diet of hardtack and beans. He might become a "pincushion" for some Native American's arrows.

The sailors of the Navy were much like sailors anywhere, at any time, footloose and satisfied if their ship was decently operated. Life at sea in the mid-1800s was no picnic. Discipline was harsh, punishment swift and often cruel, and life expectancy not long. Due to the nature of the sea tradition, there were some black sailors in the Navy at the beginning of the war.

Many of the officers serving in the armies had been classmates at West Point; others never met during their years of service. Although both Lee and Grant served in Mexico during that war, Lee did not remember Grant. Many strong friendships developed before the war and would survive, although some friends would become antagonists. Joe Johnston, the only General Officer to resign and go South, did not meet Sherman until after the Battle of Bentonville in 1865. These two would become good friends and Joe Johnston would attend Sherman's funeral in 1890, where he caught pneumonia from standing in the rain without his hat. Johnston died two weeks later.

Many of the officers, in or out of the service in 1861, were in rather unusual roles at the time the war started. Pierre G.T. Beauregard was Superintendent of West Point. William T. Sherman was head of a school in Baton Rouge, Louisiana, which later became Louisiana State University. McClellan was President of the Ohio and Mississippi Railroad in 1860. Grant was down on his luck after resigning in 1854, and he was "rescued" by the war. Joe Hooker was a farmer in California in 1861, after resigning from the Army in 1853. "Stonewall" Jackson was a professor of Artillery and Natural Philosophy (an unusual combination) at Virginia Military Institute (VMI) after resigning his Army commission in 1851. Leonidas Polk resigned his commission soon after graduation and entered the Virginia Theological Seminary in Alexandria, Virginia. By 1860, he was a bishop in the Episcopal Church in Louisiana.

POPULATION AS SHOWN IN THE 1860 CENSUS

The best picture we can get of the available manpower for the opposing sides in the war is that derived from the census of 1860. The figures are revealing in that they show a very wide disparity between the North and South in available white manpower.

The total population for the country was 34,399,301, which included 29,257,471 whites and 4,441,830 blacks (slave and free) in all the states and the District of Columbia.

Of the white population, 20,010,771 lived outside the fifteen slave states, 5,447,220 within the eleven seceding slave states, and 1,499,480 in the four nonseceding slave states.

Blacks living in the eleven seceding slave states numbered 3,521,130 slaves and only 132,760 free, while those in the four nonseceding slave states had a population of 429,401 slaves and 118,027 free. Blacks living outside the slave states numbered 240,512.

The white population of the eleven seceding states was only 27 percent of the Northern white population—not much of a manpower pool.

The black population of the eleven seceding states was 60 percent of their white population. Of their black population, free blacks were only 3.6 percent of the white population (and most of these blacks were in Virginia, North Carolina, and Louisiana).

During the period of the Civil War, immigration to the Union never ceased, but it was stopped to the Southern states. During this period, about 233,000 Germans, 196,000 Irish, and 85,000 English immigrated to the United States.

THE SOCIETY AND ECONOMIES OF THE NORTH VERSUS THE SOUTH

By 1860, American society was largely concentrated in the few major cities of the North and the South. Southern ladies travelled to New York and Philadelphia on shopping trips and their men bought the latest in mechanical innovations there. Little manufacture was done in the South.

The United States was largely agricultural in 1860. Large cities were few. In that census year, only nine cities had a population of over 100,000, and only seven other cities had a population of over 50,000, none of the latter being in the South. The 1860 census shows the following populations for the major cities involved in the war:

The nine cities in the United States with a population of over 100,000 were: New York (805,651), Philadelphia (562,529), Brooklyn (266,661), Baltimore (212,418), Boston (177,812), New Orleans (168,675), Cincinnati (161,044), St. Louis (160,773), and Chicago (109,260).

The seven cities with more than 50,000 but fewer than 100,000 included the largest, Buffalo (81,129), and the smallest, Providence, R.I. (50,666). Washington, D.C. (61,122) ranked fifth in this category. The others were Newark (71,914), Louisville (68,033), Albany (62,367), and San Francisco (56,802).

Major southern cities, other than New Orleans, all had fewer than 50,000 inhabitants. These included Charleston, S.C. (40,578), Richmond (37,190), Montgomery (35,967), Mobile (29,508), Memphis (22,623), and Savannah (22,292). Other cities smaller than those just mentioned also played a prominent part in the war. These included Nashville, Natchez, Vicksburg, Chattanooga, Atlanta, Raleigh, and Columbia, S.C.

The amount of land under cultivation, the value of the products produced by that land, the livestock supported and used, and the use of products also varied greatly between North and South. The generalized figures, taken from the 1860 census, show the wide disparity.

Improved farmland accounted for more than 106 million acres in the North and a little over 57 million acres in the South. The cash value of the land in the North was in excess of 4.7 billion dollars, as opposed to 1.8 billion dollars in the South.

The North had nearly three times as many horses, and nearly twice the number of working oxen. In milk and beef cattle, sheep and swine, the North far outweighed the South. Only in the production of peas, beans, sweet potatoes, cotton and rice did the South exceed the North. The production of "truck garden" products for sale and preserving was much greater in the North than it was in the South. This category of food production had considerable impact in feeding both the civilian and military population.

The North far exceeded the South in exports and imports in 1860. With incomplete returns for the South, the North exceeded the South by about $195 million in exports and $321 million in imports. The largest ports were New York and New Orleans.

It is obvious from the above figures that the North was in better shape economically at the beginning of the war.

THE ISSUE OF STATES' RIGHTS

In 1798 the four Alien and Sedition Acts were passed by Congress to give then-President John Adams the authority to banish or imprison any foreigner he thought to be dangerous to the government. These acts were never used by President Adams; they were meant to embarrass and defeat Thomas Jefferson, who was running for the Presidency. Jefferson and his friend James Madison instigated legislation in the states of Virginia and Kentucky to proclaim the Alien and Sedition Acts unconstitutional, essentially stating that any act passed by Congress with which the individual state did not agree could be nullified within that state. The concepts of "states' rights" and "nullification" were born.

One major problem was that the Constitution did not provide a means for a law passed by Congress to be declared unconstitutional after it had been signed by the President. During the framing of the Constitution it was assumed that the courts would assume this function, but this did not occur until 1803, when the U.S. Supreme Court stated that the courts had the right to pass on the constitutionality of any act passed by Congress.

This situation simmered during the settlement of the Northwest Territories (later to become the states of Ohio, Indiana, Illinois, Michigan and Wisconsin). There was much sentiment in the Territories for nullification, partly as a resentment against the New England states, which were strongly represented in Congress and, in some cases, laid claim to land in the Territories. Unpopular laws were being passed, as the "westerners" saw it, without due consideration for their own situation. From this area came most of the "western" armies of the Civil War; more than 90 percent of Sherman's army was composed of westerners. Paradoxically, although the western states often wished to counter New England's policies, they were strongly in favor of a central government, which they felt would best protect their interests.

No further overt action was proposed on nullification until 1828, when Congress passed a tariff law, and Senator John C. Calhoun of South Carolina wrote a document called the "South Carolina Exposition," in which was discussed the problem caused by the rising industrial strength of the Northeast influencing Congress to pass protective tariffs that greatly cut the availability of goods in the South. South Carolina even talked of secession. Calhoun's reason for recommending nullification was as an alternative to secession. His argument was that the states had given certain powers to Congress, and that the states alone had the right to say if Congress had exceeded its powers. The "states' rights" were being violated. The great Hayne-Webster debate of 1830 on the floor of Congress was the direct result of Calhoun's document.

Feelings were running very high in the South, and, in particular, in South Carolina. By 1831 the question of states' rights so preyed on the mind of one South Carolinian that he named his son States Rights Gist. Born on September 3, 1831, States Rights attended South Carolina College and went on to Harvard University Law School before setting up a law practice and becoming very active in the militia in his home state. He would later be one of six Confederate generals to die at the Battle of Franklin, Tenn., on November 30, 1864.

Congress again passed a protective tariff in 1832. This prompted South Carolina to declare both the 1828 and 1832 Acts null and void within its boundaries. It even stated its intention of leaving the Union if the laws were enforced. President Andrew Jackson replied with a proclamation to the effect that the tariffs would be collected and the

Medical chest used during the Civil War; many soldiers were very sick, often mortally so, with viral-type diseases that the doctors knew little about.

laws would be enforced. After Congress passed a Force Bill to uphold the President, South Carolina backed off. The concept of nullification died at this time. The concept of states' rights did not die so readily.

MEDICAL PRACTICES AND SERVICES AVAILABLE IN 1861
Union Medical Service and the U.S. Sanitary Commission

Prior to the firing on Ft. Sumter in 1861, the U.S. Army lacked good medical services. The Chief Medical Officer of the Army was a veteran of the War of 1812, fought 47 years previously. He was a martinet who was extremely harsh on his staff and on the doctors serving throughout the country. He is reported to have flown into a rage when he learned that one post actually had two sets of surgical instruments.

The Union Medical Service was tradition-bound, bureaucratic, and slow to respond. Fortunately for the common soldier, this was not to last long. The United States Sanitary Commission was formed early in the war, and took an immediate active interest in the welfare of the troops.

The mobilization of the Union Army in 1861 led to many immediate problems, not the least of which was the availability of doctors for the combat units. The Regular Army Medical Service used its normal procedure of inducting doctors who had recently completed medical school. The states, responsible for the mobilization of the regiments, appointed their own doctors to the various regiments. In many cases the doctor was appointed, like the colonel commanding the regiment, because of political favoritism and not necessarily his qualifications. Some of the governors of the states required examinations, some did not. Among those from the western states (Indiana, Ohio, Iowa, Wisconsin, Minnesota, Kansas, etc.), the doctors from Ohio were among the best. In New England, those from Vermont and Massachusetts were well screened.

The overall medical staff at the beginning of the war consisted of the Surgeon General, 30 surgeons, and 83 assistant surgeons. Pictured here are Confederate surgeons Dr. Wilson Randolph, Dr. Kidder Taylor, Dr. John Randolph Page, and body servant Ben Harris.

One of the major duties of the regimental doctors was the examination of enlistees from their states before their muster into service. Of the first-call volunteers, about 20 percent were discharged for disabilities incurred prior to entering the Army—syphilitics, men over 60 years old, those with hernias, those with no teeth, some with missing fingers. One instance was reported where a doctor "examined" over 90 recruits in one hour. In one Chicago regiment the doctor had recruits parade past him and he passed the entire group en masse. Most often, these unfit men clogged the hospitals and took needed facilities from the troops who were sick or injured after coming into the service. One state, New York, conducted a reexamination of the troops furnished to the Federal service. Of the

farms in isolated or semi-isolated areas, the men came into contact with few people, and with even fewer strangers. The eastern states, with their larger cities, provided a more fertile bed for "childhood" diseases to immunize the citizenry.

A major problem in the initial stages of the war was training the troops in field sanitation. Because most of the western troops, and Southern as well, were from farms, their idea of personal hygiene and the use of toilets was somewhat lacking. The problem was less in those units which were officered by current or former Regular Army officers. Sherman, upon taking command of a regiment early in the war, immediately indoctrinated his junior officers in the use of field latrines and demanded enforcement of good sanitation measures. His personal inspections of his troops' living and mess conditions brought home the message loud and clear. As a consequence, the sick rate in his units was low.

Intestinal infections increased dramatically during the first two years of war. Typhoid fever, caused by polluted water (polluted usually by human feces) caused 17 percent of the deaths in 1861. By 1865, the mortality rate from typhoid had reached 56 percent of those ill with the disease. Diarrhoea and dysentery caused a high sick rate of 64 percent (of all the forces) in the first year of the war, and this increased to 99.5 percent in 1862. Improved field-sanitation conditions brought this rate down dramatically later in the war.

When French military observers visited Union Army troop sites during the period 1861–1862, the drawings and instructions on how to construct a pit latrine were among the more popular items taken back to France.

The Sanitary Commission prepared pamphlets for issue to the troops on the preparation and use of latrines, as well as on personal hygiene items such as bathing. The commission believed that field sanitation was the responsibility of the line officer,

Portrait of Union Army militia drummers

47,417 men initially "accepted" for service, a special board of doctors weeded out 5,554. It was unfortunate that more states did not emulate New York.

By May 1861, around 30 percent of all the troops mustered had been on the sick list at least once. Mostly the complaint was "acute diarrhoea." The health of the troops from the eastern states was better than that of those from the western states, especially concerning communicable diseases such as measles, chicken pox, mumps, and smallpox. Because of the rural environments of the western states, where cities were small, towns and villages even smaller, and most of the population lived on

from the colonel down through the lieutenant.

Other major contributors to poor health were the clothing and food issued to the troops. Initially, the states were responsible for the "outfitting" of the regiments. This included providing them with proper uniforms (including undergarments), blankets, eating utensils, and weapons. When a regiment was equipped and mustered into Federal service, the state would then present a bill to the Federal government for the cost. Governments being what they are, this worked well in some cases, but not so well in others. Some troops were provided shoddy uniforms, and the state "contractors" were paid in full for the equipment.

Food was a major problem once the troops went into camp. Rather than use a common kitchen for an entire company, usually about 100 men, the men formed themselves into informal "messes," where resources were "pooled" and the individual who knew how to boil water was appointed cook. If no one knew how to boil water, they drew straws. The results of this arrangement can be imagined. The food, in most cases, was almost inedible after being cooked. The type of food was somewhat limited; usually it was a hard-baked (water, salt and flour) cracker, salt pork in various stages of preservation, beans, and coffee. Sometimes the hardtack crackers were ground using stones (or one-half of an old mess kit with nail holes in it to make a grater), and then added to other items or combined with water, formed into cakes and fried in bacon fat. The troops fried rice and beans, they fried beef, they fried everything they could get into their skillets. The doctors often referred to their ailments as "death from the frying pan."

Seldom were fresh vegetables issued. If they were available locally, the price was usually much higher than normal, due to price-gouging by local farmers. Late in 1862, the Union Army tried a new dried-vegetable mixture called "desiccated vegetables" (referred to by the troops as "decimated vegetables"). It was described variously as "not fit for the hogs," "tasteless to the extreme," and these were some of the nicer descriptions. It did have one advantage in that it stored well, and thousands of tons of it were issued from Virginia to Georgia for the Union troops. The results of this diet could be easily predicted—stomach ailments, scurvy, and general ill health.

Another problem was that several days' rations were issued at one time, and the soldier would eat his three days of food in one day. He then went hungry for the following two days. There were numerous instances where soldiers in formation would faint from weakness because they had not eaten for two or three days.

U.S. Army–issued crackers; hardtack crackers had to be soaked in water, coffee, or some other liquid to make them even chewable.

Confederate Medical Service

The Confederate government had an entirely different problem. There were neither established offices nor channels for the army medical profession in 1861. These had to be created, using what personnel they had gained from the U.S. Army, and from the volunteers available.

While rapid progress was made in most areas of organization and administration, the greatest advance was in the organization of the hospital system throughout the South. By the end of 1863, approximately 18 months after the First Battle of Bull Run (Manassas), the medical service had organized military hospitals in many locations. Among these were Virginia (39), North Carolina (21), South

Carolina (12), Georgia (50), Alabama (23), Mississippi (3), Florida (4), and Tennessee (2).

The number of men flowing in and out of Confederate hospitals equalled the number in the Northern hospitals, and surpassed it in many ways. The South's largest hospital, the Chimborazo in Richmond, had a very impressive record in treatment and humanity. Always working with limited resources, during the period from Nov. 1, 1861, to 1863, that hospital admitted 47,176 patients, of whom 17,384 were transferred, 17,845 returned to duty, 4,378 were furloughed, 635 were discharged, 846 deserted, and 3,031 died. This was a very low mortality rate, a little over 6 percent, considering the conditions. The number of desertions is surprising. The number returned to duty during this two-year period represents two Confederate corps, or more.

Within the Department of Virginia during the period Sept. 1862–Dec. 1863, the 39 hospitals in service processed 293,165 patients, as if all of Lee's army had been admitted to the hospital three times. Of this number, 95,875 were returned to duty, 2,807 were discharged as unfit for duty, 4,446 deserted, and 19,248 died. The toll in human suffering was vast and far-reaching.

UNITED STATES SANITARY COMMISSION

The origin of the Sanitary Commission and its growth during the early part of the war presents a study in organizational capabilities. Originally just one of several organizations that provided much needed succor to the troops, it grew rapidly, and, as its organization was superior to that of other groups, it rapidly became the controlling force that coordinated relief efforts.

The original groups were formed by women, usually mothers, sisters or wives of soldiers, who felt that they should do "their part" for the Union. The initial efforts were to manufacture and organize the supply of hospital necessities, such as bandages and

Savage Station, Va., field hospital, June 30, 1862

Sanitary Commission rest house in Washington, D.C., c. 1861–69

lint. This further spread to the making of shirts, drawers, hospital gowns, bedding kits, etc., as well as the collection of money to furnish such items as sewing kits, writing paper, and stamped envelopes.

At the beginning, there was much duplicated effort, resulting in a glut of some items and an extreme shortage of others. Too, the packing of the items was somewhat less than efficient, and many packages were spoiled when food (packed with clothing) turned rancid or rotted. The Commission eventually organized depots where local support groups sent their contributions. At these places, all packages were opened, examined, and repackaged. Like items were packed together—shirts with shirts, drawers with drawers, etc.—and all items were clearly stamped with indelible ink stating they were from the Commission. Packages were clearly

labelled with their contents, and with Commission markings. This prevented the looting of the supplies by transportation handlers, etc., who might sell the items to the soldiers for their own profit.

The object of the Sanitary Commission was to cut the government red tape, and to provide the necessary support in a flexible and efficient manner, something no government had ever achieved. The Commission began with a Doctor Bellows, who visited Washington in 1861 and went back to New York with a plan of organization and the blessings of the President and the Secretary of War. The highest officials of the government felt that the Commission "could do no harm."

All major officials of the Commission were medical professionals who devoted much time and money to the effort. The Commission doctors were sent to inspect the camps and the mess facilities to garner information on which to base recommendations. Their primary concern was the health of the troops. Early in the war, the Commission published 18 pamphlets dealing with field sanitation in the camps, handling of the sick and wounded, the use and storage of medicines, etc. These pamphlets proved invaluable to the government in the control of disease and the alleviation of suffering.

Several innovations were instituted by the Commission. Among these were the development and use of wheeled kettles in which soup was prepared in the rear areas of the battlefield to be served to the wounded or injured, even while the battle was raging.

The Commission also established a series of "Soldiers' Homes" or "Soldiers' Rests" along the routes the soldiers followed going to and from the fighting areas. A forerunner of the USO as we know it, these "rest stops" furnished dormitories, good food, libraries, bathing and laundry facilities, etc., to all who needed them. During the war, over 800,000 soldiers availed themselves of these services, eating over 4,500,000 meals and lodging for 1,000,000 nights. All of this was furnished to the troops free. The cost was paid by the communities and by donations of food and services.

There was no Federal allotment of money to the families of the troops during the war. Some states did provide a small allowance, but this was not common. The Commission established a "Claim Agency" to help the soldiers obtain their "bounty" payments when they were in arrears. A "Pension Agency" was also established to aid the soldier who was discharged for disability (often because of an amputation) to get his pension from laggard government agencies. It also had a "Back Pay Agency," which helped the soldier whose paybook was lost (or otherwise not usable) to gain his pay. This was a very useful service in an army where many were illiterate.

A locator service, called the "Hospital Directory," was established where information on patients and invalids in the 233 general hospitals could be found. These directories were established in Washington, Philadelphia, New York, and Louisville, where the names of more than 600,000 men were registered.

During a battle or engagement the Commission was always on the battlefield to care for the wounded and to relieve suffering.

GENERAL TACTICS AND STRATEGY IN 1861

The military tactics used by both sides were identical in most cases. There were very few surprises in the way the troops were handled, and in the way the logistics problems were solved. Depending upon the individual commander (some being stronger in defense than offense), the formations were alike, and artillery was handled similarly. Several of the general officers on both sides had spent time in Europe during the Crimean War or visiting the old Napoleonic battlefields such as Waterloo (Jackson had visited the latter, McClellan the Crimea). Frontal assaults were in vogue, and if a flank attack could be developed, so much the better. Infantry formations were elbow to elbow. The belief was that mutual support could be gained by the physical presence of one's comrades. Such formations also provided easier control of the troops by the company line officers. Since all communication was by voice (with the exception of some drums), the proximity of the commander to those being commanded was essential.

Artillery was used aggressively by both sides, the guns being placed as far forward as possible in direct support of the infantry. Both sides used identical guns. As opposed to modern American military designations of millimetres of diameter (105 mm, 155 mm, etc.), the guns were measured in "inches of bore" or by the weight of the missile, such as the "22-pounder," etc. The guns were usually of bronze- or cast-iron-based metal. Ranges for the weapons varied with the size and temperature of the gun tube at the time of firing. Massed guns were desired, but seldom achieved. Gettysburg was one of the exceptions, where over 100 guns were brought to bear on a single target.

Cavalry, as a combat arm, was not widely developed. There were few battles where cavalry action was the major factor in a win or loss. In general the terrain over which the battles were fought was not suitable for large cavalry formations, unlike the terrain in Europe. Some commanders, such as Nathan Bedford Forrest, used the cavalry effectively by mounting Confederate infantry for transportation to the battle site in order to rapidly close with the enemy—an effective stratagem, but not widely used by either side. In general, cavalry was used for scouting and for protecting the flanks of troops during a battle.

LOGISTICS

There has never been a war won without a major effort made in logistics. The glory goes to the infantry or to other combat arms, but the real battle is fought with rations, shelter, ammunition, transportation, and medical support. Of the commanders, North and South, going to war in 1861, there were few who had any experience in the logistics of waging a long campaign. For starters, the governments had never fielded such large armies.

General Joseph Hooker's division fords a creek to attack Confederate forces during the Battle of Antietam, September 1862.

Considering the transportation available at the beginning of the war and its vulnerability to attack, there were some very rude lessons to be learned by some very senior commanders. Think about the feeding of the men and animals in McDowell's army that fought at 1st Manassas. How would you start to feed 35,000 men three times a day and provide forage for over 1,000 animals? With poorly developed food storage capabilities (the preservation of vegetables, etc., in metal cans was not widely developed), the rations had to be salt-cured or fresh. This led to maintaining large herds of cattle on the hoof, and using cured bacon and hams (generally referred to as salt horse). Few advances were made in this area (except in the drying of vegetables) during the war.

Road transportation was always a major problem. Roads that could support troops and artillery in large numbers, in all weather, were few. Both armies were disadvantaged by the use of long wagon trains carrying war materiél. Grant's trains leaving the Wilderness were more than 25 miles long, and they moved extremely slowly.

Railroads were used for the first time tactically (for the movement of troops to a battle) and strategically (such as Sherman's movement of supply bases forward to support his Atlanta campaign). This was done at a very high cost in manpower to guard the railroad lines from guerrilla or other attack. The Union developed the most efficient means of replacing destroyed track or laying new track. At the beginning of the war, the North

The Orange and Alexandria Railroad, an intrastate Virginia railroad, played a crucial role as one of the most fought-over railroads during the Civil War. Shown here is the Union Mills Station in Clifton.

was far better equipped to move large volumes of matériel and troops than was the South. In 1860 the South had about 8,500 miles of track (over 1,700 of these were in Virginia) compared to over 22,000 miles in the North. The North had more connecting lines, facilitating the movement of traffic. Before the war was over, the Northern U.S. military railroads alone would have 2,105 miles of track with over 400 locomotives and 6,000 railway cars.

The South had only one direct route from Richmond to Memphis (via Chattanooga). Many of the Southern tracks were of different gauge (the measured distance between the rails) and this meant changing trains often during a journey. The South had fewer locomotive construction resources to call on, and, consequently, it was faced with an ever increasing problem of repair and maintenance.

Some innovations were made in the outfitting of railcars for the transportation of wounded by slinging litters in leather straps within the cars. Little of this was done, however; the wounded were laid on straw in boxcars that had previously carried supplies or animals.

COMMUNICATIONS AND TRANSPORTATION

The United States Mail was the primary means of communication between the various parts of the country in 1861. Mail was still being delivered to South Carolina and the other Confederate states as late as April 1861. The Confederate mail service was adapted directly from the U.S. Mail, using the same facilities and personnel. There was a system devised in late 1863 between the opposing governments whereby mail could be delivered under a "flag of truce." The troops of the Kentucky "Orphan Brigade" used this method to communicate with their families in Union-held Kentucky. U.S. postage was required, however.

The telegraph was much more widely used in the North than it was in the South, even before the war. The more industrialized North had installed over 15,000 miles of lines for the operation of the U.S. Military Telegraph, used by the Union forces during the war. The South, short of trained operators and equipment, never reached the capacity of the North, and it even lost ground as the Union occupied Southern territory.

The steam riverboat had not been around for very many years before the war began, but in a span of about 30 years the number of steamboats available had steadily proliferated. The boats were generally of shallow draft and could navigate most of the rivers, North and South. The larger boats, of course, ran the Mississippi, Ohio, and Missouri Rivers. Some of the larger and many of the medium-size boats navigated the Cumberland and Tennessee Rivers in Kentucky and Tennessee, as well as the other rivers of the South. The smaller boats, of which there were hundreds, were used as "local" transportation to service the smaller towns along the waterways for both passenger and freight traffic. Boat transportation was both cheap and reliable.

Railroads were much more prominent in the North even at the beginning of the war. The North used a common gauge of track (something the South failed to do) and had many more connecting lines between major railroad trunks. Each line built its own railway stations, some cities having as many as three stations. The concept of bringing all tracks into a common "Union" station had not been developed. In the early stages of the war, troops from Massachusetts marching from one station to another in Baltimore were set upon by a pro-Southern mob, resulting in the death of some of the demonstrators.

Field telegraph battery wagon—telegraph wires usually followed railroad tracks from city to city, and the lack of track in the South was a real handicap.

1861

This country will be drenched in blood. God only knows
how it will end. Perhaps the liberties of the whole country,
of every section and every man will be destroyed. . . .

—William T. Sherman, December 1860

⤙ PRELUDE ⤚

TERRIBLE AGONY AFFLICTED THOSE of the North and South who wished to find some way of reconciling the differences between the regions. South Carolina, with fire-eaters in control, had dealt the fatal blow by seceding from the Union. These same people blamed the Federal government and the Republican Party for their own departure, ignoring Lincoln's message at the Cooper Union in February 1860 on South Carolina's excuses for dissolving the Union. At that time, Lincoln reminded the South:

> Under all these circumstances, do you really feel yourself justified to break up this Government, unless such a court decision as yours is shall be at once submitted to as a conclusive and final rule of political action?
>
> But you will not abide the election of a Republican President! In that supposed event, you say, you will destroy the Union; and then, you say, the great crime of having destroyed it will be upon us?
>
> This is cool. A highwayman holds a pistol to my ear, and mutters through his teeth, "Stand and deliver, or I shall kill you, and then you will be a murderer!"
>
> To be sure, what the robber demanded of me—my money—was my own, and I had a clear right to keep it; but it was no more my own than my vote is my own; and the threat of death to me, to extort my money, and the threat of destruction to the Union to extort my vote, can scarcely be distinguished in principle.

Among the officers of the United States Army and Navy located around the country, it was a time for soul-searching and heart-wrenching decisions. For those of Southern birth it was especially difficult: Having served the Union for so long, where did their loyalty lie? Many others were faced with the separation of business and personal ties. In Louisiana, where William T. Sherman was the head of the Louisiana State Seminary of Learning and Military Academy later to become Louisiana State University at Baton Rouge, the decision had been made. In late December of the previous year he stated his position clearly:

> If Louisiana assumes a position of hostility toward the government, then this Seminary becomes an arsenal and a fort, and I quit. . . . I will do no act, breathe no word, think no thought hostile to the government of the United States. . . . You may assert that in no event will I forego my allegiance as long as a single state is true to the old Constitution.

When Christmas Eve of 1860 arrived, and Sherman was nearly alone in the Seminary in Baton Rouge, the newspapers brought news of South Carolina's secession. Sherman, in the depths of despair, addressed his friend David F. Boyd, who was Professor of Ancient History at the Seminary, on the effects of this secession:

> You, you the people of the South, believe there can be such a thing as peaceable secession. You don't know what you are doing. I know there can be no

Abraham Lincoln (1809–65) served as the 16th President of the United States from March 1861 until his assassination in April of 1865.

PRECEDING PAGES: Union soldiers of the 12th New York State Militia in formation at Franklin Square, Washington, D.C., June 11, 1861

such thing . . . If you will have it, the North must fight you for its own preservation. Yes, South Carolina has by this act precipitated war. . . . This country will be drenched in blood. God only knows how it will end. Perhaps the liberties of the whole country, of every section and every man will be destroyed, and yet you know that within the Union no man's liberty or property in all the South is endangered. . . .

You people speak so lightly of war. You don't know what you are talking about. War is a terrible thing. I know you are a brave, fighting people, but for every day of actual fighting, there are months of marching, exposure and suffering. More men die in war from sickness than are killed in battle. At best war is a frightful loss of life and property, and worse still is the demoralization of the people. . . .

You mistake, too, the people of the North. They are a peaceable people, but an earnest people and will fight too, and they are not going to let this country be destroyed without a mighty effort to save it.

Besides, where are your men and appliances of war to contend against them? The Northern people not only greatly outnumber the whites at the South, but they are a mechanical people with manufactures of every kind, while you are only agriculturists—a sparse population covering a large extent of territory, and in all history no nation of mere agriculturists ever made successful war against a nation of mechanics. . . .

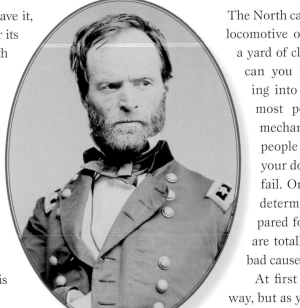

William Tecumseh Sherman
(1820–91), Union Army General

The North can make steam-engine, locomotive or railway car; hardly a yard of cloth or a pair of shoes can you make. You are rushing into war with one of the most powerful, ingeniously mechanical and determined people on earth—right at your doors. You are bound to fail. Only in your spirit and determination are you prepared for war. In all else you are totally unprepared, with a bad cause to start with.

At first you will make headway, but as your limited resources begin to fail, and shut out from the markets of Europe by blockade, as you will be, your cause will begin to wane . . . if your people would but stop and think, they must see that in the end you will surely fail . . .

Braxton Bragg, an old friend of Sherman's from Army service and West Point, was out of the Army and in business in Louisiana. He had been appointed by the Governor of Louisiana to "organize the Commonwealth against the danger of war." Realizing that Sherman was going North, he wrote his thoughts on secession to Sherman late in December 1860:

You are acting on a conviction of duty to yourself and to your family and friends. A similar duty on my part may throw us into an apparent hostile attitude, but it is too terrible to contemplate and I will not discuss it.

You see the course of events—South Carolina is gone, nothing can recall her. The Union is already dissolved. . . . The only question is: can we reconstruct any government without bloodshed? I do not think we can—a few old political hacks and barroom bullies are leading public opinion. . . . They can easily pull down a government, but when another is to be built who will confide in them? Yet no one seems to reflect that anything more is necessary than to secede.

Major Robert Anderson, USMA class of '25, was 56 years old in 1861, and a veteran of the Black Hawk, Seminole, and Mexican wars. A native Kentuckian, he would remain with the Union. Since November 1860, Anderson had been commanding the Army garrison at Ft. Moultrie, S.C., at the mouth of Charleston Harbor. When seriously threatened after South Carolina seceded, he moved his entire garrison to the island of Ft. Sumter under the cover of darkness. The South Carolinians were outraged at having been tricked. A delegation from Charleston met with no success in getting Anderson to remove himself from Sumter.

JANUARY 1861

JANUARY 3 THURSDAY
The War Department cancelled plans to ship guns from Pittsburgh to the forts in the South. Former Secretary of War Floyd, who resigned and went South, had been shipping weapons and large guns South for the past several months to help build up the Southern arsenal. Delaware rejected a proposal that it join the South in seceding.

JANUARY 6 SUNDAY
The U.S. Arsenal at Apalachicola, Fla., was seized by the state with no resistance.

The governor of Maryland sent a message to the people strongly opposing Maryland's secession from the Union.

JANUARY 9 WEDNESDAY
In Jackson, Miss., the State Convention met and voted 84 to 15 to secede. Mississippi was the second state to leave the Union.

JANUARY 10 THURSDAY
Braxton Bragg and the militia seized the United States forts and arsenals in Louisiana. Sherman spurred his horse to Alexandria and resigned.

At Tallahassee, the Florida Convention voted for secession 62 to 7, making it the third state to secede.

William H. Seward, Lincoln's old opponent for the Republican presidential nomination, accepted the post of Secretary of State.

In the United States Senate, Jefferson Davis called upon the Senate to act. This call came from a senator representing a state that had already seceded from the Union. In his call he stated:

> Senators, we are rapidly drifting into a position in which this is to become a Government of the Army and Navy in which the authority of the United States is to be maintained, not by law, not by constitutional agreement between the States, but by physical force; and you will stand still and see this policy consummated?

According to Davis, "If secession was necessary, it was a quarrel not of the South's making and if allowed to separate peacefully, there need be no difficulty."

JANUARY 11 FRIDAY
By a vote of 61 to 39, the State of Alabama left the Union. The vote against secession was higher here than it was in the preceding three states. In Montgomery, as in Jackson, the crowds cheered and set off fireworks when the news was announced. In Charleston, the surrender of Sumter was again demanded and was again refused by the dauntless Anderson.

Mass meetings and demonstrations continued in the North and South.

JANUARY 12 SATURDAY
The State of Mississippi, having left the Union, withdrew its Representatives from the House. At the same time, artillery seized from the Federal arsenals was ordered to Vicksburg in order to stop shipping on the Mississippi.

As the satirical cartoon indicates, in early 1861, relations between Washington and South Carolina were strained, with Governor Pickens demanding control of Fort Sumter. On January 13, President Buchanan, who had mere months left in office, declared that Sumter would not be surrendered under any circumstance.

JANUARY 19 SATURDAY

In a State Convention at Milledgeville, Georgia became the fifth state to secede by a vote of 208 to 89—a large majority. This was a turnaround from the sentiment before the 1860 national elections. Before Lincoln was elected, a majority of Georgians were pro-Union.

Virginia, in an attempt to settle matters peacefully, called for a convention of all the Southern states in Richmond to "discuss the problem."

JANUARY 25 FRIDAY

Many naval officers resigned their commissions and joined the Confederate Navy. This was very upsetting to Capt. Samuel F. Du Pont (of the Delaware Du Ponts) who wrote Commander, later Admiral, Andrew Hull Foote:

> What made me most sick at heart, is the resignations from the Navy. . . . I [have been] nurtured, fed and clothed by the general government for over forty years, paid whether employed or not, and for what—why to stand by the country, whether assailed by enemies from without or foes within—my oath declared "allegiance to the United States" as well as to support the Constitution. . . . I stick by the flag and the national government as long as we have one, whether my state does or not and she knows it.

JANUARY 26 SATURDAY

Louisiana voted for secession 113 to 17. Business in New Orleans was almost at a standstill because the Mississippi was closed to both Northern river traffic and to foreign ships coming in from the Gulf.

JANUARY 29 TUESDAY

Kansas was admitted to the Union as the thirty-fourth state. Largely pro-Union, it would be racked by guerrilla warfare and border raids from Missouri.

JANUARY 31 THURSDAY

In New Orleans, the U.S. Branch Mint, located on the waterfront of the Mississippi River, was seized by the state troops, as was the Revenue Schooner *Washington*.

∞ FEBRUARY 1861 ∞

A NEW GOVERNMENT WOULD BE formed in Alabama that would assume the responsibilities of creating a new nation during the turmoil of a civil war. In Washington, many were still trying for compromise—a hopeless undertaking.

FEBRUARY 1 FRIDAY

A convention in Texas voted for secession 166 to 7 and set the date for departure at February 23rd.

Lt. Col. Robert E. Lee, a veteran of nearly 32 years of service in the U.S. Army, departed Texas for Virginia upon the secession of Texas from the Union.

Robert Edward Lee, a native Virginian, born in 1807, son of "Light Horse Harry" Lee, the Revolutionary War cavalry hero, was graduated second in his class from West Point in 1829. A veteran of the Mexican War of 1849, he served as the Engineering Officer for that expedition. He was later Superintendent of West Point during a three-year period, 1852–55. Lee served with the cavalry in Texas in 1856–57 and was on leave visiting his wife's home, "Arlington," in 1859 when he was assigned to command a detachment of marines to capture John Brown at Harpers Ferry. He returned to Texas in 1860 to rejoin his regiment and was there when Texas seceded from the Union. He returned to "Arlington" to await developments.

General Robert E. Lee on his favorite horse, "Traveler"

Jefferson Davis (1808–89) resigned as a U.S. Senator representing the State of Mississippi upon learning that Mississippi had seceded from the Union. He was elected President of the Confederate States of America in February of 1861 and remained in office until the end of the war.

Vice-President of the Confederacy, Alexander Stephens (1812–83) served as a U.S. Representative from Georgia both before and after the war.

FEBRUARY 4 MONDAY

A Convention of the seceded states met to form the Confederacy and elect their officials in Montgomery.

FEBRUARY 9 SATURDAY

Jefferson Davis was elected President for six years with no option for reelection. Alexander Stephens of Georgia was elected Vice President. In a little twist, the Convention declared all United States laws to remain in force unless they conflicted with the new Confederate Constitution.

In Tennessee, voters rejected the proposal to call a convention to consider secession by nearly 10,000 votes. It would remain for the state politicians to finagle the State of Tennessee out of the Union.

The United States Mail continued to be delivered everywhere, North and South. Commerce went on almost as it had before, with some slowdown on river traffic in the west.

The Southern Congress, in an attempt to court the old Northwestern states of Indiana, Ohio, Michigan, Illinois, and Wisconsin, voted to keep the Mississippi open for navigation of commerce.

FEBRUARY 11 MONDAY

The previous day in Mississippi, Jefferson Davis was in the garden with his wife, Varina, pruning rosebushes. A courier arrived and Davis learned he was the new President of the Confederacy.

The train was leaving Springfield at 8 o'clock on this drizzly morning for Washington. Aboard would be President-elect Lincoln and his party of 15. With saddened face, Lincoln addressed his hometown crowd for the last time:

> My friends, no one not in my situation can appreciate my feeling of sadness at this parting. To this place and the kindness of these people I owe everything. Here I

have lived for a quarter of a century, and have passed from a young man to an old man. Here my children have been born, and one is buried. I now leave, not knowing when, or whether ever, I may return, with a task before me greater than that which rested upon Washington. Without the assistance of that Divine Being who ever attended him, I cannot succeed. With that assistance I cannot fail. Trusting in Him who can go with me and remain with you and be everywhere for good, let us confidently hope that all will yet be well. To His care commending you, as I hope in your prayers you will commend me, I bid you an affectionate farewell.

FEBRUARY 16 SATURDAY

In Montgomery, Davis arrived to serve as President of the Confederacy. He exclaimed, "We ask nothing; we want nothing; we have no complications."

FEBRUARY 18 MONDAY

This day saw the inauguration of Jefferson Davis, amid much fanfare and highly emotional speeches.

FEBRUARY 20 WEDNESDAY

In Montgomery, the Confederate Navy was officially established.

FEBRUARY 22 FRIDAY

In Philadelphia, on the anniversary of George Washington's birth, Lincoln spoke at Independence Hall:

I have never had a feeling politically that did not spring from the sentiments embodied in the Declaration of Independence. It was that which gave promise that in due time the weights should be lifted from

the shoulders of all men, and that all men should have an equal chance.

FEBRUARY 23 SATURDAY

After traveling all night from Harrisburg via Philadelphia and Baltimore, Lincoln arrived in Washington at 6 AM.

In Texas the voters approved secession by a vote of 34,794 to 11,235.

FEBRUARY 27 WEDNESDAY

In Washington, Congress was vainly attempting to arrive at some solution to the problem of slavery and states' rights. All amendments failed and the end of compromise drew closer.

Gov. Pickens of South Carolina wrote President Davis that "we feel that our honor and safety require that Ft. Sumter should be in our possession at the very earliest moment."

FEBRUARY 28 THURSDAY

In Washington, Congress voted to form the Territory of Colorado as a part of the Union. In Congress also, the House passed an amendment, approved by the President-elect, stating that slavery could not be interfered with in those states where it already existed.

In Raleigh, N.C., a majority of 651 votes showed the state rejecting a state convention on secession and a very strong pro-Union sentiment emerging. The same sentiment was present in eastern Tennessee, where the request for a similar convention was defeated by more than 10,000 votes. This sentiment was also present in western South Carolina, and in northwestern Georgia. Most of these areas were not slaveholding.

At Montgomery, Ala., the Confederate Congress decided to borrow $15,000,000 to support the government. More would be asked for.

The inauguration of Jefferson Davis in Montgomery, Alabama, February 18, 1861

∽ MARCH 1861 ∽

IN THE SOUTH, tension was building to a fever pitch. So far, seven states had left the Union and set up their own government. Would it last? Would the North demand the price for secession in blood? In Washington, President Buchanan's administration awaited the inauguration of the new President, doing nothing in the meantime. This somewhat rural city was flooded with newcomers seeking office and appointments. In just a few days, the destiny of the nation would be in the hands of a new leader and no one knew to what pressure he would bow.

MARCH 1 FRIDAY

At Charleston, S.C., Gen. Pierre G. T. Beauregard was assigned command of the area for the Confederacy.

Major Robert Anderson still held Ft. Sumter and maintained such friendly relations with the Charlestonians that rations were supplied to the fort from the city. The Confederates were, however, building forts themselves to threaten Sumter.

Pierre Gustave Toutant Beauregard was born in St. Bernard Parish, La., on May 28, 1819. Of Creole parentage, he spoke French before he spoke English. He was graduated from West Point, class of '38, ranking second in a class of 45. He served as an engineer in the Mexican War, receiving two wounds and two brevets for gallantry. Appointed as Commandant of West Point as a Major in January 1861, he shortly resigned his commission and joined the Confederate Army as a Brigadier General. At the end of the war he returned to New Orleans, where he served as the supervisor of the state lottery and

An illustration depicting various Confederate uniforms in 1861

as the state Adjutant General. He died in New Orleans on February 20, 1893.

In Richmond, tension mounted as the decision to secede came closer and more pressure was placed on the state government to act.

MARCH 2 SATURDAY

The Territory of Nevada was added to the Union as was the Dakota Territory, which contained what would become both North and South Dakota and most of Wyoming and Montana. In a bald-faced attempt to appease the Southern states, Congress offered an amendment to the Constitution to provide that " . . . no amendment shall be made to the Constitution which will authorize or give Congress the power to abolish or interfere within any State with the domestic institutions thereof, including that of persons held to labor or service by said State." While this was never approved by the several States, it was indicative of the mood of the times and the reconciliation attempts being made.

In Montgomery, Ala., the Confederacy admitted Texas into its new government.

MARCH 4 MONDAY

Inauguration Day in Washington. Lincoln would become the 16th President of the United States and would preside over one of the deadliest wars in history.

Lincoln's address was clear and simple:

In your hands, my dissatisfied fellow countrymen, and not in mine, is the momentous issue of civil war. The government shall not assail you. You can have no conflict, without being yourselves the aggressors. You have no oath registered in Heaven to destroy the government, while I have the most solemn one to "preserve, protect and defend" it.

General Pierre G. T. Beauregard (1818–93) served the Confederate Army and had many nicknames, including "Little Napoleon."

MARCH 11 MONDAY

The Confederate Congress in Montgomery adopted the Constitution of the Confederacy, which would be ratified by the end of April 1861.

Brigadier Gen. Braxton Bragg of North Carolina assumed command of all Confederate forces in Florida.

Gen. Scott replied to Lincoln that it was uncertain how long Major Anderson could hold out at Fort Sumter.

MARCH 16 SATURDAY

The Territory of Arizona declared itself out of the Union.

Lt. Col. Robert E. Lee, United States Army, was promoted to Colonel of the 1st U.S. Cavalry. The commission was signed by Lincoln on March 28.

MARCH 18 MONDAY

In Texas, old Sam Houston, now Governor, refused to take an oath of allegiance to the Confederacy. He didn't think that just because Texas had seceded from the Union it owed any allegiance to the Confederacy. At Montgomery, Davis told Pickens that he would prefer Major Anderson leave Sumter peacefully.

MARCH 25 MONDAY

Tensions were mounting hourly in Charleston. Col. Ward H. Lamon, who accompanied Lincoln by train from Harrisburg, visited Charleston and conferred with both Gov. Pickens and Gen. Beauregard.

MARCH 29 FRIDAY

Having been deposed as Governor of Texas, Sam Houston refused an offer of the Federal government to reestablish him in that post.

Lincoln made his decision to hold both Sumter and Ft. Pickens at the mouth of the Pensacola Bay in Florida, ordering an expedition to accomplish this to be ready to sail by April 6th. The Cabinet was still split on the decision: 3 to 2 in favor.

∞ APRIL 1861 ∞

THIS MONTH ARRIVED WITH A FEELING of dread for some, elation for others. The elation was in the South, where the hot-blooded zealots believed that the war would be short-lived and they would soon be left to their own devices. That not all so believed was shown by the opposing votes of the various state conventions; there were still strong ties to the Union.

In the North, the abolitionists felt that their chance had finally come to free the country of the stain of slavery. Not all felt the same way. Many would prefer to let well enough alone and let the "peculiar institution" die a natural death.

The storm clouds of war were gathering.

Lincoln was inaugurated on March 4, 1861, on a special platform built upon the portico of the still-under-construction Capitol.

APRIL 3 WEDNESDAY

The South Carolina State Convention met and approved the Constitution of the Confederate States by a margin of 114 to 16; there were some who would not give up the old government easily.

John Sherman, brother to William T. (called "Cump" by his family and friends), and a U.S. Senator, had been trying to get "Cump" to take a position in the government in Washington. Sherman, then in St. Louis, Mo., had recently taken a job there and was somewhat settled.

APRIL 4 THURSDAY

In Richmond, the Virginia State Convention rejected by a vote of 89 to 45 a motion to pass an ordinance of secession and have it voted on by state residents.

The former naval officer G. V. Fox was informed that the expedition to relieve Sumter would go on or about April 11th or 12th. A letter was sent to Major Anderson at Sumter asking that he hold on until the expedition arrived, if that was possible. The following day, Secretary of the Navy Gideon Welles ordered ships to Charleston to provision Sumter. The *Powhatan*, previously secretly dispatched by Lincoln, was en route to Ft. Pickens and would miss the show at Charleston.

General Braxton Bragg (1817–76) entered the Confederate Army as a Brigadier General in March 1861, and was promoted to Major General a year later.

APRIL 6 SATURDAY

Lincoln, in Washington, sent an emissary to Gov. Pickens in Columbia, S.C., to inform the Governor that Ft. Sumter would be supplied with provisions only, no reinforcements of men or guns. The plan to relieve Ft. Pickens was foiled by the Federal naval commander, who decided that he did not have the authority to cancel an agreement made by the Buchanan administration about the supply of the fort.

APRIL 7 SUNDAY

Gen. Beauregard today notified Major Robert Anderson that no further interaction would be allowed between Ft. Sumter and Charleston. The fort was now essentially cut off and could only be reached by sea.

Naval Lt. John L. Worden was dispatched to Ft. Pickens with specific orders for the landing of troops by the Navy. Gen. Braxton Bragg, the local Confederate commander, requested permission from his Secretary of War to fire on any attempt to land troops at Pickens.

APRIL 8 MONDAY

The Confederate Secretary of War, Leroy P. Walker, gave Bragg permission to resist any attempt to reinforce Ft. Pickens. Sherman replied to Montgomery Blair's offer of employment in the War Department by saying, "I cannot accept." This led several Cabinet members to believe that Sherman planned to join the Confederacy if war came.

APRIL 9 TUESDAY

The Confederate government was in a quandary. If it allowed the resupply of the forts at Charleston and Pensacola, it was tacitly agreeing that they belonged to the Union government, and that the

secession movement was meaningless. If it repelled the resupply and reinforcement, it meant that it, the Confederacy, would be branded the aggressor. Confederate Secretary of State Robert Toombs told Davis that to fire on the national flag would be "suicide, murder and will lose us every friend at the North. You will wantonly strike a hornet's nest which extends from mountain to ocean, and legions now quiet will swarm out and sting us to death. It is unnecessary; it puts us in the wrong; it is fatal."

APRIL 10 WEDNESDAY

The Confederate Secretary of War informed Beauregard that if he was sure that the attempt would be made to resupply the fort, he should demand its immediate surrender and evacuation. If refused, Beauregard was to take whatever action he deemed necessary to reduce the fort.

APRIL 11 THURSDAY

Col. James Chesnut a former U.S. Senator and the husband of the famed Civil War diarist Mary Chesnut, Capt. Stephen D. Lee, late of the U.S. Army, and Lt. Col. A. R. Chisolm, a representative of Gov. Pickens, left the dock at Charleston and went to Ft. Sumter to demand its immediate surrender. There they met with Major Robert Anderson and discussed the demand. After a consultation, Anderson declined to surrender, but stated that he would probably be starved out in a few days anyway, if not battered to pieces by artillery. Beauregard, not wishing to create more blood-

Captain Abner Doubleday, as second-in-command at Fort Sumter, used this sword to signal the firing of the first Federal shot of the Civil War on April 12, 1861.

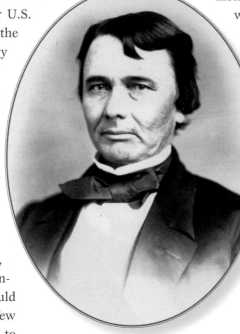

Before the war, Col. James Chesnut Jr. (1815–85) was a U.S. Senator representing South Carolina.

shed than necessary, asked Walker, the Confederate Secretary of War if he could outwait Anderson. Walker replied that Beauregard should seek to get a definite time for the evacuation of the fort.

APRIL 12 FRIDAY

Shortly past midnight, Roger Pryor and three men were sent out in a boat flying a white flag to Ft. Sumter to again confer with Major Robert Anderson about the surrender of the fort. To these men Anderson replied that he would evacuate the fort on the 15th unless he received additional instructions or supplies, not realizing that a relief fleet was lying just outside the harbor, awaiting daylight to enter. To the men in the boat, anything less than immediate surrender was not acceptable. They then informed Anderson that firing would commence within one hour if he did not surrender. Anderson, realizing what was coming, shook the hands of the four men and told them, "If we do not meet again in

Bombardment of Fort Sumter, Charleston Harbor, April 12 and 13, 1861

this world, I hope we may meet in the better one." The boat left for Cummings Point about 3:20 AM, arriving there at 4 AM.

At Cummings Point, Roger Pryor, a Virginian, was offered the honor of firing the first shot and he declined. Another Virginian, a 67-year-old fire-eater and avid secessionist, Edmund Ruffin, gladly accepted the honor, and at 4:30 AM pulled the lanyard on the gun. Sumter was fired upon. The war had begun.

In Charleston, people gathered on the rooftops to watch the display of artillery as Beauregard's 47 guns began the bombardment. The crowd, in a holiday mood, cheered as the shells struck home and the fort was battered. Beauregard's gunners threw over 4,000 rounds at the fort, tearing up the earthworks, dismantling guns, and making life miserable

for the defenders. The flag was shot from its staff only to be nailed up again by a courageous Sergeant. There could be no doubt of the outcome. Anderson was outgunned and beyond hope of help from the outside. The firing continued all day Friday and through the night.

At Pensacola, Federal troops were landed on Santa Rosa Island to reinforce Ft. Pickens. The Confederates were unable to prevent the landings and the fort would remain in Federal hands throughout the war, thereby denying the use of the harbor to the Confederates.

APRIL 13 SATURDAY

The firing on Sumter continued. Anderson capitulated and agreed to the surrender terms offered on Thursday, the 11th. Roger Pryor returned to Sumter to participate in the ceremonies. No casualties had

On April 18, 1861, the Army Arsenal at Harpers Ferry was abandoned by its garrison and many of the buildings were burned.

occurred on either side. The surrender was signed and Anderson was permitted to fire a fifty-gun salute to his flag. The flag was lowered and given to Anderson, who packed it with his personal effects. This same flag was hoisted over Sumter after four long years of blood and agony.

APRIL 14 SUNDAY

The evacuation of Sumter was complete. The news spread rapidly throughout the South, uplifting spirits and firming decisions for those who were wavering on the subject of secession.

APRIL 15 MONDAY

In Washington, Lincoln issued a call for 75,000 volunteers to serve for three months and called for a special session of Congress for July 4th. While the Northern states quickly affirmed their commitment to supply troops, North Carolina and Kentucky just as quickly refused.

APRIL 16 TUESDAY

Throughout the North, the firing on Sumter was a unifying experience, awakening the strong bonds of Union within the people.

The calls to the then-border states of Virginia, North Carolina, Tennessee, and Arkansas for troops led to action to join the South, in most cases. In Tennessee, Gov. Isham Harris, who had already started raising a "State Militia," declared, "Tennessee will furnish not a single man for the purpose of coercion, but fifty thousand if necessary for the defense of our rights and those of our Southern brothers."

APRIL 17 WEDNESDAY

Kentucky also refused to send troops. The Governor of Missouri called the requisition "illegal, unconstitutional, revolutionary, inhuman, diabolical and cannot be complied with."

Virginia, upon receiving the call for troops, replied that since Lincoln had chosen to "inaugurate the war," Virginia would send no troops. The Governor declared that "the people of this Commonwealth are free men, not slaves." So, in a secret ballot, a Secession Convention, by a majority of 88 to 55, voted to join the Confederacy.

Jefferson Davis issued a proclamation inviting all interested in "service in private armed vessels on the high seas" to apply for Letters of Marque and Reprisal—an accepted method at the time to set up legalized piracy.

APRIL 19 FRIDAY

The 6th Massachusetts Volunteer Infantry Regiment arrived in Baltimore and was marching from one station to another, en route to Washington, when a large crowd of Southern sympathizers began to throw rocks and bricks and fired into the ranks of the troops. The troops returned fire, killing twelve civilians and wounding several more.

In Washington, Lincoln declared a blockade of the Southern ports.

Col. Robert E. Lee learned of the secession action of the Virginia Convention. While friends and relatives gathered at "Arlington" to discuss the situation, Lee walked alone in the garden, trying to make his decision. He later returned to his room and paced the floor for several hours. Shortly after midnight, he emerged with his resignation from the United States Army after 32 years of service.

APRIL 20 SATURDAY

Out in the Shenandoah Valley at Lexington, the Virginia Military Institute cadets were ordered to Richmond by the governor. Thomas J. Jackson, the senior military officer present, was to command the cadets.

Thomas Jonathan "Stonewall" Jackson was born in Clarksburg, Va., now W.Va., on January 21, 1824. His parents died when he was quite young and he was raised by his uncle. He entered West Point in 1842 and was graduated in 1846. He served in Mexico during that war and resigned in 1851 to become a professor of artillery and natural philosophy at Virginia Military Institute (VMI). At the onset of war, he was sent to Richmond with the cadets from VMI and assimilated into the Confederate Army

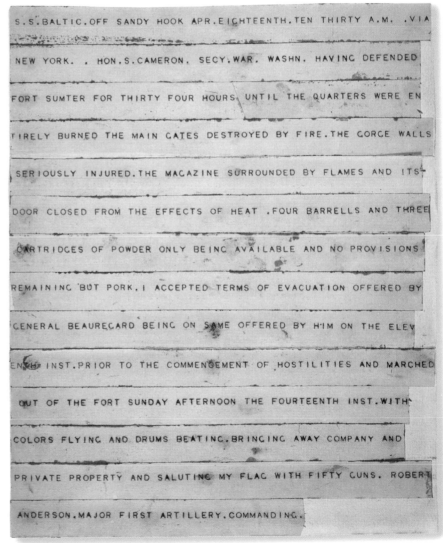

Major Robert Anderson's April 18, 1861, telegram describing the surrender of Ft. Sumter

as a Colonel. He served brilliantly in the Valley Campaign of 1862 and at Chancellorsville in May 1863, where he was accidentally killed by his own troops. He died on May 10, 1863, and was buried at Lexington, Va.

APRIL 21
SUNDAY

A delegation from Baltimore called upon Lincoln to protest the killings of citizens in Baltimore the previous Friday the 19th, calling it "a pollution" of Maryland soil. Lincoln replied that he must have troops to defend the capital. Dissatisfied, the Marylanders returned to Baltimore and cut the telegraph wires, burned bridges, and tore up miles of track. The city of Washington was now cut off from any rail support, Harpers Ferry being held by Confederate militia.

Washington began to look like a beleaguered city. Public buildings were barricaded with sandbags, troops were quartered under the unfinished Capitol dome. The Willard Hotel had fewer than 100 guests. Many of the residents, expecting the Confederate troops to enter the city at any time, wore secessionist badges and talked openly of the occupation of the city.

The Governor of Virginia asked Robert E. Lee to take command of Virginia's defenses. Lee accepted and departed for Richmond.

APRIL 23 TUESDAY

Robert E. Lee, having gone to Richmond and now formally a Major General in the Virginia forces, assumed command of all State troops.

In Washington, Lincoln was still awaiting more troops to defend the capital.

Thomas Jonathan "Stonewall" Jackson (1824–63) commanded Confederate soldiers in the Shenandoah Valley for the first two years of the war.

APRIL 25
THURSDAY

Federal troops finally arrived in Washington. First it was the 7th New York, followed by the Rhode Island Militiamen, and a group of 1,200 from Massachusetts, who had repaired a damaged engine and relaid the rails torn up by the "rowdies" of Baltimore between Annapolis and Washington.

In Richmond, Thomas J. Jackson was commissioned a Major of Engineers. He had been more than slighted, considering the West Point diploma, the Mexican War, and his experience in training. Jackson was a very unhappy man.

APRIL 26 FRIDAY

In Virginia, Major Gen. Joseph E. Johnston, of the Virginia Volunteers, was assigned to command all Virginia State forces in and around Richmond. On this day, Jackson's friend J. M. Bennett, discovering Jackson's fate, called on the Governor of Virginia and told him that this was a terrible waste of talent. The Governor agreed and promoted Jackson to Colonel and sent him to Harpers Ferry to see what mischief he could do there.

Both North and South, the people felt that the war would not last long. War fever ran high, and volunteers in both areas were fast pouring in.

APRIL 27 SATURDAY

A naval blockade, previously covering only the southern tier of states, was extended to Virginia and North Carolina by Lincoln. He also suspended the writ of *habeas corpus*, for reasons of public safety.

Richmond extended an invitation to the Confederate government to make it the capital of the Confederacy because of limited facilities in Montgomery.

APRIL 28 SUNDAY

Charles W. Wills was 21 years old in April 1861, a native of Illinois and a graduate of the State Normal School at Bloomington. When the first call came for volunteers to serve for three months, he joined Company E, 8th Illinois Infantry, on April 26, 1861. The organization was sent to Cairo, Illinois, to protect the confluence of the Ohio and Mississippi Rivers. He wrote:

> We started from Peoria last Wednesday at 11 AM amid such a scene as I never saw before. Shouting, crying, praying, and shaking hands were the exercises. Along the whole line from Peoria to Springfield, from every house we had cheers and waving of handkerchiefs.

The war fever in the South was as virulent as in the North, if not more so. Julius D. Allen was born in Salisbury, N.C., on October 22, 1837. Sixteen days after Sumter was fired upon, Allen was in Asheville, N.C. He wrote his parents:

> There has been a great deal of excitement in this place since I came here. . . . All the Union men here have become Secessionists, and the flag of the Southern Confederacy floats in triumph over this place.
>
> No one deplores the state of affairs in this county more deeply than I do, but it is the work of fire-eaters, and I can do nothing to save my country, or I would do it gladly. I have no sympathy for secession, and am still for the Union for which our fathers fought, bled and died; but I cannot express myself here. I do not think I shall ever fight under the banner of the Southern Confederacy. Please give me your sentiments, and tell me

what are the views of the people of Davidson in the present crisis.

APRIL 29 MONDAY

In Annapolis, the Maryland House of Delegates voted 53 to 13 against secession. This would not settle matters from a practical viewpoint, since much of Maryland's Eastern Shore was pro-South and they would cooperate with the South whenever possible.

The "Hero of Sumter," Major Robert Anderson, was promoted on April 30, 1861, to Brigadier General and sent to his native Kentucky to help keep that state in the Union. Kentucky being neutral, he established headquarters in Cincinnati.

∞ MAY 1861 ∞

THE DANGEROUS GAME of war began, albeit slowly. On both sides there was a feeling of unreality. Suddenly, this argument was getting serious.

The border states presented Lincoln with a special problem, Kentucky in particular. The proximity to Tennessee made it easy for pro-Confederate Kentuckians to leave the state and form military units in Tennessee. Lincoln, desirous of furnishing arms to the Kentucky Unionists without providing them to the State government, finally found a means of doing this "unofficially." The answer was found in one William Nelson.

Drawing of President Lincoln and Gen. Scott reviewing regiments on Pennsylvania Avenue, in front of the White House, c. 1861

MAY 1 WEDNESDAY

In Boston, the soldiers killed by the mob in Baltimore were afforded full military honors at their burial. The city that had seen much of the Revolutionary War now buried the first dead of the Civil War. The Governor of Tennessee was authorized to enter into league with the Confederacy by the State Legislature.

MAY 2 THURSDAY

The aging Gen. Winfield Scott had not lost his eye for strategic operations. In a letter to Major Gen. George B. McClellan, he cited his views:

We rely greatly on the sure operation of a complete blockade of the Atlantic and Gulf ports soon to commence. In connection with such a blockade, we propose a powerful movement down the Mississippi to the ocean, with a cordon of posts at proper points . . . the object being to clear out and keep open this great line of communication in connection with the strict blockade of the seaboard, so as to envelop the insurgent States and bring them to terms with less bloodshed than by any other plan.

MAY 3 FRIDAY

Expanding his troop requirements beyond the 75,000 in the first call, Lincoln now called for an additional 42,000 volunteers to serve for three years. Lincoln also expanded the regular Army to nearly 23,000 and authorized enlistment of naval personnel to 18,000. All of this was done without the approval of Congress.

MAY 4
SATURDAY

In western Virginia, several pro-Union groups were meeting to discuss possible secession from Virginia.

MAY 6 MONDAY

The states of Tennessee and Arkansas passed Secession Ordinances and left the Union officially, the 9th and 10th states to join the Confederacy. In Montgomery, Ala., President Davis approved a bill declaring war. In London, the government recognized the Confederacy as a belligerent, but not as a separate nation.

In St. Louis, there resided one Capt. Nathaniel Lyon,

a hard-bitten New Englander, and a graduate of West Point, class of '41. A red-headed, hot-tempered Unionist, he believed that anything was legal to keep the pro-Southern Governor of Missouri from getting the arms stored in the local arsenal. When Gov. Jackson called out the local state militia, Lyon disguised himself as a farm woman, complete with veil to hide his red hair and beard, and toured the local militia camps in a horse-drawn vehicle. He carried a wicker basket with two loaded revolvers in it. Using the intelligence he gathered, which was probably already available elsewhere, he planned his attack.

Clement L. Vallandigham (1820–71), a U.S. Representative from the state of Ohio, was a proponent of states' rights who vocally expressed his support of the South and was eventually exiled to the Confederacy in 1863.

MAY 7 TUESDAY

Isham Harris, Governor of Tennessee, took action within the Legislature to join the state to the Confederacy; this was done without a vote by the citizens of the state. Eastern Tennessee was very strong for the Union, and would remain so for the duration of the war.

MAY 10 FRIDAY

After assessing the information gained on the 6th, Capt. Lyon decided that the militia was really meant to seize the arsenal, so he took it upon himself to surround the camp with his own troops and those of Frank Blair's Home Guards, and capture it. The odds were definitely lopsided: Lyon's nearly 7,000 to his opponent's 700. He marched the would-be rebel soldiers off to prison through the streets of the city, causing a disturbance. Lyon's troops, many of them of German descent, were met with cries of "Damn the Dutch" and some drunk fired into the troops as they marched. The regiments turned and fired into the crowd, killing twenty-eight men, women, and children.

There were two observers in St. Louis that day. W. T. Sherman was walking on the streets with his son and his brother-in-law when the shots cut the leaves from the trees above them. These were the first shots Sherman ever heard fired in anger. He grabbed his son Willy, and, dropping down into a gully, raced for home. The other observer was Ulysses S. Grant, now a Colonel of the 21st Illinois Volunteer Infantry.

MAY 11 SATURDAY

Slowly the people of St. Louis calmed down and the interminable discussions began about which way Missouri should go—North or South.

Barber, Pvt., Co. D, 15th Illinois Volunteer Infantry, Freeport, Illinois, wrote of his departure:

> . . . the usually quiet streets of Marengo were thronged with spectators, friends and relatives of the soldiers who had come to witness their departure. A few hours before leaving, the ladies of Marengo presented the Company with a fine flag and 'neath its folds we took a solemn vow never to disgrace it or bring it back until our flag could wave in triumph over all our land.
>
> The shrill snort of the iron horse now told us that the hour had come to sever home associations and take the tented field. Amidst the tears and benedictions of our friends, the train moved on. Smothering the pent-up emotions which were surging in my soul, I looked forward to the time when I could greet them all again, when peace had folded her mantle over a rescued country.

MAY 13 MONDAY

In Kentucky, there lived a family named Nelson who produced a son, named William, who grew to be a very large man. His six-foot, four-inch, 300-pound frame contained a steel-trap mind and a prodigious memory. After completing two years at Norwich University, he was appointed a midshipman in the U.S. Navy in 1840, and spent 21 years in the naval service, rising to the rank of Lieutenant.

In early 1861 Nelson contacted Lincoln, an old family friend, to discuss Nelson's recent trip to Kentucky. Lincoln, ever mindful of the sensitive local issues in Kentucky, was seeking a means to supply the pro-Unionists with arms without funnelling the arms through the State government, which was pro-Confederate (supposedly neutral). Nelson volunteered for the job of distributing the weapons. Lincoln ordered 5,000 muskets and had them shipped to Cincinnati. Nelson went to Ohio, and shortly thereafter the guns found their way into the hands of the pro-Union forces.

From St. Louis, where he was awaiting developments, Sherman wrote his friend Boyd one last letter. In this letter he said:

> Already Missouri is humbled. I have witnessed it; my personal friends here, many of them Southern, admit that Missouri's fate is sealed. I have no doubt 100,000 disciplined men will be in Louisiana by Christmas next. The Mississippi River will be a grand theater of war. . . . It is horrible to contemplate but it cannot be avoided. I know that I individually would not do any human being a wrong, take from him a cent or molest any of his rights or property, yet I admit fully the fact that Lincoln was bound to call on the country to rally and save our constitution and government. Had I responded to his call for volunteers I know that I would now be a Major-General. But my feelings prompted me to forbear and the consequence is my family and friends are almost cold to me and they feel and say that I have failed at the critical moment of

Union militia soldiers stand at attention in front of the
U.S. Capitol, May 13, 1861

my life. It may be I am but a chip on the whirling tide of time destined to be cast on the shore as a worthless weed.

In London, Queen Victoria announced England's stance of strict neutrality—no recognition of the South as a nation.

Major Gen. Benjamin Butler occupied Baltimore.

MAY 14 TUESDAY
William T. Sherman returned to the Army, accepting a commission as the commander of the newly formed 13th Infantry Regulars.

MAY 17 FRIDAY
Gov. Isham Harris of Tennessee finally achieved his purpose: Tennessee was admitted to the Confederacy on May 16.

Nathaniel Lyon, captain of militia, was promoted to Brigadier General in the Union Army. He mounted a campaign to drive the pro-Southern forces from Missouri. He would die leading his troops at the Battle of Wilson's Creek on August 10th.

Joseph Hooker, 49 years old, West Point, class of '37, veteran of the Mexican War, where he won a Brevet Lt. Colonelcy at Chapultepec, had been farming in California. After the Mexican War, he had fallen into disfavor with Gen. Winfield Scott, and he resigned from the Army in 1853. At the outset of the war he volunteered, but was rejected, by Scott, who had a long memory. However, on this date, he was appointed Brigadier General of Volunteers and assigned to the Washington defenses.

North Carolina was admitted to the Confederacy, contingent upon ratification of the Constitution.

MAY 18 SATURDAY

Arkansas was admitted to the Confederacy.

Barber, Pvt., Co. D, 15th Illinois Volunteer Infantry, Freeport, Illinois, wrote:

> On the 18th we were sworn into the State service. Here some were rejected on account of height and physical disability, five feet and six inches being the shortest to insure acceptance. So eager were some of the boys to be accepted they would attempt to conceal their deformities and would appear as tall as possible when passing before the mustering officer. Some felt so bad as to shed tears at their rejection. . . .

MAY 20 MONDAY

Throughout the North on this day, U.S. Marshals "raided" the telegraph offices and confiscated all files of telegrams sent during the past calendar year. It was hoped that this would reveal spy sources and personnel. In some cases this was successful.

North Carolina officially seceded from the Union. This made the 11th state to leave the Union, and the last. While North Carolina may have been the last to leave, she furnished more troops and suffered more casualties than any other Southern state during the war.

Kentucky declared her neutrality and forbade the movement of any troops on state soil. This would be a very difficult position to maintain and would not last long before being violated by both sides.

The Confederate Congress voted to move the capital of the Confederacy to Richmond.

MAY 23 THURSDAY

Virginia completed her vote for secession. The vote went 3 to 1 in the eastern and central parts of the state. There was still much pro-Union sentiment in the mountains to the west.

Wills, Pvt., 8th Illinois Infantry, Cairo, Illinois, wrote:

> Lots of men come through here with their backs blue and bloody from beatings; and nine in ten of them got their marks in Memphis. A man from St. Louis was in camp a few days since with one-half of his head shaved, one-half of a heavy beard taken off, two teeth knocked out and his lips all cut with blows from a club. This was done in Memphis the day before I saw him. . . . I never enjoyed anything in the world as I do this life, and as for its spoiling me, you'll see if I don't come out a better man than when I went in. . . . The companies here with inexperienced officers have worlds of trouble, and five captains and one lieutenant, though good men at home, have resigned at the wish of their companies. Four of these companies tried to get our first lieutenant for captain, but he won't leave us. . . .

MAY 24 FRIDAY

Col. Elmer Ellsworth was killed. At the age of 24, he had organized the First Fire Zouaves (11th New York), and brought them to Washington for the defense of the capital. He was killed by hotel owner James Jackson, after Ellsworth had removed a Confederate flag from the roof of the hotel. Ellsworth would be given a lavish funeral and become a martyr, as would Jackson.

At Ft. Monroe, Ben Butler stirred the pot by refusing to release three Negro slaves who had entered his lines, stating that they were "contraband of war," thus giving a new twist to the slave issue.

MAY 30 THURSDAY

Yesterday, in Washington, Miss Dorothea Dix was finally authorized by Simon Cameron to organize and establish military hospitals.

A further blow to the South came when Secretary of War Simon Cameron notified Ben Butler in Ft. Monroe, Va., that he should retain any slaves entering his lines, employ them and keep records of their service.

MAY 31 FRIDAY

The Confederacy named Gen. Pierre Gustave Toutant Beauregard to command their forces on the "Alexandria Line," which included all of northern Virginia.

∞ JUNE 1861 ∞

THERE WAS A FLURRY OF ACTIVITY both North and South as young men flocked to the colors. In both areas there were many who had been no further than to the local county seat, and the glamour of the uniform, the drums, and the adventure were all powerful incentives. In both North and South there was a severe shortage of rifles for the infantry. Many of the state arsenals were equipped with old flintlock muskets, last used in the Mexican War, and few rifled weapons were available.

The two main arms manufacturing sites were at Springfield, Mass., and Harpers Ferry, Va.; the latter site was now lost and the equipment shipped south by Col. Thomas J. Jackson.

JUNE 1 SATURDAY

Federal cavalry moved into Fairfax Court House, Va., about 20 miles south of Washington, entering the town on a north road. Confederate military forces consisting of a cavalry company from Prince William County, another company of cavalry from Rappahannock County, and the Warrenton Rifles, commanded by Capt. John Q. Marr, were in the town at the time. The cavalry was composed of raw recruits who soon bolted and left the Warrenton Rifles holding the bag. The Rifles made a good accounting of themselves, sending the Union cavalry back with several empty saddles. A search of the area found Capt. Marr's body in a clover patch, shot through the heart. His body

An illustration of temporary barracks erected in New York City, 1861

was taken back to Warrenton, where he was interred with honors. He became one of the first Southern casualties of the war.

The blockade of the Southern ports and the use of privateers gained immediate foreign attention, especially in England, one of the major consumers of Southern cotton. Capt. Du Pont at the Philadelphia Navy Yard wrote:

> I do not like the tone of things in England. . . . Lord Derby and Granville, etc., talk of two thousand miles of coast to be blockaded! They seem to forget so far as their rights and international interests are concerned we have only to blockade the ports of entry—from Chesapeake to Galveston—any . . . venture into any other harbors or inlets of any kind is liable to capture as a smuggler. . . .

JUNE 2 SUNDAY

Gen. Pierre Gustave Toutant Beauregard, often called "the Creole," took command of the Confederate forces in northern Virginia. Among other names, this collection of units would be referred to as the Army of Northern Virginia, a name which would see much glory.

JUNE 4 TUESDAY

At Philippi, in western Virginia, the Union troops consolidated their gains, got some sleep, and prepared to move on Beverly, to the south. Beauregard inspected his organization in preparation for the defense of northern Virginia. More troops were being brought into this area, some from as far away as Louisiana.

JUNE 5 WEDNESDAY

Beauregard, consolidating his Army of Northern Virginia at Manassas, issued a proclamation to the people of northern Virginia:

> A reckless and unprincipled tyrant has invaded your soil. Abraham Lincoln, regardless of all moral, legal, and constitutional restraints, has thrown his abolition hosts among you, who are murdering and imprisoning your citizens, confiscating and destroying your property, and committing other acts of violence and outrage too shocking and revolting to humanity to be enumerated.

JUNE 8 SATURDAY

By a margin of slightly over 2 to 1, the voters in western Tennessee approved secession. The same ratio in reverse was voted in eastern Tennessee. In any case, the vote was a little late, since the state had already joined the Confederacy as a result of actions by Gov. Isham Harris.

The United States Sanitary Commission was authorized by Lincoln and Secretary of War Simon Cameron.

The blockade of Key West, Fla., was established by the U.S.S. *Mississippi.*

JUNE 9 SUNDAY

In the worst nightmare that a commander could imagine, the Federal troops moving from Newport News and Ft. Monroe became confused in the dark and began firing into their neighboring units. This was not uncommon when green troops were placed in a frightening situation and lacked the discipline that only comes with long campaigning.

JUNE 10 MONDAY

The first serious battle of the war was fought at Big Bethel, Va., between 2,500 Federals from Ft. Monroe and 1,200 Confederates. The Federals lost 18. The Confederates lost 1 man.

JUNE 11 TUESDAY

At Wheeling, in western Virginia, pro-Unionists met to organize a separate state government which would be loyal to the Union. This eventually became the basis for the West Virginia government.

JUNE 13 THURSDAY

Col. Lew Wallace, later the author of *Ben Hur,* entered Romney, western Virginia, after a long march from Cumberland, Md. Lewis Wallace was born in Brookville, Ind., on April 10, 1827. Wallace, a political general, served in the Mexican War and then returned to his legal and political careers. When the Civil War started, he organized the 11th Indiana Infantry Regiment and was appointed Colonel of that regiment. He was appointed Brigadier General of Volunteers on September 3, 1861. He served with Grant during the Ft. Donelson campaign and was promoted to Major General on March 21, 1862. During the Battle of Shiloh his performance was less than satisfactory, and he was removed from command of troops. He would end the war in an administrative post after his failure at Shiloh. After the war, he served as Governor of

New Mexico and Minister to Turkey. He died at Crawfordsville, Ind., on February 15, 1905.

Confederate Gen. Joseph E. Johnston, former Brigadier General of the United States Army and the highest ranking army officer to "go South," now commanded the troops around Harpers Ferry. He expressed doubts about holding the area without reinforcements.

JUNE 15 SATURDAY

Federal Gen. Robert Patterson, a 69-year-old Irish immigrant, veteran of the War of 1812 and the Mexican War, and in general slow to react, cautiously moved into the space vacated by Johnston. Slow and timid, Patterson would make a poor showing. Winfield Scott would remove him from command on July 19th.

Jefferson City, Mo., was occupied by Federal forces under Gen. Nathaniel Lyon, the Missouri militia having departed the city, heading west

After setting fire to the bridge across the Potomac, Gen. Joe Johnston evacuated Harpers Ferry on June 15, 1861, and moved south towards Winchester.

towards Boonville. The type of warfare to prevail in Missouri was beginning to surface, with guerrilla raids increasing.

JUNE 17 MONDAY

Gen. Lyon, after occupying Jefferson City, Mo., moved about 1,700 men by boat to Boonville. After a short fight, the forces of Gov. Jackson departed the area and left Lyon with the town. This was a minor action that had far-reaching consequences; the Federals now controlled most of the northern part of the state and the Missouri River.

JUNE 18 TUESDAY

The supply of small arms for the Union forces was becoming very crucial. The old arsenals were inadequate to meet the demand, and it took time to gear up new ones and get them into production. As a stopgap measure, arms were brought in from commercial manufacturers.

Barber, Pvt., Co. D, 15th Illinois Volunteer Infantry, en route to Alton, Illinois, wrote:

> . . . we were ordered to move camp to Alton, Illinois. At this time we had more baggage in one company than would be allowed in a whole brigade in one of Sherman's campaigns. It took two heavy trains to remove the regiment. We were vociferously cheered all along the route, the fair sex singing patriotic songs wherever we stopped and expressing their sympathy in various other ways.

General Irvin McDowell (1818–85), West Point Class of '38, had been promoted to Brigadier General of the Union Army on May 14, 1861.

citizens in mostly rural areas (only 10 towns had more than 500 inhabitants), Kansas would provide over 20,000 troops by the end of the war, suffering nearly 8,500 casualties—the highest rate per capita for any Northern state.

JUNE 20 THURSDAY

Kansas was becoming embroiled in the border dispute with Missouri. With only about 100,000

JUNE 22 SATURDAY

In western Virginia, Major Gen. George B. McClellan trumpeted the success of the Union forces there and, of course, took all credit for that success.

JUNE 23 SUNDAY

Gen. McClellan proclaimed that he would now "prosecute the war vigorously," a promise that never came true.

JUNE 24 MONDAY

In Washington, J. D. Mills of New York became the world's first machine-gun salesman. Mills called it "the Union Repeating Gun. . . . An Army in six feet square." Lincoln, being fascinated with gadgets, had to see this one. In the hayloft of Hall's carriage shop across Pennsylvania Avenue from the Willard Hotel the device was displayed for Lincoln, and he was allowed to operate it.

Lincoln called it what it reminded him of—a coffee mill—and the name stuck for the rest of the war.

JUNE 29 SATURDAY

Gen. Irvin McDowell outlined his plans for attacking the Confederate force at Manassas Junction at a staff meeting with the cabinet.

JUNE 30 SUNDAY

Allen, Co. K, 10th Illinois Calvary, Asheville, N.C., wrote:

> I do not read the papers much, as there are so many lies in them that I do not know what to believe. . . . They say that the United States soldiers, or "Yankees" as they call them, are the poorest marksmen and the greatest cowards in the world, and that there is no fight in them. The object of all of these lies that are told and published is to keep up the spirits of the people and secure more volunteers. . . . Some things are getting to be very dear here. Coffee is selling at the rate of three pounds to the dollar. If the war lasts long, times will be very hard. . . .

∞ JULY 1861 ∞

THE FEVER FOR WAR WAS BURNING both North and South. No major engagements had as yet been fought and the bravado on both sides was sometimes amusing—deadly, but amusing. It was obvious that the two armies at Manassas Junction and Washington, so close to each other, would collide soon, but no one could really predict the results.

JULY 2 TUESDAY

Lincoln authorized Gen. Winfield Scott to suspend the writ of *habeas corpus* on, or near, any military line between Washington and New York.

Federal troops under Brigadier Gen. Robert Patterson, a sixty-nine-year-old veteran of the War of 1812, crossed the Potomac at Williamsport, Md., into the Shenandoah Valley. Patterson was to keep the Confederate forces under Gen. Joseph E. Johnston occupied while McDowell moved against Manassas. Johnston and Beauregard had similar plans: to hold Patterson in the Valley and then quickly shift Johnston's troops to the aid of "the Creole" at Manassas. Moving

Major General William S. Rosecrans (1819–98) was appointed Brigadier General in the Regular Army on May 16, 1861, and was assigned to the Department of the Ohio under McClellan.

briskly, Patterson advanced towards Martinsburg, western Virginia.

In Washington, Lincoln conferred with Major Gen. John C. Frémont, "the Pathfinder," before Frémont departed for St. Louis to command in Missouri. Frémont, age 48, was already a national figure and was one of the four Major Generals appointed by Lincoln at the beginning of the war. The appointment to command the Western Department was given at the urging of Frémont's friends. Lincoln would long regret this action.

JULY 4 THURSDAY

On Independence Day, celebrations were held both North and South, the colonial forefathers being venerated equally in both places. At a special session of Congress, Lincoln requested "at least four hundred thousand men and four hundred million dollars" to pursue the war to a speedy conclusion.

Barber, Pvt., Co. D, 15th Illinois Volunteer Infantry, Alton, Illinois, wrote:

> The Fourth of July was duly observed and celebrated in an appropriate manner. The boys were all allowed a day of freedom and were put upon their honor as men and soldiers to conduct themselves properly. . . . A novel mode of punishment was now inaugurated for very fractious soldiers, which consisted in drumming them out of camp, by two men walking behind the offender with fixed bayonets pressing pretty close to his rear, and two musicians in front playing the rogues' march, passing between two lines of soldiers drawn up for the occasion, his head shaved clean on one side, his clothes turned wrong side out, hooted and jeered at by his

A Confederate Army wooden canteen

companions as he passed along, until he was out of camp. Such cases received very little sympathy from good soldiers, as they were always bringing trouble. . . .

JULY 5 FRIDAY

Missouri Gov. Claiborne Jackson, pro-Confederate, got a little nervous about Gen. Nathaniel Lyon in his rear, only to find out that Brigadier Gen. Franz Sigel was in front of him. Jackson's force waited for Sigel's attack, then assaulted both ends of his line. Sigel retired and retreated through Carthage, Mo., giving the Federal advance a serious setback. Jackson moved to link up with Sterling Price and his force.

JULY 7 SUNDAY

Two torpedoes (mines) were picked up in the Potomac River by the U.S.S. *Resolute*, Acting Master W. Budd. This was the first record of such deployment.

JULY 10 WEDNESDAY

In western Virginia, McClellan placed three brigades at Buckhannon and another at Philippi, ready to move against Confederate Gen. Robert S. Garnett's smaller forces at Rich Mountain and Laurel Hill. A general who would become prominent later, William Stark Rosecrans, attacked at Rich Mountain. Rich Mountain was not much of a battle, but it demonstrated Rosecrans's initiative and drive.

The Tsar of All the Russias informed Washington of Russia's policy of neutrality towards the belligerents.

Barber, Pvt., Co. D, 15th Illinois Volunteer Infantry, Alton, Illinois, wrote:

> Sickness now began to prevail to a considerable extent, over two hundred being on the sick list at one time. Several deaths occurred

while we camped here. A considerable number were being discharged. Surgeons at this time would make out discharges for slight causes, and, if an order from the War Department had not put a stop to it, our army would soon have become badly decimated.

JULY 11 THURSDAY

At Rich Mountain, Rosecrans, with 2,000 troops, attacked the rear of Confederate Lt. Col. John Pegram's force of 1,300, cutting off their retreat. McClellan was supposed to attack at the same time that Rosecrans did, but held his position. Nonetheless, McClellan took credit for the victory, not unusual for McClellan.

JULY 12 FRIDAY

Confederate Brigadier Gen. Robert Selden Garnett was retreating into the Cheat River valley. Part of the troops from Rich Mountain escaped to Staunton, Va. McClellan came into Beverly, western Virginia, about noon.

JULY 13 SATURDAY

Garnett's troops crossed Cheat Mountain in the rain and entered the Cheat River valley. About noon the Federals caught up, and there was a fight at Corrick's Ford in which Garnett was killed, giving him the dubious honor of being the first general to be killed, North or South. His body was recovered by Federal troops, who returned it to his family. Pegram was forced to surrender 555 of his troops.

JULY 14 SUNDAY

McDowell, with the largest American army ever assembled (even Winfield Scott had only about 14,000 men during the Mexican War), considered leaving his stinking camps around Alexandria and Washington for Manassas. With 35,000 men, McDowell outnumbered Beauregard by at least 10,000, but the addition of Johnston's Valley troops would make the odds even. Both North and South, the troops lacked combat experience.

JULY 15 MONDAY

As the news spread of the victories along the Cheat River in western Virginia, the name McClellan became a household word. The first real "hero" had arrived! The campaign, well planned by McClellan, was better executed by his subordinates, with "Little Mac" getting the lion's share of the credit. His ego, already large, soared to new heights.

JULY 16 TUESDAY

Out from the camps around Alexandria and Washington moved McDowell's over 1,400 officers and 30,000 men. All five of the division commanders and eight of the 11 brigade commanders were Regular Army officers, some with much field experience. The march to Manassas Centreville was a nightmare.

The troops had little training in marching and water discipline. The long lines of troops and artillery would move a short distance, stop for a while, repeat. This was done in a hot sun, and with troops that drank all their water in the first three hours and had no place to get more.

There was much breaking of ranks to sit in the shade or to pick blackberries. Equipment that seemed light enough in Alexandria now weighed tons, and was discarded along the road.

JULY 17 WEDNESDAY

McDowell's army finally reached Fairfax C. H. Discipline on the march had not improved. Among the brigades en route to Manassas was one commanded by Col. William T. Sherman, until recently assigned as an inspector for Gen. Scott.

Meanwhile, President Davis had ordered Joseph E. Johnston to shake loose from Gen. Patterson in the lower Shenandoah Valley and to join Beauregard at Manassas. This was no problem because Patterson, in defiance of his orders, had withdrawn from the Winchester area to Charles Town, leaving Johnston to go where he would. Johnston headed his troops to the nearest railhead to shuttle them to Manassas Junction.

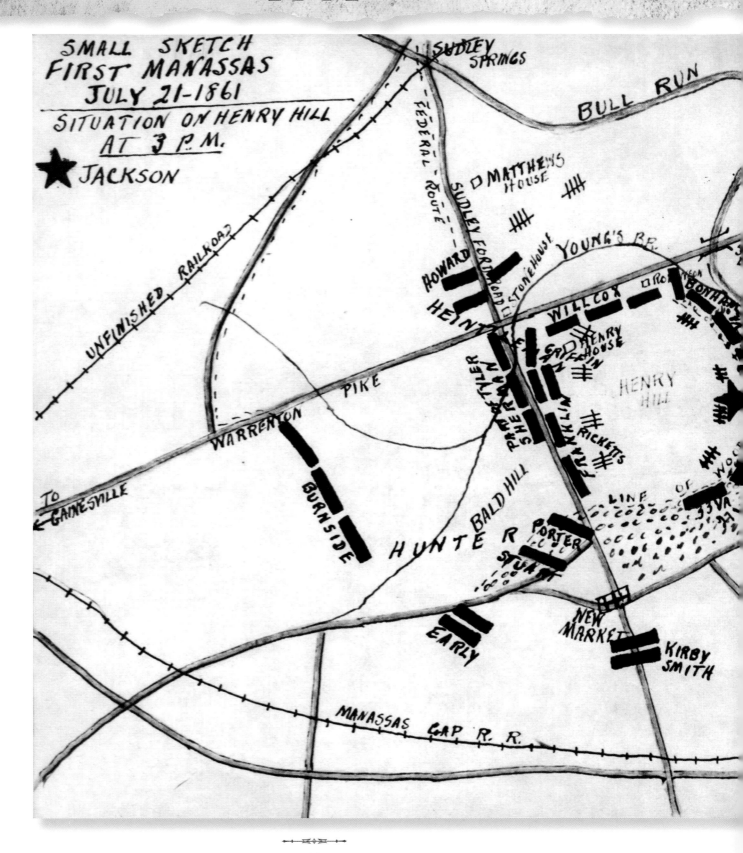

SMALL SKETCH
FIRST MANASSAS
JULY 21-1861
SITUATION ON HENRY HILL
AT 3 P.M.
★ JACKSON

SUDLEY SPRINGS
BULL RUN
FEDERAL ROUTE
MATTHEWS HOUSE
SUDLEY FORD ROAD
YOUNG'S BR.
HOWARD
STONEHOUSE
WILLCOX
BONHAM
HEINTZELMAN
3RD HENRY HOUSE
HENRY HILL
PORTER SHERMAN
FRANKLIN
RICKETTS
UNFINISHED RAILROAD
PIKE
WARRENTON
BURNSIDE
HUNTER
BALD HILL
LINE OF WOODS
PORTER
STUART
33 VA
TO GAINESVILLE
EARLY
NEW MARKET
KIRBY SMITH
MANASSAS GAP R. R.

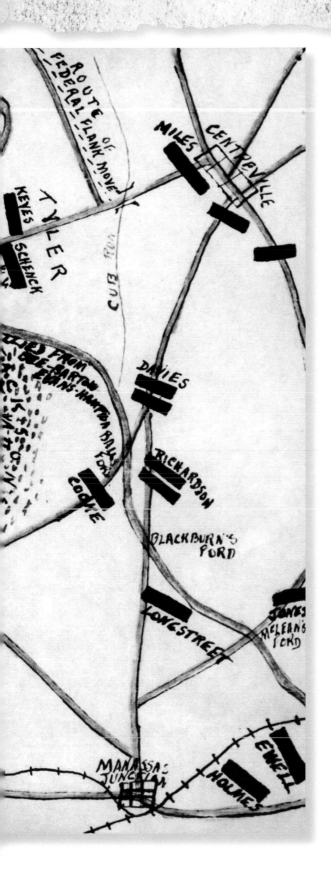

JULY 18 THURSDAY

At about noon McDowell's army approached Centreville. The temperature was nearing 90°, the men were out of water.

McDowell decided to reconnoitre the area and sent a brigade-size force from Brigadier Gen. Daniel Tyler's division to Blackburn Ford, where Col. I.B. Richardson took the brigade further than it was supposed to go and met Beauregard's troops in a bloody clash which accomplished little or nothing, but caused the Federals to retreat.

JULY 19 FRIDAY

At Centreville, Va., all day was used to get McDowell's army fed and regrouped. Stragglers came in at all hours. At Manassas Junction nearby, Gen. Thomas J. Jackson arrived with his Confederate brigade in advance of Joe Johnston's force moving from Winchester. The battle loomed.

Major Gen. McClellan issued congratulations to his army, and to himself, on their conduct in the western Virginia campaign.

JULY 20 SATURDAY

Barber, Pvt., Co. D, 15th Illinois Volunteer Infantry, St. Charles, Mo., wrote:

> We proceeded up the river as far as St. Charles, Mo., where we arrived the next evening, July 20th, and we immediately disembarked and went into camp one mile above the city. We apprehended some trouble on landing, as the rebels were rampant, but no serious difficulty occurred. We were now for the first time in what we considered an enemy's country.

JULY 21 SUNDAY

Davis took a train to Manassas from Richmond to find out what was going on, arriving in midafternoon while the battle was in progress.

Map of Manassas, July 21, 1861: "Situation on Henry Hill at 3 PM"

Knowing that the battle would be on this day, several U.S. Congressmen and their ladies travelled to Centreville by carriage to see it. Picnics and wine were on the menu for most. Their traffic and constant jockeying for position on the field interfered with the troop movements and control.

Each general attempted to outflank the other's left flank. The end result was almost a disaster for both sides. The Confederates were in trouble until Johnston's main force arrived from the Valley. This made the difference and gave enough weight to the line to start the Union rout.

Jackson, who had spent a year in Europe studying the battlefields of the Napoleonic Wars, remembered the Battle of Waterloo and used the same tactic by screening his men just below the crest of the hill where they could fire over it without the risk of being fired into. Not being in too much danger, his troops were holding steady when Gen. Bee, attempting to rally his own men, cried, "There is Jackson

The Battle of Bull Run, July 21, 1861: No pursuit was made by the Confederates, primarily because they were almost as confused as the retreating Federals.

standing like a stone wall. Rally on the Virginians."

As the battle progressed, the Federal troops became confused, and finally a retreat turned into a rout. The fleeing troops mingled with the sightseeing civilians from Washington, and the scene quickly became one of bedlam.

Edmonds, S. Emma E., Union Field Nurse, Georgetown Hospital, Washington, D.C., wrote:

> The hospitals in Washington, Alexandria and Georgetown were crowded with wounded, sick, discouraged soldiers. That extraordinary march from Bull Run, through rain, mud, chagrin, did more towards filling the hospitals than did the battle itself. . . .

JULY 22 MONDAY

Gloom and surprise spread over the North as the results of Bull Run were learned. Recriminations were passed around wholesale, with McDowell getting most of the blame. For all the failure, his was a good plan, and his actions during the battle were correct. The army was ill trained and disciplined.

The "Crittenden Resolution," passed by the House of Representatives, stated that the war was being waged "to defend and maintain the supremacy of the Constitution and to preserve the Union," and *not to interfere with slavery or subjugate the South.*

Lincoln sent for McClellan to take command of the Federal forces around Washington.

Barber, Pvt., Co. D, 15th Illinois Volunteer Infantry, St. Charles, Mo., wrote:

> We could say now that our actual military life had just begun. I was placed on picket the first night at St. Charles, and well I remember my feelings on that occasion. . . . Every noise was noticed and every dark object turned into imaginary rebels. . . . The fellow that was with me was completely demoralized, hence it required greater vigi-

lance on my part. He deserted the same night and nothing have I heard of him since.

> Here we heard of the terrible and disastrous battle of Bull Run, and a deep, burning shame crimsoned our cheeks at the defeat and disgrace of our arms.

The following day (the 24th), Gen. Jacob D. Cox's soldiers attacked the Confederates of Gen. Henry A. Wise, only to see the Confederates retreat towards Gauley Bridge while the Federals took the city.

JULY 25 THURSDAY

By a vote of 30 to 5, the U.S. Senate passed the Crittenden Resolution.

JULY 27 SATURDAY

Major Gen. George B. McClellan assumed command of the newly formed Army of the Potomac.

JULY 28 SUNDAY

The Seventh U.S. Infantry, all ten companies, surrendered to a Confederate force at St. Augustine Springs, New Mexico Territory, without a shot.

JULY 30 TUESDAY

At Ft. Monroe, Hampton Roads, Va., Maj. Gen. Ben Butler wrote to Secretary of War Simon Cameron on the continuing problem of Negroes entering his lines to seek freedom. At this time he had about nine hundred former slaves in his care.

Barber, Pvt., Co. D, 15th Illinois Volunteer Infantry, Mexico, Mo., wrote:

> We now practiced target-shooting daily. . . . We now began to get a foretaste of army fare. Our bacon was so maggoty that it could almost walk, and our hard-tack so hard we could hardly break it.

JULY 31 WEDNESDAY

Lincoln nominated Col. Ulysses S. Grant, among others, to be Brigadier General of Volunteers.

∾ AUGUST 1861 ∾

IT WAS OBVIOUS THAT THE WAR was going to last much longer than expected. Stockpiling of supplies and materials began, and considerations were given to the future strength of the forces.

A major problem was arming the troops. The capacity of the Springfield Mass. Arsenal was insufficient to meet the demand, so action was taken to obtain arms in Europe.

Not much activity had taken place in the Ohio and Mississippi valleys up to this time. Kentucky was still "on the fence." Forces for both South and North were actively trying to sway events there. Missouri was in a state of disarray.

AUGUST 1 THURSDAY

Confederate Gen. Robert E. Lee, advisor to President Davis, arrived in western Virginia on a mission to "inspect and coordinate" the Southern forces in Virginia's western counties. He shortly took command from Gen. W. W. Loring and began developing a strategy to hold the area for the Confederacy.

Lincoln appointed ex-naval officer Gustavus Vasa Fox as Assistant Secretary of the Navy, a promotion from Chief Clerk of the Navy Department. One of his major strengths was the network of acquaintances he had throughout the Navy. He could, and did, use these contacts to get things done, and to smooth ruffled feathers.

AUGUST 2 FRIDAY

Major Gen. Ben Butler, at Ft. Monroe on Hampton Roads, banned the sale of all intoxicating beverages to the soldiers. This type of action has never, in history, been effective. Whiskey was found stored in the barrels of the big guns, canteens and gun barrels of the pickets, and any other container imaginable.

Col. William T. Sherman, already commanding a brigade, was promoted to Brigadier General of Volunteers.

Wills, Pvt., 8th Illinois Infantry, Cairo, Illinois, wrote:

> Hot! You don't know what that word means. I feel that I have always been ignorant of its true meaning till this week, but am posted now, sure. The supposed-to-be "never failing cool, delicious breeze" that I have talked about so much, seems to be at "parade rest" now and—I can't do justice to the subject . . . We drill now five hours a day, under a sun that cooks eggs in 13 minutes, but we think we feel the heat no more walking than lying around the quarters. . . .

AUGUST 3 SATURDAY

Napoleon III of France visited Lincoln at the White House and remarked on the notable lack of ceremony at the official residence of the President. He later dined with the President and Mrs. Lincoln at a state dinner.

AUGUST 5 MONDAY

Barber, Pvt., Co. D, 15th Illinois Volunteer Infantry, Mexico, Mo., wrote:

> Some of the boys began to get sick here on account of the poor water we had to use, and our rations grew no better very fast. Some of the boys positively asserted that our bacon had followed us from St. Charles, and our hard-tack was harder still . . .

AUGUST 7 WEDNESDAY

Confederate Gen. John B. Magruder burned Hampton, Va., because he said that he had learned that Gen. Ben Butler intended to use the village as a holding point for "runaway slaves" whom he considered as "contraband of war." According to Butler, Magruder only gave the residents fifteen minutes to leave before the fires were lit, and Butler declared it a "wanton act of war."

AUGUST 8 THURSDAY

Barber, Pvt., Co. D, 15th Illinois Volunteer Infantry, Fulton, Mo., wrote:

Our camp was situated near where was fought one of the first battles in Missouri for the Union, and there was great danger of being attacked during the night. . . . We were on the move before daylight the next morning. I was feeling some better but I had no appetite for breakfast. We had fifteen miles to march and we made it before ten o'clock. . . . Some of the time we made four miles per hour. We halted at one of the churches in Fulton and rested. A collection was taken up to procure a dinner, and we had the satisfaction of soon sitting down to a nice, warm meal. My appetite had now returned and I ate heartily and felt much refreshed. . . .

Our situation here was a dangerous one. We had only four hundred men and were isolated from any other command, and out of reach of assistance if overpowered, in an ene-my's country, with spies lurking all around us. . . . We were always on the alert and prepared for emergencies. . . . Our position was admirably situated for defensive operations. . . .

AUGUST 9 FRIDAY

In Missouri, Confederate Gen. Ben McCulloch led the Southern forces; the ill-equipped Missouri state troops were led by Sterling Price. They neared Springfield with a combined force of nearly 11,000 men. Concentration would be made around an area filled with underbrush and thickets of stunted oaks.

In Springfield, Union Gen. Nathaniel Lyon gathered his 5,400 men and set off to find the secessionist army. The odds were greater than 2 to 1.

AUGUST 10 SATURDAY

The second major battle of the Civil War was fought. Lyon divided his inferior force, sending Franz Sigel to make a rear attack. Sigel's attack came to nothing: His troops were routed and he was out of the battle without having contributed much except confusion.

What was left after the burning of Hampton, Va., by Confederate Gen. John B. Magruder on August 7, 1861

Lyon drove the Confederates back at first but they rallied, and, with their superior numbers, eventually won the day. Lyon was killed leading his men. With Lyon dead, the Federals withdrew and the Confederates were too worn out to follow. The Federals left 1,317 of their force dead along Bloody Ridge, nearly 25 percent of their original force. No other battle in the state would be as heavy during the war.

AUGUST 12 MONDAY

In the aftermath of the Battle of Wilson's Creek and the Federal retreat, the Confederate commander,

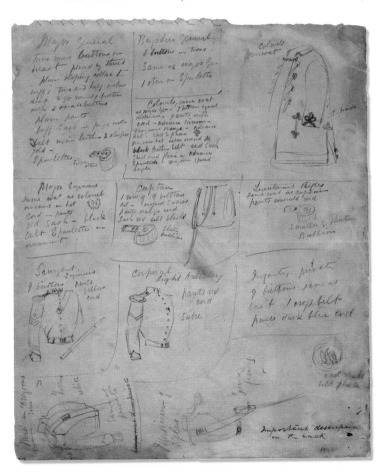

This undated sketch of the uniforms of the Army of the Potomac was made by Alfred R. Waud (1828–91). Its extensive descriptions show distinctions in uniforms by rank and branch of service, and were probably intended for the use of engravers doing the illustrations for newspapers.

Gen. Ben McCulloch, said that the Union people in Missouri would be protected, but that the time had come for them to choose sides, North or South.

At Cairo, Illinois, three new wooden gunboats, *Tyler*, *Conestoga*, and *Lexington*, arrived to cover operations until such time as ironclads could be built.

AUGUST 13 TUESDAY

In Washington, President Lincoln dined with the newly promoted Brigadier Gen. Robert Anderson, hero of Ft. Sumter. The discussion surely included the assignment of Anderson to Kentucky.

AUGUST 14 WEDNESDAY

In Richmond, President Davis proclaimed the banishment of foreigners who did not recognize the government of the Confederacy. In St. Louis, Major Gen. Charles Frémont declared martial law and suppressed two local newspapers for Southern sympathies.

AUGUST 15 THURSDAY

Brigadier Gen. Robert Anderson was named the new commander of the Department of the Cumberland, which consisted of Kentucky and Tennessee. To spare his native state the embarrassment of setting up headquarters there, he moved his headquarters to Cincinnati, Ohio.

Frémont, in Missouri, called for reinforcements, fearing that Confederate Generals McCulloch and Price would again advance.

AUGUST 17 SATURDAY

The main army of the eastern area was formed this day with the merger of the Departments of Northeastern Virginia, Washington, and the Shenandoah into the Army of the Potomac. This army would carry the brunt of the war in the east and be much maligned, poorly led, and much bloodied. Major Gen. Henry W. "Old Brains" Halleck was appointed a Major General in the Regular Army.

The first combined amphibious operation of the war took place on August 27, 1861, at Hatteras Inlet, N.C., where the forces of Flag Officer Stringham and Major General Butler allied to capture Fort Hatteras and Fort Clark. The scene is depicted in this lithograph by Currier & Ives.

Major Gen. Benjamin F. Butler, later of New Orleans fame, began to organize forces to capture the Cape Hatteras, N.C., area, after turning over his Department of Virginia to Major Gen. John E. Wool.

AUGUST 20 TUESDAY

Major Gen. George Brinton McClellan assumed command of the Army of the Potomac.

A convention was held in Wheeling, western Virginia, to consider the separation of the western counties from the Old Dominion.

Barber, Pvt., Co. D, 15th Illinois Volunteer Infantry, Rolla, Mo., wrote:

> Rolla at this time . . . contained but two or three hundred inhabitants. . . . We found in camp here the 13th Illinois Volunteer Infantry . . . Maj-Gen John C. Frémont was in command of the Western Department and he now advanced out of his own pocket $10.00 to each man on our wages, an act of generosity on his part which we never forgot. We had not been in camp but a few days before Sigel's brave and shattered army came straggling in. It was sorrowful to look at them. Some were sorely wounded and it must have been very painful for them to march, but they seemed to be cheerful, though all looked nearly worn out. Their clothes were in tatters. Footsore and weary, they struggled on. Brave men! They deserved a better fate. . . .

AUGUST 24 SATURDAY

In Washington, the spy Mrs. Rose Greenhow was arrested, along with Mrs. Philip Phillips, on charges of corresponding with the Confederates.

AUGUST 26 MONDAY

On the western rivers, Navy Capt. Andrew Foote assumed command of the river forces, relieving John Rodgers. Foote turned out to be an excellent choice, working well with the Army commanders.

AUGUST 28 WEDNESDAY

In St. Louis, Gen. Nathaniel Lyon, killed at Wilson's Creek, was buried with appropriate ceremony.

AUGUST 30 FRIDAY

From his luxurious headquarters in St. Louis, Mo., Major Gen. John Charles Frémont, late of California and more politician than general, issued his own emancipation proclamation and order of confiscation. This, of course, was entirely unauthorized, and would create endless headaches for Lincoln.

Frémont thought big. He declared martial law throughout Missouri, and confiscated the property of "those who shall take up arms against the United States," and stated that "their slaves, if any they have, are hereby declared free men." Anyone found in the Union-controlled areas with guns in their hands would be tried by military courts-martial and shot, if found guilty. This also applied to all those who were "proven to have taken an active part with their enemies in the field."

AUGUST 31 SATURDAY

In Richmond, the government announced the appointment of five full generals. This was somewhat unprecedented in American military procedures. There had been few full generals of four-star rank in American history. Washington was the only one of the Revolutionary War. The only other major figure was Winfield Scott.

The appointments were made, in order of seniority, as follows: Samuel Cooper; Albert Sidney Johnston; Robert Edward Lee; Joseph Eggleston Johnston; Pierre Gustav Toutant Beauregard.

SEPTEMBER 1861

SEPTEMBER 1861 was a time for soul-searching. The Battle of Manassas (Bull Run) was sobering to both North and South. The North found their leaders to be lacking, and had assigned Major Gen. George B. McClellan to command the Army of the Potomac. He had begun his task of reorganization and training. Not the least of the problems was the question of weapons for the troops. This problem, still unresolved, would plague the military for two years.

Leonidas Polk (1806–64) was a bishop of the Episcopal Church in Louisiana before he became a Major General in the Confederate Army. He assumed control of the forces in Arkansas and Missouri on September 2, 1861.

In the South, the government agencies and departments were finding that their resources were limited. The seceding states, so eager to leave the Federal "yoke," were also rather restive under their new "yoke."

SEPTEMBER 1 SUNDAY

Wills, Pvt., 8th Illinois Infantry, Cairo, Illinois, wrote:

> We had blankets given us this last week and new accoutrements throughout. If they would only change our guns now we would have nothing but a move to ask for. A uniform was also furnished us last week. . . . I have been visiting Col. Raritan's and Hick's Camp this PM They have no guns yet and their sentinels stand guard with sticks. Looks funny. We have about 50 prisoners here now. They think they are treated splendidly and say that if any of our boys fall into their hands they will remember it. . . .
>
> We have had some fighting in camp lately. An artillery man stabbed one of the 9th and got knocked, kicked and bayoneted for it. . . .

The news arrived in Washington about the successful operations at Hatteras in North Carolina. This was a major morale booster to the North, considering the low morale following the defeat at Manassas.

SEPTEMBER 2 MONDAY

On August 30th, Major Gen. Frémont issued an unauthorized proclamation freeing the slaves of owners who fought for the South, confiscating the owners' property and assigning death sentences to the owners. Lincoln notified Frémont to "modify" (essentially rescind) this order because of the effect on border states such as Kentucky.

SEPTEMBER 3 TUESDAY

Confederate forces commanded by Major Gen. Gideon Pillow marched into Kentucky en route to Columbus, Ky., on the Mississippi River. Kentucky was no longer neutral.

SEPTEMBER 6 FRIDAY

Grant landed Federal troops from transports, protected by gunboats, at Paducah, Ky., to prevent the Confederates from occupying the city. The city was captured without a shot. The later capture of Smithland at the junction of the Ohio and the Cumberland prevented the South from claiming Kentucky by planting the Confederate flag on the Ohio River. Both rivers, the Tennessee and Cumberland, would play prominent roles in later campaigns.

SEPTEMBER 7 SATURDAY

The furor over Frémont in Missouri reached new heights when reports arrived about the lavish expenditures he and his staff had made in St. Louis. He had spent nearly $12 million for steamboats, fortifications, uniforms, food and parties, in a spending spree that seemed to have no end. Most of this was blamed on his staff of "California robbers and scoundrels." Lincoln asked Gen. David Hunter to go to St. Louis and "assist" Frémont in the administration of the Department.

Major General John Charles Frémont (1813–90), seen in this undated portrait by photographer Matthew Brady, was not only the commander of the Army's Department of the West, he was also an explorer who had previously collected and discovered a number of plant species. In 1864, he ran for president against Abraham Lincoln, eventually withdrawing from the race.

Things got worse in Missouri, with bushwhackers running rampant in the countryside. Confederate Sterling Price was refitting his troops, largely with arms picked up from the Wilson's Creek battlefield, and preparing to move on Lexington, Mo.

SEPTEMBER 10 TUESDAY

In the west, Gen. Albert Sidney Johnston was appointed head of Tennessee, Missouri, Arkansas and Kentucky for the Confederate government.

In St. Louis Frémont waited six days to respond that he would not rescind the emancipation order. However, if the President so ordered, he would do it. The antislavery radicals in the North were ecstatic. Further, Frémont sent his reply in care of Mrs. Frémont, who was something of a fire-eater herself. Lincoln, not pleased with the letter, showed his displeasure, and Mrs. Frémont showed her temper and explained that Frémont was "above and beyond" the ordinary run of soldiers. She left the White House in a huff to return to Missouri.

In western Virginia, Federal Gen. Rosecrans attacked the Confederates at Carnifix Ferry, but was unable to break their lines.

SEPTEMBER 11 WEDNESDAY

In western Virginia, Lee commenced his five-pronged attack against the Union forces. The weather was stormy with heavy rains, slowing movement in the heavily wooded, mountainous area.

SEPTEMBER 12 THURSDAY

In western Kentucky, the 8th Illinois Infantry marched to Paducah to "relieve" an expected attack on Federals in that location.

Wills, Pvt., 8th Illinois Infantry, Camp Norfolk, Ky., wrote:

> Agreeable to our very short notice, we packed our knapsacks, put three days' rations in our haversacks, were carried across the river to Bird's Point in two boats, and just at

dark, started out through the woods. 'Twas a confounded, dark, dirty, narrow road and I was right glad when the word "halt" was given and preparations made for bunking in for the night. The next morning we started again along down the river, the gunboats, two of them, keeping a couple of miles ahead of us . . . We advanced about 5 miles when the gunboats, which were about a mile and one-half ahead of us, opened mouth, and thunder! What a rumpus they did keep up. We could not see them for the thick brush between us and the river, but we thought sure our little fight had come at last. . . .

> While they were gone we ate our dinners and made ready for the expected march and fight. But the colonel . . . scooted us back to our morning's starting place . . . About an hour after we started back, 15 of our cavalry scouts were run in, through the place where we took dinner, by 60 or 70 secesh cavalry. Three or four were wounded and our boys say that they killed several of the Rebels. . . . I fell in love with Paducah while I was there and I think I will settle there when the war is over. . . .

In Missouri, Sterling Price began his assault on Lexington by besieging Mulligan's Irish Guard, a 2,800-man force in trenches on the campus of the Masonic College. In St. Louis, Frémont was startled and decided to act.

SEPTEMBER 14 SATURDAY

In St. Louis, there was much stirring about in Frémont's camps. He was organizing 38,000 troops to relieve Mulligan at Lexington, Mo.

SEPTEMBER 15 SUNDAY

Frémont continued to "get ready" for his relief of Lexington. In Washington, Lincoln met with his Cabinet to discuss the dismissal of Frémont. Lee closed his campaign in western Virginia.

This drawing of the destruction of Fort Ocracoke, on the Outer Banks of North Carolina, depicts the Union tugboat *Fanny* in the foreground. The expedition was led by Lieutenant Eastman aboard the USS *Pawnee* on September 17, 1861.

SEPTEMBER 16 MONDAY

William Nelson, the huge Kentuckian who was so instrumental in getting guns to the Unionists in Kentucky earlier in the year, was promoted to Brigadier General.

Wills, Sgt., 8th Illinois Infantry, Camp Norfolk, Ky., wrote:

> Yesterday Sunday the *Yankee* came up and shelled the woods where we were the day before. She tried to throw some shells into our camp but they didn't reach us by a mile and a half. One of our gunboats has to lay here all the time or the *Yankee* would make us skedaddle out of this on double quick. . . .

SEPTEMBER 17 TUESDAY

At Ocracoke Inlet, N.C., the Federal Navy destroyed

the fort defending the inlet and thus closed another port for blockade runners.

Grant's campaign to hold Paducah, Ky., was successful. Wills, Sgt., 8th Illinois Infantry, Camp Norfolk, Ky., wrote:

> Well, I've slept half of this day and feel sleepy yet. I had a tough time on picket last night. We were divided into four squads, and owing to the small number of men we had out (only 50), the corporals had to stand guard as privates; so I had all the stationing of reliefs to do myself and did not get a minute's sleep all night. We were not troubled any by the enemy but the mosquitoes and fleas gave us the devil. . . .
>
> We are rapidly learning to appropriate and confiscate. On our last scout one of our boys rode a stray horse back and another came in

with a female jackass and her child. Chickens are very scarce here now and the natives complain that sweet potato hills have turned into holes since we have been here. Our mess have this PM confiscated the roof of a man's barn to cover our cook house with.

The Union Navy took possession of Ship Island, Miss., with the landing party from the USS *Massachusetts*. The island would become an important staging and refueling site for the blockading squadrons.

SEPTEMBER 20 FRIDAY

At Lexington, Mo., the siege that began on the 12th was ended with the surrender of Col. James A. Mulligan's Irish Guard command of 2,800 Federals. The Confederate commander, Maj. Gen. Sterling Price, former Governor of Missouri, delayed assaulting for five days while Mulligan waited for relief from Union forces under Gen. John Frémont that never came. On the 18th, Price assaulted the works to

no avail. An attempt was made again on the 19th with more success; this time the Confederates used dampened bales of hemp, rolling them forward as they advanced to protect the assaulting troops. Finally, Mulligan capitulated. Barber, Pvt., Co. D, 15th Illinois Volunteer Infantry, Rolla, Mo., wrote:

Rumors of an attack now became rife in camp. Price and McCulloch were reported to be near with a large army. This just served to keep up excitement enough to destroy the ennui of army life. Maj. Gen. Hunter was in command of the post now. He received a wound at the battle of Bull Run. We made several forced marches out to meet the enemy, but each time failed to bring them to an engagement; as soon as our backs were turned, they would commence bushwhacking. A great many of the citizens adopted the role of being friends to our face and foes to our back.

The siege of Lexington, Mo.—depicted in this illustration from *Frank Leslie's Pictorial History of the American Civil War*—ended on September 20, 1861.

This group of "contrabands"—escaped slaves who came into the possession of Union forces—was photographed in May of 1862 at a farmhouse, near Yorktown, Va., which had served as the headquarters of General Lafayette during the American Revolution.

SEPTEMBER 22 SUNDAY

In St. Louis, the lack of energy on the part of Frémont in the relief of Lexington brought down a storm of criticism on his head.

Kansas Jayhawkers, led by James H. Lane, raided, looted and burned the town of Osceola, Mo., in yet another example of terror on the Kansas–Missouri border. No military advantage was gained in this senseless act.

Wills, Sgt., 8th Illinois Infantry, Camp Norfolk, Ky., wrote:

> We are all again bored to death with lying still, but patience and we'll get what we want in time. We have the report here to-day that Col. Mulligan has capitulated to Price . . . at

Lexington. . . . I'm getting perfectly indifferent about Frémont's being superseded . . . With at least 75,000 troops at Paducah, Cairo and in Missouri, to allow the gallant Mulligan to be forced to surrender is perfectly shameful . . . if this war goes against us 'twill be the fault of our commanders, and not of the men, sure. . . .

SEPTEMBER 25 WEDNESDAY

Secretary of the Navy Welles, in a historic command, instructed Flag Officer Du Pont, Commander of the South Atlantic Blockading Squadron:

> The Department finds it necessary to adopt a regulation with respect to the large and increasing number of persons of color,

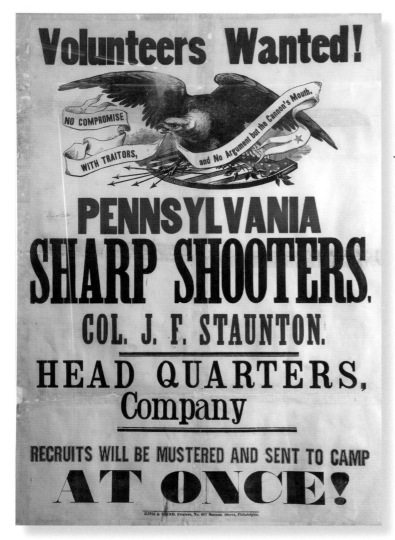

An early Civil War recruitment poster. Some states were so successful at enlisting volunteers that they didn't need to rely heavily on conscription.

commonly known as "contrabands," now subsisted at the navy yards and on board ships-of-war. These can neither be expelled from the service, to which they have resorted, nor can they be maintained unemployed, and it is not proper that they should be compelled to render necessary and regular services without compensation. You are therefore authorized, when their services can be made useful, to enlist them for the naval service, under the same forms and regulations as apply to other enlistments. They will be allowed, however, no higher rating than "boys" at a compensation of ten dollars per month and one ration a day.

SEPTEMBER 26 THURSDAY

John S. Jackman, a native Kentuckian, born in December 1841, began one of the most important periods of his life when he left Kentucky for service in the 1st Kentucky Brigade, later to be known as "The Orphan Brigade," of the Confederate Army. He was to serve until the end of the war as a private. His story, in this chronicle, begins here:

The first six months of my "soldier life" I let pass without making notes of any kind. To make my Journal more complete, I shall write up that period from memory. I shall use no dates but those positively known to be correct.

Late in the afternoon left home with the intention of making my way to Green River, where the advance of the Confederate Army was then encamped . . . On the evening mentioned I walked down to the Depot . . . and as I was passing in, W.S. said to me, "Let us go to Bloomfield to-night and join the party going through to Dixie!". . . I mounted my horse and joined W.S. at his home. We were soon in the road, two modern Don Quixotes starting to seek adventure.

They were then rendezvousing at Camp "Charity"—so called because the people furnished us rations while there encamped—several companies from different counties, and among them was one from Bardstown, the "Allsin Greys." To this company we purposed to attach ourselves . . .

There were several recruits from Samuel's Depot neighborhoods going to Camp "Charity" that night . . . [W]e were riding along in high glee, and were suddenly challenged, "Who goes there?" Silence came over our party immediately and Capt. G., who was at the head, answered promptly, "Recruits for the Rebel Army." We were then commanded to halt, and a picket came forward to inspect. This was something novel to me—this was soldiering in reality. As the picket advanced, I caught a glimpse of his polished bayonet as it gleamed in the moonlight. That was the first bayonet I had seen in actual use, to overturn the "best government the world ever saw." I shall never forget my feelings at first beholding that polished steel glittering in the moon beams.

After being satisfied that we were all right, the picket conducted us to the stand, and another one set out with us, to show us the way to camp. Being then midnight, and all the fires having burnt down, we were very close to the camp before we knew it. A sentinel on post challenged us, and I distinctly heard the clicking of his lock, as he drew the hammer back. I thought this extreme vigilance. After parlaying sometime with the sentinel, who was green, we were taken in by Capt. W., afterward Lieut. Col., and conducted to the bivouac of his company. A fire was "recruited," and we sat around chatting awhile with James H. and others hailing from about Samuel's who had preceded us the day before. Being weary I soon rolled myself up in my shawl, and tumbled down under a large beech tree to sleep. I lay a moment watching the "lamps of heaven" as they twinkled through the foliage of the old tree, my thoughts busy contemplating the *sublimeness* of soldiering; then I sank into a restless slumber.

SEPTEMBER 27 FRIDAY

In Washington, a rather heated discussion developed when the lack of aggressive activity on McClellan's part was brought into a discussion at a Cabinet meeting attended by McClellan.

In Kentucky, Jackman began to get a taste of his future life in the Confederate Army.

Jackman, Pvt., "The Orphan Brigade," Camp Charity, Ky., wrote:

At 9 AM was placed on guard, and for the first time "buckled on my armor." How proud I felt as I paced to and fro in my beat, with a long sabre bayonet on my gun which glittered not a little in the sun beams. . . . That night until the moon came up, was black as Erebus, and my beat was back of the camp in a dense wood. . . . I heard two fellows coming to the spring which was just inside my beat . . . I halted them "instanter." They commenced begging me to let them in, but I pompously told them *my duty* kept me from letting anyone pass my post unless first giving the countersign, which they did not have. The next moment "Corporal of the guard, post no. 8" was bawled out by me in my best military manner. It was passed from sentinel to sentinel to my entire satisfaction . . . Presently I heard the Corporal coming, tumbling over logs, and swearing true trooper style. The "Corp" let the water-hunters in, and I was left to pace my beat, "solitary and alone." Two years after, I met the Corporal—then a Lieutenant—at Dalton, Ga., and I told him how I played off on him. He laughed heartily.

SEPTEMBER 28 SATURDAY

Jackman, Pvt., "The Orphan Brigade," Green River, Ky., wrote:

At 2 o'clock our little army took up its line of march for Green River. We had been recruited to upwards of 400—about equally divided foot and horse. Our departure was amid tears of the gentler sex, who were present to bid relatives farewell. The column moved off, nearly all joining in singing a war-song. Many who then marched away with buoyant step were doomed never to return. They found graves far from home— far from kindred!

SEPTEMBER 29 SUNDAY

Gov. Oliver P. Morton of Indiana was complaining that Lincoln was not paying enough attention to Kentucky. Morton, at age 38, was a hard-headed fire-eater. Early in the war, getting no immediate support from the Federal government, he suspended the State Legislature and directed State funds to the arming and outfitting of Union regiments. He established his own arms factory when rifles were not forthcoming, keeping this going throughout the war. Mostly through his efforts, Indiana furnished nearly 150,000 troops during the war, with little resort to the draft.

SEPTEMBER 30 MONDAY

In Washington, Lincoln was still wrestling with the problem of Frémont. Meanwhile, McClellan was sitting in Virginia doing little except admiring himself and "his" army. Lincoln was getting testy.

The month came to a quiet and not very successful end for either side of the struggle.

∞ OCTOBER 1861 ∞

THE ARMY OF THE POTOMAC lay idle and nothing seemed to move McClellan into action. McClellan was organizing and training "his" army into one of the finest and best organized armies ever seen on the continent. All he needed to do now was to use it for its intended purpose. McClellan was also having his problems with both Winfield Scott and the President. They were, after all, either too old or too uninitiated to "understand" his overall designs.

In Richmond, and elsewhere in the South, the puzzlement over the "nonevents" at Manassas was the talk of the town. Just why was Gen. Joseph E. Johnston sitting on his hands and not taking the offensive? Richmond was also concerned about the recognition of the Confederacy by foreign governments. This act would place the stamp of legitimacy on secession in the eyes of the world.

Kentucky had lost its neutrality and was being somewhat "occupied" by the Northern armies. All key cities were firmly in control of Federal troops.

In the west, Missouri still needed attention with Frémont in command. His "order of emancipation and confiscation" still rankled the administration.

OCTOBER 1 TUESDAY

At Centreville, Va., President Jefferson Davis and Generals Joe Johnston, Pierre Beauregard, and G. W. Smith held a council of war and strategy. The sentiment was to concentrate the armies in the east and to await Union attack in the spring. This recommendation, of course, would not satisfy the fire-eaters of the South, but it was most practical, considering the manpower and matériel available.

Pamlico Sound in North Carolina was the scene of a lopsided battle and victory for the Confederacy when the CSS *Curlew*, *Raleigh* and *Junaluska* under Flag Officer William F. Lynch, CSN, captured the steamer *Fanny*, which was loaded with arms and troops. This gave the South a boost in morale and provided some much needed supplies and arms.

The question of issuing "letters of marque," which allowed privateering on the high seas, was finally settled for the Union when Secretary of the Navy Gideon Welles refused to issue such letters on the grounds that they would be "a recognition of the assumption of the insurgents that they were a distinct and independent nationality."

Jackman, Pvt., "The Orphan Brigade," Camp Charity, wrote:

We commenced camp life—learning how to cook, pitch tents, drill, etc., etc. I could not walk about much, my feet were so sore. Afterwards all the nails came off my toes. Saw my brother Jo and several old acquaintances in the 2d. I had expected to see the soldiers better clad than I found them—they were very ragged and dirty.

OCTOBER 2 WEDNESDAY

Wills, Sgt., 8th Illinois Infantry, Bird's Point, opposite Cairo, Illinois, wrote:

Just at noon yesterday orders came to strike tents and in an hour we were under way and have come to a halt in this forsaken hole. It seems the 8th can't get out of hearing of the Cairo morning and evening gun anyway. Our major says they are talking of chucking us into Cairo and making us garrison it this winter.

This engraving, depicting Confederate prisoners being held in the basement of the state capitol building in Jefferson City, Missouri, was published in *Harper's Weekly* on October 5, 1861.

I'll be tempted to desert if 'tis so. The 22d call us the featherbed regiment now, and if they keep us this way much longer we will be tender as women. . . . You scout the idea of one's liking such a life as this. I tell you that I never was so well satisfied in my life as I have been since I joined the army . . . Nobody ever heard me grumble a word about soldiering and never will if they don't station us in Cairo.

OCTOBER 4 FRIDAY

The USS *South Carolina* captured 4,000 to 5,000 stands of arms when the Confederate schooners *Ezilda* and *Joseph H. Toone* were taken near South Pass of the Mississippi River, south of New Orleans.

OCTOBER 5 SATURDAY

In England, the London *Post* published an editorial backing the Confederacy, while the London *Times* leaned towards the Union.

Jackman, Pvt., "The Orphan Brigade," Bowling Green, Ky., wrote:

In the evening two companies took the train for Bowling Green and arrived there just after dark. When we saw the camp fires in the suburbs, all said the world was there encamped. We knew little about armies then. . . .

Barber, Pvt., Co. D, 15th Illinois Volunteer Infantry, Jefferson City, Mo., wrote:

When we arrived at Jefferson City, we were ordered to keep on the train in the pelting storm until further orders, but those orders came right speedily.

Our company took up their quarters in the Senate Chamber, where only a few months before the traitor Governor of Missouri, Jackson, and his Confederates were plotting treason and endeavoring to drag Missouri into the whirlpool of secession . . .

The streets of the city wore a desolate aspect. War's rude finger had left its mark. Traitors and patriots met on the street with set teeth and blazing eyes, brother against brother, and father against son. Missouri at this time was in a terrible state of anarchy. . . .

OCTOBER 6 SUNDAY

Barber, Pvt., Co. D, 15th Illinois Volunteer Infantry, Tipton, Mo., wrote:

Tipton is a nice village, containing one thousand inhabitants, surrounded by as splendid a country as the eye ever looked upon. Here Frémont's grand army was concentrating preparatory to that grand campaign which was to sweep the rebel horde from Missouri, but strange to say, Frémont permitted Price and his army which had been up to Lexington and captured Mulligan and his command, to pass back across his flank without molesting him. While we were camped here, we received a visit from the Secretary of War—Cameron . . .

OCTOBER 7 MONDAY

In Missouri, Frémont, late and slow, left St. Louis for Springfield to command the chase after Sterling Price, who was withdrawing towards Lexington.

OCTOBER 12 SATURDAY

In a historic engagement, three Confederate ships attacked five Federal ships near Head of Passes, south of New Orleans in the Mississippi delta. The *Manassas* rammed the USS *Richmond* and forced her and the USS *Vincennes* aground under heavy fire before the Confederate ram withdrew. Acting Master Edward F. Devens of the *Vincennes* reported:

From the appearance of the *Richmond*'s side in the vicinity of the hole, I should say that the ram had claws or hooks attached to her . . . for the purpose of tearing out the plank from the ship's side. It is a most destructive invention . . .

Another historic event took place at Carondelet, Mo., when the first Federal ironclad, the *St. Louis*, was launched.

OCTOBER 15 TUESDAY

In Missouri, self-promoted Gen. Merriwether Jeff Thompson, normally called "Jeff," burned the Big River Bridge near Potosi and captured some Federal troops. This followed by one day his announcement to the local citizens to "drive the invaders from your soil or die among your native hills." Thompson, a native of Harpers Ferry, western Virginia, at age 35 had been involved in many things since leaving his native state. He was rejected by both West Point and the Virginia Military Institute, but still aspired to a military career. At the beginning of the war, he organized a battalion of volunteers and offered their services to the Governor. This was rejected, so he began his own war on the Union, operating in the swampy areas and raiding the countryside. He became known as the "Swamp Fox of the Confederacy," operating both as a part of other Confederate forces and as an independent command.

OCTOBER 20 SUNDAY

A lady visited the Confederate War Office in Richmond and left a "programme of the enemy's contemplated movements." The lady in question, not identified, had recently reached Richmond from Washington, where she had attended a dinner party with Gen. John A. Dix, at which the deployment strategy was discussed. The movements included Bank's advance on Manassas after crossing the Potomac near Leesburg, and the expeditions of Generals Burnside (into North Carolina) and Butler (into Louisiana).

Brigadier Gen. Charles P. Stone crossed some troops at Edwards Ferry–Ball's Bluff on a short

reconnaissance and then withdrew them after a short time. Reconnaissances were also made to Hunter's Mill and Thornton Station in northern Virginia.

OCTOBER 21 MONDAY

At Ball's Bluff on the Potomac, a disaster awaited Union forces. Brig. Gen. Charles P. Stone ferried his troops across the river in wholly inadequate boats to the base of the bluff and downstream of Edwards Ferry. The immediate commander at Ball's Bluff was one Col. Edward D. Baker, U.S. Senator from Oregon and a personal friend of Lincoln's. After light skirmishing in the morning, the Confederates drove the Federals back to the edge of the bluff in the afternoon. A mass exodus began. Col. Baker was killed, the boats got swamped in the water; men drowned, were captured or fled on foot. Each

Col. Edward D. Baker, whose death is depicted in this c. 1862 engraving, was one of the Union casualties in the skirmish at Ball's Bluff, near Leesburg, Va., on October 21, 1861.

The deck and turret of the USS *Monitor*, photographed on July 9, 1862

side had about 1,700 troops committed during the battle. The Union lost 49 killed, 158 wounded and 714 missing—a total of 921 casualties. The South lost only 36 killed, 117 wounded and 2 missing. The blame was placed on Stone, and he was accused of treason. Later imprisoned, he was released and restored to duty, but his career was ruined. McClellan, who ordered this debacle, escaped criticism.

OCTOBER 23 WEDNESDAY

Barber, Pvt., Co. D, 15th Illinois Volunteer Infantry, opposite Warsaw, Mo., wrote:

The next morning we were early on the move; marched twenty miles, and on the 23rd we camped on the south side of the Osage opposite the ruined city of Warsaw. We laid over here one day—for what purpose I do not know. Price was reported only twenty-five miles off. We gave him an opportunity to disband that portion of his army who lived in the country through which he passed and rest the remainder. Then we started after him again. We got as far as Mt. Au Revoir and halted again. We were pressing Price too hard. It would never do. We must wait and let him get farther ahead. So we waited a week.

OCTOBER 24 THURSDAY

In western Virginia, the people voted overwhelmingly to form a new state.

Colonel and Senator Baker had his funeral today in Washington, attended by the President and many members of Congress. Lincoln also informed Brigadier Gen. R. S. Curtis that he should deliver enclosed orders to Major Gen. Frémont and Gen. David Hunter. The orders were to relieve Frémont of command and place Hunter in his stead. If, however, Frémont had won a battle, or a battle was pending in the interim, the orders were not to be delivered.

The USS *Monitor* was designed by John Ericsson, a Swedish engineer, and was sometimes described as a "cheesebox on a raft."

OCTOBER 25 FRIDAY

The charge of Frémont's cavalry into Springfield, Mo., was a gallant affair, even if the opposition was almost nonexistent. Much was made of this by Frémont's supporters, but he knew the game was up and was making sure that no one could reach him with reassignment orders. His actions did little to halt the retreat of Price from Lexington, and nothing to affect the overall military situation.

At Greenpoint, N.Y., the keel was laid for the USS *Monitor*, a historic ship that would make the existing navies of the world obsolete.

Confederate General Simon Bolivar Buckner (1823–1914), seen in this undated portrait, became governor of Kentucky in 1887.

OCTOBER 27 SUNDAY

In Springfield, Mo., Frémont stated he would pursue Price, who was believed to be advancing on the city. Actually, Price was in full retreat in the opposite direction.

OCTOBER 28 MONDAY

In a command change in the west, Gen. Albert Sydney Johnston assumed command of the Army of Central Kentucky at Bowling Green, where Gen. Simon Bolivar Buckner was holding the fort.

OCTOBER 29 TUESDAY

A fleet of 77 vessels, the largest Federal fleet assembled to date, sailed from Ft. Monroe on Hampton Roads for Port Royal, S.C. The fleet was commanded by Flag Officer Du Pont, and was carrying over 16,000 troops, commanded by Brigadier Gen. Thomas W. Sherman. The intent of this massive array of armament was to take Port Royal for a refueling and servicing station for the blockading squadrons.

OCTOBER 30 WEDNESDAY

Barber, Pvt., Co. D, 15th Illinois Volunteer Infantry, Mt. Au Revoir, Mo., wrote:

> It was a very common sight to see three or four able-bodied young men at the different farm houses along the route, eyeing us with a look of triumph. They all professed to be peaceful citizens and perfectly neutral. I never had a doubt in my own mind but what Price disbanded a large part of his army in this way. He knew perfectly well that he could not cope with us in battle and so he adopted that plan as the most feasible way of saving his army and annoying us. He succeeded but too well.

OCTOBER 31 THURSDAY

Day, Pvt., Co. B, 25th Massachusetts Volunteer Infantry, Worcester, Mass., wrote:

> It seems that at last we have been ordered from these cold, frosty climes, to a warmer and more genial one—the Sunny South. . . . Here were leave takings that required some nerve to suppress the rising tear. Probably some of us have seen our friends for the last time on earth, and bade them the last good-bye. But we will go forward to duty, trusting in God, and hoping for the best.

NOVEMBER 1861

THIS MONTH FOUND BOTH North and South having gained no advantage in the seven months since Sumter was fired upon. There had been some battles in the east and west, but nothing very decisive that could break the stalemate. Both presidents were urging their respective field commanders to "do something," but this came to naught. Neither Johnston in Virginia nor Frémont in Missouri were advancing their causes. Many of the troops were looking towards winter quarters.

NOVEMBER 1 FRIDAY

At Springfield, Mo., Frémont had learned that the order removing him from command had been sent from Washington. He immediately closed off access to himself so that the order could not be delivered. Gen. Curtis, who was sent by Lincoln to deliver the order, had the order sent by a captain disguised as a local farmer. When the captain gained his audience, he handed Frémont the order and was placed under arrest to keep the news quiet. Frémont then finally set out to attack Sterling Price, only to find that Price had fallen back sixty miles and was beyond his immediate reach.

Barber, Pvt., Co. D, 15th Illinois Volunteer Infantry, Mt. Au Revoir, Mo., wrote:

> One day one of these neutral rebs came into camp with a load of apples to sell. He

inadvertently betrayed his sentiments and, with the permission of Col. Ellis, the boys relieved him of his apples in less time than it takes to write it. Rollin and Milton, who were always on hand at such a time, managed to secure two bushels for tent No. 6. The fellow was lucky in getting off as well as he did. We soon resumed our march. . . . The last day but one before reaching Springfield, we had marched twenty-seven miles . . . when an order came for us to reach Springfield by daylight, if possible, as a battle was expected the next day.

NOVEMBER 2 SATURDAY

After being in command for 100 days, spending in excess of $12 million, issuing an unauthorized emancipation declaration and refusing to bow to the commands of the President of the United States, John C. Frémont sent a farewell address to his command and returned to his wife in St. Louis, Mo. There were some protests about his removal but these soon died.

Barber, Pvt., Co. D, 15th Illinois Volunteer Infantry, Springfield, Mo., wrote:

We had twenty-seven miles to go yet, but . . . it was long past daylight before our division came in sight of the city, and then only about one-third of the command came in together. The rest were worn out for want of sleep and rest and stopped on the road. . . . We had marched nearly sixty miles without sleep and very little rest, and to our mortification there was no prospect of a battle at that time. . . . A few days before, Frémont's body guard, under command of Maj. Zagonyi, had had a severe battle at Springfield. With this small body of men, he

Major Gen. David Hunter (1802–86) succeeded John Charles Frémont as commander of the Western Department. He later served as president of the military commission that tried the conspirators involved in Lincoln's assassination.

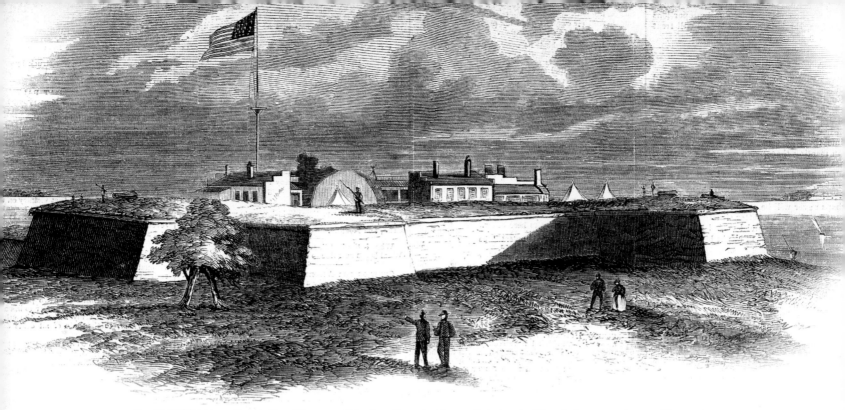

Fort McHenry, where Francis Scott Key wrote "The Star-Spangled Banner" during the War of 1812, served as a military prison and an artillery training outpost during the Civil War.

charged twenty times his number and drove the enemy from town, but over one-half of his command perished in the fight. . . .

Gen. Frémont is now relieved of his command and Gen. Hunter assumed temporary command. . . . After resting for a few days, we were ordered to counter-march, this leaving all southern Missouri open again to the ravages of the enemy, besides having the miserable consciousness that our campaign had been a miserable failure. . . .

NOVEMBER 3 SUNDAY

Major Gen. David Hunter was now in command, relieving Frémont on this day.

At Fairfax Court House, Va., Gen. Thomas J. "Stonewall" Jackson readied to leave for Winchester to begin his Valley Campaign.

NOVEMBER 4 MONDAY

Day, Pvt., Co. B, 25th Massachusetts Volunteer Infantry, Annapolis, Md., wrote:

. . . morning in Baltimore, and a stiller or more quiet place I never saw. . . . As we steamed past old Ft. McHenry, I was reminded of an interesting scrap of history connected with this fort. When the British fleet bombarded this fort during the last war with England, there was aboard one of the ships an American prisoner, a Mr. Key, I think his name was, who watched with the most intense anxiety the result of the bombardment, and during its progress, wrote the song that has since become famous as one of our national anthems, The Star-Spangled Banner. . . . Arrived at Annapolis about noon and marched up to the Naval Academy where we quartered and took dinner with the 21st Massachusetts, now doing garrison duty at this post. . . .

FACING PAGE: Prof. Thaddeus S. C. Lowe (1832–1913) was appointed the Chief Aeronaut of the Union Army Balloon Corps in July of 1861. This 1862 photograph shows Lowe at Fair Oaks, Va., in his balloon *Intrepid*.

NOVEMBER 7
THURSDAY

Brigadier Gen. U. S. Grant fought his first battle, capturing a Confederate fortified position near Belmont, Mo.: The Confederate General Polk sent troops across the river to counterattack and Grant was forced to retreat. Neither side gained an advantage, but Grant learned some lessons here that would do him good later.

NOVEMBER 8
FRIDAY

Lt. James E. Jouett of the USS *Santee* organized a "cutting out" expedition of small boats near Galveston, Tex., where the schooner *Royal Yacht* was captured and burned. These types of expeditions were very popular in naval warfare during this period. Usually they consisted of two or more ship's boats loaded with sailors and marines who used the cover of darkness and muffled oars to approach the target ship.

Lee arrived in Savannah to take command of a very large territory which was blockaded and poorly manned.

NOVEMBER 9 SATURDAY

The Federal force in South Carolina captured Beaufort without a fight and blocked the Broad River, effectively cutting water communications between Charleston and Savannah.

In the west there were some command changes which would do much to shape later events. Major Gen. Henry W. Halleck was assigned command of the Department of the Missouri, which included Grant's command. Gen. William T. Sherman was

Confederate Lieut. Gen. Nathan Bedford Forrest (1821–77) was the oldest of twelve children born to a poverty-stricken blacksmith in Chapel Hill, Tennessee. He had to take over the support of his family when he was 16, following the death of his father.

also replaced in command by Gen. Don Carlos Buell, with Sherman leaving under a cloud.

NOVEMBER 10
SUNDAY

Federal troops expanded their hold on Port Royal, S.C., by carrying out an expedition against Braddock's Point.

NOVEMBER 11 MONDAY

Near Ft. Monroe, Professor Thaddeus Lowe was making history by raising the balloon from the deck of the balloon-boat *G. W. Parke Custis.*

NOVEMBER 16 SATURDAY

Day, Pvt., Co. B, 25th Massachusetts Volunteer Infantry, near Annapolis, Md., wrote:

We begin to see a little something of the peculiar institution—slavery. There are a great many negroes strolling around the camps, most of them runaways, and as Maryland is supposed to be a loyal state, we have no right to take sides and afford them protection. . . . The masters and hunters are frequently here looking up their boys, as they call them, and we generally manage to put them on the wrong track and then run the boys into other camps, and they run into the woods. . . .

NOVEMBER 24 SUNDAY

Today an almost obscure Confederate undertook an expedition into Kentucky from Tennessee. Nathan Bedford Forrest was beginning his career as one of the cavalry geniuses of the war. Forrest was to become a legend during the war and certainly had something heroic in his personality. His exploits during the war and his capability as a cavalry commander made his tactics memorable, and they were studied for generations thereafter. He rightfully was called a "wizard of the saddle."

NOVEMBER 29 FRIDAY

Along the coast of South Carolina and Georgia, fires could be seen where planters were burning cotton to prevent it falling into the hands of the North. The Charleston *Mercury* exclaimed, "Let the torch be applied whenever the invader pollutes our soil."

∞ DECEMBER 1861 ∞

ALONG THE ATLANTIC SEABOARD smoke columns arose from the pyres of burning cotton set ablaze by the planters to prevent it being seized by the Yankees. Lincoln was readying his address to Congress. In both North and South, the soldiers were settling into winter camps and long sessions of drill, drill, and more drill. Most were learning to cope with living outdoors, using inadequate shelter for the first time.

DECEMBER 1 SUNDAY

Lincoln, becoming impatient, sent a memorandum to McClellan inquiring "just *how* long would it require to actually get in motion?" Off the coast of Georgia, the USS *Seminole*, Commander John S. Missroon, with a small group of other ships, captured the sloop *Lida*, with a cargo of coffee, lead, and sugar. The noose of the blockade was tightening.

DECEMBER 2 MONDAY

Lincoln authorized Major Gen. Henry Halleck in the Department of Missouri to suspend the writ of *habeas corpus* in areas where he found it necessary. This was a considerable widening of the original suspension, which covered only an area along the eastern seaboard.

Secretary of the Navy Gideon Welles sent his first annual report to the President containing an upbeat note. Things were looking fairly well for the Union, as regarded the Navy.

DECEMBER 4 WEDNESDAY

The United States Senate voted 36 to 0 to expel Senator John C. Breckinridge of Kentucky. Breckinridge, having served as Buchanan's Vice President, was elected to the Senate in 1860. He remained in the Senate hoping to find some peaceful solution to the problem, but, seeing this as an impossible task, joined the Confederate Army in November. He was appointed Commander of the 1st Kentucky Brigade, which became known as "The Orphan Brigade."

DECEMBER 9
MONDAY

The first of the "oversight" committees to be set up by Congress over the years, the Joint Committee on the Conduct of the War was authorized on this date. Little would escape its attention and investi-

After his service in the Confederate Army, John Breckinridge (1821–75) became Confederate Secretary of War in 1865. At the end of the war, he escaped to Cuba, where he remained in exile for three years before returning to Kentucky to resume his law practice.

gations. Probably many millions of man-hours were wasted in testimony to this committee.

DECEMBER 10 TUESDAY

In Richmond, the State of Kentucky was admitted to the Confederacy, making the 13th, and final, state. The Confederate government of Kentucky had no permanent home, and it moved around frequently.

Barber, Pvt., Co. D, 15th Illinois Volunteer Infantry, Otterville, Mo., wrote:

We made frequent forays out into the country and confiscated corn, etc., from the rebels; on such occasions, there was usually a scrambling to see who would go. Almost invariably the boys would come in loaded down with the best that the country afforded. The weather became so intensely cold that we had to adopt some plan to keep from freezing. We pegged our tent as close to the ground as possible, and covered over the lap with dirt. We then built a sort of fire-place at the foot, with the chimney just outside the tent, and got a good bed of twigs and straw to lie on; had the opening of

On the night of December 11, 1861, a raging fire swept the business district of Charleston, S.C. Coupled with the shortages created by the blockade, the fire was a new and unwanted blow to the economy. This 1865 photograph shows the damage to the Roman Catholic Cathedral of St. John and St. Finbar caused by the fire.

the tent so arranged that we could fasten it tight, and at night, beneath our heavy covering, we nestled together like a litter of young pigs. Though the thermometer was ten below zero, we slept warm and comfortable. . . .

We were now set to work building winter quarters. . . .

DECEMBER 16 MONDAY
Today the Stonewall Brigade left camp at Winchester, Va., and marched to the bluffs overlooking Dam No. 5 of the Chesapeake and Ohio Canal.

DECEMBER 17 TUESDAY
Near Dam No. 5 of the C&O Canal, the Stonewall Brigade huddled in the bitter cold all day waiting for darkness to begin their destruction of the dam. At darkness, thirty members of the group went to the dam and began to dismantle it.

DECEMBER 18 WEDNESDAY
At daylight, the Federals discovered the Stonewall Brigade's presence at Dam No. 5 of the C&O Canal and began firing at the soldiers working on the destruction of the dam. Jackson brought his artillery to bear, but this was replied to by Federal artillery, so operations were suspended until dark. Jackson's men were hiding in the old mill on the Virginia side of the Potomac when this building was brought under fire by Federal artillery, causing a sudden evacuation of Confederates.

DECEMBER 20 FRIDAY
After waiting out the long, cold day yesterday to get back to the destruction of Dam No. 5 on the C&O Canal, Jackson moved some of his men upriver and the Federals followed, thinking he was headed for Dam No. 4. Immediately, the destroyers returned to Dam No. 5 and fell to with vigor in the icy water. The Federals did not return to Dam No. 5. The Brigade completed their work of destruction on Dam

No. 5 and prepared to depart. The final work had been free of Federal interference.

DECEMBER 26 THURSDAY
Martial law was declared in St. Louis, and along all railroads operating in the state of Missouri.

Day, Pvt., Co. B, 25th Massachusetts Volunteer Infantry, near Annapolis, Md., wrote:

Christmas went off very pleasantly and apparently to the satisfaction of all. . . . The Irishmen had their Christmas box, the Germans their song and lager, while ball playing and other athletic sports used up the day and music and dancing were the order of the evening. Santa Claus came with a Christmas dinner for a few, but more of us he passed by; however, I think the old gentleman has got a store for us somewhere on the way. . . .

DECEMBER 30 MONDAY
Banks in the United States suspended the practice of redeeming paper money for metal currency, a practice that would continue until 1879.

DECEMBER 31 TUESDAY
Things were not going at all well for Lincoln or his cause. He tried to sort some sense out of the command structure in the west by asking both Buell and Halleck if they were doing any joint planning. The replies he got were not encouraging. Buell replied that he had no provision for concerted action, and Halleck said he didn't know what Buell was doing and couldn't cooperate in any case. Lincoln wired both generals to do some cooperating and then visited the Quartermaster General of the Army, Montgomery C. Meigs. During his visit he asked:

General, what shall I do? The people are impatient; Chase has no money, and tells me he can raise no more; the General of the Army has typhoid fever. The bottom is out of the tub. What shall I do?

1862

This is no time for man to war against man. The forces of
Heaven are loose and in all their fury, the wind howls, the
sea rages, the eternal is here in all his majesty. . . .

—Private Day, off Cape Hatteras, N.C., January 1862

∽ JANUARY 1862 ∽

JANUARY 1, 1862, was bright with promise for some, and looked upon with dread by others. It was a cold, bitter winter for the soldiers. Most of the soldiers in the armies were not psychologically prepared for a long war. Many, especially in the South, were just settling in after enlistments, which were for the duration of the war. They could not easily adapt to camp life without some hardship.

JANUARY 1 WEDNESDAY

Lincoln and his Cabinet held the traditional New Year's reception. The entire diplomatic corps was in attendance. General George McClellan, who had not made an aggressive move for five months, was ill.

In the Shenandoah Valley, Gen. Thomas J. Jackson began his movement towards Romney in western Virginia. His ultimate goal was the Baltimore and Ohio Railroad and the locks of the Chesapeake and Ohio Canal—an attempt to cut communications with the west.

JANUARY 2 THURSDAY

After much confusion and delay on the part of Gen. Ripley, Chief of Ordnance, the Union finally received a quantity of machine guns. These were the "coffee mill" guns first demonstrated to Lincoln on June 24, 1861, in Washington. Col. John W. Geary, commanding the 28th Pennsylvania Infantry, had the dubious honor of receiving these guns for use in the field.

JANUARY 3 FRIDAY

The diseases that ravaged many of the new camps left few untouched. It was not uncommon for a company that began with 100 or more men to lose 20 or more during the first few months to disease, accident or disability.

Statistics were to show that during the first year and a half of the war the Union lost 2.01 percent of its force to disease. The figures for the Confederate forces were higher, at 3.81 percent. Nearly half again as many Rebels died of diarrhea and dysentery as the Yanks. Nearly five times as many Rebels died of pulmonary diseases.

Jackman, Pvt., "The Orphan Brigade," in a Kentucky camp, wrote:

> We had been in camp but a few days when Billie S.N. was sent to the hospital with the typhoid fever and soon after died. A week or two afterward three others of the mess were sent off—"Bro Don," H.O.

PRECEDING PAGES: The 21st Wisconsin Volunteer Infantry Regiment crossing a pontoon bridge over the Ohio River near Cincinnati on Saturday, September 13, 1862

ABOVE: An Ager "coffee mill gun" in the hands of the 96th Pennsylvania Volunteer Regiment, Camp Northumberland, northern Virginia, February 1862

and "Capt." G.—Billie A.G.P. and myself were all that remained. Four of the company died in hospital while encamped at "Clear Water" and retreating, left A.O. at Gallatin, Tenn., who died.

JANUARY 5 SUNDAY

Early yesterday morning, Jackson captured Bath, chasing the Federals to the Potomac. The town of Hancock refused to surrender, and, after giving time to remove the women and children, a few shells were lobbed into the town. The Arkansas troops with Jackson burned the railroad bridge over the Great Cacapon River in western Virginia.

Barber, Pvt., Co. D, 15th Illinois Volunteer Infantry, Otterville, Mo., wrote:

> We now received another installment of pay. A good many of the boys had acquired the habit of gambling. "Chuck Luck" was their favorite game. . . . Many a soldier would venture all his hard earnings on the throw of the dice, and thus lose in a few hours what it had taken him months to earn. This species of gaming was carried on to such an extent that an order was issued prohibiting it. If anyone was caught at it, he was arrested and his money confiscated, but this did not stop the practice. . . . Gaming engendered other vices and too many of the boys gave free rein to their passions and indulged in all manner of excesses of the grossest nature.

JANUARY 6 MONDAY

The Union force near Hancock, in western Virginia, got reinforcements and Jackson withdrew his men, abandoning any chance of crossing the Potomac and raiding north.

Lincoln again rejected suggestions from some of

FOR New Orleans AND A MARKET.

With the advent of the Union blockade of Confederate ports, blockade runners—boats that tried to work their way past Federal ships—proliferated. This cartoon, depicting a Confederate blockade runner, suggests that the only successful way to run a blockade would have been aboard an alligator.

the senators that McClellan be removed for inaction. Lincoln also was after Buell again on the east Tennessee situation.

JANUARY 8 WEDNESDAY

President Davis was still badgering the various governors of the Confederate States for more support and troops. The reluctance of the governors was growing.

JANUARY 9 THURSDAY

In Cairo, Illinois, Grant was preparing to conduct a reconnaissance-in-force towards Columbus, Ky., on the Mississippi.

In New Orleans, the blockade was causing considerable concern. The Commercial Bulletin, a local New Orleans paper, reported:

> The situation of this port makes it a matter of vast moment to the whole Confederate State that it should be opened to the commerce of the world within the least possible period. . . .

In Philadelphia, orders reached Flag Officer Farragut assigning him to command the Western Gulf Blockading Squadron to cover an area from west Florida to the Rio Grande. His primary mission, however, was to gain access to the Mississippi and to capture New Orleans, and then go upriver to connect with Grant coming downriver.

Day, Pvt., Co. B, 25th Massachusetts Volunteer Infantry, aboard the steamer *New York*, Chesapeake Bay, wrote:

> . . . We passed the mouth of the Potomac river a little before sunset and shortly after dropped anchor for the night.

JANUARY 10 FRIDAY

There were increasing charges against the War Department for corruption, and murmurs were rising for the resignation of Simon Cameron, the Secretary of War.

The cooperation between the Union Army and Navy was paying off in the Port Royal area of South Carolina on the Coosaw River. Confederate Brigadier Gen. John C. Pemberton described the effectiveness of this teamwork:

> Although the enemy did not land in force at Page's Point or Cunningham's Bluff, it was entirely practicable for him to have done so under the cover of his gunboats. . . . At no time during his occupation of the river bank did he leave their [the gunboats,] protection, and, finally, when withdrawing to the island, did so under a fire from his vessels almost as heavy as that under which he had landed . . . by far the larger proportion of the [Confederate] casualties being from the shells of the fleet.

JANUARY 11 SATURDAY

In Washington, Simon Cameron resigned as Secretary of War. Lincoln accepted with alacrity.

Day, Pvt., Co. B, 25th Massachusetts Volunteer Infantry, steamer *New York*, Hampton Roads, Va., wrote:

> As I look out on the Old Dominion, the Mother of presidents, statesmen and heroes, my mind is filled with historical reminiscences of its past greatness and glory. Alas! that Virginia, a state that bore such a proud record in the history of our country . . . should now be sunk in the mire and slough of rebellion. There is no appearance of leaving here today. . . .

JANUARY 13 MONDAY

In Washington, Lincoln indicated he would nominate Edwin M. Stanton as the new Secretary of War, replacing Cameron. Lincoln also held a meeting of the Cabinet and a council of generals, including McClellan, to discuss the plans for the war. McClellan refused to discuss his operational plans, resenting the interference of Lincoln and the other generals. Lincoln let this slide for the time being, hoping "Little Mac" did, indeed, have a plan.

Day, Pvt., Co. B, 25th Massachusetts Volunteer Infantry, aboard the steamer *New York*, Hatteras Lighthouse, N.C., wrote:

> Going on deck this morning, I found we were riding at anchor in sight of Hatteras light. . . . As they weighed anchor, the boat rose and fell with the swells. I rather enjoyed this and thought it very nice. . . . Mr. Mulligan said, "We are going to have a great storm and Hatteras is a bad place to be caught in a storm." . . . At 1 PM we dropped anchor in front of the battery at Hatteras inlet, in the midst of a terrific southeast storm . . . . This is indeed the grandest, wildest scene I ever beheld! As far as the eye can reach, the water is rolling, foaming and dashing over the shoals, throwing its white spray far into the air, as though the sea and sky met. This is no time for man to war against man. The forces of Heaven are loose and in all their

fury, the wind howls, the sea rages, the eternal is here in all his majesty. . . .

JANUARY 15 WEDNESDAY

Stanton was confirmed by the Senate as the new Secretary of War. This would prove to be a mixed blessing. He was a friend of McClellan's, and not so friendly with Lincoln.

Jackson's column finally reached Romney, western Virginia, after two weeks on the march.

JANUARY 18 SATURDAY

In Kentucky, the Virginian who had remained loyal to the Union, George H. Thomas, brought his troops closer to the confrontation with Brigadier Gen. George B. Crittenden, CSA, on the Cumberland River. Crittenden had his back to the river and was in a poorly defined position.

Jackson finally ordered his troops into winter quarters at Bath Berkeley Springs and Moorefield.

JANUARY 19 SUNDAY

The Battle of Mill Springs was fought near the banks of the Cumberland River in Kentucky, between Federal forces under Brigadier Gen. George H. Thomas, and Confederate generals Crittenden and Zollicoffer. Crittenden escaped the Federals and left the area in a pouring rain. Zollicoffer wore a white raincoat during the engagement and was killed. The Rebels escaped across the river, leaving only discarded equipment and supplies. The Confederate defense line in Kentucky had been broken and would never be repaired—a demoralizing effect on all, except for the Federals, who gained support in eastern Kentucky and Tennessee.

Day, Pvt., Co. B, 25th Massachusetts Volunteer Infantry, Hatteras Inlet, N.C., wrote:

> Of all the lonely, God-forsaken looking places I ever saw, this Hatteras island takes the premium. It is simply a sandbar rising a little above the water, and the shoals extend nearly 100 miles out to sea. The water is never still and fair weather is never known; storms and sea gulls are the only productions. . . . It is the key, or gate-way, to nearly all of eastern North Carolina and places us directly in the rear of Norfolk, Va. . . .

JANUARY 20 MONDAY

At Hatteras Inlet, N.C., the amphibious operations fleet had arrived on the 13th and was preparing for the assault on Roanoke Island. The CSS *Sea Bird*, Flag Officer Lynch, reported that he had visited the Hatteras Inlet and "there saw a large fleet of steam-

David Glasgow Farragut (1801–70) was born in Tennessee, but moved north at the beginning of the war because of his loyalty to the Union. He was the first Rear Admiral and Vice Admiral in U.S. naval history.

ers and transports." He further wrote to Confederate Secretary of the Navy Mallory of the importance of the area which Roanoke Island controlled, "Here is the great thoroughfare from Albemarle Sound and its tributaries, and if the enemy obtain lodgements or succeed in passing here he will cut off a very rich country from Norfolk market."

With the arrival of Flag Officer Farragut in the Gulf of Mexico, the operational areas were split, giving Farragut the area from west Florida to Mexico. His main mission, however, was to capture New Orleans.

Wills, 3rd Sgt., Co. E, 8th Illinois Infantry, near Columbus, Ky., wrote:

We went out to Little Meadows which is about eight or nine miles from Columbus and halted. Taylor's battery . . . now unlimbered and planted their guns. . . . We waited here two hours and then formed again and returned to our camp of the previous night. It had turned warm by this time and the slush was six inches deep on our backward march. Slept in the mud that night and remained in camp all next day, during which it rained every hour.

Sunday we started for the river and of all the marches, that beats! We waded through at least eight streams from one to two feet deep and five to ten yards wide. . . . Object of expedish, don't know, don't care, only know that it did me good. I feel 100 percent better than I did when I started.

Col. Pitt Kellogg has brought me my commission as 1st Lieutenant in his regiment, and I am adjutant in the 3d battalion, Major Rawalts. I go to Cape Girardeau the last of this week.

JANUARY 21 TUESDAY

After remaining in Romney, western Virginia, since the 16th, Jackson ordered Garnett and the Stonewall Brigade back to Winchester. Jackson went with his old brigade. It was Jackson's 38th birthday.

JANUARY 23 THURSDAY

Day, Pvt., Co. B, 25th Massachusetts Volunteer Infantry, Hatteras Inlet, N.C., wrote:

Another great storm. The wind is blowing a gale and the sea is dashing, foaming and threatening everything with destruction. The camps on shore are flooded, the soldiers driven into the fort or up the island; more vessels ashore and the fleet going to the devil. A great many of the men are beginning to despond. . . . I have always had rather a desire for a sea voyage, but I am willing to confess that that wish is fully gratified. This being "rocked in the cradle of the deep" sounds all very pretty in song and romance, but the romance is played out with me, and I think the person who wrote the song "A Life on the Ocean Wave" must have been a proper subject for a lunatic asylum.

JANUARY 25 SATURDAY

The struggle continued to move the troop transports across the sandbar at Hatteras Inlet into Pamlico Sound. This had to be done before operations against Roanoke Island could be accomplished.

JANUARY 26 SUNDAY

"The Creole," Gen. Pierre G. T. Beauregard, was ordered to Tennessee to be second-in-command to Gen. Albert Sidney Johnston. Beauregard, the hero of Sumter and Manassas, previously served with Gen. Joseph E. Johnston, commanding the Confederates in Virginia.

JANUARY 27 MONDAY

President Lincoln, finally weary of McClellan's inactivity, issued General War Order No. 1, which declared that on February 22, 1862, all land and sea forces would attack the insurgents. It was, in fact, an act of desperation on Lincoln's part. No one seemed eager to get moving, in particular McClellan.

Confederate Secretary of War Judah Benjamin issued an order to Gen. Wise, who was commanding the troops at Roanoke Island, to hold the island at all costs. The odds were 5 to l in favor of the Federals.

JANUARY 28 TUESDAY

Flag Officer Foote notified Gen. Henry Halleck that he and Gen. Grant were of the opinion that Ft. Henry might be taken with four gunboats and the troops available. Halleck considered the condition of the river and notified Grant that the order would be issued as soon as he determined the conditions of the roads. Foote, impatient, told Halleck that the river was at flood stage and this was the time to make the attack using the river. Halleck waited.

JANUARY 29 WEDNESDAY

At Hatteras Inlet, the troop ships were still not all over the sandbar. Supplying fresh water to the troops on the ships was a real problem, and it got worse daily.

JANUARY 30 THURSDAY

A landmark in history was reached today when the USS *Monitor* was launched at Greenpoint, Long Island.

Day, Pvt., Co. B, 25th Massachusetts Volunteer Infantry, Hatteras Inlet, N.C., wrote:

> Our canteens are again filled with contraband water so we shall be alright today as far as that is concerned. Some of the boys made a raid last night on the sutler's stuff and appropriated to themselves pretty much what he had. I cannot approve of that, as the sutler is at a good deal of trouble and expense to get a few notions for us and probably sells them as cheap as he can afford. . . .

Julia Ward Howe, author of the lyrics to "The Battle Hymn of the Republic," was familiar with the 1855 abolitionist song "Glory Hallelujah" and composed her poem with its tune in mind.

JANUARY 31 FRIDAY

Lincoln, to supplement his General War Order No. 1, issued Special War Order No. 1, which was directed specifically at Major Gen. George B. McClellan. In this order, Lincoln directed that action be taken against Manassas before February 22nd. "Little Mac" ignored the whole thing.

FEBRUARY 1862

IN THE WINTERING ARMIES, the troops sickened with the usual colds, flu and other maladies common to large groups of people. The Southern coast, already in peril, braced itself for more troubles as the Union advanced towards Roanoke Island and Savannah. Few Southern ports were open for even the occasional blockade runner. The noose tightened.

In the west, especially on the Tennessee and Cumberland rivers, the Federal gunboats reigned supreme. The Confederate Navy was nonexistent on these waters, and Flag Officer Foote was having things his way. The February *Atlantic Monthly* published the latest poem by Julia Ward Howe, which was almost immediately translated into song as "The Battle Hymn of the Republic."

FEBRUARY 1 SATURDAY

The assault on Forts Henry and Donelson was getting underway. Flag Officer Foote telegraphed Washington, "I leave early to-morrow with four armored gunboats on an expedition cooperating with the Army Senior officer will telegraph you during my absence. . . ."

FEBRUARY 3 MONDAY

In Washington, President Lincoln declined the offer of war elephants from the King of Siam, stating that the weather "does not reach a latitude so low as to favor the multiplication of the elephant."

Day, Pvt., Co. B, 25th Massachusetts Volunteer Infantry, Hatteras Sound, N.C., wrote:

> Business is brisk today; all the boats are in the sound and the schooners are alongside of them supplying them with coal, water and rations, preparatory to a trip up the sound. Everything now seems to be nearly ready, and I expect that some fine morning we will make a call on our southern friends. . . . I would much rather they welcome us to a good dinner of fishballs than cannon balls; but I suppose they will have their own choice of reception and we must reciprocate the best we can.

FEBRUARY 4 TUESDAY

In Richmond, the Virginia House of Delegates discussed enlisting free Negroes in the Confederate forces. In many Southern units the terms of enlistment were about to expire, and the commanders were appealing to the troops to stay on.

FEBRUARY 5 WEDNESDAY

At Ft. Henry, the river had flooded a good portion of the lower fort, and Gen. Tilghman's troops were having a hard time with morale. They had only 3,000 or so men to defend the fort.

Day, Pvt., Co. B, 25th Massachusetts Volunteer Infantry, Albemarle Sound, N.C., wrote:

> . . . [H]ere we go for a trip up the sound, probably for Roanoke island. . . . It is quite an important point and we learn is strongly defended. Our fleet consists of about seventy sail of all kinds and makes an imposing appearance. . . .

FEBRUARY 6 THURSDAY

The Navy stole the march on the Army today when Flag Officer Foote and his gunboat armada captured Ft. Henry with ground troops. Using four armored and three wooden gunboats, the fire from the fleet was sufficient to cause Brigadier Gen. Tilghman to surrender his reduced strength command, having sent most of his men cross-country to Ft. Donelson.

Gen. Albert S. Johnston, CSA, noted:

> The capture of that Fort [Henry] by the enemy gives them the control of the navigation of the Tennessee River, and their gunboats are now ascending the river to Florence [Alabama]. . . . Should Ft. Donelson be taken it will open the route to the enemy to Nashville, giving them the means of breaking the bridges and destroying the ferryboats on the river as far as navigable.

In North Carolina, the transports were all across the sandbar and preparations for the assault on Roanoke Island proceeded.

FEBRUARY 7 FRIDAY

The assault on Roanoke Island finally got underway today. The gunboats leading, the assault force

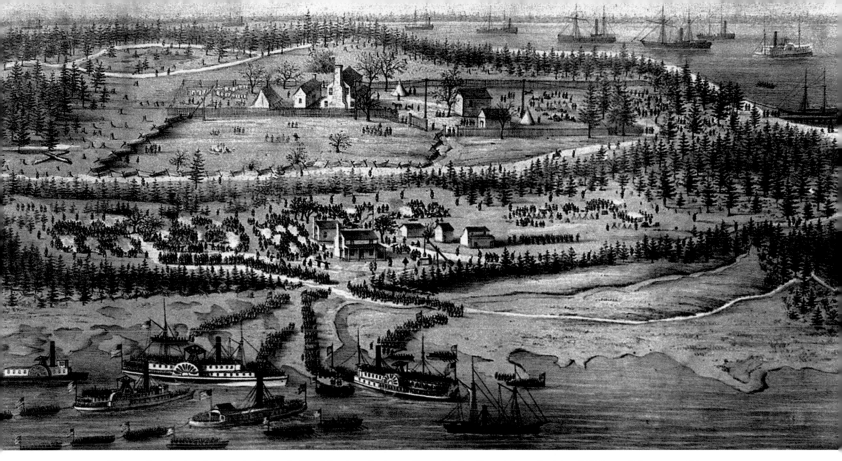

This undated print depicts the forces led by Brig. Gen. Ambrose Burnside landing at Roanoke Island, N.C., on February 7, 1862.

headed into the battle with the heavy bombardment of Ft. Barrow at Pork Point. An eyewitness on a troop ship told the story.

Day, Pvt., Co. B, 25th Massachusetts Volunteer Infantry, Bombardment of Roanoke Island, N.C., wrote:

[A]t about 10 o'clock we saw a white cloud rise from one of the boats and the next moment a huge column of dirt and sand rose from the enemy's works . . . The fort replied from all its guns, but their shots fell short as the boats lay beyond their range. The bombardment now commenced in earnest, the boats sailing in a circle and delivering their fire as they passed the fort. Their firing was not rapid, but well directed. . . . At noon the transports commenced the passage of the narrow channel into Croatan sound. From here we had a much nearer and better view of the bombardment. The boats were sailing much nearer the fort and firing more rapidly. They had driven the men from the guns on the fort and their fire was feebly replied to. At this time the shells from the boats had set the barracks and other buildings near the fort on fire. Great clouds of smoke and flame rose from the burning buildings and the boats belched forth their fire more furiously than ever, the shots tearing up the parapet of the fort or burying themselves in the mound of sand covering the magazine. It was truly a grand and fearful exhibition! Thousands looked on with breathless suspense, expecting every moment to see the magazine blow up or the rebels strike their colors.

The enemy's gunboats which had been idle spectators behind the blockade now came to the rescue; but a few well directed shots from 100-pounder rifles sent them reeling back to their places. . . .

About 2 PM. . . . I was standing near Col. Upton at the gangway forward of the wheelhouse as the Pilot Boy ran alongside and heard Gen. Foster tell the colonel to order his men to load with ball cartridge, take three days' rations and come aboard his boat and the barges as soon as possible. This loading with ball cartridge was a new order to me; it implied that our holiday soldiering was over. A peculiar feeling such as I had never before experienced came over me; I felt it to the very taps of my brogans and thought I would rather be excused. . . .

5 PM Foster's brigade had all landed and by dark nearly the whole division was ashore. Now commenced the work of carrying rails and planks to build a road across the marsh to get the howitzers of the marine artillery ashore. Soon after dark, Gen. Foster with the 21st Massachusetts and a section of the marine artillery, hauling their howitzers, went past us into the woods to establish his picket line. After a while the general returned and said we might build fires and make ourselves comfortable.

FEBRUARY 8
SATURDAY

The battle for Roanoke Island resumed about 9 AM. By 4 PM the obstructions sunk by the Confederates had been cleared sufficiently for the Federal gunboats to enter Albemarle Sound. The Confederate gunboats offered only token resistance, being overwhelmed by the Federal fleet.

The back door to Norfolk was now open.

Day, Pvt., Co. B, 25th Massachusetts Volunteer Infantry, Battle of Roanoke Island, N.C., wrote:

At daylight, the order to fall in was heard on all sides. Putting on my equipment and taking Spitfire and a big sweet potato which I had, with much labor, succeeded in baking, I took my place in my company. . . .

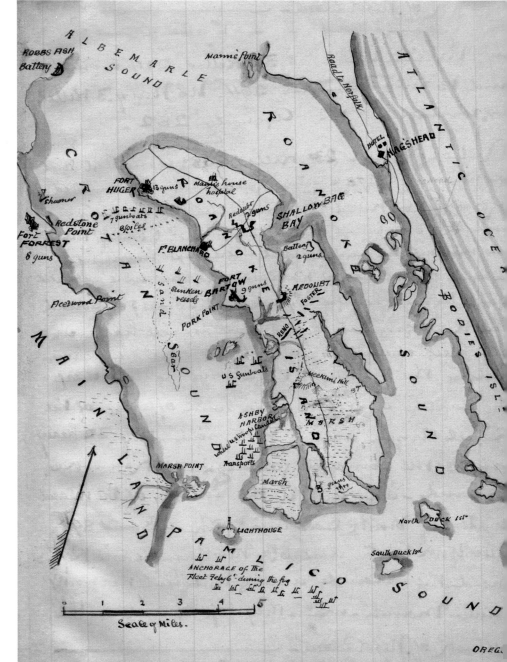

A map of Roanoke Island, showing the location of Confederate forces on the eve of battle

Company A, Capt. Pickett, was thrown out as skirmishers. They soon fell in with the enemy's pickets and drove them in. . . .

We were now in line in the swamp and, facing to the front, commenced firing. The battery had already opened the ball and were receiving the attention of the enemy in front. We could see nothing to shoot at, but taking our range by the smoke of the enemy's guns, we blazed away. We fired high, low, and obliquely, thinking if we covered a wide range of ground we might possibly lame somebody and it seemed our shots must have proved troublesome for they turned their attention to us, pouring musketry and canister shot without stint into the swamp. We were up to our knees in mud and water so their shot passed over us without doing much damage.

Capt. Foster of company D was the first man I saw hit. I was watching him as he stood on a bog, cutting away the briars with his sword and thinking of him as colonel of the old 8th regiment Massachusetts volunteer militia, in which I used to muster. The shot struck him in the eye. He whirled round on the bog and would have fallen had not three of his men caught him and led him to the rear. . . .

By cutting and crowding ourselves through the briars, we advanced to within about 300 yards of the enemy. Our ammunition being now exhausted and having been in the swamp about three hours, we were ordered out. . . . Seeing that all was now lost, the rebels took to their heels for the head of the island, followed by Reno and Foster's brigades. At the head of the island, near the enemy's camp, was Gen. Burnside with the 24th Massachusetts regiment to whom Col. Shaw, in command of the Confederate forces, surrendered. By this, about 3,000 prisoners, with their arms, ammunition and stores, fell into our hands. But the greatest prize of all, old ex-Governor Wise, slipped through our fingers. . . .

During the action I had seen quite a number hit and led back to the rear, but I had little time to think much about it. After the chase commenced and we marched through the little redoubt and over the ground held by the enemy and I began to see the mangled forms of dead and dying men, I was filled with an indescribable horror and wanted to go right home. I now began to realize what we had been doing, and thought that if in this age of the world, with all our boasted civilization and education, men could not settle their differences short of cutting each other's throats, we were not far removed from barbarism. But I suppose as long as the nature of man is ambitious and selfish, he will try to obtain by force what he cannot attain by other means. . . .

FEBRUARY 10 MONDAY

In the west, Gen. Halleck was sending urgent messages to Flag Officer Foote to provide gunboats for the troops on the Cumberland River who would soon assault Ft. Donelson. Meanwhile, Foote was trying mightily to repair battle damage to his small fleet of gunboats.

Down in the Gulf of Mexico, Flag Officer Farragut was assembling the ships and mortar boats which would comprise the fleet attempting to capture New Orleans. His progress was watched keenly by the Confederate spies in the area.

FEBRUARY 12 WEDNESDAY

In the area around Ft. Donelson, Grant now had his troops in a ring around the fort, which was anchored on the river. He awaited the arrival of Foote and his gunboats, which were on the way.

Flag Officer Foote left Cairo last night after notifying Secretary of War Gideon Welles:

I leave Cairo again to-night with the Louisville, Pittsburg, and St Louis for the Cumberland River to cooperate with the army in the attack on Ft. Donelson. . . . I shall do all in my power to render the gunboats effective in the fight, although they are not properly manned. . . . If we could wait ten days, and I had men, I would go with eight mortar boats and six armored boats and conquer.

FEBRUARY 14 FRIDAY

The assault on Ft. Donelson was made by Gen. Grant and Flag Officer Foote. The fort, being situated on high ground, could subject the fleet to plunging fire (i.e., the shells falling nearly vertically) into areas on the gunboats which were lightly protected. Despite this, Foote ordered his boats into the battle. The USS *St. Louis*, Foote's flagship, was hit 59 times, lost her steering and began to drift downriver. Foote, injured during the melee, would have to give up command of the flotilla later because of the injury. The gunboat attack was broken off for the time being.

Barber, Pvt., Co. D, 15th Illinois Volunteer Infantry, Cairo, Illinois, wrote:

. . . February 14th we arrived at Cairo where we halted for orders. . . . [W]e learned that a fierce and bloody battle was in progress at Ft. Donelson on the Cumberland river . . . We had no doubt now of our destination.

FEBRUARY 15 SATURDAY

The gunboats of Flag Officer Foote were back on the Cumberland River in support of the assault of Ft. Donelson. Major Gen. Lew Wallace summed up the role of the Navy in this engagement:

I recollect yet the positive pleasure the sounds [naval gunfire] gave me . . . the obstinacy and courage of the Commodore.

The efforts of Flag Officer Andrew Hull Foote (1806–63) contributed greatly to Gen. Ulysses S. Grant's success in the battle at Ft. Donelson.

. . . Was the attack of assistance to us? I don't think there is room to question it. It distracted the enemy's attention, and I fully believe it was the gunboats . . . that operated to prevent a general movement of the rebels up the river or across it, the night before the surrender.

One commander within the fort was thinking of everything but surrender. Tonight, Nathan Bedford Forrest would lead his cavalry out of Donelson, through a freezing swamp, and to safety. His would be the only organized body of troops to escape.

This illustration, published in the March 8, 1862, edition of *Harper's Weekly*, depicts the search by torchlight for wounded soldiers after the battle at Ft. Donelson.

FEBRUARY 16 SUNDAY

Gen. Simon B. Buckner in Ft. Donelson asked Grant for terms for surrender. Grant gave his now famous reply: "No terms except unconditional and immediate surrender can be accepted. I propose to move immediately upon your works." Buckner believed and accepted.

FEBRUARY 17 MONDAY

Generals Floyd and Pillow arrived in Nashville to be greeted by Gen. Albert S. Johnston. Forrest would arrive with his cavalry tomorrow. The South was in turmoil, and Nashville in a panic. Many of the citizens were packing to leave for points unknown.

Grant, now known as "Unconditional Surrender" Grant, was promoted to Major General of Volunteers by a grateful government in Washington.

FEBRUARY 18 TUESDAY

Barber, Pvt., Co. D, 15th Illinois Volunteer Infantry, Ft. Donelson, Tenn., wrote:

Volunteers were called for to help attend to the wounded and place them on transports.

It was a pitiful and sickening sight to see such a mass of mangled limbs and mutilated bodies, but the patience with which they bore their injuries excited our admiration. Of the twenty which I helped carry on the boat, not one uttered a complaint, even though a leg or an arm were missing. The next day we took a stroll over the battlefield. We saw sights that fairly froze the blood in our veins. The dead lay as they had fallen, in every conceivable shape, some grasping their guns as though they were in the act of firing, while others, with a cartridge in their icy grasp, were in the act of loading. Some of the countenances wore a peaceful, glad smile, while on others rested a fiendish look of hate. It looked as though each countenance was the exact counterpart of the thoughts that were passing through the mind when the death messenger laid them low. Perhaps that noble looking youth, with his smiling up-turned face, with his glossy ringlets matted with his own life-blood, felt a mother's prayer stealing over his senses as his young life went out. Near him lay a young husband with a prayer for his wife and little one yet lingering on his lips. Youth and age, virtue and evil, were represented on those ghastly countenances. Before us lay the charred and blackened remains of some who had been burnt alive. They were wounded too badly to move and the fierce elements consumed them. We now came to where the rebels made their last desperate effort to break our lines, and in a small cleared field the dead were piled up, friend and foe alike in death struggle.

Jackman, Pvt., "The Orphan Brigade," in hospital, en route to Gallatin, Tenn., wrote:

> . . . until daylight the next morning we were on the road to Gallatin. The weather turned cold that night and a snow two or three inches deep fell. The train was so heavy, the engineer said, that he could not pull it. I believe he wanted it captured. I did not sleep a moment that night. The car was crowded to overflowing with sick and I had to stand up a great deal of the time.

Day, Pvt., Co. B, 25th Massachusetts Volunteer Infantry, Roanoke Island, N.C., wrote:

> The prisoners are all paroled, and were sent off to-day. Paroling the prisoners was rather interesting to the lookers on. They were required to affix their autographs to the parole, and it was curious to observe that a large majority of them wrote it the same way, simply making the letter X. Capt. Messenger, the provost marshal, was master of ceremonies. . . .

FEBRUARY 19 WEDNESDAY

Robert E. Lee, charged with the defenses of the Florida district, was having a very difficult time with this assignment. He had few troops to work with and little artillery for shore batteries, and the rail network in this part of the country was less than satisfactory. He looked long and hard at the defenses on the many islands on the coast and wrote Brigadier Gen. Trapier:

> In looking at the whole defense of Florida, it becomes important to ascertain what points can probably be held and what points had better be relinquished. The force that the enemy can bring against any position where he can concentrate his floating batteries renders it prudent and proper to withdraw from the islands to the main-land and be prepared to contest his advance into the interior. Where an island offers the best point of defense, and is so connected with the main that its communications cannot be cut off, it may be retained. Otherwise, it should be abandoned.

FEBRUARY 20 THURSDAY

In Washington, William Wallace "Willie" Lincoln died at the age of 11 of typhoid fever. The tragedy overwhelmed the President, who tried to console his wife. They were not the only ones suffering from the loss of loved ones. The casualty notices from Ft. Donelson were being posted, both North and South, in all the towns and villages that had sent their men to war.

Flag Officer Farragut arrived at Ship Island, Miss., to begin his assault on New Orleans. Earlier, Gen. Braxton Bragg, CSA, had reported to Richmond that large bodies of troops and quantities of supplies were being landed at the island.

At Nashville, Governor Isham Harris abandoned the city by moving the State government to Memphis.

FEBRUARY 22 SATURDAY

President Davis was inaugurated today in Richmond as the first President of the Confederacy.

FEBRUARY 25 TUESDAY

Federal troops in large numbers were now in Nashville, and the city remained in Federal hands for the duration of the war. The loss of the city by the

Willie Lincoln (1850–62), President Lincoln's son, poses in this 1861 photo with his cousin Lockwood Todd, on the left, and brother Thomas, known as Tad (1853–71), on the right. Willie died at the age of 11, on February 20, 1862, of typhoid fever.

Confederates was more than a moral loss: Huge quantities of supplies had been stockpiled there for distribution to the Confederate forces in Virginia and elsewhere.

FEBRUARY 27 THURSDAY

In Richmond, the Confederate Congress gave President Davis the right to suspend *habeas corpus*, something that Lincoln had already done. Davis, unlike Lincoln, would use this power very little during the war.

Brig. Gen. Charles Ferguson Smith (1807–62) was injured in the battle of Pittsburg Landing when he slipped and badly scraped his shin while entering a small boat. The wound refused to heal, and he died of the resulting infection.

MARCH 1862

THERE HAD BEEN MANY CHANGES since March 1861. One year previously, the first blush of war had not been dimmed by the battle casualties of Bull Run and Forts Henry and Donelson. At that time, troops were gaily preparing for a war that no one believed would last long. Now, the outlook was much more grim and realistic. The casualty lists had been posted, a major city of the Confederacy had been lost and, for all practical purposes, Tennessee had been lost as well. North Carolina was almost sealed from the sea, and South Carolina's major harbors were either blockaded or occupied. In the North, little seemed right. McClellan was still waiting for an opportune time to move. It was clear that the war would not be won overnight.

MARCH 3 MONDAY

Union General John Pope began his assault on New Madrid, Mo., today while Federal troops occupied Columbus, Ky., to the north. Gen. Halleck, in a snit because Grant got the glory for the capture of Forts Henry and Donelson, accused Grant of not reporting properly during those operations and other, largely unspecified, misconduct a rumored charge of drunkenness. Halleck got authorization from Washington, and placed Brig. Gen. C. F. Smith in charge of the Union forces going up the Tennessee River.

Barber, Pvt., Co. D, 15th Illinois Volunteer Infantry, near Pittsburg Landing, Tenn., wrote:

> . . . [W]e marched to a landing four miles above Ft. Henry. . . . Here an immense fleet of transports had collected, which was to convey the army up to a point near Corinth, to operate against the rebel army which was concentrating all its available forces at the latter place.

MARCH 5 WEDNESDAY

In the Shenandoah Valley, Union Gen. Nathaniel Banks moved his troops south, up the Valley, towards Winchester, where "Stonewall" Jackson waited.

The first of Gen. C. F. Smith's forces reached Savannah, Tenn., just northeast of Corinth, Miss. Another 80 troop transports, escorted by gunboats, soon followed. The buildup was increasing rapidly.

Flag Officer Foote's gunboats needed repair badly after their service at Forts Henry and Donelson. While Halleck urged him to immediately attack Island No. 10, he declined because:

> . . . [t]he gunboats have been so much cut up in the late engagements at Forts Henry and Donelson in the pilot houses, hulls and disabled machinery that I could not induce the pilots to go in them again in a fight until they are repaired. I regret this, as we ought to move in the quickest possible time, but I have declined doing it, being utterly unprepared. . . .

Barber, Pvt., Co. D, 15th Illinois Volunteer Infantry, Pittsburg Landing [Shiloh], Tenn., wrote:

> Four divisions of the army now proceeded up the river twenty miles and disembarked at Pittsburg Landing. A gunboat had had a fight here a few days before with a land battery on the river bank. The place was almost a wilderness. A few log shanties were the only signs of human habitation. . . . The fourth division was the first to land. Our camp was situated one and a half miles from the landing and in the center of the military position of the army. On our right were Sherman and Prentiss, on the left, McClernand. Wallace's division landed at Crump Landing a few miles below. The landing of the army on this side of the river was a bold move in Grant as it placed him between the rebel army and the river, thus cutting off his retreat in case of disaster.

MARCH 6 THURSDAY

North of Fayetteville, Ark., four blue-clad divisions under the command of Brigadier Gen. Samuel R. Curtis were dug in along Sugar Creek, awaiting an assault by the Confederate forces of Earl Van Dorn. Van Dorn, not liking the odds, decided to move around the flank of the Federals during the night and attack their rear at Pea Ridge.

The USS *Monitor*, after several problems, sailed from Long Island for Hampton Roads, Va., where destiny awaited.

MARCH 7 FRIDAY

In northwest Arkansas, Gen. Earl Van Dorn's columns had passed around the flank and attacked Brigadier Gen. Curtis's Federal force from the rear. The Federals reacted quickly and fought strongly all day. Brigadier Gen. Benjamin McCulloch was killed by a sharpshooter during the fight, causing much confusion in the Confederate ranks. Confederate Brigadier Gen. James McIntosh was also killed. Curtis concentrated his forces at nightfall and awaited the attack by Van Dorn on Saturday

In Virginia, McClellan finally got moving south amid bands blaring and drums beating. Joe Johnston, not really looking for a fight, retreated ahead of "Little Mac."

MARCH 8 SATURDAY

The Battle of Pea Ridge ended today, with the Confederates retreating hastily towards the Arkansas River. Gen. Curtis wrote his brother:

> The enemy is again far away in the Boston Mountains. The scene is silent and sad—the vulture and the wolf now have the dominion and the dead friends and foes sleep in the same lonely graves.

At Hampton Roads, Va., the ironclad CSS *Virginia* steamed out of Norfolk under command of Flag Officer Buchanan, and created havoc among the Federal fleet. Her opponents were mostly wooden ships that could not withstand a ram from the *Virginia* or the weight of her guns.

MARCH 9 SUNDAY

Today began a new age in naval warfare. In an engagement that began at about 9 AM and lasted nearly four hours, the ironclads USS *Monitor* and CSS *Virginia* stood toe to toe and slugged it out on the waters of Hampton Roads, Va. Neither won the contest, but the reverberations of this battle were felt worldwide. As Capt. Dahlgren phrased it, "Now comes the reign of iron—and cased sloops are to take the place of wooden ships."

Gen. Joe Johnston's Confederate troops withdrew slowly south towards Rappahannock Station. McClellan's army stopped its southward progress and returned to its bases around Alexandria, Va.

Barber, Pvt., Co. D, 15th Illinois Volunteer Infantry, Pittsburg Landing, Tenn., wrote:

The rebels were concentrating all their available forces at Corinth, only twenty miles from us, and the two armies lay watching each other for several weeks, like ferocious bull dogs eager for a fight. Grant was waiting for Buell to come to his assistance before he commenced offensive operations, but all the while threatening the rebel army. Our camp was a very pleasant one and had been selected with some care. . . .

As depicted by this c. 1889 print, the fierce battle between the USS *Monitor* and the CSS *Virginia* (built from the remains of the USS *Merrimack*) on March 9, 1862, was the first encounter between "ironclads," or armored warships.

MARCH 11 TUESDAY

In Washington there was a new order of command. McClellan was relieved as General-in-Chief, but was retained as Commander of the Army of the Potomac. Other similar command changes occurred. All Department Commanders now reported directly to the Secretary of War.

At Winchester, Jackson withdrew his 4,600 men southward, followed closely by Banks.

In Richmond, President Davis refused to accept or acknowledge the reports sent by Generals Floyd and Pillow, who had fled Ft. Donelson. Both were relieved from command.

MARCH 12 WEDNESDAY

Federal troops occupied Winchester, on the heels of Jackson's retreating men. This town would change hands many times during the war, almost like a seesaw.

There was a degree of panic in Richmond as the citizens learned that McClellan was going to York Peninsula. The proximity to Richmond caused a rush on the "passport" office of those wanting to leave the city.

MARCH 13 THURSDAY

At a conference at Fairfax Court House, Va., McClellan pressed his plan to move the Army of the Potomac to the York Peninsula and James River, for an assault on Richmond. Lincoln reminded McClellan that the city of Washington must be kept covered by adequate troops at all times.

In New Bern, N.C., Gen. Burnside's troops landed under cover of naval bombardment on the west bank of the Neuse River and began to advance on the city.

Gen. Lee returned to Richmond today after his assignment as Commander of the Department of Florida.

Day, Pvt., Co. B, 25th Massachusetts Volunteer Infantry, ashore at New Bern, N.C., wrote:

The morning of the 13th was dark and rainy. . . . Before noon the troops were all landed, and the march commenced. The 25th taking the advance, we marched up the river bank about a mile, the gun-boats shelling the woods in advance of us. We then struck into the woods. . . . We soon came out to a cart road, or horse path, along which we followed for a couple of miles, when we came to a deserted cavalry camp. . . . A little further on, we came to the carriage road. . . .

The deep mud in the road, together with the heat, began to tell on the boys, and many of them were obliged to fall out by the way. Our march began to grow slower, and when about dusk it commenced raining again, we turned into the woods at the right of the road, where we were to bivouac for the night. . . .

MARCH 14 FRIDAY

The advancing Federals at New Madrid, Mo., found their enemy had evacuated to Island No. 10 or across the river, to the eastern bank of the Mississippi. Gen. John Pope still did not have Island No. 10 in his possession, but he was plugging away at it.

Flag Officer Foote at Cairo, Ill., departed with seven gunboats and ten mortar boats to attack Island No. 10.

At New Bern, N.C., Burnside's 11,000 men moved on the town and captured it, after some minor fighting, from a force of about 4,000 Confederates. The attack had been carried out through pouring rain and over muddy roads. With this city taken, another port and useful supply point was established.

Day, Pvt., Co. B, 25th Massachusetts Volunteer Infantry, Battle of New Bern, N.C., wrote:

We were within a half mile of the enemy's line, and Reno's and Parke's brigades were deploying in front of them, on the center and left of our line. . . . We filed out of the road to the right, moving towards the river. As we moved out we were honored with a salute from one of the enemy's batteries, but the shots passed harmlessly over our heads. The boys looked a little wild, but with steady step, moved on. . . . The howitzer battery now came up, took position in the road between the 24th and 27th Massachusetts, and commenced firing. . . . We advanced nearly to the edge of the woods, and only a short distance from the enemy's line. I was running my eye along it to see where and how it ended, expecting every moment to hear the order to charge, but just then the boats commenced throwing shell over us towards the Confederate line. They had got a low range and the shells were coming dangerously near. . . . In this condition of affairs, we were compelled to fall back. The boats, however, were soon notified of their mistake and ceased firing.

We again advanced, going over and beyond where we fell back, when all at once we received a galling flank fire from an unseen battery. We again fell back a few rods, dressing the line, and again cautiously advanced. We now discovered that their works curved and connected with a large water battery. . . . In the rear of this battery were mounted old 32-pounder marine guns. . . . From these guns they fired grape shot. . . . To charge was hopeless, and in falling back we received another fire from this battery. From these we lost quite a number of men, killed and wounded. I had the honor of stopping one ball myself; it struck a tree, however, before it did me. Having got back from under the guns of this battery, Col. Upton reported the situation to Gen. Foster, who ordered him to move his regiment to the left of the 24th Massachusetts and support the howitzer battery.

During all this time, however, the battle was raging furiously along the center and left. In front of our battery the enemy had a large gun which commanded the road. . . . This gun, after each discharge, was hauled around, and again back into position by a pair of mules. After each discharge, a young dare-devil of a marine lieutenant would run down the road almost to the gun to see what they were up to. On one of these excursions he discovered one of the mules down, probably from a stray shot. He came running back up the road like a wild man swinging his cap and shouting at the top of his voice: "Come on, come on! for God's sake, come on. Now is your time." The 25th, without any other order, sprang forward, followed by the 24th Massachusetts and all the line. On the charge, they received a heavy fire from the enfilading battery, but on they went, scaling the ditch and parapet like blackbirds, but no enemy was there. Seeing us coming, they took that as a notice to leave, and acted on it immediately. . . .

The 25th reformed and marching a short distance to the rear charged across the railroad into the swamp, capturing Col. Avery and his South Carolina regiment who were covering the retreat. Thus, after five hours hard fighting, ended the battle of New Bern. . . . Although the battle resulted as I wished, I certainly did not feel like glorying, for who can compute the woe, anguish and sorrow of this day's work? I cannot get over my horror of a battle. . . .

This map—created by Union Army cartographer Robert Knox Sneden—of the Battle of New Bern, N.C., which took place on March 14, 1862, shows the area between Old Beaufort Road and the Neuse River to the north and Evan's Mill Pond to the south. The locations of Forts Lane, Ellis, Thompson and Dixie are also indicated. Color coding denotes the position of Union and Confederate forces.

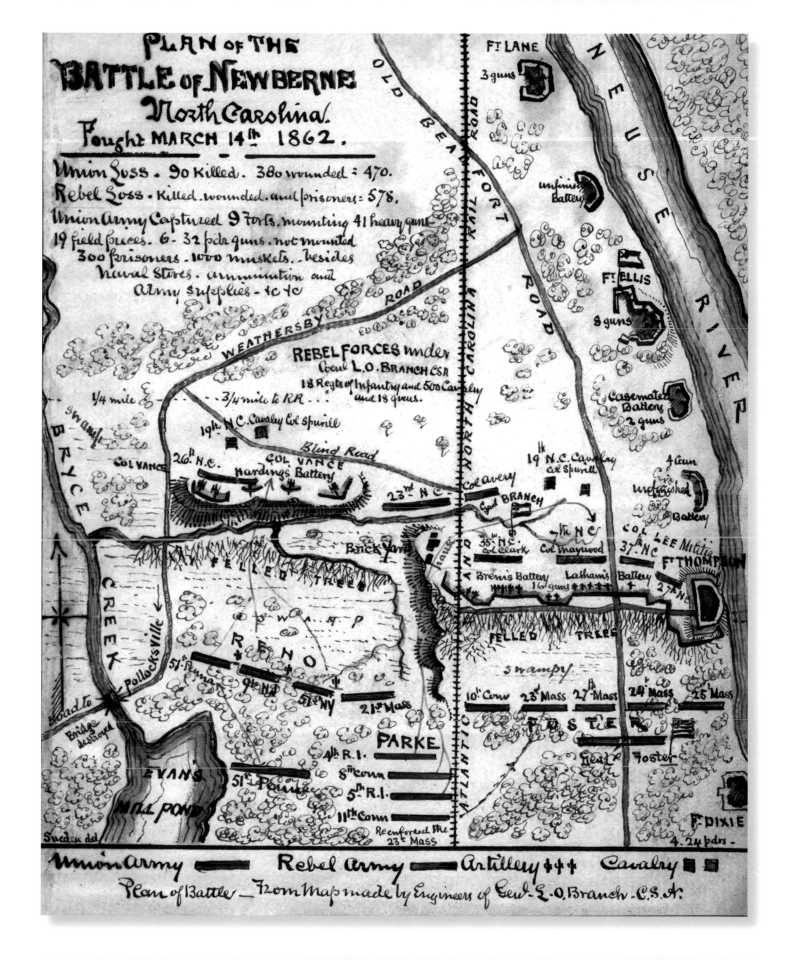

PLAN OF THE
BATTLE of NEWBERNE
North Carolina.
Fought MARCH 14th 1862.

Union Loss. 90 Killed. 380 wounded = 470.
Rebel Loss - Killed. wounded. and prisoners = 578.
Union Army Captured 9 forts. mounting 41 heavy guns
19 field pieces. 6 - 32 pdr guns. not mounted
300 prisoners. 1000 muskets. besides
Naval Stores. Ammunition and
Army supplies - &c &c

FT LANE
3 guns

NEUSE RIVER

OLD BEAUFORT ROAD

unfinished Battery

Ft ELLIS
9 guns

WEATHERSBY ROAD

REBEL FORCES under
Genl L.O. BRANCH CSA
18 Regts of Infantry and 500 Cavalry
and 18 guns.

Casemated Battery
2 guns

¼ mile   ¾ mile to RR

19th N.C. Cavalry Col Spruill

26th N.C.
COL VANCE
COL VANCE
Hardings Battery

Blind Road

23rd N.C.

Col Avery

Genl BRANCH

19 N.C. Cavalry
Col Spruill

4 Gun
unfinished
Battery

COL VANCE

BRYCE

SWAMP

COL VANCE

Brick Yard

35th N.C.
Col Clark

7th N.C.
Col Maywood

COL LEE Militia
37th N.C.
Ft THOMPSON

Brem's Battery   Latham's Battery
16 guns

27th N.C.

FELLED TREES

CREEK

FELLED TREES
SWAMP

Swamp

Pollocksville

RENO
51st Penna
9th N.J.
51st NY
21st Mass

10th Conn   23d Mass   27th Mass   24th Mass   25th Mass

FOSTER

PARKE

4th R.I.

8th Conn
5th R.I.

11th Conn

Road to
Bridge destroyed

Reinforced the
23d Mass

West   Foster

EVANS
MILL POND

F. DIXIE

51st Penna

Sweden del

4. 24 pdrs -

Union Army   Rebel Army   Artillery ♦♦♦   Cavalry ■▢

Plan of Battle — From Map made by Engineers of Genl. L.O. Branch - C.S.A.

MARCH 15 SATURDAY

Flag Officer Foote's flotilla of gunboats and mortar boats reached the area above Island No. 10, but dense fog and rain prevented any action.

The divisions of Sherman and Hurlbut arrived at the landing docks of Pittsburg Landing on the Tennessee River. Major Gen. Don Carlos Buell was ordered from Nashville to the area around Savannah, Tenn., which was close by. Halleck, on one of his better days, dismissed the rather superficial charges against Grant, and restored him to command in Tennessee. Grant replaced Gen. C. F. Smith, who had injured his leg getting into a boat. Forces were concentrating around Pittsburg Landing.

MARCH 17 MONDAY

Grant arrived at Pittsburg Landing and assumed command, placing his headquarters at Savannah, north of the Landing.

In Alexandria, Va., long blue lines of soldiers marched through the streets to board waiting transports to carry them to York Peninsula for the assault on Richmond.

MARCH 19 WEDNESDAY

The defenders of Island No. 10 on the Mississippi River still provided strong resistance to Flag Officer Foote's floating artillery. Foote said this place "is harder to conquer than Columbus, as the island shores are lined with forts, each fort commanding the one above it."

The Confederate Fort Darling, at Drewry's Bluff near Richmond, Va., served as the headquarters for the Confederate States Marine Corps. The photograph of the fort was taken in April of 1865, after the Confederates had abandoned the facility.

MARCH 20 THURSDAY

At Ship Island, Miss., Major Gen. Benjamin F. Butler assumed command of the troops that would make the assault on New Orleans and southern Louisiana.

In Richmond, President Davis wrote regarding the defense of the James River approach to the city:

> The position of Drewry's Bluff, seven or eight miles below Richmond . . . was chosen to obstruct the river against such vessels as the *Monitor.* The work is being rapidly completed. Either Ft. Powhatan or Kennon's Marsh, if found to be the proper positions, will be fortified and obstructed as at Drewry's Bluff, to prevent the ascent of the river by ironclad vessels. . . .

Drewry's Bluff remained in business until April 1865, when it was abandoned by the Confederates after Richmond fell.

Federals near Strasburg, threatened by Ashby's cavalry, moved back towards Winchester. "Stonewall" rested his infantry near Mt. Jackson, Va.

In North Carolina, Burnside's troops moved from New Bern towards Washington, N.C., without opposition.

MARCH 21 FRIDAY

On the Mississippi, Flag Officer Foote's guns still pounded Island No. 10, which still held out. Halleck expressed his appreciation to Foote for his efforts.

MARCH 23 SUNDAY

At about 2 PM, Jackson's "Stonewall Brigade" approached the village of Kernstown, which was located about three miles from Winchester. Jackson immediately went into battle with 2,700 men against 11,000 (some reports say Jackson had 3,500 and Shields 9,000). He lost, but said that if he had had another 2,000 men he would have won. The battle was a complete success in that it

caused the officials in Washington to send over 60,000 men after him, thus tying up resources that could have been used on the Peninsula. Jackson's men fell back to Newton Stephens City. This marked the beginning of the famous Shenandoah Valley campaign.

MARCH 29 SATURDAY

Along an old road leading to the Shenandoah Valley was the little town of Middleburg. The 28th Pennsylvania Infantry, commanded by Col. John W. Geary, reached Middleburg, and its passage was contested by a group of Confederate cavalry and infantry based in the town. The interesting thing about this action was that for the first time a machine gun (Lincoln's "coffee mill") was employed against enemy troops. One Capt. Bartlett, describing the action about a month later, said, "One of these guns was brought to bear on a squadron of cavalry at 800 yards, and it cut them to pieces terribly, quickly forcing them to fly." One of the deadliest weapons invented had had its first field trial in combat.

At Corinth, Miss., the Confederate Army of the Kentucky and that of the Mississippi were consolidated under one command, that of Gen. Albert Sydney Johnston.

MARCH 30 SUNDAY

Jackman, Pvt., "The Orphan Brigade," Burnsville, Miss., wrote:

> Being Sunday morning, the boys are rubbing up for inspection to be at 2 o'clock PM. Drill in camp. Am not well.
>
> Evening—Heavy firing of artillery in the direction of the Tennessee. First hostile guns heard. The firing lasted some time and made me feel "devilish" as the deep thunder came rolling over the hills. All on the qui vive to know the cause. The company ordered to be ready to march at 5, morning.

⁓ APRIL 1862 ⁓

AT LAST THE NORTHERN ARMIES were moving. Long columns of troops were departing Alexandria, Va., for York Peninsula around Norfolk and Yorktown. McClellan was finally doing something with the thousands of men he had been training for the past several months.

In the west, Island No. 10 on the Mississippi was under siege, and Federal gunboats were slipping past the island to the broad stretches of river previously under Confederate control. Memphis was threatened. If Grant could succeed in his bid for control of

Uniform coat of General Ulysses S. Grant worn after the war in 1866, when he was General of the Army

the Tennessee and Cumberland rivers, the western part of Tennessee would be lost to the South, and Mississippi would be threatened from above.

On the coastal areas, Maj. Gen. Burnside's troops were besieging Ft. Macon and already a large piece of the Pamlico Sound area was in Federal hands.

APRIL 1 TUESDAY

The Army of the Potomac, "Little Mac's" army, boarded steamers in seemingly continuous streams and headed for the wharfs and piers of the Peninsula. The army was strong, well-equipped and itching for battle.

APRIL 2 WEDNESDAY

Gen. McClellan and his staff arrived at Ft. Monroe aboard the steamer *Commodore.* "Little Mac" intended to outflank the Confederates, using his naval superiority on the James River. Federal gunboats began a bombardment of Yorktown which would continue until the Confederates evacuated the city early in May.

At Pittsburg Landing, near the meeting house at Shiloh, Grant awaited reinforcements prior to moving on the Confederates at Corinth.

APRIL 3 THURSDAY

Jackman, Pvt., "The Orphan Brigade," Burnsville, Miss., wrote:

> Through the day drew and cooked up three days' rations; and forty rounds issued to the man. After dark, the regiment was drawn up before the Colonel's tent and a battle order given.

Grant's army was still unaware of the approaching Confederate force although there had been some skirmishing around Shiloh Church. Reinforcements were arriving and being placed as rapidly as possible. Sherman was placid, believing the Confederates would not attack.

Lincoln, disturbed because only twenty thousand troops had been left to guard Washington when

McClellan moved the Army of the Potomac south, ordered the Secretary of War, Stanton, to keep in northern Virginia one of the corps destined for the Peninsula. McDowell's Corps was retained. McClellan, protesting, as he always would, that he would not have enough troops for the coming battle, was left with only 100,000 troops to fulfill his battle plan. He was initially opposed by Confederate Gen. Magruder with 20,000. Lincoln directed McClellan to advance at once.

The United States Senate voted to abolish slavery in the District of Columbia by a vote of 29 to 14.

APRIL 4 FRIDAY

More delays for the Confederate forces around Shiloh. Nothing seemed to be working right for Gen. A. S. Johnston in getting his attack on Grant moving. Johnston believed that any real chance of surprise was gone. Still, the Union forces didn't realize what was happening.

Barber, Pvt., Co. D, 15th Illinois Volunteer Infantry, Shiloh, Tenn., wrote:

> . . . we were soon awakened from our repose by a spirited dash of the enemy into our very midst making a reconnaissance. This was the Friday before the battle. The 15th was called upon to repulse this attack from the enemy. Promptly and quietly they obeyed the order and [were] the first regiment on hand from the fourth division. We received great credit for our behavior on this occasion. . . .

On York Peninsula, McClellan moved his 100,000 against Magruder's less than 20,000, and still called for more reinforcements.

Wills, 1st Lt., Adj., HQ, 3rd Battalion, 7th Illinois Cavalry, near Pt. Pleasant, Mo., wrote:

> This fuss about "Island 10" I think is all humbug. Don't believe they have attacked it yet. It don't sound like Foote's fighting. Look on the map and see what a nice pen there is between the rivers Tennessee and Mississippi. Don't it look that if Grant and company can whip them out at Corinth, that we'll have all the forces at Memphis and intermediate points to "Island 10" in a bag that they'll have trouble in getting through? . . . I firmly believe the summer will see the war ended. But it will also see a host of us upended if we have to fight over such ground as this. . . .

APRIL 5 SATURDAY

McClellan, in front of Yorktown, Va., had been held at bay by Magruder, who marched his men around in circles, letting the Federals see the long columns of troops through a gap in the fortifications. McClellan believed what he saw and thought that Magruder was being reinforced by thousands more troops. Meanwhile Joe Johnston was shifting his troops as rapidly as possible to help Magruder.

In the west, Albert Sidney Johnston again failed to attack. He didn't get his troops aligned until late in the day, and decided to wait until tomorrow. The Federals still did not realize that the Rebels were nearly on them. Some pickets reported large troop movements, but no one, including Sherman, believed them.

In the west, the news of the gunboat running past Island No. 10 had electrified the local troops. The Northern papers, including Greeley's Tribune, made light of the announcement at first.

Wills, 1st Lt., Adj., HQ, 3rd Battalion, 7th Illinois Cavalry, near Pt. Pleasant, Mo., wrote:

> One of our boys has just returned from Madrid and says he saw our gunboat Cairo there. She slipped by the batteries at "Island No. 10" in the storm last night.

On the Mississippi approach to New Orleans, Flag Officer Farragut took a personal look at the defenses of Forts Jackson and St. Philip.

1862

APRIL 6 SUNDAY

In the early morning hours, Confederate Gen. Albert Sidney Johnston finally got all his troops together and sent them screaming into the still unsuspecting Union lines around Shiloh Church. As the picket firing increased dramatically, some Union troops reacted but most did not and were unprepared for the charge that burst upon them. Grant, at his headquarters in Savannah, Tenn., several miles north, was alerted and immediately went to Pittsburg Landing. He also ordered Maj. Gen. Lew Wallace at Crump's Landing to march immediately to Shiloh Church. The first units of Maj. Gen. Don Carlos Buell's army were at Savannah, Tenn., under Brig. Gen. William Nelson. Most of Buell's troops were still en route.

Barber, Pvt., Co. D, 15th Illinois Volunteer Infantry, Shiloh, Tenn., wrote:

> . . . The camp was alarmed . . . by the rapid firing of the pickets, who soon came in with the report that the enemy was marching on us in overwhelming numbers. . . . The enemy was in camp before it had time to arouse and form a line. Some were shot in their sleep, never knowing what hurt them. . . . Rally[ing] amidst a perfect storm of bullets, shot and shell, [Union soldiers] tried to form a new line, and as the infuriated enemy, made mad with whisky and gunpowder, hurled themselves against the line, it gradually fell back, step by step, forming new and stronger lines and leaving their track strewn with the dead and dying. The onset of the foe was terrific, but instead of the easy victory that had been promised them, they were met with a valor superior to their own, as the cool aim of our boys which strewed the ground with dead

This c. 1885 print depicts some of the horror and destruction of the Battle at Shiloh.

amply testified. . . I heard the distant rattling of musketry and first thought it was something else. . . . In less than five minutes from the time the bugle was sounded, the regiment was on the march to the scene of conflict. . . .

We had not proceeded far before we met crowds of stragglers skulking to the rear. It was a humiliating sight, and our boys heaped curses, bitter and cutting, on their cowardly heads. . . . Long trains of ambulances now passed us going to the rear, loaded with the wounded. We saw two long lines of troops engaged in terrific fighting—long sheets of fire and smoke from one end of the line to the other; shot answering shot; charge meeting charge; and the wild shouts of the combatants at each successive turn of the battle presented to us a scene terribly sublime. . . .

. . . The clear tones of Colonel Ellis now recalled our wandering minds, and the word, "Forward" was given. . . . We took our position a little forward of a rise of ground. . . .

We had hardly gotten our line formed before the enemy opened on us with grape and canister. At first it fell short of its mark, but nearer and nearer the death-dealing missiles strike, tearing up the earth and filling the eyes with dust. . . . Thick and fast the iron hail comes. Groans reach us as the soldiers, wounded and mangled, crawl to the rear. The emboldened enemy now advanced in solid column, having ten to our one. The 53rd Ohio, appalled at the sight, broke and ran without firing a gun and we were left single-handed to contend against these fearful odds. We were now ordered to rise and commence firing. Rapidly and coolly we poured our deadly fire into the advancing column. Now a rebel sergeant, in front of us, performed a brave act worthy of

a better cause. He advanced in front of his command and with his own hands planted the rebel flag on a piece of our artillery that they had captured; but this act sealed his doom. He fell, pierced and riddled with bullets. I shot at him, but I hope that it was not my bullet that sealed his eyes in death. The enemy now opened a fire upon us so terrific that our little band seemed likely to be annihilated. Our brave boys were dropping by scores. A ball struck the stock of my musket, shivering it and nearly knocking it from my grasp. Another ball passed through my canteen, while another cut the straps to my haversack. Thick as hailstones the bullets whistled through my hair and around my cheek, still I remained unhurt.

Early in the action as Col. Ellis was standing on a log watching with eager eyes the motions of the enemy, a ball passed through his wrist. Lieut. Smith tied a handkerchief around it and Col. Ellis continued giving his orders as coolly as though nothing had happened, but soon an unerring shot pierced his noble heart. . . . Soon I saw Major Goddard receive his death wound while standing a few feet from me. . . . Capt. Wayne now came to me and called my attention to the rebel soldier concealed behind a root. He turned and immediately received his death wound. Lieut. Fred A. Smith was now in command. He was struck by a ball while standing by my side and knocked to the ground. As he was falling, he reached his hands out to me for assistance; almost involuntarily I bore him to the rear over the brow of the hill, took his handkerchief and bound up his wound as well as I could, then gave him in charge of Lieut. Bradley, of Company C, who was passing. I then hastened back to rejoin my company, but what was my astonishment to find not one living member of the 15th Regiment. It seems that as soon as Fred was wounded, our boys, to prevent being surrounded and taken prisoners, broke and retreated in disorder and in the tumult, I had not noticed it, so instead of finding our regiment where I left it, I found the ground swarming with rebels. Something said to me, "This is not a safe place for Luke Barber," and that if I wanted to live to fight another day, I must retreat out of that, and retreat I did, very rapidly too. . . .

I tried hard to find where the regiment was. . . . Failing in this, I found an Iowa regiment belonging to our division and fought with them until two o'clock PM. Here I had the satisfaction of seeing the rebels run. Back and forth the tide surged. I had now expended all of my ammunition and there being a lull in the fight, I determined to again seek for what was left of the 15th regiment. . . . Gen. Hurlbut was forming a new line, the strongest that had yet been formed, and all attempts of the enemy to force it back were fruitless. He had a large number of siege guns planted where they were protected by heavy works and it was impossible for the enemy to face the fire of these monsters. In their last attack they were handsomely repulsed. Their line was formed within half a mile of the landing. The enemy had spent their strength and their best efforts could not move us now. Our cause began to brighten. Gen. Grant had made every disposition to take the offensive in the morning and it is my unshaken belief that if Buell had not arrived during the night the result would have been the same. During the afternoon the rebel General A. Sidney Johnson was killed, and much of the life of the rebel army went out with his death. He was a brave man and an able officer. After his death, it was plainly seen that the rebel army was not handled as skillfully as before and the remark that Gen. Beauregard made, that he would water his horse in the Tennessee or in hell was not realized. The enemy occupied our camp that night and the thought was not very consoling, as all our things were left lying around in the tent in a very loose manner, which did not look very well to receive company.

I started out again to look for the regiment, and this time I had the unspeakable pleasure of being successful. I found them down at the landing. . . . In the morning we mustered five hundred and fifty men. Now scarcely two hundred answered to their names. Company D had only thirteen men out of fifty that were mustered in the morning. . . .

Hurlbut, with a greatly reduced command, organized a new line around Pittsburg Landing and the resistance to the Confederate advance stiffened, troops who had been hiding under the bluffs next to the river joining in the defense. Prentiss, with his gallant division, held the Rebels at the Hornets Nest until finally overcome by superior numbers, and he surrendered the remnants of his division. The reinforcements of Gen. Nelson also organized a supporting line.

Sometime around 3 o'clock in the afternoon, Gen. Albert S. Johnston, commanding the Confederate forces, was wounded in the leg. At first it did not seem serious, and he continued to direct the battle. He slowly bled to death, his boot filling with blood. Falling from his horse, he died shortly thereafter, and the command of the troops passed to Gen. Pierre G. T. Beauregard. "The Creole" attempted to gather the scattered army and get it into some fighting shape, but time was against him, and he would have to wait for the morrow.

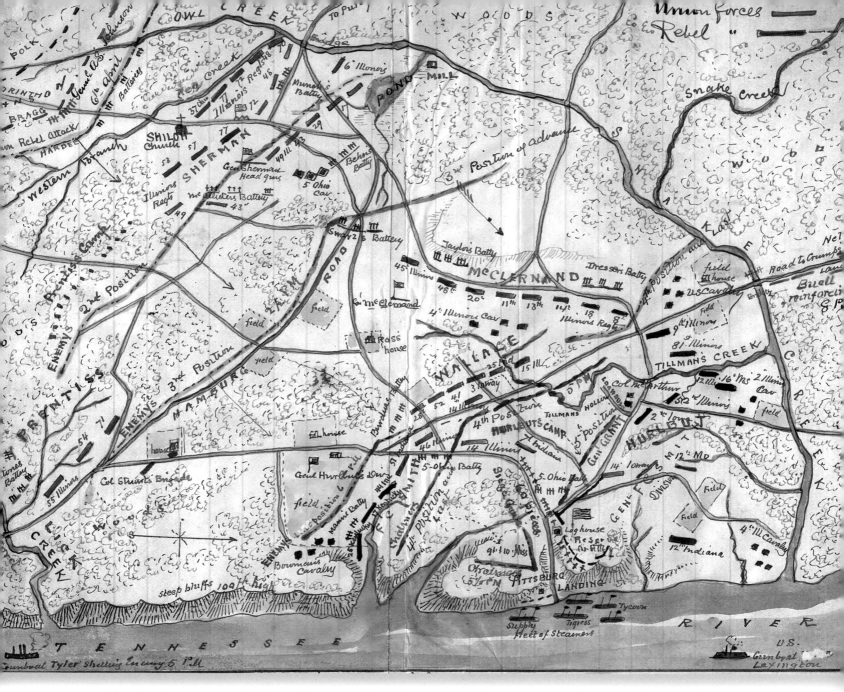

Robert Knox Sneden's map of Owl Creek, Pittsburg Landing and the Tennessee River shows the position of the Union Army before and after the battle of Shiloh.

Taylor, Surgeon, U.S. Army, attached to Buell's Army, Shiloh, Tenn., wrote:

Heard the firing early Sunday morning at Pittsburg and knew the fight had become general. Waited on orders to march from Genl. Grant—did not receive any up to one o'clock. Genl. Nelson started the column— when within 2 miles of the battle field, Genl. Grant's aide overtook us with orders to hurry up in double quick or the day was lost. Arrived at the river at 3. Genl. Ammon crossed the river in time to save the day, but for it the whole army would have gone up.

Jackman, Pvt., "The Orphan Brigade," Shiloh, Tenn., wrote:

> This day will long be remembered. Soon after the sun had risen, the firing of artillery became so general and the roar of musketry could be heard as distinctly, I knew the battle had commenced. . . . Met a man on horseback with a stand of captured colors. We were now in proximity of the fighting and we met crowds of men, some crippling along wounded in the legs or about the body, others no blood could be seen about them yet all seemed bent on getting away. . . .
>
> While passing a hospital in the roadside, I happened to see one of our company lying by a tent wounded. I went out to see him and there found the brigade hospital established. There were heaps of wounded lying about, many of them I knew and first one then another would ask me to give him water or some other favor for him. While thus occupied, Dr. P. told me to stay with him, that I was not able to go on the field, that I would be captured. There was no one to help him and I turned surgeon, pro tempore. I was not able to do much but rendered all the assistance in my power. Part of my duties was to put patients under the influence of chloroform. I kept my handkerchief saturated all the time and was often dizzy from the effects of it myself. It was about one o'clock in the day when I got there.
>
> All day long the battle raged. Occasionally there would be a lull for a short time, but the cannon were never completely hushed. They would break out in increased thunder and the roar of musketry would roll up and down the lines vibrating almost regularly from one extreme to the other. All day long the ambulances continued to discharge their loads of wounded. At last, night set in and the musketry ceased, but the Federal gunboats continued shelling awhile after dusk. Nearly midnight when we got through with the wounded. A heavy rain set in. I was tired, sick and all covered with blood. But I was in far better fix than many that were there. I sat on a medicine chest in the surgeon's tent and "nodded" the long night through.

During the night, in a raging storm, Gen. Buell landed more of his troops at Pittsburg Landing. The Confederates had lost the battle from this point. Grant had been surprised, but not beaten. Tomorrow would be another bloody day, but the conflict would be settled.

On the Mississippi, Gen. John Pope finalized his plans for the assault on Island No. 10. He would also attack the Rebel troops at Tiptonville, Tenn.

Meanwhile, at Yorktown, Va., McClellan was still preparing his siege lines. Lincoln, impatient with the inactivity of the Army of the Potomac, urged "Little Mac" to move. As usual, McClellan called for more troops and supplies. Confederate Joe Johnston was hurrying his troops to Magruder's aid.

APRIL 7 MONDAY

On this morning, Gen. Lew Wallace's division finally arrived at Pittsburg Landing after a long, wearying march. Gen. Don Carlos Buell had also arrived with the remainder of his troops. Grant assaulted early, and quickly regained his old camps and most of the ground lost on the previous day.

Barber, Pvt., Co. D, 15th Illinois Volunteer Infantry, Shiloh, Tenn., wrote:

> The army was astir early Monday morning. In consideration of our disorganized state, we were held in reserve for the greater portion of the day. Company D could only muster thirteen men this morning. We were commanded by Corporal Handy. Lieutenant-Colonel Cam was assigned to command the

regiment. As we filed along to our place in line, Gen. Hurlbut gazed on our decimated ranks with watery eyes. . . . Now the rattling of musketry, increasing in volume every moment, tell us that the ball has been opened by General Grant. The now discouraged rebels begin to yield before our resistless advance. Soon the action became general, and deafening discharges sweep along the whole line. . . . By noon we had passed our

Maj. Gen. Don Carlos Buell (1818–98) had previously served with distinction in the Mexican War.

camp. Faster and faster the enemy begin to yield. Harder and harder now press on our victorious troops. . . . Occasionally the line would halt for a few moments and our tired boys would instantly fall into a doze. . . . A heavy battery of Parrott guns was placed in our rear and fired over our heads. Even this would fail to arouse us, but when the shouts of victory from our boys rent the air as the rebs were once more hurled back, then we would start up and again advance.

About three o'clock PM we received an order which effectually banished sleep from our eyelids. We were ordered to the front to prepare for a charge. . . . Soon the line was formed. . . . General Grant was here in person to superintend the charge and as he rode to the front of the line, he was greeted with tremendous cheers. Soon the brave McCook rode to the front, drew his sword, waved it over his head and shouted: "Now give them a touch of Illinois! Forward! Charge!" and with one wild shout, we sprang forward, making the earth tremble beneath our feet. The rebels shrank back dismayed before this charge.

In wild panic and confusion they broke and ran. The defeat had now turned into a perfect rout. Through woods and swamps, over hills and through valleys, we pursued the flying foe until sheer exhaustion compelled us to stop. . . . Our poor and insufficient cavalry followed them a short distance. If we had had good cavalry, the rebel army would have been completely destroyed. . . . Thus ended the memorable battle of Shiloh.

Jackman, Pvt., "The Orphan Brigade," Shiloh, Tenn., wrote:

With the dawn came the roar of battle; but the combat did not wax very warm until later in the day. . . . Once that morning a body of Federal cavalry came close enough to fire on us, tearing up the tents but fortunately hurting no one. Dr. P. and I were standing close together talking when a ball passed between our noses which instantly stopped our conversation. . . . A little after the middle of the day, the battle raged terribly—it was the last struggle of the confederates, ending in defeat. Soon after I saw Genl. Beauregard, accompanied by one or two of his staff, ride leisurely back to the rear as cool and unperturbed as if nothing had happened. A line was being formed in the rear of us and we had to move. Jim B. and I put the only remaining wounded of our regiment who could be moved into a large spring wagon and started back. We had to leave some that it would have been death to put them in wagons. We hated to do so but we could not do otherwise. . . .

In the bloodiest battle fought to date, the losses were staggering. Union forces lost 13,047, of which 1,754 were killed. Rebel losses were 10,694, a total of 1,723 killed. Combined, nearly 24,000 Americans had been killed, wounded or were missing in two days. This total was larger than the population of most cities in Indiana or Illinois. There were more casualties here than at the Battle of Waterloo, where Napoleon met his fate. Unfortunately, there would be many Waterloos to come.

On the Mississippi, opposite Island No. 10, Gen. John Pope got his floating artillery. The USS *Carondelet* had now been joined by the USS *Pittsburg*, Lt. Egbert Thompson, south of the island and was now in a position to assault Tiptonville on the Tennessee side of the river. Pope wasted no time in using his gunboats to hammer the Rebel gun positions, driving the crews from their guns. Landing under the cover of the gunboats, the troops quickly cut off the escape of the Rebels. The Rebels, after a not-too-outstanding defense, surrendered both at Tiptonville and at Island No. 10. The Mississippi was open to Memphis.

Island No. 10, the "key" to the Mississippi, surrendered to the naval forces of Flag Officer Foote.

On the Mississippi, the Confederates at Island No. 10 formally surrendered to the Federal forces under Gen. John Pope.

APRIL 9 WEDNESDAY

In Richmond, not yet a year into the war, the Confederate Congress passed a conscription bill to get the necessary manpower for the army. Many Confederates objected to this draft law, claiming it infringed upon the liberties of the individual. It seemed those people who left the Union for "liberty infringement" were having no better luck with their new government.

In Washington, the President was trying to explain to McClellan that he had held McDowell's corps behind for the defense of the city. McClellan was turning a deaf ear and calling for more men. Lincoln was also beginning to wonder about the rather large "discrepancy" between the count of the enemy as stated by McClellan and as shown by the intelligence gathered by other sources.

In New Orleans, the threat of Farragut and his fleet was becoming more real every day, suggesting that the armed steamers sent north should be returned for the defense of the city. However, Confederate Secretary of the Navy Mallory was still convinced that Foote's gunboats north of Memphis were the real threat and refused to allow the boats to return to New Orleans. This would be a costly decision.

APRIL 10 THURSDAY

The Federal Congress passed a joint resolution calling for the gradual emancipation of the slaves in all the states. Lincoln approved the measure and signed it.

At Shiloh, the cleanup continued. Most of the dead soldiers were buried by now, and the wounded who could be moved were long gone down the Tennessee River to hospitals in the North. Private Barber reported a theme recurring among the Union troops about the Confederate dead.

Barber, Pvt., Co. D, 15th Illinois Volunteer Infantry, Shiloh, Tenn., wrote:

It was a painful task. Months passed before I recovered from the effects of it. Now we turned our attention to the rebel dead. We noticed that the faces of all of them had turned black. On examination, we found that their canteens contained whiskey and gunpowder which was, no doubt, the cause of it. It seems that this had been given to them just before going into battle to make them fight. This was the cause of the rebels fighting so like demons the first day. It took two days to bury all of them. I will not attempt to give much of a description of this battle-field. . . . On one spot of ground, where we generally had our reviews, an artillery duel was fought and the ground was so thickly strewed with dead horses that you could walk nearly all over it on the carcasses. . . .

APRIL 12 SATURDAY

In Georgia, the scene was set for one of the great adventures of the war, the Great Locomotive Chase, later to be immortalized in a 20th-century movie. A party of twenty-two Union volunteers under James J. Andrews boarded a train at Marietta, Ga., and rode it as passengers to Big Shanty. There the train stopped for breakfast, and everyone, including the crew, got off to eat. Andrews and his band detached the locomotive "General" and three freight cars and took off northward. The train crew, not even finishing their grits, started the chase in another engine, the "Texas." North of Ringgold, Ga., the hijackers ran out of fuel,

abandoned the train and took off into the woods; they were later captured. Andrews and seven others were executed, eight escaped prison, and six were paroled. The daring of Andrews captured the imagination and admiration of both the North and South.

Around Yorktown, Va., McClellan was still digging. Magruder was getting more troops; he now had about 30,000 to match "Little Mac's" 100,000.

APRIL 16 WEDNESDAY

In Richmond, President Davis signed the bill authorizing conscription of every white male between eighteen and thirty-five years of age. This bill provided for substitutions of draftees, a pattern to be followed by the North later.

On the lower Mississippi, Flag Officer Farragut moved his fleet upriver to just below Forts Jackson and St. Philip.

APRIL 20 SUNDAY

In western Tennessee, Halleck gathered his force for the assault.

Barber, Pvt., Co. D, 15th Illinois Volunteer Infantry, Shiloh, Tenn., wrote:

Colonel Turner now arrived and assumed command of the regiment. . . . We now began to prepare for an active campaign. We were reviewed and we knew that the ball would open again soon. Gen. Pope's army, the heroes of Island No. Ten, had now arrived, and, with Buell's army, our numbers were increased to one hundred thousand men. The enemy was also receiving large re-inforcements and were busily fortifying at Corinth.

APRIL 21 MONDAY

Flag Officer Farragut was delayed in his approach to New Orleans. The chains barring the river were still a problem, so he did something about them:

We have been bombarding the forts for three or four days, but the current is running so strong that we cannot stem it sufficiently to do anything with our ships . . . Captain Bell went last night to cut the chain across the river. . . . They let the chain go, but the men sent to explode the petard did not succeed; his wires broke. . . . However, the chain was divided, and it gives us space enough to go through.

APRIL 24 THURSDAY

At 2 AM the USS *Hartford*, Farragut's flagship, signaled the fleet to begin passing the forts below New Orleans. Once past the barricades, the Federal fleet faced the Confederate gunboats, including the ram *Manassas*. The ram struck both the USS *Mississippi* and *Brooklyn*, but with little damage. Most of the Confederate fleet fled upriver.

Farragut had now captured the South's largest city and its major port. With the taking of this port the Union had a base of operations to control the economy of most of the southern tier of the South.

APRIL 25 FRIDAY

Farragut moved up the Mississippi to New Orleans. The local people had set the waterfront afire, and Farragut anchored his fleet in the river away from the flames. A rude, nearly violent, and noisy throng met Farragut's officers when they landed to meet the mayor of New Orleans. The mayor claimed no authority to surrender the city. It didn't really matter much who surrendered it. It was fairly taken. It would never be taken from Federal authority again during the war.

APRIL 28 MONDAY

South of New Orleans, Fts. Jackson and St. Philip formally surrendered to Federal forces. The Mississippi River was now open for navigation—at least as far as New Orleans. At the city, Farragut threatened to bombard the city if the Rebels didn't show some respect for the Union flag.

APRIL 29 TUESDAY

Major Gen. Halleck, with over 100,000 men, prepared to attack Beauregard's nearly 65,000. Halleck would march from Pittsburg Landing for Corinth. Grant, named second-in-command, was very upset at what he considered a demotion. In all events, Halleck was not looking for a hero who would outshine him in the coming campaign.

The USS *Hartford*, seen in this c. 1905 photograph, was Admiral Farragut's flagship.

∞ MAY 1862 ∞

THINGS WERE LOOKING GRIM for the Confederacy. Tennessee had been lost for all practical purposes, most of the Atlantic coast was either occupied or blockaded, the Gulf of Mexico ports were mostly sealed and the South's largest city, New Orleans, was occupied by the blue-coats. The drastic reverses within the past 90 days offset the euphoria of the fall of '61, when the Confederacy basked in the glory of the victory at Manassas. Richmond was threatened from the Peninsula by McClellan's Army of the Potomac. Banks was in the Shenandoah Valley, and McDowell was in the vicinity of Fredericksburg, also threats to Richmond. In the west, the bloody battlefield of Shiloh had been cleaned up, but not forgotten. The forces there awaited action at Corinth. The North had to keep up the momentum.

MAY 1 THURSDAY

Union Major Gen. Benjamin F. Butler and his troops assumed control of New Orleans.

President Lincoln was concerned that McClellan had not attacked Johnston, but seemed to be preparing for a lengthy siege. He asked McClellan, one of many times, "Is anything to be done?"

A panoramic view of the encampment of the Army of the Potomac at Cumberland Landing, Va., on the Pamunkey River, May 1862

Day, Pvt., Co. B, 25th Massachusetts Volunteer Infantry, New Bern, N.C., wrote:

Martial law not being a very favorable institution for pleasure parties, I presume the usual May day festival is dispensed with here. . . . Ft. Macon surrendered to Gen. Burnside last Friday evening, after a bombardment of eleven hours . . . they hauled down their colors . . . 65 guns and 450 prisoners, with stores and ammunition, have fallen into our hands. . . .

MAY 3 SATURDAY

The Confederate forces around Yorktown withdrew from their fortifications before McClellan started his bombardment. Confederate forces numbered about 55,000, versus Union forces of over 100,000. McClellan was still calling for more manpower, even as the Rebels retreated.

MAY 4 SUNDAY

The Army of the Potomac entered Yorktown and continued towards Williamsburg. Advance Union units clashed with Confederate Generals Longstreet and D. H. Hill's troops outside of town.

In the Valley, Jackson's men boarded trains and headed for Staunton, where they arrived about 5 PM.

MAY 5 MONDAY

Lincoln decided to really play the role of Commander-in-Chief. He went to Ft. Monroe aboard the steamer *Miami*, accompanied by Secretaries Stanton and Chase. The following day he directed the gunboat operations against Sewell's Point on the James River.

Heavy fighting took place around Williamsburg, the old capital of Virginia, when McClellan's forces collided with those of Joseph Johnston. Longstreet and D. H. Hill led their Confederates well in the rearguard action that brought on more casualties than would have been expected for this type of fighting. Johnston continued his retreat up the Peninsula.

MAY 6 TUESDAY

Federal troops occupied Williamsburg, Va., on the heels of the retreating Confederates. Joe Johnston continued his retreat towards Richmond.

MAY 8 THURSDAY

The Battle of McDowell took place in western Virginia today, as Jackson's 10,000 men were attacked by about 6,000 from Frémont's command under Gen. Schenck. The Federals retreated towards Franklin and Jackson pursued. His "foot-cavalry" was making its mark.

Barber, Pvt., Co. D, 15th Illinois Volunteer Infantry, near Corinth, Miss., wrote:

When the army came to a strong position, they would throw up strong works, irregular in shape, and commanding every possible position. These fortifications were considered secure places to fall back upon in case of disaster. The whole intervening space between us and the Landing was one continual series of fortifications. General Halleck was one of those old fogy commanders with more caution than spirit. We will admit that the enemy had taught us to respect their bravery, but with the army that Halleck had, he should have marched right up to their stronghold and sat down before it and expended labor in besieging the place instead of so much in the rear to provide for contingencies.

Rumors of the evacuation of Norfolk seemed to be well founded. A tug deserting from Norfolk brought the news that the evacuation was well under way and that the CSS *Virginia* and her escort of gunboats was to proceed up the James or York River.

MAY 9 FRIDAY

On the western rivers, Flag Officer Foote was relieved of command due to injuries received at Ft. Donelson.

MAY 10 SATURDAY

The Confederates set fire to the Norfolk Navy Yard before evacuating it and moved west towards Richmond. Union troops under Major Gen. Wool crossed Hampton Roads and occupied the city.

Confederate forces began evacuating Pensacola yesterday after the fall of both Island No. 10 and New Orleans. They fired on the Navy Yard and destroyed all the ships under construction. Today, the Union Army and Navy occupied the city, and Commander David D. Porter reported, "The Rebels have done their work well. The yard is a ruin."

In New Orleans, Gen. Benjamin Butler seized $80,000 in gold from the Netherlands Consulate. An odd move, even for him.

Barber, Pvt., Co. D, 15th Illinois Volunteer Infantry, near Corinth, Miss., wrote:

> Gen. Beauregard knew what kind of man he had to deal with and shaped his plans so as to completely fool Halleck. If Sherman, Grant or Thomas had had command of the army, Beauregard would not have gotten away as slickly as he did. The nearer we approached the enemy, the more cautious he was—so cautious, that it seemed more like cowardice than prudence.

MAY 12 MONDAY

Natchez, Miss., surrendered to Farragut's fleet today. Farragut was pushing his way upriver to see how far he can go towards Foote's river fleet. The stranglehold on Memphis was tightening.

In Richmond, those who could afford to do so left.

MAY 14 WEDNESDAY

Around Corinth, Miss., the skirmishing was fairly light. Halleck had a bad case of the "slows" on this campaign. It would prove to be the only time he commanded a force in battle.

Jackman, Pvt., "The Orphan Brigade," Castillian Springs, Miss., wrote:

> Brown died in our room this morning. How little feeling soldiers have sometimes! While willing to help a comrade while living, when dead, there is never much shedding of tears for them. We were all standing around Brown's bed and when he drew his last breath one of the boys bent over him, observed him for a moment and said: "He never will draw another breath so long as he lives." This was said so simply the whole room rang out in laughter. We buried B. in the evening. Many are dying here. Intend to go to the front in a few days.

Day, Pvt., Co. B, 25th Massachusetts Volunteer Infantry, picket duty, N.C., wrote:

> I was out in the woods yesterday and last night on picket duty and picket duty is simply lying around in the brush watching the approach of outside parties. Parties approaching in the night time and failing to promptly respond to the hail of the picket are given an instantaneous passport to a land that is fairer than this. A picket is composed of three or more men stationed at convenient distances from each other along the roads, horse paths, and anywhere an enemy might be supposed to come. One keeps watch while the others sleep, but with the hooting of the owls, sand-fleas, woodticks, lizards and mosquitoes, their repose is a good deal disturbed.
>
> ... with a strong scouting party went out to Tuscarora, a little hamlet about five miles distant, where is the enemy's outpost and where is kept a post of observation. On the approach of the colonel and his party they left, but before doing so set fire to a new steam saw and grain mill which was destroyed.

MAY 15 THURSDAY

In New Orleans, Major Gen. Benjamin F. Butler created a sensation when he issued Order Number

28 to counter the treatment his soldiers had been receiving from the ladies of the city:

As the officers and soldiers of the United States have been subject to repeated insults from the women calling themselves ladies of New Orleans in return for the most scrupulous non-interference and courtesy on our part, it is ordered that hereafter when any female shall by word, gesture or movement insult or show contempt for any officer or soldier of the United States she shall be regarded and held liable to be treated as a woman of the town plying her avocation.

The ladies' reaction was to have Butler's likeness painted in the bottom of their chamber pots.

MAY 18 SUNDAY

Barber, Pvt., Co. D, 15th Illinois Volunteer Infantry, near Corinth, Miss., wrote:

The picket lines of the two opposing armies were within hearing distance, but as each side managed to keep pretty well concealed, the firing did but little damage, although occasionally one would get wounded. The night watch was the more dreary and dangerous. We knew not how many secret foes were lurking around to take advantage of every movement.

MAY 20 TUESDAY

In Richmond, President Davis, in response to a resolution of the Confederate Congress, announced that Richmond would be defended. This was still early in the war, before the casualties of Seven Days, Second Manassas, Fredericksburg, etc., were brought to Richmond. The spirit would be more subdued a year later.

This cartoon, from the July 12, 1862, issue of *Harper's Weekly*, depicts the ladies of New Orleans before (left) and after (right) the order issued by Maj. Gen. Benjamin Butler on May 15, 1862.

MAY 22 THURSDAY

Jackman, Pvt., "The Orphan Brigade," Corinth, Miss., wrote:

> Once, while fronted on the road, Genl. Breckinridge rode by. He was dressed in citizen suit with a broadrimmed felt hat on. He passed our regt. first and the boys cheered him. He said: "Boys, I shall try and be with you more today than before." When asked after the Battle of Shiloh why he was not with his old brigade more during the battle he said that he knew the Kentucky boys would fight without the presence of their Maj. Genl. but that he was needed more on other parts of the field. This was considered quite a compliment. When passing the other regiments—all cheered him loudly. Two or three miles beyond the fortifications on the left wing we formed line of battle. . . . When close to the evening, hotter, "lounged about" waiting for Van Dorn to open on the right but he failed to accomplish the flank movement intended and we marched back to camp that evening without any battle.

On May 20, 1862, the Union Army under Gen. Nathaniel Prentiss Banks entered Front Royal, Va., an event captured in this drawing by Edwin Forbes. The battle took place on May 23, 1862.

Barber, Pvt., Co. D, 15th Illinois Volunteer Infantry, near Corinth, Miss., wrote:

> A large force of our men went and drove the rebels out. In return, the rebels soon returned with large re-inforcements and our boys were compelled to give it up again. Then we had the whole division in line, supported by several batteries, and charged the rebels and again they were compelled to give way. This time they did not renew their attempt to take it as it would likely have brought on a general engagement. The next day we moved our lines forward again, but we had hard fighting. The enemy contested every inch of ground.

MAY 23 FRIDAY

Today the Battle of Front Royal took place. Jackson, approaching from the south, took Banks's troops, about 800 men, by surprise and captured many of them. As a battle it wasn't much, but it created a stir in Washington. The people of that city could see Jackson's "legions" looming in the distance.

MAY 24 SATURDAY

In the Valley, Jackson failed to trap Banks, and most of the Federals escaped towards Winchester. The advance of Turner Ashby's cavalry, supported by Poague's artillery battery, created panic among the Federals, who abandoned large quantities of provisions and equipment. Lincoln ordered McDowell to send 20,000 men towards the Shenandoah to capture Jackson. He also ordered Frémont to enter the Valley and to cut off Jackson's retreat south.

The diversion of McDowell's men to the Valley gave McClellan another excuse for not pressing his attack on the Peninsula. He continued to believe he was under strength, although he had over 100,000 men.

MAY 25 SUNDAY

At Winchester, Banks held Jackson and Ewell for a period of time before Banks's troops broke and ran for Harpers Ferry. Another great haul of supplies and munitions was garnered for the Confederacy. Jackson's legend grew. He had 16,000 against Banks's 8,000. The citizens of Winchester were jubilant, cheering in the streets. Most of the Shenandoah Valley belonged again to the Confederacy, at least for a while.

Lincoln wired McClellan that it was time to make a decision. Either attack Richmond or come back to defend Washington.

MAY 26 MONDAY

Jackman, Pvt., "The Orphan Brigade," Corinth, Miss., wrote:

> Mystery about the movements. . . . Some say retreat—some say fight. Old "Beauré" knows what he is about.

Barber, Pvt., Co. D, 15th Illinois Volunteer Infantry, near Corinth, Miss., wrote:

> We are now in hearing of the rebel camp. We could plainly hear the drums beating, the heavy lumbering of the cars as they came into Corinth. Matters seemed to be approaching a crisis. . . . We could hear the cars arriving and departing rapidly. It was evident that the rebs were either receiving large re-inforcements or were evacuating the place. The latter seemed the most plausible to us. But still Halleck, with that extreme cautiousness, crept slowly up and allowed the wily foe to slip from his grasp. The enemy kept up a heavy skirmish line to make it appear that they were still there in strength, but subsequent events showed that they were rapidly evacuating at this time. We had now began to suffer for want of water and it became absolutely necessary for the army to move forward where they could get water or retreat. The latter was not to be thought of.

MAY 27 TUESDAY
Jackson pushed on towards Harpers Ferry, with skirmishing at Loudoun Heights. At Corinth there was more skirmishing.

MAY 28 WEDNESDAY
Jackman, Pvt., "The Orphan Brigade," Corinth, Miss., wrote:

> In the morning broke up camp and started the wagon train to the rear, then marched out to the trenches where we lay in reserve all day. Our brigade is the reserve of the division and our regt. the reserve of the brigade. Heavy skirmishing along the whole line today. In the evening the enemy were close enough to throw two solid shot over us. Tonight all quiet. Cannot tell whether we are going to wait for an attack or retreat. Have been suffering for water all day.

Barber, Pvt., Co. D, 15th Illinois Volunteer Infantry, near Corinth, Miss., wrote:

> Early next morning we received ten month's pay, and we immediately started for the front again. On our way there we learned that the enemy had evacuated and that our forces held possession of the place. Soon we heard of a terrible fight in Virginia and that McClellan was defeated. The bulk of Beauregard's army was in the fight, so the campaign against Corinth was a drawn game. The rebels gained the battle in Virginia but lost possession of the stronghold of Corinth. We entered the place about ten o'clock. The rebels had destroyed everything they did not take with them. . . .

MAY 29 THURSDAY
At Harpers Ferry, there was quite a gathering in the works. Jackson had about 16,000 troops opposing Banks's 8,000. But behind Jackson, up the Valley, Frémont had about 15,000, and McDowell's 20,000 were ready to cut off Jackson's retreat. Jackson was at Halltown, watching.

Near Seven Pines on the Chickahominy there was some light skirmishing, and some further north along the South Anna River.

MAY 30 FRIDAY
Halleck sat a few miles north of Corinth, completely oblivious to the fact that Beauregard was moving his entire army towards Tupelo; there was a thin screen between Halleck and the retreating Confederates. Although Halleck called it a victory, some wondered.

In the Valley, Jackson began to fall back from Harpers Ferry to avoid the trap being laid by McDowell's troops commanded by Gen. Shields, with Frémont's forces at Front Royal.

Jackman, Pvt., "The Orphan Brigade," Corinth, Miss., wrote:

> . . . Tonight all quiet. Bivouacking in line of battle. Rations short.

MAY 31 SATURDAY
McClellan had one corps north of the Chickahominy and two south of that river. Joe Johnston's Confederates attacked the two corps at Fair Oaks (or Seven Pines). Several mistakes caused delays and the Confederate attack did not pick up momentum until 1 PM, and even then the contact was spotty. The Rebel drive was stopped when Gen. Sumner, not waiting for McClellan's order, moved his corps into the battle. At this point a chance bullet changed the way the war would be fought from this time forward in the eastern theater.

Gen. Joseph Eggleston Johnston was wounded and Robert E. Lee was given command of the Army of Northern Virginia the next day.

Jackson made good his escape, much to Lincoln's disgust.

Corinth was a victory, of sorts. The Mississippi River above New Orleans to Vicksburg was open.

The threat of the CSS *Virginia* was no more; she had been destroyed. McClellan had wasted a golden opportunity, and Jackson had escaped a trap in the Valley.

∽ JUNE 1862 ∽

THE BEGINNING OF JUNE brought Lincoln no answer to his command problems. McClellan was still timorous and crying for more men on the Peninsula. Halleck, after he had relieved Grant and taken charge of the army so that the glory could be his, lacked the stamina and nerve to attack. Banks, McDowell, and Frémont in the Valley failed to trap Stonewall Jackson, although they had more than twice his number of troops. Lincoln pondered his next step, and lived with the command that he had.

In the South, the only bright spot was that Richmond had not fallen. Tennessee was gone, along with New Orleans and most of the Mississippi River. Pensacola was in Federal hands, and much of the southern east coast was under the Stars and Stripes. Many of the residents of Richmond had fled, and Davis looked to Lee to manufacture a miracle.

JUNE 1 SUNDAY

East of Richmond, near the Chickahominy River, the last day of the Battle of Seven Pines (Fair Oaks) was fought. Lee was in charge, effective this morning, and was trying to make sense of the confusion. By 3 PM Lee had decided to have his troops withdraw to their original lines, having gained nothing except to swell the casualty list on both sides. The South had suffered over 6,000 new casualties, about 1,000 more than the North. Both sides decided to wait.

JUNE 2 MONDAY

At Fair Oaks, east of Richmond, the cleanup of the battlefield began with the burial of the dead and the gathering of scattered equipment.

Near Corinth, Gen. John Pope was following the retreating Confederates when a clash developed near Rienzi, Miss.

JUNE 4 WEDNESDAY

The evacuation of Ft. Pillow was completed tonight; the road was open to Memphis.

JUNE 6 FRIDAY

The city of Memphis, Tenn., fell to Union forces. The Federal fleet under command of Commodore Charles Davis sailed down the Mississippi and engaged the Confederate ships below the bluffs of the city. Citizens of Memphis lined the bluffs to watch the Federals be defeated. The fight became a free-for-all with gunboats and rams going in every direction, either running or attacking. After an initial assault by the rams, the gunboats took over the action and blasted the Confederate ships. Few escaped. The Confederates also lost five large transports and other vessels under construction. The battle lasted only two hours, and was completed by 7:30 AM. Most of the spectators lining the bluff went home, many in tears. At 11 AM, the mayor surrendered the city. Federal troops that were part of the flotilla occupied the city and mounted guards. The Mississippi was now open all the way to Vicksburg, Miss.

JUNE 7 SATURDAY

Federal troops shelled Chattanooga, Tenn., waking the Confederates to the realization that they had better fortify that important rail junction or lose it.

JUNE 8 SUNDAY

At Port Republic, Va., with McDowell sitting on the sidelines, Jackson faced two Federal columns under Frémont and Shields. The Federals were trying to accomplish a pincer movement on Jackson's small army. Frémont attacked at Cross Keys against the force of Gen. Richard Ewell, who fought him off,

This photograph of the battlefield at Seven Pines, Va., was taken in June of 1862. The weapon in the foreground is an 8-inch seige howitzer.

causing Frémont to partially retreat. Lincoln decided that since McDowell couldn't catch Jackson, he could just as well go back to threatening Richmond.

JUNE 9 MONDAY

Jackson pulled another one of his magic tricks at Port Republic and brought Ewell across the river in time to help punch Shields's troops in the nose before Frémont realized that he was facing only a skeleton Rebel force. This was the last battle of the Valley Campaign. In the past 38 days Jackson's "foot cavalry" had marched nearly 400 miles and kept tens of thousands of Federal troops tied up and away from the front at Richmond. This campaign, above all others, made Jackson's name legendary.

JUNE 12 THURSDAY

Confederate Gen. JEB Stuart mounted his 1,200 cavalry and began his four-day ride completely around the Army of the Potomac. While it did little in the way of military accomplishment, it was very embarrassing toGen. McClellan and it gave the South a morale boost. It also added to the Southerners' general conception that they possessed a native talent for horsemanship far exceeding that of the Northerners. It had one other effect: It stirred both North and South to equip and field more cavalry.

James Ewell Brown (JEB) Stuart fought through most of the major campaigns, serving as Lee's "eyes." His failure during the Gettysburg campaign was noteworthy. A very flamboyant character, he had many affectations, including that of wearing a plume in his hat. He was mortally wounded in a cavalry battle with Sheridan's Union cavalry at Yellow Tavern, north of Richmond, on May 11, 1864. He died the following day and was mourned by all the South; "the Cavalier of Dixie" was dead.

JUNE 15 SUNDAY

Today, Stuart arrived back in Richmond a legend. He had brought back valuable information for Lee concerning terrain, roads, etc., but his excursion may have also had a negative effect, since it alerted McClellan that the Union flanks were vulnerable.

General James Ewell Brown "JEB" Stuart (1833–64) of the Confederate States Army

JUNE 18 WEDNESDAY

A terrain feature that would be repeatedly fought over during the war was taken by Federal troops under Brigadier Gen. George W. Morgan. The Cumberland Gap, that pass through the mountains that had been used for centuries by the Indians and then by Daniel Boone to gain entry to Kentucky, that "Bloody Ground," was again being fought over.

On the Mississippi River, Vicksburg was at last paying some attention to her long-neglected defenses.

JUNE 25 WEDNESDAY

The Seven Days' Battle began today in a small and mild way when McClellan ordered his forward units to advance on his left flank which, he said, was to be a general movement forward. The troops of Gen. Samuel Heintzelman's corps clashed with the Confederates of Gen. Ben Huger, and a smart little fight began.

JUNE 26 THURSDAY

The second day of the Seven Days' Battle began with sharp fighting around Mechanicsville, when Gen. A. P. Hill attacked at 3 PM, after waiting for Jackson to come up. Hill's troops pushed through Mechanicsville, and the Federals fell back into strong prepared positions. Hill threw his men at the position and the attack failed. During the night the Federals withdrew to other prepared positions around Gaines Mill.

JUNE 27 FRIDAY

The third day of the Seven Days' Battle began with Fitz John Porter holding at Gaines Mill and the Confederates attacking about 3 PM and getting their Rebel noses severely bloodied. After dark, the Confederates under Gen. John Bell Hood and George Pickett broke the lines at Gaines Mill, but the force was not sustained, and they had to fall back. Porter lost about 6,800 men to Lee's 8,700. McClellan began his withdrawal to the James River.

At Vicksburg, the bombardment continued. In Washington, Lincoln accepted the resignation of Major Gen. Frémont from the Army. Some say it was accepted with alacrity. Frémont was at the end of his military career.

JUNE 28 SATURDAY

On the fourth day of the Seven Days' Battle it was fairly quiet. The long lines of wagons moving towards the James River marked McClellan's retreat. Lee reorganized his forces for yet another attack. McClellan sent a telegram to Lincoln saying the battle was lost because his force was too small. The General blamed the President for the failure.

At Vicksburg, Farragut's fleet moved upriver at 2 AM in an attempt to pass the defenses. At 4 AM, the air between the city and the river was full of flying shells and mortar bombs as the boats raced north and the shore guns tried to sink them. In two hours it was over. All but three of the ships made the passage despite the amount of iron flying around. Something was proven: Gunboats could pass defenses if Union losses could be held to an acceptable level.

JUNE 29 SUNDAY

The fifth day of the Seven Days' Battle. Confederate forces were closely following and attacking McClellan's retreating columns. The Federal rear guard was constantly in action and withstood the repeated assaults. Jackson was late again. Although the Federals safely withdrew, they left more than 2,500 sick and wounded at Savage's Station on the Richmond and York Railroad.

JUNE 30 MONDAY

The sixth day of the Seven Days' Battle. At White Oak Swamp, Lee's Army of Northern Virginia tried to attack McClellan across a swamp. McClellan successfully countered the attack. Longstreet could not break the lines, and, Jackson was late again. By nightfall, McClellan had drawn his lines in around Malvern Hill, where the finale would be played tomorrow.

∽ JULY 1862 ∽

THE MONTH OF JUNE had changed things drastically for the South. Jackson had proven more than a match for the Federal generals in the Valley, and Lee had firmly taken over the Army of Northern Virginia. A bloody battle was raging just east of Richmond as the new month began, its outcome uncertain. In the west, Farragut was north of Vicksburg and the Mississippi River was open from Vicksburg to New Orleans and the sea. Much had been gained here but there was still a thorn in the middle—the city of Vicksburg was still in Confederate hands. A full year would go by before that changed.

JULY 1 TUESDAY

The seventh day of the Seven Days' Battle. Lee, hoping to destroy the Federals entrenched on Malvern Hill, ordered the attack. His attacks, largely disjointed due to poor coordination, were cut to pieces by the Federal gunners and riflemen. In many cases the Confederate casualties were very heavy, as in a South Carolina regiment that began piling up its dead to serve as breastworks to resist the attack of a Union brigade.

The casualties for both sides for the Seven Days' Battle were heavy, with the South bearing the brunt of them—about 20,000, to 16,000 for the Federals. This represented a much larger percentage for the South of the total number of men engaged—about 88,000, to 115,000 for the Federals.

In the west, the saltwater fleet of Flag Officer Farragut joined the freshwater fleet of Flag Officer Davis north of Vicksburg today. The meeting of the squadrons had a great morale effect in the North, but Vicksburg was still there.

South of Corinth, in Mississippi, Col. Philip H. Sheridan, currently commanding a cavalry unit, defeated a force of Confederates.

JULY 2 WEDNESDAY

On the James River in Virginia, McClellan retreated from Malvern Hill to Harrison's Landing in a driving rain. The site had been chosen by Commander Rodgers because it was so situated that gunboats could protect both flanks of the army.

Jackman, Pvt., "The Orphan Brigade," Vicksburg, Miss., wrote:

> In the forenoon all quiet. As evening came on, moved down nearer the city in a

ravine close to where "Whistling Dick" was mounted. The upper fleet soon after commenced shelling from mortar boats and it seems they knew where we were for most of the shells fell about our ravine. . . . I felt sorry for the inhabitants [of Vicksburg]. Those that were left in the city commenced leaving town. I noticed one lady going out a street with five or six little children about her that were gamboling along unconscious, it seemed, of danger until a bomb burst almost in their midst when they all huddled about their mother for protection.

JULY 3 THURSDAY

McClellan was safely entrenched at Harrison's Landing, protected by his artillery and the Federal gunboats. Lee probed for a hole to drive his troops through. On both sides, the finger-pointing escalated, as nearly everyone was looking for scapegoats.

McClellan chose Lincoln and Congress as his patsies for having failed. After all, they hadn't given him the troops he had asked for although he outnumbered

Confederate soldiers of the 3d Georgia Infantry—two were half-brothers killed in the Battle of Malvern Hill.

Lee by 30,000. Lee was silent and was reorganizing his army while thinking of what could be done to John Pope, who was posturing in the Manassas area.

JULY 4 FRIDAY

The celebration of Independence Day was carried on in the North with great enthusiasm, despite the defeat on the Peninsula. Speeches, picnics, more speeches, parades and more speeches were the order of the day. The South did not celebrate. In fact, Nashville would not celebrate this day for a long time.

JULY 9 WEDNESDAY

In Kentucky, John Hunt Morgan was loose. Driving his cavalry hard, Morgan chased the Federals and captured Tompkinsville, Ky. Gen. Lee, opposite McClellan on the James River, tried his hand at using field artillery against the guns of the gunboats in the river.

Three gunboats, the USS *Commodore Perry*, *Shawsheen*, and *Ceres*, used field artillery in a very portable way by landing a field piece from one of the ships, accompanied by soldiers and a party of sailors, at Hamilton, N.C., where the steamer *Wilson* was captured.

JULY 11 FRIDAY

"Old Brains" Halleck was promoted to General-in-Chief of all U.S. land forces. Halleck was a fusspot, a procrastinator, an envious man, and a fairly good administrator. An excellent armchair general, as were some others in this war, he commanded the army at Corinth poorly and showed no aggressiveness.

JULY 12 SATURDAY

Morgan captured Lebanon, Ky., causing panic in the cities along the Ohio. The citizens of Cincinnati, Evansville and Louisville asked for protection.

In New Orleans, the city was reported to be cleaner than ever "in the memory of the oldest inhabitant and never more healthy at this time of the year." Although ruling the city with an iron hand, Gen. Benjamin Butler also accomplished many good things. One was the control of the dreaded and deadly yellow fever. The fever was caused by the pools of stagnant water lying in the streets and empty lots of the city where the mosquitoes bred. Butler took action to have these puddles filled with dirt and sand and, in doing so, unknowingly solved a major part of the problem.

JULY 14 MONDAY

Gen. John Hunt Morgan had now reached Cynthiana, Ky., with his raiding cavalry. The citizens of southern Indiana and Ohio were in an uproar.

JULY 16 WEDNESDAY

In Paris, Napoleon III received Confederate Commissioner John Slidell, who requested France's formal recognition of the Confederacy and the aid of French warships in breaking the blockade, in exchange for cotton. France declined.

Today a precedent was set. The first by date of rank Rear Admiral in the history of the United States was appointed: Flag Officer David G. Farragut. The Navy's overall officer rank structure was reformed to include the ranks of Commodore and Lt. Com-

Henry Wager Halleck (1815–72), seen in this undated portrait, remained General-in-Chief of all U.S. land forces until Ulysses S. Grant was appointed to that post in March of 1864.

mander. Rear Admirals were to rank with Army Major Generals, the highest rank in the Army at that time.

JULY 17
THURSDAY

The Confederacy suffered from an institution that would adversely affect the North in the future: the purchase of substitutes for those conscripted. The conscription laws, never popular, led to much evasion and subterfuge by those eligible but not willing to go.

Congress passed an act which established that:

> . . . every officer, seaman, or marine, disabled in the line of duty, shall be entitled to receive for life, or during his disability, a pension from the United States, according to the nature and degree of his disability, not exceeding in any case his monthly pay.

JULY 18 FRIDAY

In the North at this time, it was still relatively easy for a citizen to travel within the Union without restriction. The South, however, had imposed rather severe travel restrictions on all its citizens, requiring them to have "passports" to travel from place to place within the Confederacy. In essence, a person had to have a "passport" to travel from Richmond to Petersburg, Chattanooga, Knoxville, or Atlanta. Richmond, the capital, was most concerned about "spies" carrying information across the lines to the Federals.

JULY 21
MONDAY

Barber, Pvt., Co. D, 15th Illinois Volunteer Infantry, entry into Memphis, Tenn., wrote:

Isabella Marie "Belle" Boyd (1844–1900), also known as Cleopatra of the Secession, ran her spying operation from her father's hotel in Front Royal, Va.

Gen. Hurlbut . . . granted five [24 hour] passes a day from each company to go to the city. . . . Each soldier was required to go armed with a bayonet or revolver. The rebel citizens were very violent yet, and the soldiers would not brook insult or hear our flag spoken lightly of. . . . The evil disposed now began to plunge into all kinds of dissipation, frequenting drinking saloons and other places of infamous resort. . . .

JULY 23 WEDNESDAY

Major Gen. Henry Halleck assumed command of all Union Army forces today. At Carmel Church, just south of Fredericksburg, Va., Federal cavalry raided a Southern supply depot, destroying supplies.

JULY 29 TUESDAY

A woman accused of being a Confederate spy was captured near Warrenton, Va., by the Federals. Belle Boyd was accused of being a spy and mail courier and sent to the Old Capital Prison in Washington (the current site of Ft. McNair). Released on August 28th for lack of evidence, she would return to her chosen work with zeal.

JULY 31 THURSDAY

President Davis informed Gen. Lee that on July 22nd a cartel for exchange of prisoners had been signed with the Federal government. He also informed Lee that because of Gen. John Pope's declarations about treatment of citizens, any commissioned officers captured from Pope's army were to be treated as felons rather than as prisoners of war. This was a drastic step and one that Lee would invoke but sparingly.

∞ AUGUST 1862 ∞

THE HOSPITALS IN RICHMOND and the North were still fairly crowded with wounded from the Seven Days' Battle east of Richmond. Many who were badly wounded or suffered amputation had died. The crowd in Richmond of relatives who came to collect their dead or wounded was thinning out. In the west, Vicksburg still held strong against the river gunboats and Grant's army. Buell was shuffling along from Corinth to Chattanooga at a slow pace. Bragg, at Chattanooga, was getting ready for a campaign into Kentucky to rouse the state and get volunteers. He might have better luck than John Hunt Morgan did, but it was doubtful.

AUGUST 1 FRIDAY

Some in Richmond believed that because Vicksburg successfully withstood the gunboat assault, New Orleans should not have been surrendered without a battle. No comparison between terrains was taken into account. Vicksburg was on a bluff and hard to assault. New Orleans was flat and had no defense against attack from the river.

AUGUST 2 SATURDAY

The modern torpedo was being invented. William H. Aspinwall, a merchant, wrote Assistant Secretary of the Navy Fox:

> . . . [A] properly shaped cylindrical shot fired 6 or 8 feet under water will be the next improvement on iron clad vessels. At short range great effect could be attained below the iron plating. . . .

AUGUST 4 MONDAY

After over a year of trial and error, Lincoln told the military to get rid of the deadwood officers and incompetents and make an effort to promote more worthy officers.

In New Orleans, Gen. Benjamin Butler began his version of a social program by collecting a total of $341,916 from local "secessionists" for the benefit of the poor in the city.

Lincoln, offered two Negro regiments from Indiana for the Union Army, declined, suggesting they be used as laborers.

AUGUST 5 TUESDAY

Recruiting for troops in the North was going well, both to fill the old regiments and to create new ones. The problem was this: Now that some of the older regiments were decimated, were the survivors to be assigned to new units, or to fill up the old regiments? In both armies, "regimental identity" was quite often the thing that held units together. Some men, when consolidated with other regiments which had also been decimated, deserted rather than serve under a new regimental flag.

AUGUST 6 WEDNESDAY

Within gunboat range of the Mississippi River, north of Baton Rouge, Major Gen. John Cabell Breckinridge led about 2,600 Confederates through the fog and into a fight with about 2,500 Union troops commanded by Brigadier Gen. Thomas Williams. Even with limited visibility, the Rebel attack was turned aside, and the Federals ended the battle by 10 AM with the aid of the gunboats USS *Sumter*, *Cayuga*, *Kineo* and *Katahdin*. Losses were reasonably heavy for the numbers engaged. The Confederates pulled back north and began to fortify Port Hudson. The CSS *Arkansas* dropped down from Vicksburg to lend a hand and was destroyed.

On August 9, 1862, the Battle of Cedar Mountain was waged near Culpeper, Va. This photograph of a Federal battery fording the Rapidan River was taken on the morning of the battle.

AUGUST 7 THURSDAY

The Federals left Malvern Hill to the Confederates again today. This was the second time the blue-coats abandoned this defense position. This time it was voluntary.

AUGUST 8 FRIDAY

In northern Alabama there was a very serious problem of guerrillas firing into trains as they went along the tracks through the forests. To counter this, the Union commander ordered the arrest of local ministers and other leading churchmen and placed one of them a day on the trains—a rather harsh remedy, and there was no indication that it worked.

In Baltimore those avoiding the draft by leaving the area were arrested. This practice was so widespread that the War Department issued orders to prevent draft evasion throughout the rest of the North.

AUGUST 10 SUNDAY

On the Mississippi River south of Baton Rouge, Admiral Farragut carried out his threat to retaliate against the town of Donaldsonville if the local citizens didn't quit firing on the ships as they passed:

. . . [I] sent a message to the inhabitants that if they did not discontinue this practice, I would destroy the town. The last time I passed up to Baton Rouge to the support of the army, I . . . heard them firing upon the vessels coming up, first upon the

Sallie Robinson and next upon the *Brooklyn*. In the latter case they made a mistake, and it was so quickly returned that they ran away. The next night they fired again upon the *St. Charles.* I therefore ordered them to send their women and children out of the town, as I certainly intended to destroy it on my way down the river, and I fulfilled my promise to a certain extent. I burned down the hotels and wharf buildings, also the dwelling houses and other buildings of a Mr. Phillips Landry, who is said to be a captain of guerrillas.

AUGUST 11 MONDAY

Grant, near Corinth, reorganized and refitted his army. He ordered that slaves entering his lines be used for labor and paid either in wages or in kind.

AUGUST 16 SATURDAY

McClellan was finally free of the Peninsula with many of his troops now at Alexandria and Aquia Creek. He was supposed to support Pope's Army of Virginia, which was now heading into a major clash with Lee near Manassas. Lee's army, now consolidated, was moving north from Gordonsville towards Culpeper and Manassas.

AUGUST 18 MONDAY

Pope, pressed by Lee's advance, withdrew north of the Rappahannock River and waited for reinforcements from McClellan's idle legions. It would be a long wait.

AUGUST 19 TUESDAY

An uprising of the Sioux Indians that began on the 17th was still in progress. The Indians, facing starvation on their reservations, rebelled and began a bloodbath in which nearly 600 people would be killed in Minnesota. They rampaged through the countryside, killing and burning as they went.

AUGUST 20 WEDNESDAY

Skirmishing between Pope and Jackson was becoming more frequent and widespread. As Lee advanced, Pope withdrew, still waiting for reinforcements from McClellan's idle thousands.

AUGUST 22 FRIDAY

Still more skirmishing along the Rappahannock between Lee and Pope. Pope was a little embarrassed when JEB Stuart raided Catlett's Station and captured all of Pope's baggage and papers. Now he had no clean shirts, and no reinforcements.

After burning, looting and mutilating corpses around Ft. Ridgley, Minn., and being driven off, the Sioux Indians were back again, only to be repulsed again.

AUGUST 26 TUESDAY

The inevitable happened. Lee and Pope were beginning a battle which would be known as the Second Battle of Bull Run or Second Manassas.

The opening action was taken by cavalry under Fitzhugh Lee, one of Robert E. Lee's sons, when he entered Manassas Junction and captured the rail depot and cut off the communication to Washington. Jackson, on the move since the previous day, had come through the Bull Run Mountains at Thoroughfare Gap and was now positioned at Bristoe Station. The Confederates captured tons of supplies at the Manassas Junction rail depot, and begin moving much of it south.

Meanwhile, Pope didn't know where Jackson, Lee, or anyone was at the moment. McClellan was at Alexandria awaiting the remainder of his army from the Peninsula.

AUGUST 27 WEDNESDAY

Pope, already outflanked by Jackson, left his lines and moved north towards the old Manassas battlefield. Jackson, now at Manassas Junction rail depot, was destroying everything that couldn't be carried off. Longstreet was coming up in support of Jackson. Pope was in trouble, but didn't realize it.

AUGUST 28 THURSDAY

At Manassas, Pope arrived at about noon to find that Jackson had withdrawn. Pope hurried towards Centreville, where he thought Jackson had gone, and slammed into that force at Brawner's Farm without knowing that they were there. Longstreet and Lee proceeded through Thoroughfare Gap and passed to the north of Pope undetected. The stage was set for defeat.

AUGUST 29 FRIDAY

At Manassas, Pope was trying to make sense of the tactical situation. He believed that he had Jackson trapped, and he ordered attacks against Jackson's positions. Jackson had a strong position in a railroad cut at Sudley Springs and held without difficulty.

Halleck, in Washington, was urging McClellan to send troops immediately to support Pope. McClellan, having a strong dislike for Pope, "tried his best" to comply but little was done.

In Washington, Lincoln was cut off from all telegraphic communication.

AUGUST 30 SATURDAY

At Manassas, Pope believed that the Confederates had retreated. Pope attacked Jackson's line, the Confederate left flank. Longstreet attacked from the Confederate right flank and rolled up Pope's army, sending them into retreat towards Centreville. Pope had been beaten, but the army did not panic and go into a rout. While Lee won the battle, he hadn't destroyed the Union Army on the field.

It was finally over. There was enough glory (Confederate) and blame (Federal) to share. Pope had been humiliated after his

bombastic pronouncements before the campaign, and he would be sent west to command an administrative district. McClellan would deny any blame for not reinforcing Pope. Halleck had proven, once again, that he was not forceful enough in a crisis.

The Union had suffered over 16,000 casualties, and the South over 9,000. For relieving the pressure on Richmond, over 25,000 men were killed, wounded, or missing.

William Henry Fitzhugh Lee (1837–91), a son of Gen. Robert E. Lee, commanded the cavalry at the Second Battle of Bull Run in August of 1862. He later fought at Antietam under his cousin, also named Fitzhugh Lee. After the war, he became a U.S. Congressman.

This drawing by Edwin Forbes depicts the retreat of Gen. Pope's army through the town of Centreville, Va., after the Second Battle of Bull Run.

AUGUST 31 SUNDAY

A little late, two corps from the Army of the Potomac arrived to reinforce Pope. Lee, using information gathered by Stuart's cavalry scouts, got ready to attack Pope again by turning the Union right flank. He moved Jackson to a position just west of Chantilly, with Longstreet following along. The game was not over just yet.

∞ SEPTEMBER 1862 ∞

IT SEEMED THAT RICHMOND WAS safe for the time being. McClellan was back in northern Virginia strutting like a peacock about his "victory" on the Peninsula, and complaining that he hadn't received the support he had needed. Pope, thoroughly defeated at Second Manassas, was licking his wounds and awaiting Lee's further action. Washington was threatened, and Lincoln was worried.

In the west, Vicksburg was safe for the moment. Grant was east of Corinth, Miss. Bragg was to begin his campaign into Kentucky within days and some of the people in that state would welcome a return of the Confederates.

SEPTEMBER 1 MONDAY

After Manassas, Lee was not yet finished. He sent Jackson around the Federal right, where Stonewall ran into Federal Generals I. I. Stevens and Kearny. In the midst of a heavy rainstorm the fighting swirled around Chantilly until evening. During this scrap both Stevens and Kearny were killed, a real blow to the North. Pope held on and withdrew towards Centreville, pressured by Lee. As night fell, Washington was safe, but Lee was very close.

At Holly Springs, Miss., John Jackman was detailed to the regimental adjutant's office as a clerk.

SEPTEMBER 2 TUESDAY

Lincoln, reluctantly, returned McClellan to command of all the armies in northern Virginia, a move hotly opposed by Secretaries Stanton and Chase. Pope was now without a command. Lee gathered his army near Chantilly and rested the men while he thought of what to do next.

SEPTEMBER 3 WEDNESDAY

Pope, now without a command, wrote his report to Gen. Halleck in which he accused Gen. Porter of disobeying orders in the face of the enemy, and Gen. McClellan of not sending troops in a timely fashion.

SEPTEMBER 4 THURSDAY

The South's position in the outside world was not promising; neither France, England nor any other nation had recognized Southern independence. Lee felt that an invasion of the North would prove to anyone that the Confederacy had sufficient strength to stand on its own feet. With this in mind, Lee headed his troops to the crossings of the Potomac and into Maryland, where he hoped the people would rise for the South.

The movement of the Army of Northern Virginia into Maryland caused fighting at all the major fords of the Potomac.

SEPTEMBER 5 FRIDAY

In the west, Buell was withdrawing from Alabama towards Murfreesboro, Tenn. Bragg, at Sparta, Tenn., was prematurely proclaiming the state to be free.

SEPTEMBER 6 SATURDAY

Stonewall Jackson entered Frederick, Md. The Rebels expected a warm greeting and some recruits but received closed doors, locked stores and mostly a cold shoulder.

Pope was given command of a new Department of the Northwest and was sent to Minnesota to cope with the Indians who were rampaging and destroying the countryside.

SEPTEMBER 9 TUESDAY

At Frederick, Md., Lee issued his famous Special Order 191, which defined his campaign strategy. He then divided his forces, and continued on the move. He sent troops to Harpers Ferry, Boonsborough, Md., and Crampton's Gap. None of these forces was large.

SEPTEMBER 10 WEDNESDAY

In Maryland west of Washington, McClellan learned that Lee had evacuated Frederick. McClellan rushed his long blue lines to the northwest.

Barber, Pvt., Co. D, 15th Illinois Volunteer Infantry, en route to La Grange, Tenn., wrote:

> Our march lay through a swampy country, threaded by muddy creeks and rivers. The rebels had destroyed most of the bridges, hence our progress was very slow. We were obliged to take a circuitous route to avoid the enemy. . . . Guerrillas lurked in our track, picking up stragglers. Lon Howe and Emory Hiner of our company were captured within one mile of camp.

SEPTEMBER 11 THURSDAY

Kirby Smith's troops were within seven miles of Cincinnati, causing panic there. Smith had already occupied Maysville, Ky., just southwest of the city.

Lee's men were in Hagerstown, Md. There were more skirmishes as the armies drew closer together. Lee's exact whereabouts and intentions were still not known to McClellan.

A depiction of Gen. McClellan entering Frederick, Md., by artist Alfred R. Waud

SEPTEMBER 12 FRIDAY

McClellan's men moved into Frederick, Md., as Jackson was converging on Harpers Ferry. In Richmond, a debate went on about the advisability of invading the North.

SEPTEMBER 13 SATURDAY

The Union Army entered the town of Frederick, Md., almost as soon as the Confederates left the other side of town. In the Federal ranks of the 27th Indiana Volunteer Regiment, one Billy W. Mitchell found three cigars wrapped in paper lying in a fence corner. Mitchell picked up the packet and discovered that he had Gen. Robert E. Lee's Special Order No. 191 in his hand. This order contained all the details of the Confederate invasion. Lee's order was rapidly transmitted to McClellan, who was jubi-

lant over the discovery. By evening, McClellan had his long blue columns hurrying west of Frederick towards South Mountain, that long hogback dividing the valleys. Stuart and his cavalry awaited them.

SEPTEMBER 15 MONDAY

Harpers Ferry went into the hands of Stonewall Jackson today. The Federal commander, mortally wounded, offered little resistance.

SEPTEMBER 16 TUESDAY

Lee gathered his troops at Sharpsburg, leaving Gen. A. P. Hill at Harpers Ferry, but bringing Jackson and the rest of his corps to Antietam. McClellan moved cautiously, as usual, and lost a good opportunity to crush Lee while the Rebel army was still somewhat scattered.

SEPTEMBER 17 WEDNESDAY

On this day 23,110 Americans would be reported as killed, wounded or missing in action at Sharpsburg, Md., near Antietem Creek: 12,410 Union and 10,700 Confederate, initially outnumbered 2 to 1. They would fall at the rate of about 2,000 per hour, or about 35 per minute, from 6 AM to 6 PM. If laid end to end, the dead and wounded would have lined a road for 25 miles. This was the bloodiest single day in American history.

SEPTEMBER 18 THURSDAY

With dawn on this day the terrible slaughter of Antietam was more apparent. Thousands of dead were still lying in the fields and along the fence rows. Nearly 12,000 lay in Miller's cornfield. The Bloody Lane was filled with Confederate dead, in some places four deep. Lee awaited McClellan. "Little Mac" was loath to act, as usual. The wounded suffered and the dead awaited burial.

Stowe, Sgt., Co. G, 15th Massachusetts, hospital at Sharpsburg [Antietam], Md., wrote:

> Misery acute, painful misery. How I suffered last night. It was the most painful of anything have ever experienced. My leg must be broken for I cannot help myself scarcely any. I remember talking and groaning all night. Many died in calling for help. . . . Sergt Johnson who lies on the other side of the log is calling for water.
>
> Carried off the field at 10 AM by the Rebs who show much kindness but devote much time to plundering the dead bodies of our men. . . . Water very short. We suffer very much.

SEPTEMBER 19 FRIDAY

At Sharpsburg, Lee began his retreat across the Potomac, and McClellan crowed about his victory although he went through the battle without committing over 30,000 of his soldiers, who could have overwhelmingly defeated the Confederate force. He allowed Lee to disengage and to escape with no pursuit. The news getting to Richmond was garbled.

The Sanitary Commission reacted to the carnage of Antietam by bringing in supplies, as well as food, to treat the wounded. . . . as well as food—all donated by Northern volunteers and communities—to treat the wounded

SEPTEMBER 20 SATURDAY

Lee moved his divisions across the Potomac unopposed. This was McClellan's major blunder; he could have trapped Lee's army against the flooding river. Instead, he sent his cavalry to harass the gray columns and sat in Antietam. This would be McClellan's last battle.

SEPTEMBER 21 SUNDAY

More wounded leaving today at Antietam. Slowly, ever so slowly, the dead were buried and the dying given their final solace. Many wounded, especially amputees, would die from infections caused by the unsanitary "operating room" conditions.

McClellan sat, while Lee withdrew into Virginia.

SEPTEMBER 22 MONDAY

Lincoln issued his "preliminary" Emancipation Proclamation today. It did little except free the slaves in the states not held by the Union.

At Antietam, the wounded were still dying at a tremendous rate.

Stowe, Sgt., Co. G, 15th Massachusetts, hospital at Sharpsburg [Antietam], Md., wrote:

> Two men died last night. . . . How painful my stump is. I did not know [I] was capable of enduring so much pain. How very meager are accommodations—no chamber pots & nobody to find or rig up one. How ludicrous for 2 score amputated men to help themselves with diarrhea.

THE BATTLE OF ANTIETAM

SEPTEMBER 17, 1862

*David Thomson, a member of the 9th New York Volunteers,
describes the battle on Burnside Bridge.*

About noon the battle began afresh. This must have been Franklin's men of the Sixth Corps, for the firing was nearer. Suddenly a stir beginning far up on the right, and running like a wave along the line, brought the regiment to its feet. A silence fell on every one at once, for each that felt that the momentous "now" had come. Just as we started I saw, with a little shock, a line officer take out his watch to note the hour, as though the affair beyond the creek were a business appointment which he was going to keep.

When we reached the brow of the hill the fringe of trees along the creek screened the fighting entirely, and we were deployed as skirmishers under their cover. We sat there for two hours. All that time the rest of the corps had been moving over the stone bridge and going into position on the other side of the creek. Then we were ordered over at a ford which had been found below the bridge, where the water was waist-deep. One man was shot in mid-stream. At the foot of the slope on the opposite side the line was formed and we moved up through the thin woods. Reaching the

Burnside Bridge, Antietam, photographed in 1862

level we lay down behind a battery which seemed to have been disabled. There, if anywhere, I should have remembered that I was soaking wet from my waist down. So great was the excitement, however, that I have never been able to recall it. . . .

Our knapsacks were left on the ground behind us. At the word a rush was made for the fences. The line was so disordered by the time the second fence was passed that we hurried forward to a shallow undulation a few feet ahead, and lay down among the furrows to re-form, doing so by crawling up into line. A hundred feet or so ahead was a similar undulation to which we ran for a second shelter. The battery, which at first had not seemed to notice us, now, apprised of its danger, opened fire upon us. We were getting ready now for the charge proper, but were still lying on our faces. Lieutenant-Colonel Kimball was ramping up and down the line. The discreet regiment behind the fence was silent. Now and then a bullet from them cut the air over our heads, but generally they were reserving their fire for that better shot which they knew they would get in a few minutes.

As the range grew better, the firing became more rapid, the situation desperate and exasperating to the last degree. Human nature was on the rack, and there burst forth from it the most vehement, terrible swearing I have ever heard. Certainly the joy of conflict was not ours that day. The suspense was only for a moment, however, for the order to charge came just after. Whether the regiment was thrown into disorder or not, I never knew. I only remember that as we rose and started all the fire that had been held back so long was loosed. In a second the air was full of the hiss of bullets and the hurtle of grape-shot. The mental strain was so great that I saw at that moment the singular effect mentioned, I think, in the life of Goethe on a similar occasion—the whole landscape for an instant turned slightly red. I see again as I saw it then in a flash, a man just in front of me drop his musket and throw up his hands, stung into vigorous swearing by a bullet behind the ear. Many men fell going up the hill, but it seemed to be all over in a moment, and I found myself passing a hollow where a dozen wounded men lay—among them our sergeant-major, who was calling me to come down. . . .

Members of the 93rd New York Infantry in Antietam, taken on September 16, 1862, the day before the battle

We lay there until dusk, perhaps an hour, while the bullets snipped the leaves from a young locust-tree, growing at the edge of the hollow and powdered us with the fragments, we had time to speculate on many things—among others, on the impatience with which men clamor, in dull times, to be led into a fight. We heard all through the war that the army "was eager to be led against the enemy." It must have been so, for truthful correspondents said so, and editors confirmed it. But when you came to hunt for this particular itch, it was always the next regiment that had it. The truth is, when bullets are whacking against tree-trunks and solid shot are cracking skulls like egg-shells, the consuming passion in the breast of the average man is to get out of the way. . . .

Night fell, preventing further struggle. Of 600 men of the regiment who crossed the creek at 3 o'clock that afternoon, 45 were killed and 176 wounded. The Confederates held possession of that part of the field over which we had moved, and just after dusk they sent out detachments to collect arms and bring in prisoners. When they came to our hollow all the unwounded and slightly wounded there were marched to the rear—prisoners of the 15th Georgia. We slept on the ground that night without protection of any kind; for, with a recklessness quite common throughout the war, we had thrown away every incumbrance on going into the fight.

FACING PAGE: Map of the Antietam battlefield

BELOW: Bodies of the Confederate dead await burial after the Battle of Antietam

MAP OF THE
Battlefield of Antietam,
Prepared by
LIEUT. WM. H. WILLCOX, TOP. OFF. & A.A.D.C.
ON
BRIG. GEN. DOUBLEDAY'S STAFF.
FROM ACTUAL SURVEYS
UNION FORCES. REBEL FORCES.
Scale of Miles

1862

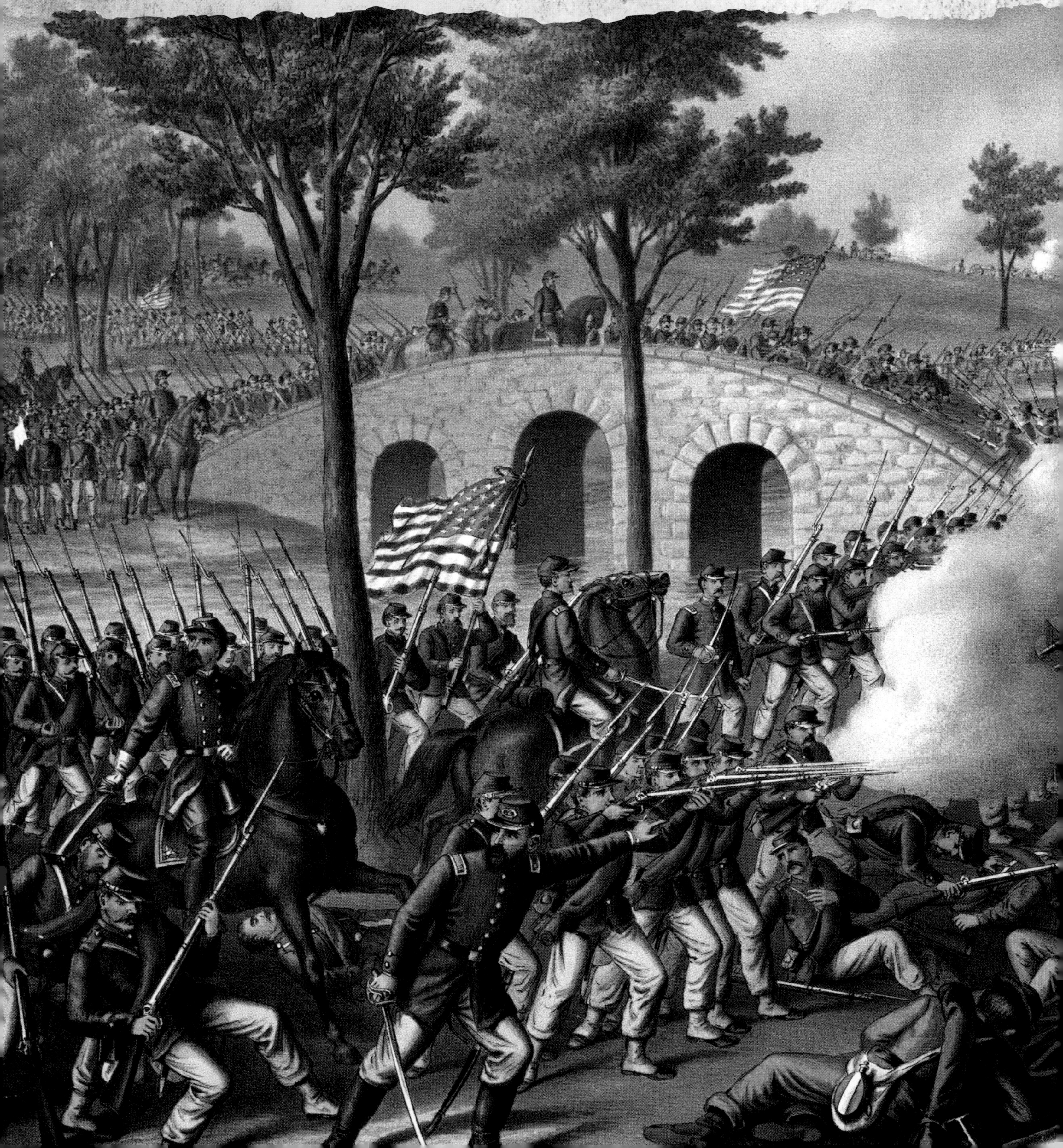

1862

SEPTEMBER 27 SATURDAY

Lincoln was becoming annoyed with McClellan, who sat and crowed about his "victory."

A first: A regiment of free Negroes was mustered in at New Orleans as the First Regiment Louisiana Native Guards.

The Battle of Antietam, September 17, 1862, as interpreted by the Chicago lithographers Kurz & Allison

SEPTEMBER 29 MONDAY

At 7:54 this evening, Sgt. Stowe had a telegram sent to J. W. Stowe as follows: "Dangerously wounded at Hoffmans hospital near Sharpsburg. Come instantly."

It was too late. On October 1, Stowe died of his wounds and the amputation.

OCTOBER 1862

SEPTEMBER WAS OVER and the aftermath of Antietam was still with both sides in the form of the
wounded and dying. It would be months before
many of these men could shoulder a musket, and
for some it would be a long trip home—minus an
arm or a leg. The long wagon trains of wounded
coming back into Virginia had unloaded their cargo
at train depots, and the wounded who could travel
were sent on to Richmond and other military hospitals for better care. Those who were native to the
Valley were taken home to recuperate. Many Union
soldiers went home, others to the large hospitals
around Washington, and slowly, ever so slowly, the
wounded were shipped out during the cooler days
and crisp nights.

OCTOBER 3 FRIDAY

Near Corinth, Miss., the Confederates attacked
Rosecrans's lines and drove them in towards the
town. The attack, led by Van Dorn and Sterling
Price, was made to force the Federals to withdraw
into Tennessee.

OCTOBER 4 SATURDAY

The second day of battle near Corinth saw Van
Dorn renewing his attacks on Rosecrans. The
battle swayed back and forth with attack and
counterattack until midafternoon, when Van Dorn
withdrew to the northwest around the town of
Chewalla. So far the Union had lost about 2,500
and the Confederates a little over 4,200. The result
of the battle was a draw. The rail center of Corinth
was still in Federal hands.

OCTOBER 5 SUNDAY

Van Dorn, while not hotly pursued by Rosecrans,
was ambushed by Federal troops under General E.
O. C. Ord at the Hatchie River, where a stiff fight
took place.

OCTOBER 8 WEDNESDAY

The only major battle fought on Kentucky soil was
fought today at Perryville. Major Gen. Don Carlos Buell's Union army clashed with Gen. Braxton
Bragg's Confederates. In total forces, the Union outnumbered the Confederates by more than 2 to 1. It
was a partial victory for the North, and in one way a
total victory, in that no major invasion of Kentucky
was attempted again by the South.

OCTOBER 11 SATURDAY

JEB Stuart entered Chambersburg, Pa., where he cut
the telegraph lines, seized horses, wrecked everything in sight that looked useful and couldn't be
carried away and left in the afternoon, going south
towards Emmitsburg, Md.

OCTOBER 14 TUESDAY

Today, elections held in several of the midwestern
states elected Democrats to Congress, except in
Iowa, which was solidly Republican.

Brigadier Gen. James Birdseye McPherson today
became a Division Commander in Grant's army.
He would distinguish himself many times before he
was killed outside Atlanta.

OCTOBER 19 SUNDAY

Yesterday near Lexington, Ky., the cavalry of John
Hunt Morgan defeated a Union cavalry force,
entered the city, captured the garrison, paroled the
prisoners and went away.

OCTOBER 24 FRIDAY

Don Carlos Buell was removed from command in
Kentucky and replaced by Major Gen. William S.
Rosecrans. Rosecrans had a little over two months
before his major battle at Stone's River.

On October 3, 1862, President Lincoln visited Gen. George
McClellan in Antietam, Md. This photograph shows the
president and McClellan conferring in the general's tent.

02

OCTOBER 25 SATURDAY

In the west, Major Gen. Grant assumed command of the Thirteenth Army Corps and the Department of the Tennessee.

OCTOBER 26 SUNDAY

The Army of the Potomac began crossing the river and into Virginia. This was its first major move in more than two months. The movement was not rapid.

OCTOBER 30 THURSDAY

The United States Navy Department had offered a reward of $500,000 for the capture of the CSS *Alabama,* or $300,000 if she were destroyed. A dozen ships were chasing her.

OCTOBER 31 FRIDAY

The Confederate Congress authorized a Torpedo Bureau under Brigadier Gen. Gabriel J. Rains and a Naval Submarine Battery Service under Lt. Hunter Davidson. The purpose was to organize and improve methods of torpedo mine warfare.

❧ NOVEMBER 1862 ❧

OCTOBER HAD BEEN A MONTH of healing and trying to forget. The ranks of the armies, North and South, were missing messmates who were left at Antietam's Stone Bridge or Bloody Lane, some field near Corinth, or a fence corner at Perryville.

McClellan had finally started moving again, albeit slowly. Lee sat at Winchester and considered a move to Gordonsville, where he could protect Richmond better. Bragg and his battered and weary legions were back in Tennessee after a long and arduous campaign that had gained little. Rosecrans had beaten Van Dorn at Corinth, and the Confederate Army in that area retreated. Vicksburg was under siege, but lightly.

NOVEMBER 1 SATURDAY

In Kentucky, the new Federal commander, Major Gen. William S. Rosecrans, prepared his troops for the move back into Tennessee and the search for Braxton Bragg. On the Mississippi River, Grant was preparing an overland campaign against Vicksburg, despite the political machinations being carried on by Major Gen. John McClernand in Illinois.

A naval task force, under the overall command of Commander Davenport, was formed yesterday to support the Army in its assault on Plymouth and Hamilton, N.C.

Barber, Cpl., Co. D, 15th Illinois Volunteer Infantry, Oxford, Miss., wrote:

> We continued to push the enemy until they crossed the Tallahatchie. Here they seemed disposed to make a stand, and well they might. The place was impregnable against a direct assault . . . but the invincible Sherman soon flanked them with his division and they beat a precipitate retreat. . . . Soon the beautiful city of Oxford was reached and we marched triumphantly through its streets.

NOVEMBER 3 MONDAY

Longstreet arrived with his corps at Culpeper C.H., Va., moving in from the Valley to get in front of McClellan, who was now at Warrenton. No contact had been made yet.

NOVEMBER 4 TUESDAY

In the North, the Democrats won the elections in some states, notably New York, New Jersey, Illinois and Wisconsin. This raised the hopes of the Southerners, who believed that the Democrats would be able to contain the hated Lincoln and bring peace, especially on their terms. Not all was good news for the Democrats, however. The control of the House of Representatives remained with the Republicans.

THE REBEL FORAY IN PENNSYLVANIA—GENERAL VIEW OF CHAMBERSBURG.—SKETCHED BY MR. DAVIS.—[SEE PAGE 698.]

In the November 1, 1862, issue of *Harper's Weekly*, artist Theodore Davis published these drawings illustrating the previous month's Confederate infiltration of Chambersburg, Pa. At the top is a general view of Chambersburg; at the lower left, Confederate soldiers exchange their rags for overcoats; at the bottom right, townspeople watch the engine house and machine shops as they burn.

NOVEMBER 5 WEDNESDAY

In what would be a shock to McClellan, President Lincoln ordered him replaced, assigning Major Gen. Ambrose E. Burnside as the commander of the Army of the Potomac. Burnside, an able general at some levels, realized his shortcomings and told Lincoln that he did not want the command and that he was unfit for it. This brought an end to McClellan's military career. McClellan's departure created much controversy in the ranks of the Army of the Potomac, which venerated him. At the same time, Major Gen. Fitz John Porter was relieved from command and was replaced by Major Gen. Joseph Hooker.

NOVEMBER 6 THURSDAY

In Richmond, the promotions of James Longstreet and Stonewall Jackson from Major Gen. to Lieutenant Gen. were announced, as were their assignments to the First and Second Army Corps.

NOVEMBER 8 SATURDAY

In New Orleans, Major Gen. Benjamin F. Butler ordered all the breweries and distilleries in the city closed. In Washington, the President appointed Major Gen. Nathaniel Banks, late of the Shenandoah Valley, to replace Butler. Banks was given specific instructions that his job was to open the Mississippi River, not to worry about breweries.

NOVEMBER 9 SUNDAY

Major Gen. Ambrose E. Burnside today assumed command of the Army of the Potomac, then at Warrenton, Va., about 40 miles southwest of Washington.

NOVEMBER 10 MONDAY

Major Gen. George B. McClellan, at age 36, had commanded more men than any other general in American history. He took a dispirited army and, with his unique organizational skills, built it into a magnificent body of men, the like of which had never been seen on the continent. For all his virtues, and there were many, he had a failing that could not be tolerated in a general: he would not commit his men to battle with a will to win.

NOVEMBER 15 SATURDAY

Barber, Cpl., Co. D, 15th Illinois Volunteer Infantry, to Abbeyville, Miss., wrote:

Ambrose Everett Burnside (1824–81) was born in Liberty, Ind., the son of a former slave owner from South Carolina who had moved to Indiana after freeing his slaves.

Aquia Creek, a tributary of the Potomac River in northern Virginia, served as a supply base for the Army of the Potomac. This illustration of the facility appeared in an 1862 edition of *Harper's Weekly*.

One morning, just before marching, a very serious affray occurred in Company F. Two men, Ser. Hill and Ser. _____, got into a dispute about some trifling matter. Words led to blows and _____ drew his knife and, before any of us could interfere, stabbed Hill through the abdomen. The wound was supposed to be mortal and the surgeon left him at a plantation near Springdale. One of his comrades volunteered to stay and nurse him. It was a noble act. The would-be murderer was arrested on the spot. A double guard was placed around him, but notwithstanding, he made his escape. He went back to his wounded victim, asked and received his pardon for his rash act; nursed him until he was nearly well and then left for the rebel army. The other two men were made prisoners, paroled and eventually got back to the regiment.

NOVEMBER 19 WEDNESDAY

Lt. Gen. James Longstreet brought his corps onto Marye's Heights near Fredericksburg today after a march from Culpeper. Burnside arrived at Falmouth, across the river.

NOVEMBER 21 FRIDAY

Gen. Nathan Bedford Forrest was sent to western Tennessee by Bragg to cut the communications of both Grant's and Rosecrans's armies. He would do a good job of it, being a constant fly in the ointment.

On the Rappahannock, Burnside asked that the city of Fredericksburg surrender; it refused. The bombardment of the town was threatened, and the Mayor requested time to remove the sick, wounded, women and children. Jackson was hurrying from the Valley.

NOVEMBER 27 THURSDAY

President Lincoln arrived at Aquia Creek yesterday. He conferred with Gen. Burnside on the plans for a new offensive. Their plans differed.

Rear Admiral Farragut wrote from New Orleans:

> I am still doing nothing, but waiting for the tide of events and doing all I can to hold what I have, & blockade Mobile. So soon as the river rises, we will have Porter down from above, who now commands the upper squadron, and then I shall probably go outside. . . . We shall spoil unless we have a fight occasionally.

The month ended on a quiet note. This month saw much jockeying for position, both east and west, in both armies. A time of rest before the storm.

⚬ DECEMBER 1862 ⚬

DECEMBER ARRIVED ALMOST WITHOUT ANYONE prepared for it. In Richmond, Vicksburg and Mobile, the citizens were short of many of the commodities they had taken for granted just a short year ago. Clothing was getting to be in short supply. Cooking fuel was very expensive, and often so expensive that it could not be spared for heating a parlor. Meat was expensive, as was cornmeal, butter and flour. The value of Confederate money shrank as inflationary pressures ate away at the currency. The North was in better shape economically. While inflation had some effect, food was still plentiful, as was clothing and other necessities.

On the war front, Bragg was at Murfreesboro, Tenn., and planning an operation to drive the Union forces out of the state. Rosecrans, in Nashville, had other ideas. Grant was near Holly Springs and working on his plans for Vicksburg. Burnside and Lee faced each other over the Rappahannock in Fredericksburg. The battles were building.

DECEMBER 1 MONDAY

Near Fredericksburg, Jackson arrived from the Valley with his corps ready for a fight. Lee awaited Burnside's actions.

DECEMBER 2 TUESDAY

There was minor skirmishing along the Rappahannock between Lee's and Burnside's forces, but nothing major. Civilians evacuated Fredericksburg as fast as they could. Many took trains to Richmond. Many sent their slaves to points south to prevent them from either escaping into the Federal lines or being freed by the Federals. Once within the blue lines, they were usually gone forever.

DECEMBER 4 THURSDAY

Gen. Joseph Eggleston Johnston assumed command of the Confederate armies in the west today.

DECEMBER 7 SUNDAY

About 12 miles from Fayetteville, Ark., two evenly matched armies got into a fight in freezing weather in what later became known as the Battle of Prairie Grove. Gen. Thomas C. Hindman's 10,000 Confederates attacked the combined Union force of Generals James Blunt and Francis J. Herron, also with 10,000. The casualties were about even: 1,251 Federals and 1,317 Confederates.

At Hartsville, Tenn., John Hunt Morgan and his cavalrymen waged a small battle with Col. A. B. Moore's garrison and took them lock, stock and barrel. Moore lost over 2,000 men, 1,800 of them captured.

DECEMBER 9 TUESDAY

There was increased activity at Falmouth just across the river from Fredericksburg. Burnside issued orders for his Grand Division commanders to issue 60 rounds per man, prepare three days' cooked rations and be prepared for an assault on the Rebels across the river. Pontoon bridges were coming up to span the Rappahannock for the crossing.

DECEMBER 10 WEDNESDAY

The U.S. House of Representatives passed a bill creating the new state of West Virginia; the same bill had passed a Senate vote the previous July.

All day the officers of the Union army scrambled to ensure that everything was in order for the assault tomorrow on Fredericksburg. Details were checked, rechecked and checked again.

DECEMBER 11 THURSDAY

In the predawn darkness at 4:45 AM the alert was given to the Confederates that the Yankees were building their bridges for the assault. The Confederates came up to their positions. Barksdale's Mississippians were placed in the brick buildings whose blank rear walls faced the river to the west. Loopholes were knocked in the brick and firing posts assigned. They looked directly out on the bridges. At daylight, the firing began and it became downright dangerous to be on the bridges. The engineers left their positions to scamper back out of the fire only to be driven back to work by their officers. Finally, at 10 AM, Burnside had enough of this. He ordered his artillery to demolish those houses, and they certainly did. Over 140 guns poured nearly 5,000 rounds of heavy artillery into the city. Barksdale's men came back, however, and shot a few more of the engineers. Eventually, a bridgehead was established and the Yanks poured over the bridges and into the city. The Confederates withdrew and it was nearly 7:30 PM by the time the last of the Mississippians were back into their own lines. It would be a long night for everyone.

Fredericksburg, Va., in 1863

Colonel of 20th Maine Volunteers, General Joshua L. Chamberlain
describes the night of December 13–14.

The desperate charge was over. We had not reached the enemy's fortifications, but only that fatal crest where we had seen five lines of battle mount but to be cut to earth as by a sword-swoop of fire. We had that costly honor which sometimes falls to the "reserve"—to go in when all is havoc and confusion, through storm and slaughter, to cover the broken and depleted ranks of comrades and take the battle from their hands. Thus we had replaced the gallant few still struggling on the crest, and received that withering fire, which nothing could withstand, by throwing ourselves flat in a slight hollow of the ground, within pistol shot of the enemy's works; and, mingled with the dead and dying that strewed the field, we returned the fire till it reddened into night, and at last fell away through darkness into silence.

But out of that silence from the battle's crash and roar rose new sounds more appalling still; rose or fell, you knew not which, or whether from the earth or air; a strange ventriloquism, of which you could not locate the source, a smothered moan that seemed to come from distances beyond reach of the natural sense, a wail so fat and deep and wide, as if a thousand discords were flowing together into a key-note weird, unearthly, terrible to hear and hear, yet startling with its nearness; the writhing concord broken by cries for help, pierced by shrieks of paroxysm; some begging for a drop of water; some calling on God for pity; and some on friendly hands to finish what the enemy had so horribly begun; some with delirious, dreamy voices murmuring loved names, as if the dearest were bending over them; some gathering their last strength to fire a musket to call attention to them where they lay helpless and deserted; and underneath, all the time, that deep bass note from closed lips too hopeless or too heroic to articulate their agony.

Who could sleep, or who would? Our position was isolated and exposed. Officers must be on the alert with their command. But the human took the mastery of the official; sympathy of soldiership. Command could be devolved; but pity, not. So with a staff officer I sallied forth to see what we could do where the helpers seemed so few. Taking some observations in order not to lose the bearing of our own position, we guided our steps by the most piteous of the cries. Our part was but little; to relieve a painful posture; to give a cooling draught to fevered lips; to compress a severed artery, as we had learned to do, though in bungling

Confederate Army officer's uniform coat worn by LTC William H. Fulkerson of the 63d Tennessee Infantry.

FACING PAGE: This April 1864 photograph shows the damage inflicted upon surrounding houses during the Battle of Fredericksburg.

fashion; to apply a rude bandage, which yet might prolong the life to saving; to take a token or farewell message for some stricken home; it was but little, yet it was an endless task. We had moved towards the right and rear of our own position—the part of the field immediately above the city. The farther we went the more the need deepened, and the calls multiplied. Numbers half wakening from the lethargy of death, or of despair, by sounds of succor, begged us to take them quickly to a surgeon; and when we could not do that, imploring us to do the next most merciful service and give them quick dispatch out of their misery. Right glad were we when, after midnight, the shadowy ambulances came gliding along, and the kindly hospital stewards, with stretchers and soothing appliances, let us feel that we might return to our proper duty.

Above: Charles Memorial Hamilton (1840–70), a member of the 5th Pennsylvania Reserve Infantry, was wounded and captured during the Battle of Fredericksburg. He was released a month later as part of an exchange.

Right: The Battle of Fredericksburg, December 13, 1862

DECEMBER 13 SATURDAY

All was ready at Fredericksburg. At ten o'clock the fog thinned and the artillery began to roar. On Marye's Heights, the Confederates watched as the Federals aligned their ranks and prepared for the charge up the hill. It finally came at 11:30 AM when the assault began and the Yankees assaulted Longstreet's men who were positioned behind a stone wall and at a higher elevation. It was slaughter of the worst kind. Wave after wave of blue-clad troops lined up and went up the hill only to be shot down. Six charges had been made by 6 PM, all repulsed. It had been a futile exercise that killed nearly 1,300 Union troops, wounded about 9,600 and left almost 1,800 as prisoners. The South lost about 600 killed, 4,100 wounded and 650 missing.

DECEMBER 14 SUNDAY

Burnside was ready to order another assault on Lee but was dissuaded by his commanders. Lee rightly declined to leave his prepared position and attack Burnside. He had no pontoons to cross the river and, besides, there was a mighty array of cannon to face. The cleanup of the battlefield began with the searching for the wounded and the burying of the dead.

DECEMBER 15 MONDAY

While the rest of Burnside's men withdrew across the Rappahannock, the recriminations began. Hooker would be one of the most vocal of Burnside's critics, a fact that would be remembered by Lincoln in the days to come.

This drawing by Alonzo Chappel depicts Union soldiers landing on the shore of the Rappahannock River, pulling up pontoon bridges and maneuvering in the foreground; the buildings of Fredericksburg burn in the background.

DECEMBER 16 TUESDAY

The Army of the Potomac was licking its wounds at Falmouth and at Stafford Heights near Fredericksburg. The army would winter here, denuding the countryside for miles around for firewood. The soil, lacking the living vegetation to hold it, would become a quagmire and erosion would strip the land of its rich topsoil. Many years would pass before the land returned to its 1861 condition.

DECEMBER 17 WEDNESDAY

Grant, out in Holly Springs, Miss., was plagued with cotton speculators who roamed his lines looking for plantation owners who wanted to sell their cotton. There was also the usual plague of peddlers, unauthorized sutlers and just plain sharks who traveled over the area taking advantage of the troops. Finally, Grant reached his limit of endurance and issued his famous General Order No. 11, which stated, "The Jews, as a class violating every regulation of trade established by the Treasury Department and also department orders, are hereby expelled from the department within twenty-four hours from the receipt of this order," a strong statement that would be rescinded by both Lincoln and Halleck on the 4th of the next month. This would follow Grant for years, well into his Presidency.

In Washington, Lincoln had more troubles than Grant. Salmon P. Chase was constantly intriguing with members of Congress to gain the upper hand over Seward. This came to a head when Seward offered to resign from the Cabinet. The resignation was declined by Lincoln.

DECEMBER 18 THURSDAY

Grant announced the organization of his army. Sherman, Hurlbut, McPherson and McClernand were to be corps commanders. McClernand was satisfied, at least temporarily, with his new assignment.

At Chattanooga, Jefferson Davis reported that Bragg's troops at Murfreesboro were in fine shape and were ready for the coming campaign.

DECEMBER 20 SATURDAY

The Cabinet crisis ended today when Chase offered his resignation. To Chase's great surprise and discomfort, Lincoln accepted it. Chase had presidential ambitions and had been plotting to discredit Lincoln almost from the time he had joined the Cabinet. While Lincoln accepted the paper, he declined to put it into force. Lincoln had, however, a sword to hold over Chase's head, since he could accept the resignation at any time.

DECEMBER 21
SUNDAY

Today, the U.S. Congress authorized the Medal of Honor, the nation's highest award, to be awarded to such Navy personnel as distinguished themselves by their gallantry inaction. During the war, a total of 327 sailors and marines were awarded the Medal of Honor.

DECEMBER 24
WEDNESDAY

Christmas Eve of the first full year of war. Around many campfires the soldiers were feeling homesick, lonely and discouraged, no matter which uniform they wore.

DECEMBER 25 THURSDAY

President and Mrs. Lincoln visited hospitals in Washington today.

The holiday meant little to John Hunt Morgan's men as they continued their Kentucky raid, with fighting at Green's Chapel and Bear Wallow.

DECEMBER 27 SATURDAY

Sherman's men were approaching Vicksburg's defenses on the north, while Pemberton was bringing in more troops for the defense of the city. A stalemate would soon develop.

Rosecrans's army was moving slowly towards Bragg at Murfreesboro. Contact had been made and there was some skirmishing between the forces.

Morgan's men were as far north as Elizabethtown, Ky., on their current raid. Tomorrow he would destroy a bridge near Muldraugh's Hill near the site of the present Ft. Knox, and then run for Tennessee.

DECEMBER 29
MONDAY

Sherman's troops fought the Battle of Chickasaw Bayou to gain the bluffs on the north side of Vicksburg. The terrain was not friendly and all the work of the campaign went for nothing. The positions were too strong to take by frontal assault. Sherman awaited developments.

Outside Murfreesboro, Tenn., the contact between Bragg and Rosecrans was heavier and the fighting became more frequent between the pickets. In one case, General Joseph Wheeler's cavalry, having completed the screening of the Confederate flank, swept down on a Federal brigade and captured 20 wagons loaded with supplies for Crittenden's men. Morgan was fighting his way back into Tennessee at Springfield and New Haven, Ky.

Medal of Honor, c. 1862–96

DECEMBER 30 TUESDAY

Lincoln finished his draft of the Emancipation Proclamation. He circulated it to the Cabinet for comment. The document stated that all slaves in *Confederate-held* territory were free, but *not* those in Union territory. This, in effect, did not free a single slave. It did, however, have the very far-reaching effect of preventing France and England from recognizing the Confederate government; to have done so would have meant recognition of a slave-holding government.

Sherman remained in position near Chickasaw Bayou at Vicksburg hoping for a break so that he could capture the city. His plans for withdrawal were still in effect.

At Murfreesboro, it was obvious that a major battle was taking place. Fighting began with an unexpected assault on the Federal lines, which drove the Union forces back through the woods. Things might have been different if Sheridan had not been there with his division. He held, although he would lose his three brigade commanders before the day was over. At night the firing faded and the commanders prohibited the troops from building fires to warm themselves. In the bitter cold, everyone had a miserable night.

Wounded soldiers and hospital staff in a ward at the Armory Square Hospital in Washington, D.C.

1863

... [B]ut just then a white flag was seen to flutter from the rebel works, which proclaimed that the finale had been reached. Then one long, joyous shout echoed and re-echoed along our lines. Its cadence rang long and deep over hill and valley until we caught the glad anthem and swelled the chorus with our voices in one glad shout of joy. It was a glorious opening for the Fourth of July ...

—Corporal Barber, at the surrender of Vicksburg, July 1863

PRECEDING PAGES: This c. 1888 lithograph depicts the siege and surrender of Vicksburg on July 4, 1863.

ABOVE: The Emancipation Proclamation declared the freedom of all slaves in any Confederate state that refused to return to the Union by January 1, 1863.

JANUARY 1 THURSDAY

As the new year began, the Battle of Murfreesboro (Stone's River) continued. Lincoln's Emancipation Proclamation went into effect. It did nothing to free the slaves in the Northern states, but it was a major moral force in the South.

JANUARY 2 FRIDAY

More fighting at Stone's River this day. Breckinridge's "Orphan Brigade" managed to take a small hill but were driven from it with heavy losses. Everyone took another breather. Bragg announced to Richmond that he had a great victory.

JANUARY 3 SATURDAY

Gen. Braxton Bragg determined that he could not hold the positions at Murfreesboro, and he retreated to Manchester, leaving Rosecrans in possession of the field. The cleanup began. Jackman found a good meal and began the march.

JANUARY 6 TUESDAY

Jackman and the "Orphans" went into winter quarters at Manchester. The pace was slow, the duty dull, the recreation better than average.

JANUARY 7 WEDNESDAY

In Tennessee, Grant rescinded his General Order No. 11, which had expelled the Jews.

Since the Emancipation Proclamation was issued on January 1, slaves in the South had been celebrating as best they could. For many years, even into the 20th century, that day was celebrated as "Freedom Day."

JANUARY 9 FRIDAY

At Arkansas Post on the Arkansas River, Major Gen. McClernand's troops were landed under the cover of naval gunfire, which drove the enemy from their rifle pits. This enabled McClernand's men to approach Ft. Hindman unseen. Grant evacuated Holly Springs, Miss.

Lt. John N. Maffitt (1819–86), left, was compared by a journalist at the *New York Herald* to Capt. Raphael Semmes (1809–77), right. Both men were commanders in the Confederate States Navy. Semmes was photographed standing on the deck of the CSS *Alabama* in 1863.

JANUARY 11 SUNDAY

On this morning the bombardment of Ft. Hindman was continued from the gunboats and "after a well directed fire of about two and one-half hours every gun in the fort was dismounted or disabled and the fort knocked to pieces. . . ." Brig. Gen. Thomas J. Churchill, CSA, surrendered the fort after a gallant resistance.

JANUARY 19 MONDAY

At Fredericksburg, Burnside had convinced Lincoln that a new attack across the Rappahannock was possible. The troops of the Army of the Potomac started upriver towards the U.S. Ford.

A letter, intercepted coming out of Nassau, Bahamas, showed the effect of the blockade on the South:

> There are men here who are making immense fortunes by shipping goods to Dixie. . . . It is a speculation by which one makes either 600 to 800 percent or loses all.

JANUARY 20 TUESDAY

In Havana, Cuba, a correspondent for the *New York Herald* described Lt. John N. Maffitt, commander of the raider CSS *Florida*, which had just come into port:

> Captain Maffitt is no ordinary character. He is vigorous, energetic, bold, quick and dashing, and the sooner he is caught and hung the better it will be for the interest of our commercial community. He is decidedly popular here, and you can scarcely imagine the anxiety evinced to get a glance at him. . . . Nobody, unless informed, would have imagined the small, black-eyed, poetic-looking gentleman, with his romantic appearance, to be a second Semmes, probably in time to be a more celebrated and more dangerous pirate.

JANUARY 21 WEDNESDAY

Along the Rappahannock in Virginia, the famous "Mud March" of the Army of the Potomac was about to begin. The Army having gone to U.S. Ford to effect a crossing, the rains swelled the river to prevent any such activity and created mud, mud and more mud.

JANUARY 22 THURSDAY

Grant, finally tired of McClernand's grandstand plays, assumed command of all troops in Arkansas; this reduced McClernand from commander of the expedition to a corps commander. McClernand was furious and went to Lincoln with his problem. Lincoln told him to calm himself.

JANUARY 25 SUNDAY

Lincoln met with Burnside, who argued, unsuccessfully, for removal of the Generals Hooker, W. B. Franklin and W. F. Smith. If this was not done, said Burnside, he would resign from the Army of the Potomac. Lincoln appointed Hooker the new commander and relieved Generals E. V. Sumner and W. B. Franklin. Burnside, who never wanted the command to begin with, settled for this.

JANUARY 26 MONDAY

At Fredericksburg (actually across the river at Falmouth), Major Gen. Joseph Hooker took command of the Army of the Potomac, a job for which he had been angling for months. Lincoln wrote a letter to Hooker regarding his assignment:

> Jan 26, 1863.
>
> Major-General Hooker.
>
> . . . Only those generals who gain success can set up as dictators. What I ask of you is military success, and I will risk the dictatorship. The Government will support you to the utmost of its ability, which is neither more nor less than it has done and will do for all commanders. . . .
>
> And now, beware of rashness! Beware of rashness! But with energy and sleepless vigilance, go forward and give us victories. . . .

JANUARY 30 FRIDAY

The *Richmond Dispatch* printed a listing showing the price of groceries had increased tenfold since the war had started.

JANUARY 31 SATURDAY

Two Confederate rams left Charleston Harbor in an early-morning fog and attacked the blockading fleet. The rams successfully destroyed two Federal blockading ships. Gen. P. T. G. Beauregard, commander of the Charleston district, claimed that the blockade had been lifted. More Federal ships arrived.

∞ FEBRUARY 1863 ∞

THERE WAS LITTLE ACTIVITY as the armies lay in their respective camps, trying to stay warm and outwait the weather until the spring campaigns could begin. The blockade vessels on the coasts continued their endless patrols, occasionally catching a blockade runner. The Army of Tennessee huddled in its tents at Manchester, Tenn., and tried to build a social life in the town. Grant was constantly probing for a way to get into Vicksburg. A quiet time in the war.

FEBRUARY 2 MONDAY

Col. C. R. Ellet, commander of the ram USS *Queen of the West*, had her decks covered with confiscated cotton bales for protection, and her paddle wheels boarded over with heavy planks. She, in effect, looked like a floating box with a long snout. Ellet intended to take the ship under the guns of Vicksburg to ram and sink the steamer *City of Vicksburg* early that morning. The shore batteries opened fire but hit her only three times before she reached her target.

FEBRUARY 3 TUESDAY

North of Vicksburg, the Federals blew up the levee, creating a gap almost 75 yards wide. The Mississippi River gushed through, flooding the Yazoo Pass. It was hoped that gunboats and transports could go over this flood to attack Vicksburg from the rear.

In Washington, the French minister, M. Mercier, hoping to get a mediation going between North and South, made his offer to "chair" such a meeting to Secretary of State Seward. Seward was more than a little offended by what he called "interference by a foreign power in a family dispute," and turned down the offer. Congress, when it learned of the offer, was also highly incensed.

FEBRUARY 5 THURSDAY

At Falmouth, Va., Hooker was busy reorganizing the Army of the Potomac into corps, eliminating Burnside's Grand Divisions. Eight corps were formed, and the cavalry was placed in a separate command under Stoneman. This command arrangement would remain essentially the same for the remainder of the war.

FEBRUARY 14 SATURDAY

The USS *Queen of the West* met her fate today when she came under heavy fire from the shore batteries at Gordon's Landing on the Black River. Attempting to back down the river, she ran aground directly under the guns of the shore batteries, which poured shot into the ship with every broadside. The ram was abandoned and fell into Confederate hands. The crew escaped primarily by floating downriver on cotton bales; they were picked up by the *De Soto*, an Army steamer.

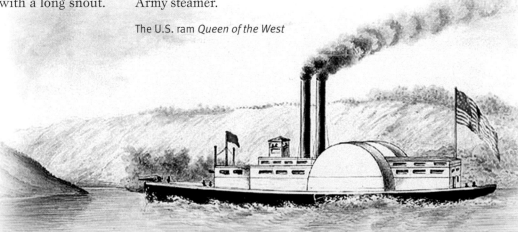

The U.S. ram *Queen of the West*

FEBRUARY 16 MONDAY

In a landmark decision that would cause much turmoil, the U.S. Senate passed the Conscription Act. The South had been conscripting men for more than a year at this time.

FEBRUARY 19 THURSDAY

There was heavy skirmishing along the Yazoo River where Grant was trying to get at the Vicksburg defenses.

There were mass rallies in support of the Emancipation Proclamation at Liverpool and Carlisle, England. Because of popular support for the freedom of the slaves, if the British government endorsed the South, it would be against the will of the people. Britain hereafter stayed neutral.

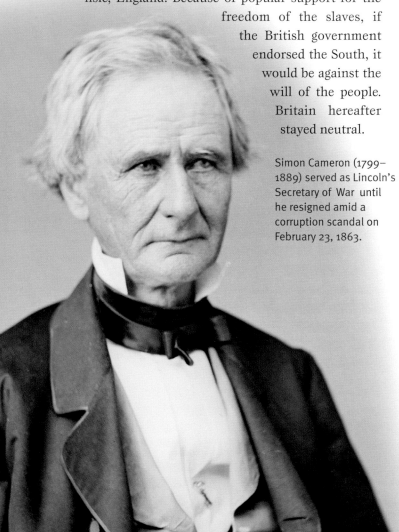

Simon Cameron (1799–1889) served as Lincoln's Secretary of War until he resigned amid a corruption scandal on February 23, 1863.

FEBRUARY 21 SATURDAY

Jackson, at Moss Neck, Va., worked on more court-martial proceedings for deserters.

FEBRUARY 22 SUNDAY

Allen, Pvt., Co. K, 1st Batallion, 10th Illinois Cavalry, Helena, Ark., wrote:

As no one speaks or writes without saying something about the war, I will give my humble opinion in as few words as possible: I believe that with proper management the accursed rebellion can be put down and could have been put down long ago; but that with management like the past, it will never be put down. I approve of the acts of the Administration, except the Emancipation Proclamation which virtually amounts to nothing, as the act for freeing the slaves and confiscating the property of rebels accomplishes all that the Proclamation can do, besides the latter excites some discontent in the army, and more among the people of loyal States. In regard to the arming of the blacks, I have no very great objection to that if the white and black soldiers are kept distinct and separate; but I think we have plenty of white men to whip the damned rebels. . . .

FEBRUARY 23 MONDAY

Simon Cameron, former governor of Pennsylvania, political boss of a corrupt machine, Secretary of War who was (essentially) fired by Lincoln, today resigned his post as Ambassador to Russia. Cameron's tour as Secretary of War initiated one of the most corrupt eras ever seen in this country of wholesale bilking of the government for war matériel.

FEBRUARY 24 TUESDAY

In perhaps one of the most poignant diary entries ever written in the war, James K. Boswell, who had served as an aide-de-camp to Jackson for one year, recorded:

> How long it seems since that day; it appears more like ten years than one; the truth is that I have thought, felt and acted more in the last year than in all the rest of my life. . . . I have been once with Gen. Jackson when he was defeated, and nine times when he was victorious; in some of these battles I have been exposed to death in all its forms, and in others I have been exposed but little. I have heard the wild cry of victory as it rose above the roar of cannon and musket. I have seen the field strewn with thousands of corpses, both of friend and foe. I have heard the groans of the wounded and dying. . . . I have seen towns ransacked, and hundreds, nay thousands, of helpless women and children thrown homeless upon the world. . . . O war, why art thou called glorious when such are thy fruits? How long must our dear land be desolated by the ravages and our bravest sacrificed upon thy altars? One year ago I was full of life and animation, hope dressed the future in "couleur de rose," all my dreams were cherished as though I were sure of their realization.

James K. Boswell would have his rendezvous with death in early May at the Battle of Chancellorsville, just west of Fredericksburg, Va.

FEBRUARY 25 WEDNESDAY

In Washington, Lincoln signed the act authorizing the national bank and national currency system.

FEBRUARY 27 FRIDAY

Confederate General Joseph E. Johnston was unhappy with the command arrangements in the west. He said his armies were too scattered for offensive operations, and were too small for good defensive operations. He asked to be relieved and assigned some other command.

MARCH 1863

EVEN IN THE "SUNNY" SOUTH there was bitter cold and deep snows to contend with. The food distribution system was still in need of repair and there was near famine in the larger cities, such as Richmond. Vicksburg still stood, as did Port Hudson. Little progress had been made over the winter. In the camps, the soldiers still outwaited the weather and hoped for dry roads.

MARCH 1 SUNDAY

On this date a new national color was presented to the colonel of the 11th Connecticut Volunteers by a Miss Julia A. Beach of Wallingford, Conn. It was to replace the old flag, presented to the regiment in 1861, which had been carried through many battles. The new flag and what remained of the old one were placed on the same staff and carried until the end of the war.

MARCH 5 THURSDAY

The Union Army finally acknowledged that the practice of the men doing their own cooking was both bad for their digestion and for their morale. Cooking was a major problem in both Northern and Southern armies. Most of the men were not familiar with the preparation of food (their mothers or their wives did this for them), and the consequent product was often inedible and generally very greasy.

A real problem, just being dealt with, was the conduct of the officers who commanded the regiments. Most of these officers were "rewarded" for forming the regiments (sometimes at their own expense) by being appointed colonel of the regiment. In all too many cases they had no experience in military matters, and, in some cases, no desire to learn. This was true, unfortunately, both for North and South.

MARCH 8 SUNDAY

In Richmond, Judge Samuel A. Meredith had stated an opinion that foreigners, Marylanders, and others

A man cooks on a stove in the camp of the 153rd New York infantry in this undated photograph.

who had served in the Army had become domiciled, and were thus liable for conscription. There was a rush for passports to leave the Confederacy.

MARCH 9 MONDAY

In Tennessee, Rosecrans braced for a Confederate attack.

Grant, just having a little fun on the Mississippi, sent a second fake ironclad past the batteries of Vicksburg, drawing a tremendous amount of fire. The "gunboat" was made of logs with barrels for smokestacks.

This evening at Fairfax C.H., south of Washington, Union Gen. Edwin H. Stoughton and his staff were captured in their beds by Confederate John S. Mosby and his band. This was most embarrassing for the

general since he was supposed to be out to capture Mosby. The officers were taken to Confederate lines and turned over as prisoners-of-war. They were later exchanged.

MARCH 12 THURSDAY

Admiral Farragut arrived at Baton Rouge aboard his flagship, the USS *Hartford*, to finalize the plans for the assault on Port Hudson. The USS *Richmond*, Capt. James Alden, was at Baton Rouge awaiting Farragut's arrival.

MARCH 13 FRIDAY

At the Richmond Arsenal, located near the James River, at the foot of 7th Street in Richmond, the building was shaken when the Confederate States

Laboratory on nearby Brown's Island exploded. Forty-five women and children were killed in the explosion.

MARCH 14 SATURDAY

On the Mississippi River, Admiral Farragut sent his squadron of seven ships against the shore batteries of Port Hudson, attempting to run past them. All made it to safety except for the *Mississippi*, which had blown up.

MARCH 17 TUESDAY

At Kelly's Ford on the Rappahannock, Federal cavalry under Gen. William W. Averell crossed the river and ran into a nasty group of Confederates who gave them a stiff fight in brushy and second-growth timber country. The South lost one of its favorite sons, young John Pelham, age 25, known as "the gallant Pelham," who was killed while observing the fight.

MARCH 18 WEDNESDAY

Day, Pvt., Co. B, 25th Massachusetts Volunteer Infantry, New Bern, N.C., wrote:

> After months of idleness in camp, at last comes a change. At 4 o'clock PM orders came to break camp, pick up our traps and be ready to march in half an hour. . . .
>
> In Richmond, Hood's Texans were marching through the city, going back north to join Lee's army, south of Fredericksburg.

MARCH 20 FRIDAY

Farragut, below Warrenton, Miss., sent a message to Grant and Admiral Porter offering his assistance in stopping the supplies from crossing at the mouth of the Red River. He also asked for coal to resupply his two ships. Grant floated a coal barge down past the guns of Vicksburg for the resupply.

MARCH 22 SUNDAY

The water-borne expeditions to attack Vicksburg from the rear had now been canceled. Admiral D. D.

Porter described them as "a most novel expedition. Never did those people expect to see ironclads floating where the keel of a flat boat never passed."

Day, Pvt., Co. B, 25th Massachusetts Volunteer Infantry, Plymouth, N.C., wrote:

> This town has undergone quite a change since we were here last fall. During the winter the enemy made a dash in here, setting the town on fire, burning up the central and business portion of it. These people have singular ideas; they seem to think that by destroying their property, they are in some way damaging us, but if we destroy any property, it is a great piece of vandalism. . . .

MARCH 23 MONDAY

Admiral Farragut wrote his wife from his flagship below Vicksburg. In this letter he clearly stated the credo of every good military leader in history:

> I passed the batteries of Port Hudson with my chicken USS *Albatross* under my wing. We came through in safety. . . . Would to God I only knew that our friends on the other ships were as well as we are! We are all in the same hands, and He disposes of us as He thinks best. . . . You know my creed: I never send others in advance when there is a doubt, and, being one on whom the country has bestowed its greatest honors, I thought I ought to take the risks which belong to them. So I took the lead. . . .

MARCH 25 WEDNESDAY

Barber, Cpl., Co. D, 15th Illinois Volunteer Infantry, Memphis, Tenn., wrote:

> Col. Richardson, a noted guerrilla, now began to harass us. Several regiments of the 4th division were sent out to disperse this band. They were strongly posted in a low, swampy ground, accessible only on one side by the artillery. A sharp fight ensued.

We lost several killed and wounded. A Major in an Iowa regiment was killed.

MARCH 26 THURSDAY

A Frenchman named Brutus de Villeroi designed a semi-submarine boat and sold it to the government in Washington. This contraption was 46 feet long, 4½ feet wide, and carried a crew of 17. It originally was propelled by oars, but these were replaced at the Washington Navy Yard by a hand-operated screw propeller. This "ship," called the *Alligator*, was sent to Admiral Du Pont to be used as a reconnaissance craft.

MARCH 29 SUNDAY

Commander Duncan, USS *Norwich*, reported the evacuation of Jacksonville, Fla., by Union forces after they destroyed the greater part of the city.

The USS *Alligator*, seen in this undated illustration, left Washington for Port Royal on March 31, 1863. It was towed by the USS *Sumpter*. On April 2, a storm forced the *Sumpter* to cut the submarine adrift near the Cape Hatteras coast. According to reports sent to Secretary of the Navy Welles, the *Alligator* was then lost at sea.

MARCH 30 MONDAY

In the words of Lt. Maffitt, CSS *Florida*, the crew were "living like lords on Yankee plunder" from the provisions taken from the seized bark *M. J. Colcord.* The ship, loaded with provisions and bound for Cape Town, South Africa, was taken, the provisions transferred to the *Florida*, the crew to a Danish brig, *Christian*, and the *Colcord* destroyed.

MARCH 31 TUESDAY

The Confederate Army forces launched a large attack on the Union garrison at Washington, N.C. The Confederate forces were supported by large numbers of artillery to cope with Union gunboats. This siege would last till mid-April with the garrison being supplied by gunboats running past the artillery batteries of Gen. A. P. Hill.

Meanwhile, Gen. McClernand's troops had left Milliken's Bend and were en route to New Carthage, on the west bank of the Mississippi.

APRIL 1863

SPRING CREPT THROUGH THE SOUTH, greening the laurel bushes, setting the woods ablaze with blooming dogwood trees and lifting the heart of civilian and soldier alike. The runoff of the snows into the streams made the larger rivers, like the Mississippi, Ohio, Cumberland and Tennessee, flood and fill with hazards to navigation. In the camps, the soldiers stretched their aching muscles, long stiffened from winter's inactivity, and prepared for the coming campaigns. In the distance, the summer bugles called the men to arms.

APRIL 1 WEDNESDAY

On April 1, as the soldiers and sailors from the USS *Commodore Morris* prepared to remove 22,000 bushels of grain from Patterson Smith's plantation on the Ware River in Virginia to the ship, the landing party was attacked by Confederate cavalry. The landing party immediately formed into ranks, the guns from the ship fired on the cavalry, the Union men charged and the Confederates were routed. What grain could not be removed to the ship was burned.

Barber, Cpl., Co. D, 15th Illinois Volunteer Infantry, Memphis, Tenn., wrote:

Our picket duty here required the utmost vigilance. Rank rebels of both sexes, under the guise of peaceful citizens, obtained passes to go beyond the lines. . . . It was soon discovered that these persons carried on a regular system of smuggling through contraband articles. . . . Things, calling themselves ladies, were caught with quinine and other articles secreted in their crinolines. Gen. Veatch now issued an order that all ladies of suspicious character should be searched before passing out. . . .

APRIL 3 FRIDAY

There was no mention of yesterday's "food riot" in the Richmond papers this day. Crowds of women and other "non-draftable" individuals still gathered on street corners asking for food. The City Battalion, charged with keeping the peace, was finally called in, and the crowds dispersed.

APRIL 4 SATURDAY

Admiral Du Pont issued his order of battle for the attack on Charleston.

APRIL 5 SUNDAY

At New Carthage, Grant's troops were preparing to cross the Mississippi south of Grand Gulf, in the attack to take Vicksburg in the rear.

APRIL 6 MONDAY

Lincoln, visiting Hooker at Fredericksburg, expressed his opinion that "our prime object is the enemies' army in front of us, and is not with, or about, Richmond. . . ." This would be his constant message and it would not be understood until Grant took command eleven months later.

APRIL 7 TUESDAY

Admiral Du Pont attacked Charleston but was rebuffed. Du Pont told Gen. David Hunter that he now believed that the port could not be taken by a sea assault.

APRIL 10 FRIDAY

In Richmond, President Davis called for the people to plant "truck gardens" to grow vegetables for the army's use. This effort was very successful. After all, the South couldn't sell cotton at this time.

APRIL 11 SATURDAY

At Charleston, S.C., Gen. P. T. G. Beauregard commanded the defenses of the harbor. He believed that Du Pont would attack again.

Col. A. D. Streight moved out from Nashville with 1,700 Federal cavalry mounted on mules, for a raid into Georgia.

APRIL 12 SUNDAY

Gen. Hooker, at Falmouth, Va., evidently was not listening to Lincoln about what the real objective was for the Army of the Potomac—Lee's army. He wrote Lincoln with a plan to go around Lee's left flank and cut him off from Richmond. What he intended to do with Lee after he cut him off was not stated.

On the Mississippi River above Vicksburg, Admiral D. D. Porter got ready to move most of his gunboats past the Vicksburg guns to support Grant's attack from New Carthage on the west bank to Grand Gulf on the east bank.

APRIL 15 WEDNESDAY

In the west, Grant's forces continued to concentrate at, or near, New Carthage, La., getting ready for the

crossing. The Confederates withdrew from the assault on Washington, N.C., which had been going on since the end of the previous month. A relief expedition of Union gunboats and troops was coming up and it would overpower Confederate strength.

Barber, Cpl., Co. D, 15th Illinois Volunteer Infantry, Memphis, Tenn., wrote:

> So foul had the morals of the city become that Gen. Veatch issued an order expelling two boat loads of fallen humanity. Indeed, matters had come to such a pass that a decent lady was ashamed to be seen on the street, and stringent measures had to be resorted to to remedy the evil. All the bad passions of the naturally dissipated in our division were brought to light here, and too often were the young and noble drawn into this whirlpool of vice.

APRIL 17 FRIDAY

Col. Benjamin H. Grierson led 1,700 Union cavalry from LaGrange, Tenn., on a raid through Mississippi and Louisiana. This raid was later immortalized in the movie *Horse Soldiers.* The raid, which lasted 16 days, covered 600 miles.

APRIL 19 SUNDAY

On this day a Union soldier recorded in his diary that "Mr. Howe is now visiting us. His son has been discharged, the old gent, I believe, also." This was in reference to Elias Howe, the inventor of the sewing machine. The editor of the diary, Edward Marcus, footnotes the entry with:

> Although he was clubfooted and in his forties, Elias Howe, inventor of the sewing

The Union cavalry leaders featured in this collection of portraits include, from top left across and then down (by row): William W. Averill, Hugh J. Kilpatrick, August Kautz, David McMurtrie Gregg, Philip Sheridan, George Armstrong Custer, Abel D. Streight, Benjamin H. Grierson, James H. Wilson, George Stoneman, Wesley Merritt and Alfred Thomas Archimedes Torbert.

machine, served with the 17th Connecticut Regiment but was never officially mustered in. His son, Elias, Jr., enlisted in Company D on August 28, 1862, serving to the end of the war. Elias Howe, then a wealthy man, made himself responsible for many of the expenses of the 17th. When the regiment had gone three months without pay early in 1863, he gave the paymaster his personal check to cover what was due all officers and men. Then, the story goes, he went back into line and drew $39, his pay for three months as a private.

APRIL 20 MONDAY

Lincoln declared that the new State of West Virginia would join the Union on June 20th of this year.

Barber, Cpl., Co. D, 15th Illinois Volunteer Infantry, Memphis, Tenn., wrote:

> An order from the Secretary of War now permitted the enlistment of colored troops and the appointment of white officers to

command them. I was offered a recommendation by the adjutant of the regiment for a commission, but I preferred my present position to any in a Negro company. Several members of the 15th did receive commissions. . . .

APRIL 21 TUESDAY

Gen. Lee reported to the Confederate War Department today that his men subsisted on a daily ration of one-quarter pound of meat and a pound of flour. In addition, they received a pound of rice for every ten men, two to three times a week. Scurvy and typhoid fever were breaking out among the men.

APRIL 24 FRIDAY

Day, Pvt., Co. B, 25th Massachusetts Volunteer Infantry, Plymouth, N.C., wrote:

> The noise of the battle is over and we are no longer harassed by war's dread alarms, but can now sit down, eat our fresh shad

Company E of the 4th U.S. Colored Infantry of the Union Army

and herring and drink our peach and honey in peace and quiet.

APRIL 25 SATURDAY

News of Grierson's raid into Mississippi had reached Richmond, causing much consternation among the people.

APRIL 27 MONDAY

The Army of the Potomac was on the move from its winter quarters at Falmouth. They marched up the Rappahannock towards the fords which would take them to Lee's rear.

APRIL 28 TUESDAY

Hooker's Army of the Potomac began crossing the Rappahannock upstream from Fredericksburg, leaving Major Gen. John "Uncle John" Sedgwick racing Lee. At Fredericksburg the bells of the Episcopal Church rang out the alarm for the Confederates.

APRIL 29 WEDNESDAY

On the Mississippi at Grand Gulf, Admiral D. D. Porter's gunboats engaged the fortifications at that city for five and one-half hours while Grant's troop transports passed the guns at night.

APRIL 30 THURSDAY

At Chancellorsville, Hooker, in his exuberance, prepared a message to be read to the troops on May 1, in which he informed his army that "the operations of the last three days have determined that our enemy must ingloriously fly, or come out from behind their defenses and give us battle on our ground, where certain destruction awaits him."

Grant's first landing of troops on the east bank of the Mississippi River near Bruinsburg met with success. The final stages of the Vicksburg campaign were set.

The friends of the Seventh and Eighth Regiments, New York Volunteers, welcome the return of their heroes to New York on April 28, 1863.

∽ MAY 1863 ∽

AT THE BEGINNING OF MAY 1863, major actions were pending in Virginia and Mississippi. The Army of the Potomac had left its muddy, sprawling camps in the denuded countryside around Falmouth and had moved to the fords of the Rappahannock and Rapidan, poised for an assault on Lee. Grant, in the west, was across the Mississippi at Grand Gulf, tightening the noose around Vicksburg.

MAY 1 FRIDAY

Hooker, with 70,000 men, crossed the fords and began the Battle of Chancellorsville. Lee hurriedly withdrew all but Jubal Early and 10,000 Confederates, whom he left facing Major Gen. Sedgwick's 40,000, and with 47,000 men turned to face Hooker.

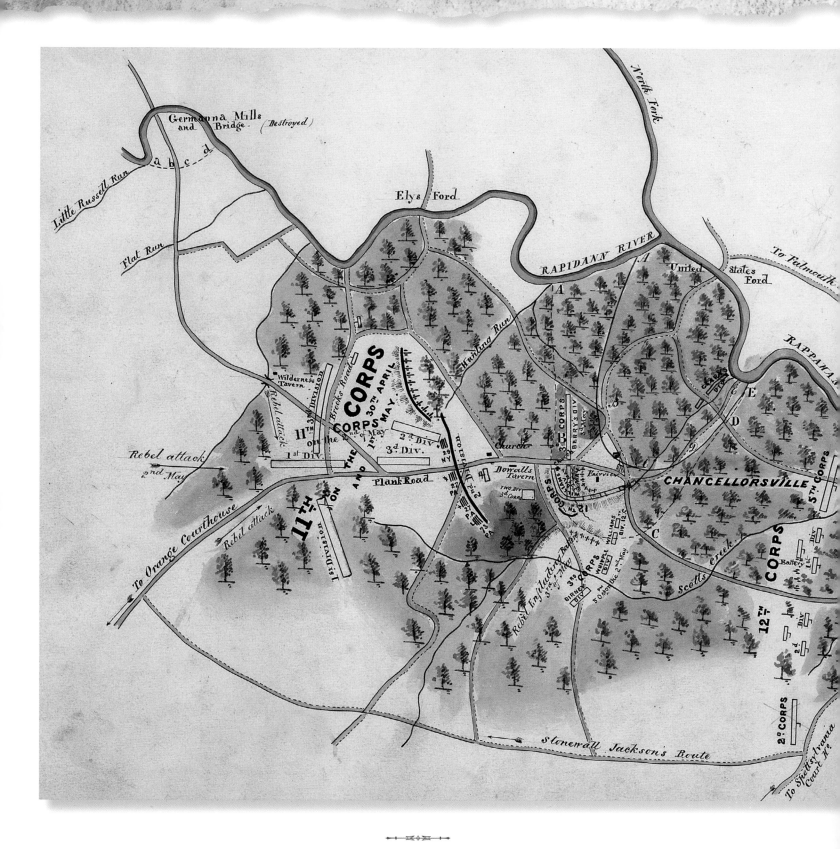

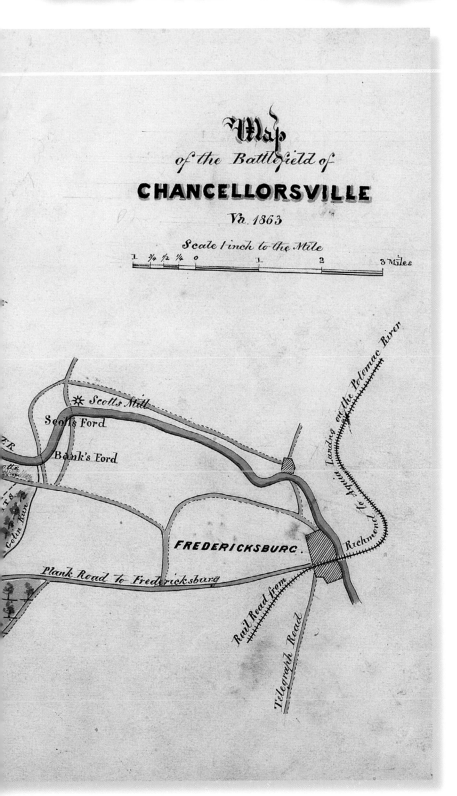

Map of the Battlefield of

CHANCELLORSVILLE

Va. 1863

Scale 1 inch to the Mile

1   ¾ ½ ¼   0   1   2   3 Miles

Scotts Mill
Scotts Ford
Bank's Ford
Aquia Landing on the Potomac River
FREDERICKSBURG.
Richmond to Aquia
Plank Road to Fredericksburg
Rail Road from
Telegraph Road

The Army of the Potomac moved forward, and then in the afternoon Hooker stunned his own officers and Lee by withdrawing and concentrating in a small area near Chancellorsville. With little or no fighting, "Fighting Joe" Hooker went on the defensive.

That night Lee and Jackson talked in the now famous "cracker barrel" conference which resulted in Jackson taking 26,000 of the 47,000 available forces around the left flank to attack Hooker's right flank.

Barber, Cpl., Co. D, 15th Illinois Volunteer Infantry, Vicksburg, Miss., wrote:

> It was with some regret, but no reluctance, that I bade adieu to Memphis. . . . Our brave comrades, in their grapple with the rebel "Gibraltar of the West"—Vicksburg, needed our assistance. . . .

Confederate Secretary of the Navy Mallory solved a sticky problem by getting the Congress to create a Provisional Navy.

MAY 2 SATURDAY

Early in the morning, Jackson's corps was moving deeper into the Wilderness, going past Catherine Furnace at a rapid pace. At 6 PM he gave the order which opened the assault against the unsuspecting Federals' right flank. On the Federal left flank, Lee opened fire against George Meade's men to draw attention from Jackson.

The Federal right flank fell back in confusion and panic and rolled up like a carpet. Few of the units fought well, most fleeing back towards the main body of the army at Chancellorsville.

In the twilight, Jackson and some of this staff were riding on a recon when they were mistaken for Federals and fired upon by their own troops. Jackson, struck twice in the left arm and once through the palm of the right hand, was taken to a nearby farmhouse, where his arm was amputated later that evening.

An 1863 map of the Chancellorsville, Va., battlefield

∞ THE BATTLE OF CHANCELLORSVILLE ∞

APRIL 30 TO MAY 6, 1863

The Reverend James Power Smith, "Stonewall" Jackson's aide-de-camp, describes the injury that first cost Jackson his left arm—which was amputated—and eventually his life.

When Jackson had reached the point where his line now crossed the turnpike, scarcely a mile west of Chancellorsville, and not half a mile from a line of Federal troops, he had found his front line unfit for the farther and vigorous advance he desired, by reason of the irregular character of the fighting, now right, now left, and because of the dense thickets, through which it was impossible to preserve alignment. Division commanders found it more and more difficult as the twilight deepened to hold their broken brigades in hand. Regretting the necessity of relieving the troops in front, General Jackson had ordered A. P. Hill's division, his third and reserve line, to be placed in front.

While this change was being effected, impatient and anxious, the general rode forward on the turnpike, followed by two or three of his staff and a number of couriers and signal sergeants. He passed the swampy depression and began the ascent of the hill toward Chancellorsville, when he came upon a line of the Federal infantry lying on their arms. Fired at by one or two muskets (two musket-balls from the enemy whistled over my head as I came to the front), he turned and came back toward his line, upon the side of the road to his left.

As he rode near to the Confederate troops, just placed in position and ignorant that he was in the front, the

This lithograph depicts the fatal wounding of General Jackson during the Battle of Chancellorsville, May 2, 1863.

left company began firing to the front, and two of his party fell from their saddles dead—Captain Boswell of the Engineers, and Sergeant Cunliffe, of the Signal Corps. Spurring his horse across the road to his right, he was met by a second volley from the right company of Pender's North Carolina brigade. Under this volley, when not two rods from the troops, the general received three balls at the same instant. One penetrated the palm of his right hand and was cut out that night from the back of his hand. A second passed around the wrist of the left arm and out through the left hand. A third ball passed through the left arm half-way from shoulder to elbow. The large bone of the upper arm was splintered to the elbow joint, and the wound bled freely. His horse turned quickly from the fire, through the thick bushes which swept the cap from the general's head, and scratched his forehead, leaving drops of blood to stain his face.

As he lost his hold upon the bridle-rein, he reeled from the saddle, and was caught by the arms of Captain Wilbourn, of the Signal Corps. Laid upon the ground, there came at once to his succor General A. P. Hill and members of his staff. The writer reached his side a minute after, to find General Hill holding the head and shoulders of the wounded chief. Cutting open the coat-sleeve from wrist to shoulder, I found the wound in the upper arm, and with my handkerchief I bound the arm above the wound to stem the flow of blood. Couriers were sent for Dr. Hunter McGuire, the surgeon of the corps and the general's trusted friend, and for an ambulance. Being outside of our lines, it was urgent that he be moved at once. With difficulty litter-bearers were brought from the line nearby, and the general was placed upon the litter and carefully raised to the shoulder, I myself bearing one corner. . . .

Soon an ambulance was reached, and stopping to seek some stimulant at Chancellor's (Dowdall's Tavern), we were found by Dr. McGuire, who at once took charge of the wounded man. Passing back

The Wilderness Church in Chancellorsville, Va., was the site of an attack by Gen. Stonewall Jackson against the Union forces of Maj. Gen. Carl Schurz.

over the battle-field of the afternoon, we reached the Wilderness store, and then, in a field on the north, the field-hospital of our corps under Dr. Harvey Black. Here we found a tent prepared, and after midnight the left arm was amputated near the left shoulder, and a ball taken from the right hand. . . .

On Monday the general was carried in an ambulance, by way of Spotsylvania Court House, to most comfortable lodging at Chandlerss, near Guinea's Station, on the Richmond, Fredericksburg and Potomac railroad. And here, against our hopes, notwithstanding the skill and care of wise and watchful surgeons, attended day and night by wife and friends, amid the prayers and tears of all the Southern land, thinking not of himself, but of the cause he loved, and for the troops who had followed him so well and given him so great a name, our chief sank, day by day, with symptoms of pneumonia and some pains of pleurisy, until, at 3:15 PM on the quiet of the Sabbath afternoon, May 10th, 1863, he raised himself from his bed, saying, "No, no, let us pass over the river, and rest under the shade of the trees"; and, falling again to his pillow, he passed away, "over the river, where, in a land where warfare is not known or feared, he rests forever 'under the trees.'"

Wounded soldiers after the Battle of Chancellorsville

On this night Hooker ordered Sedgwick to assault Lee from the rear; this action brought on the Second Battle of Fredericksburg.

MAY 3 SUNDAY

Hooker ordered a retreat, and Gen. Darius Couch organized the movement across the Rapidan.

Sedgwick twice attacked Marye's Heights and finally drove Early off the Heights, but with tremendous casualties. Lee's line finally gave way, and Early retreated. Lee, using some of the troops awaiting Hooker's assault, turned and stopped Sedgwick at Salem Church late in the afternoon.

MAY 4 MONDAY

Things were a mess for the Union forces in the area west of Fredericksburg. Hooker, losing his nerve and the initiative, ordered his Army of the Potomac back across U.S. Ford on the Rapidan River, disengaging from Lee's Army of Northern Virginia.

Grant was still pulling his troops across the river at Bruinsburg and pushing them east towards Jackson, Miss., as rapidly as possible.

MAY 5 TUESDAY

Lee prepared his forces to attack Hooker but found that the Federals were moving back across the Rappahannock in defeat. The Battle of Chancellorsville was over, as was the Second Battle of Fredericksburg. The Union fielded nearly 134,000 men, suffering almost 17,300 casualties. Confederate losses were about 12,800 from an effective force of nearly 60,000 (nearly 20 percent) a loss that they could ill afford. But perhaps the greatest loss to the Confederacy in this battle was "Stonewall" Jackson; there was no replacement for him.

MAY 6 WEDNESDAY

Confederate General Ambrose Powell (A. P.) Hill was assigned Jackson's old corps. Jackson was lying in a house at Guiney's Station. His wife would join him there and remain with him until his death.

MAY 7 THURSDAY

At Falmouth, Va., Lincoln and Gen. Halleck concluded their meeting with Hooker and returned to Washington. Lincoln was very concerned about the effect of the defeat on the people of the North.

Sherman was now across the river from Milliken's Bend with his large corps and started moving towards Jackson, Miss., directly east of Vicksburg to cut the rail lines of supply. In an early lesson on foraging, Grant's orders were to "live off the country." The countryside was soon stripped.

MAY 9 SATURDAY

With Charleston more and more bottled up, and New Orleans gone, the blockade runners were concentrating more on Wilmington, N.C., which would become the principal port for such activity.

Grant was now at Utica, about 20 miles southwest of Jackson, Miss., and driving hard.

MAY 10 SUNDAY

On this Sunday in a small house south of Fredericksburg, near Guiney's Station, the mighty "Stonewall" Jackson died, his last words being "Let us cross over the river and rest under the shade of the trees."

MAY 12 TUESDAY

In Massachusetts, Col. Robert Shaw had exceeded his 1,000-man limit in recruiting the first all-black regiment in the Union army—the 54th Massachusetts. The spillover in manpower was used to form the second black regiment—the 55th Massachusetts.

Grant decided to handle the city of Jackson first and then go on to Vicksburg.

MAY 13 WEDNESDAY

Beleaguered Vicksburg was calling for more support, and the Confederate Secretary of War was pulling troops from Charleston and other areas to help.

Beauregard, commander at Charleston, warned that this would drastically weaken that port's defenses.

MAY 14 THURSDAY

Gen. Nathaniel Banks embarked on his mission to capture Port Hudson, the Confederate fortification south of Vicksburg.

Sherman's and McPherson's corps neared Jackson, Miss., in midmorning. Joe Johnston, knowing he had little hope against Grant's superior force, evacuated as much of the vital supplies as he could and sent two brigades to delay the Yankees.

MAY 16 SATURDAY

The Battle of Champion's Hill was fought. Grant, moving fast towards Edward's Station, blocked a move by Pemberton to join Johnston, and the two forces collided at Champion's Hill. By mid-afternoon the hill had changed hands three times, and the Confederates had had enough, beginning their withdrawal towards Vicksburg and towards the bridge crossing the Big Black River. The Confederates had lost about 3,850 men at Champion's Hill as opposed to 2,440 Union lost. Pemberton could not afford such losses for long. Johnston never got into the fight.

MAY 18 MONDAY

Things were heating up in the Vicksburg area. Grant was back from Jackson and the Battle of Champion's Hill was over. On this day, Grant invested Vicksburg. The fortifications were completely surrounded on the land side, and the gunboats were on the river. No escape now for Pemberton's army.

MAY 22 FRIDAY

At Vicksburg, Grant lost almost 3,200 of his total force of 45,000 in a large-scale attack on the Confederate defenses. The Confederate losses were less than 500.

Barber, Cpl., Co. D, 15th Illinois Volunteer Infantry, Vicksburg, Miss., wrote:

It was fifteen miles to Vicksburg and we could plainly hear the heavy notes of artillery. On the 18th and 22d, when the charges were made, the hills fairly shook with the shock of artillery. Grant saw what a sacrifice of life it would cost to take the place by storm, so he waited the slow and surer operations of a siege. . . .

MAY 26 TUESDAY

Barber, Cpl., Co. D, 15th Illinois Volunteer Infantry, Vicksburg, Miss., wrote:

. . . We were now within one and one-half miles of the rebel line and two and one-half miles from Vicksburg. In our immediate front was a strong fort, a little isolated from the others, mounting heavy siege guns.

MAY 27 WEDNESDAY

Major Gen. Nathaniel Banks today launched his long-awaited attack on Port Hudson, La., with little result other than nearly 2,000 killed, wounded or missing, out of a force of 13,000. The attack, poorly coordinated, was made through rough terrain, heavily wooded and cut with deep ravines, which caused troop alignment problems. Admiral Farragut's gunboats provided close support where possible, and continued firing on the fortifications after the attack faltered.

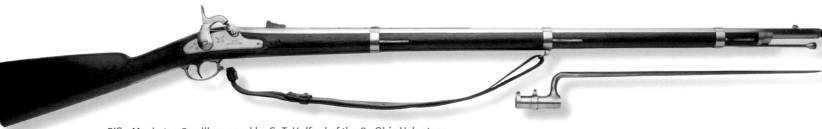

Rifle-Musket, .58 caliber, used by G. T. Holford of the 83 Ohio Volunteer Infantry, which fought in the Battle of Vicksburg

Henry A. Monroe (1845–1913) was a drummer for Company C of the 54th Massachusetts Volunteer Infantry.

MAY 28 THURSDAY

The 54th Massachusetts Volunteer Infantry left Boston for Hilton Head, S.C., the first all-black regiment to be ordered south.

MAY 30 SATURDAY

President Davis's hopes of getting enough troops to aid Pemberton were still alive, but dying rapidly. The famed "Orphan Brigade" was coming to help.

JUNE 1863

THROUGHOUT THE SOUTH, the June heat had a telling effect on the protagonists. The ironclads operating on the rivers and along the coast were like ovens most of the time, the boilers heating things up internally, the sun externally. The soldiers around Vicksburg and Port Hudson were also steaming, realizing that the worst of the summer was yet to come. In the South the prices of goods were increasing, not only from scarcity, but also due to the decreased value of the Confederate dollar. Both sides had their woes this summer.

JUNE 1 MONDAY

Ambrose E. Burnside, Major Gen., USA, closed the *Chicago Times* for publishing disloyal statements. This created a furor throughout the North among the defenders of the First Amendment.

JUNE 3 WEDNESDAY

The Gettysburg campaign began with the movement of Lee's legions from the Fredericksburg area to the west. The long gray columns quit their camps and began the trek to the Shenandoah Valley, where they would turn north for Pennsylvania. In Hooker's camps, no movement was yet to be seen. The Yankee commander was unaware that his adversary was moving.

JUNE 4 THURSDAY

Barber, Cpl., Co. D, 15th Illinois Volunteer Infantry, Vicksburg, Miss., wrote:

One day General Grant rode along the line and told the boys that he had plenty of ammunition and not to be afraid to use it. This was the signal for firing. Some of the boys expended over two hundred rounds that day. The rebs lay in their trenches, quiet as mice, not daring to show their heads. . . .

Sometimes the rebels would make a charge on our picket line in the night and try to force it back. In one of these charges, they surprised the 14th Illinois, killed and wounded seven and took twenty prisoners. . . . All this was done so quickly that we, only a short distance from them, were unable to render them any assistance. . . .

JUNE 5 FRIDAY

Hooker, trying to find where Lee's army had gone, probed the crossings at Franklin's Crossing and Deep Run, only to find them screened with pickets from A. P. Hill's corps. Lincoln suggested to Hooker that he might attack the moving Confederates, but Hooker delayed until it was too late. Lee's last corps, A. P. Hill's, was set in motion for Culpepper.

There was skirmishing again between Rosecrans's and Bragg's armies in Tennessee.

Grant and Admiral Porter were giving Vicksburg

no rest. Twenty-four hours a day the mortar boats lobbed their deadly missiles into the city. Many of the residents now lived in caves to escape the danger.

JUNE 9 TUESDAY

At Beverly and Kelly's Ford on the Rappahannock, west of Fredericksburg, Union cavalry galloped across the fords, driving in the Confederate pickets, and went looking for Lee. Stuart, at Brandy Station, was caught by surprise, and was rapidly engaged in the largest cavalry battle ever fought in North America. Almost 20,000 horsemen clashed at Stevenburg and Fleetwood Hill for about 12 hours. The Confederates held the ground at the end of the day, but it was a close thing indeed. Gen. Alfred Pleasanton's Federal cavalry had reversed the image of the North's cavalry, and had given Southern cavalry a bloody nose.

Union mortar boats were bombarding Vicksburg

After the deadly cavalry charge near Brandy Station, Va.—depicted here in a drawing by Edwin Forbes—jokes about "Who ever saw a dead cavalryman?" would no longer be in vogue in either army.

almost every hour. From dawn till noon, a total of 175 shells were fired into the city. The pounding the city was taking was severe.

Jackman, Pvt., "The Orphan Brigade," Jackson, Miss., wrote:

> Was waked up by the fire bells in the city and opening my eyes saw that the light of a fire was shining into the office—the walls of the tent being up—making it light as day. Could see the Bowman House, a large hotel near the Capitol, wrapped in flames which roared not a little in the stillness of the night. Heavy cannonading all night at Vicksburg.

JUNE 10 WEDNESDAY

One group of Confederate prisoners would not make it to their Union prison camp. Being transported to Ft. Delaware on the steamer *Maple Leaf*, they overpowered the guards, captured the ship and forced it to land below Cape Henry, Va., where they escaped.

JUNE 11 THURSDAY

On this day, the 54th Massachusetts Volunteer Infantry Regiment received its first combat experience. This, the first all-black regiment in the Union Army, went on an amphibious raid on Darien, Ga., with the 2nd South Carolina. The commander of the expedition, one Col. James Montgomery, had the town sacked and burned for no apparent reason.

JUNE 13 SATURDAY

Ewell's corps was still leading Lee's army northwest. At Winchester, the Confederates drove in the Union pickets at that city and moved on to occupy Berryville. Hooker started the blue columns north by northwest from Falmouth about three days behind Lee.

JUNE 16 TUESDAY

Lee's gray columns were strung out all over western Virginia and into Maryland. Hooker reached Fairfax C.H., about 20 miles from the capital, and between Lee and Washington.

JUNE 18 THURSDAY

Grant, who was convinced that all McClernand wanted was to make political headway, relieved him of command and sent him north.

JUNE 20 SATURDAY

The mountain counties of Virginia, having voted for separation from their parent state, were admitted into the Union as the new State of West Virginia.

Barber, Cpl., Co. D, 15th Illinois Volunteer Infantry, Vicksburg, Miss., wrote:

> We had now got so close to the enemy that in several places along the line we were at work undermining their forts with the intention of blowing them up. . . . Finally everything was in readiness, the troops were under arms, ready to make the charge if a breach was made and our boys went in.
>
> The concussion was terrific. Rebels were thrown twenty feet into the air and buried in the ruins, but so strong were the works that the explosion failed to make a breach. A fierce hand-to-hand encounter ensued over the parapet, bayonets crossed over the works and thrusts and stabs were made. Our boys finally retired, confident that victory would soon crown our efforts. The 45th Illinois stood the brunt of this engagement.

JUNE 23 TUESDAY

Lincoln finally stirred Rosecrans enough to get him moving towards Braxton Bragg at Tullahoma, Tenn. Rosecrans did well in this campaign, outflanking Bragg and forcing him to fall back towards Chattanooga.

JUNE 25 THURSDAY

Gen. Lee made a big mistake today. He gave JEB Stuart permission to leave the Army of Northern

Jubal Anderson Early (1816–94, seen here in civilian clothes many years after the war ended), initially voted against secession but volunteered for military service when Virginia left the Union. His greatest battles were in the Valley Campaigns of 1864, when he defeated several Union generals and threatened Washington. After the war, he supervised the Louisiana State Lottery, and was the first president of the Southern Historical Society.

Virginia, giving up his role of being the "eyes of the commander," and to join Lee on the other side of the Potomac. Stuart went on his way and Lee would not see him until the middle of the Battle of Gettysburg.

JUNE 26 FRIDAY

This day saw the passing of Rear Admiral Andrew Hull Foote, at age 57, in New York City. He died of the wounds received at Ft. Donelson in the spring of 1862. He was a great innovator of river warfare on the western rivers, and a great supporter of joint-service actions. He would be sorely missed.

Confederate Gen. Jubal Early passed through Gettysburg, Pa., for the first time today on his way to York, Pa. Gov. Curtin of Pennsylvania called for 60,000 volunteers to serve for 90 days to repel the invaders. Just how these raw troops were supposed to stand up to Lee's battle-hardened veterans has always remained a mystery.

JUNE 27 SATURDAY

In Washington, Lincoln did something rarely done in the annals of military history. He relieved the commander of a major army on the eve of battle. "Fighting Joe" Hooker was relieved by George Gordon Meade, Major Gen., USA, as commander of the Army of the Potomac.

JUNE 29 MONDAY

Meade wasted no time ordering the Army of the Potomac towards Gettysburg. Gen. Buford's cavalrymen were in Gettysburg already and more troops were coming up fast. Lee was calling his men in as fast as possible.

In Tennessee, Rosecrans was mixing it up with Bragg at Tullahoma, with heavy skirmishing in other points nearby.

∞ JULY 1863 ∞

THE BROILING HEAT OF JULY baked the land from Vicksburg to Gettysburg. In Pennsylvania, the blue and gray columns about to collide at Gettysburg marched down the dusty roads in sweltering sun. Water was in short supply and the troops suffered. In Vicksburg and Port Hudson, the heat was even more intense. At those places, the fortifications were bombarded incessantly, the defenders waiting with stoic patience for the outcome. In Tennessee, the elevation made the heat more tolerable but to those on the roads, no less a problem. Rosecrans drove for Chattanooga, moving Bragg into Georgia.

JULY 1 WEDNESDAY

At dawn the Confederates moved towards Gettysburg along the Chambersburg Pike, A. P. Hill's skirmishers looking for Union troops. They found them about four miles west of town in the form of Company E, 9th New York Cavalry of John Buford's cavalry division, armed with repeating rifles. By 8 AM the contact had reached a point where Buford's men were opposing two Confederate brigades, but Major Gen. John F. Reynolds's corps of infantry was coming up fast. By midmorning, the fighting was getting heavy and in the midst of battle Reynolds was killed at the edge of McPherson's Woods. The Union lines held the Confederates. The famed "fishhook" line was established on Cemetery Ridge, with the Confederates occupying Seminary Ridge across the way. All day long the Federals streamed into Gettysburg and were placed in defensive positions. There was a lot of confusion and milling about until things settled down about dark. Meade arrived on the field about midnight.

At Vicksburg the end was clear—surrender or starvation. Grant's army encircled the city with a death grip, and Gen. Joseph E. Johnston's small force to the east around Clinton, Miss., was vastly outnumbered and had little or no means to transport itself beyond the railroad line from Jackson.

JULY 2 THURSDAY

Things were stirring early at Gettysburg. Not all the Union troops had arrived as yet, the long columns

This July 1863 photograph by Alexander Gardner shows the headquarters of Gen. George Gordon Meade on Cemetery Ridge at Gettysburg.

still pouring in. Gen. Dan Sickles took things into his own hands and moved his Third Corps out of the assigned positions on the Union left and forward to the area of the Peach Orchard and Devil's Den to an exposed position. Lee wanted Longstreet to attack this salient of the Union left and Longstreet opposed the plan. Fortunately, Major Gen. Gouverneur K. Warren, the Chief Engineer of the Army of the Potomac, rode to the Little Round Top, recognized that disaster was awaiting for the left flank unless something was done and sent his aides to pull any troops off the road and send them to the hill. Meanwhile, Longstreet sent his Confederates against Sickles's exposed men and drove them from the Peach Orchard and Devil's Den to the crest of Cemetery Ridge. Gen. John Bell Hood's Texans got into a stiff fight with the 20th Maine of Col. Chamberlain on Little Round Top and the fighting was hand-to-hand and rock-to-rock. Chamberlain's men ran out of ammunition, so he ordered a bayonet charge that so demoralized the Rebels that they fled. The left flank was saved for the Union.

Gen. Jubal Early was to have attacked Culp's Hill at the same time Longstreet began his attack, but delays occurred and the charge up East Cemetery Hill did not begin until dusk. It went on until 10 PM and ended with Early back down the hill and where he started from. The day ended with many casualties, including Dan Sickles, who would lose a leg from his wounds, many deaths, but no real advantage gained by either side. Meade was fighting a defensive battle and handling it well, so far.

During the fighting, JEB Stuart arrived back at the Army of Northern Virginia, quite pleased that he had brought Gen. Lee a wagon train of supplies. Lee was angry with Stuart for his grandstand ride around Meade's army when Stuart should have been available to provide scouts for intelligence purposes. Quickly taking advantage of the situation, Lee ordered Stuart to use his cavalry to cut Meade's retreat route to the east. Stuart rested his horses and got ready.

In the area of Vicksburg, the tension was growing. Surely the city could not hold much longer. Joe Johnston's Confederates waited the outcome of the battle, knowing that when Grant was finished with Vicksburg, he would turn on the Confederate force to destroy it.

JULY 3 FRIDAY

The entrenchments began and the artillery rolled forward into place. By dawn the place known as Cemetery Ridge fairly bristled with Union muskets and artillery.

Lee had tried assaults on both flanks of Meade's army and been repulsed. Now he would try the middle. He would send 15,000 men in three divisions against the Union center in a charge that would forever be known as "Pickett's Charge," but that would be made up of troops from the divisions of Henry Heth, Dorsey Pender and Pickett's Virginians.

Longstreet again advised against the attack. Lee was adamant and the attack was ordered, beginning with a tremendous 100-gun artillery barrage against the Union lines that started at 1 PM, to be answered by about 80 guns from the Federal line.

Across the field from the Union position, the Confederates emerged from the woods and formed into lines for the attack. It was a supreme example of raw courage and one of the most heart-stopping spectacles of the war. The Union gunners waited until the gray lines were within range and then pounded them with shot and shell in a seemingly unending stream. The ranks developed wide gaps where the artillery fire took its toll and the men closed ranks, still advancing. As they came within range of the Union muskets, the Federals, behind the cemetery wall and the entrenchments, poured a rain of lead into the gray ranks. The charge had failed and the Confederates retreated across the field to be met by Lee, who kept repeating, "All this has been my fault."

This battle would cost both sides dearly. The total casualties amounted to about 43,500—23,049 Union and 20,451 Confederate—of whom over 27,000 were

This c. 1894 illustration commemorates the surrender of Vicksburg. Gen. Grant, on horseback at the far left, meets the Confederate soldiers as they march out. Gen. Pemberton and his staff stand at right, observing.

wounded. When the cleanup was being done, the burial squads picked up the muskets left on the field by the dead and wounded, affixed the bayonets, and stuck the bayonets in the ground so that the butt of each rifle was up. The 26,000 muskets thus recovered made the battlefield look like a forest of rifles.

Early that same morning in Vicksburg, the white truce flags appeared on the defenses of the city. Gen. Pemberton had bowed to a superior force and six weeks of siege after nearly a year of Union operations against him. The two generals, Grant and Pemberton, met under an oak tree to discuss the terms of surrender which would take place the next day, the Fourth of July.

Barber, Cpl., Co. D, 15th Illinois Volunteer Infantry, Vicksburg, Miss., wrote:

> The two generals met beneath the wide spreading branches of a stately oak between the lines. . . . General Grant gave him until the next morning to accede to his unconditional terms of surrender. . . . While the truce was being held, the pickets of the two armies met and conversed on friendly terms on neutral ground between the lines. Blackberries were very thick there and friend and foe picked from the same bush and vied with each other in acts of civility. . . .

JULY 4 SATURDAY

Gen. John Pemberton and about 29,000 Confederates surrendered to Gen. Grant at Vicksburg by laying down their arms and marching out of the battered city. The Mississippi was now open, save for Port Hudson, which could not hold out much longer. The citizens of Vicksburg wept with sorrow as the surrender was completed. Grant could now turn his attention to Johnston's army to the east.

Raphael Semmes, the famed Confederate commerce raider, wrote later, with keen insight, about the fall of Vicksburg and the loss at Gettysburg:

> . . . Vicksburg and Gettysburg mark an era in the war. . . . We need no better evidence of the shock which had been given to public confidence in the South, by those two disasters, than the simple fact that our currency depreciated almost immediately a thousand percent!

In Gettysburg, Lee had decided to retreat into Virginia. Late in the afternoon, in a heavy downpour the wagons filled with wounded began their

FACING PAGE: W. F. Goodhue created this map of the battlefield at Gettysburg in 1863. It shows drainage, vegetation, roads, railroads, houses and names of inhabitants, as well as the movements of the 12th Army Corps. Union and Confederate positions are shown with names of the commanding officers of some units.

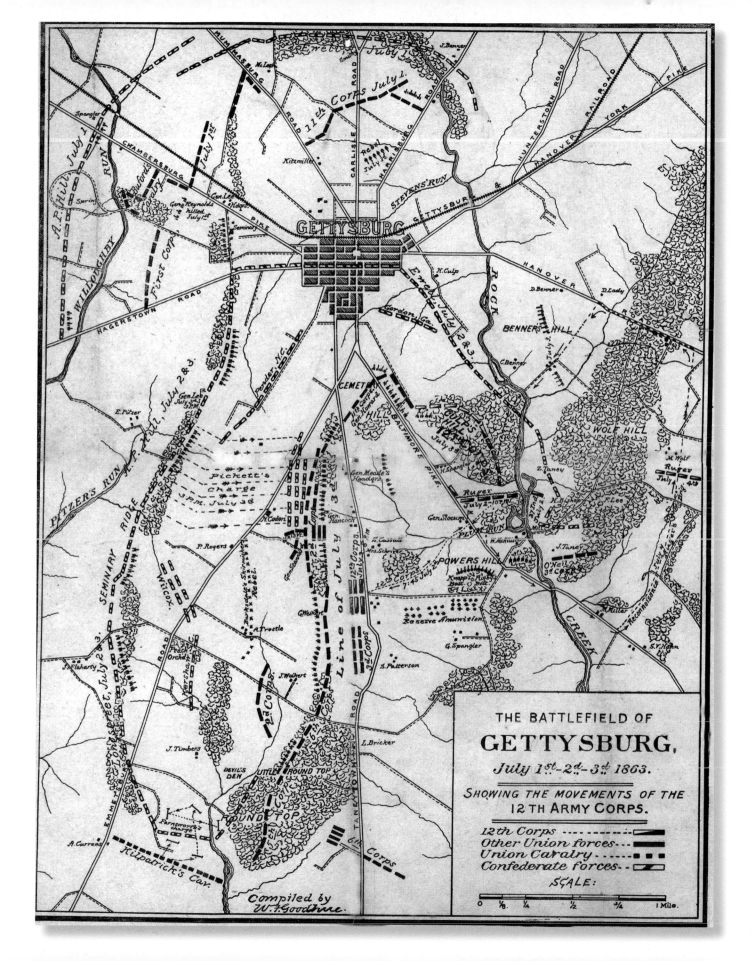

THE BATTLEFIELD OF
GETTYSBURG,
July 1st - 2nd - 3rd 1863.

SHOWING THE MOVEMENTS OF THE
12TH ARMY CORPS.

12th Corps ....
Other Union forces ....
Union Cavalry ....
Confederate forces ....

SCALE:

0   ⅛   ¼   ½   ¾   1 Mile.

Compiled by
W. F. Goodhue.

THE BATTLE OF GETTYSBURG

JULY 1 TO 3, 1863

*Augustus Buell, a cannoneer with the 1st Division of the 1st Corps
of the Army of the Potomac, describes the first day of the battle.*

We turned out the next morning about day-break, harnessed up, and, after crossing the creek, halted to let the infantry of Wadsworth's Division file by. There was no mistake now. While we stood there watching these splendid soldiers file by with their long, swinging "route step," and their muskets glittering in the rays of the rising sun, there came out of the northwest a sullen "boom! boom! boom!" of three guns, followed almost immediately by a prolonged crackling sound, which, at that distance, reminded one very much of the snapping of a dry brush-heap when you first set it on fire. We soon reasoned out the state of affairs up in front. Buford, we calculated, had engaged the leading infantry of Lee's army, and was probably trying to hold them with his cavalry in heavy skirmish line, dismounted, until our infantry could come up. . . .

The sounds of the cavalry fight had been distinct ever since we left Marsh Creek—a fitful crackle—but now we heard fierce, angry crash on crash, rapidly growing in volume and intensity signifying that our leading infantry—Cutler's and the Iron Brigade—had encountered the "doughboys" of Lee's advance. It is well known that the men of the Iron Brigade always preferred slouch hats (Western fashion), and seldom or never wore caps. At the time this heavy crashing

RIGHT: An untitled painting of the Battle of Gettysburg by an unknown artist.

Field glasses used by Union Brevet Major General G. K. Warren (1830–82) during the Battle of Gettysburg

began we were probably halfway up from Marsh Creek, and, as the Battery was marching at a walk, most of us were walking along with the guns instead of riding on the limbers. Among the Cannoneers was a man from the 2d Wisconsin (John Holland) who took great pride in the Iron Brigade. So, when that sudden crash! crash! crash! floated over the hills to our ears, John said, with visible enthusiasm, "Hear that, my son! That's the talk! The old slouch hats have got there, you bet!!"

Now the artillery began to play in earnest, and it was evident that the three batteries which had preceded us were closely engaged, while the musketry had grown from the crackling sound of the skirmishing we had heard early in the morning to an almost incessant crash, which betokened the file firing of a main line of battle. Just before reaching the brow of the hill, south of the town, where we could get our first sight of the battle itself, there was a provoking halt of nearly half an hour. We could hear every sound, even the yells of the troops fighting on the ridge beyond Gettysburg, and we could see the smoke mount up and float away lazily to the northeastward; but we could not see the combatants. While halted here Doubleday's Division passed up the road, each regiment breaking into double quick as it reached the top of the hill. The Eleventh Corps also began by this time to arrive from Emmittsburg. Finally, when the last of the Second Brigade of Doubleday's (Stone's) had passed, we got the order to advance again, and in two minutes the whole scene burst upon us like the lifting of the curtain in a grand play. The spectacle was simply stupendous. It is doubtful if there was ever a battle fought elsewhere of which such a complete view was possible from one point as we got of that battle when we reached the top of the hill abreast of Round Top. . . .

FACING PAGE: Veterans of the Battle of Gettysburg (from left): Lieutenant Colonel Myles Keogh, Major General John Buford, Captain Peter Penn-Gaskell, Captain Craig W. Wadsworth, Lieutenant Colonel Albert Payson Morrow

BELOW: The center of the Federal position viewed from Little Round Top, Gettysburg

slow, agonizing journey south. Meade, left in possession of the field, had no plans to follow Lee, although he was urged to do so by Lincoln. This would be another opportunity lost to the Army of the Potomac.

JULY 5 SUNDAY

From Gettysburg, Lee's army had moved south towards Hagerstown, Md., and Meade sat in Gettysburg—an act somewhat reminiscent of those of McClellan.

Vicksburg was in Federal hands, supplies came in for the relief of the citizens of the city, and troops occupied the public buildings. The Federals began to parole the Confederates. Sherman stirred his men out of their entrenchments and prepared for an attack towards the city of Jackson, and Joe Johnston, to the east.

Pickett's Charge is depicted in this undated oil painting by Edwin Forbes. The viewer looks toward the Confederate attack: Ziegler's Grove appears on the left.

JULY 6 MONDAY

Rear Admiral John A. Dahlgren, former commander of the Washington Navy Yard and a friend of President Lincoln, arrived in Port Royal, S.C., as the new commander of the South Atlantic Blockading Squadron, replacing Rear Admiral Samuel F. Du Pont. There had been a lot of finger-pointing about the failure of the assault on Charleston, S.C., and it appeared that the scapegoat was to be Du Pont.

There was light skirmishing between the cavalry forces of Lee and Meade as Lee withdrew through Maryland to Virginia. Meade still sat in Gettysburg, despite Lincoln's urging.

JULY 7 TUESDAY

The forces gather for the Union assault on Joe Johnston and Jackson, Miss. While the generals shuffled the maps and symbols, the troops waited.

At Port Hudson, south of Vicksburg, the last remaining Confederate bastion held out despite short rations and incessant pounding by mortar boats.

Lee, in Hagerstown, Md., notified President Davis of his retreat from Gettysburg and his decision to withdraw further south. Davis was not joyous at the news, but understanding. Lincoln received the news of Vicksburg's surrender and wrote Halleck, "Now, if General Meade can complete his work, so gloriously prosecuted thus far, by the literal or substantial destruction of Lee's army, the rebellion will be over." Lincoln was right again, but he couldn't get his commander of the Army of the Potomac to see this.

JULY 9 THURSDAY

As Sherman drew near the Mississippi capital, there was light fighting near Clinton and the approaches to the city. President Davis, wholly out of touch with the situation there, wired Johnston that he hoped Johnston might yet "attack and crush the enemy."

Port Hudson formally surrendered, clearing the last obstacle for navigation on the Mississippi from Cairo to New Orleans and the sea. There would be minor guerrilla harassment for the remainder of the war.

JULY 11 SATURDAY

Sherman had invested the city of Jackson, Miss., and the waiting began. Things remained reasonably quiet in the lines.

At Gettysburg, Meade finally got off his posterior and mounted a halfhearted general offensive against Lee's forces, which had their backs to the Potomac. Lincoln, in the wings, cheered Meade on, hoping that he would attack and destroy Lee's army.

JULY 12 SUNDAY

Lee, still with his back to the river, awaited either Meade's attack or the falling of the river so he could cross with his main force, which he hoped he could do the next day. Lincoln hoped Meade would be in time to stop Lee, but this was not to be.

In Tennessee, Bragg was now in Chattanooga, having lost the state to Rosecrans. Both commanders were reorganizing and fitting up for the next campaign.

JULY 13 MONDAY

The opposition to the Draft Law reached its culmination today with riots in New York City, Boston, Portsmouth, N.H., Rutland, Vt., Wooster, Ohio, and Troy, N.Y. The largest, of course, was in New York, where a mob stormed the draft headquarters, burned houses and looted stores. Fires broke out, and a Negro church and orphanage were burned as Negroes became the prime target for the mob, made up mostly of working-class Irish. Property losses were estimated at $1,500,000, and it was estimated that 100 people were killed or wounded during the period, which ended July 16.

JULY 14 TUESDAY

Lee crossed the Potomac and was safe, for the time being, in Virginia.

JULY 16 THURSDAY

Gen. Joseph E. Johnston decided to abandon Jackson, Miss., to its fate at Sherman's hands. Johnston pulled his men out of the city about midnight.

JULY 17 FRIDAY

Things were looking gloomy all around with Vicksburg and Port Hudson gone, Gettysburg a costly defeat and now the attack on Morris Island near Charleston.

Maj. Gen. George Gordon Meade (1815–72) was not only a career officer in the U.S. Army, but also a civil engineer. His notoriously short temper earned him the nickname Old Snapping Turtle.

JULY 18 SATURDAY

On Morris Island in Charleston Harbor, another assault was made on Ft. Wagner after a heavy pounding by mortar boats and ironclads. The assault by Brig. Gen. Truman Seymour's men was led by the 54th Massachusetts Volunteer Infantry, the first of the Negro regiments to enter the war. Of the 6,000 men in the assault, 1,515 of them would be casualties, including Col. Robert Gould Shaw, who organized and commanded the 54th Massachusetts. He would be buried in the trenches with his men. The failure of the assault would cause a change in the Federal plan of attack on Charleston from a frontal assault to a siege.

JULY 19 SUNDAY

Meade's Army of the Potomac finally crossed the Potomac after Lee, at Harpers Ferry and other fords, and moved rapidly south towards the Blue Ridge passes, which were being screened by Stuart's cavalry.

JULY 20 MONDAY

Having eluded capture the day before with about 400 of his men, John Hunt Morgan got into another scrape with Union forces at Hockingport, Ohio, before turning away from the Ohio River.

In the Blue Ridge passes, Federal and Rebel cavalry got into stiff fights with each other as Lee moved through the Shenandoah, and Meade paralleled Lee's route further east.

JULY 26 SUNDAY

Morgan was finally run to ground near the Pennsylvania line. At Salineville, Ohio, he and his spent command surrendered. He had 364 officers and men remaining. The officers were sent to the state prison at Columbus, and the enlisted men to prison camps. Morgan's raid was daring, spectacular and caused much consternation but did little else. Nothing of great military value was destroyed nor were many people killed. In many ways the raid was a great grandstand play.

AUGUST 1863

CONSIDERING THE EVENTS OF JULY, for the North things looked better. The Mississippi was open to the sea and Lee was out of Pennsylvania. The South had a different perspective. The country had been cut in two, with the trans-Mississippi area isolated and the supplies from that region no longer available for the armies in the east. Both North and South, towns and villages counted their dead and mourned for the fallen at Gettysburg, Vicksburg, Port Hudson, Tullahoma and a thousand other skirmishes. The war continued.

AUGUST 1 SATURDAY

There was another melee at Brandy Station, Va., but certainly nothing like the previous cavalry battle at the same site in early June. Opposing cavalry clashed briefly on the old battlefield, the Union looking for Lee.

Belle Boyd, an oft-arrested spy suspect, was again in custody for similar activities at the Old Capital Prison in Washington.

AUGUST 3 MONDAY

President Davis issued what was, in effect, an act of amnesty by requesting that all absentees return to their regiments. Desertion in Lee's army was reaching dramatic proportions. One man, living along the James River east of Richmond, reported more than one thousand, mostly North Carolinian, soldiers crossing there heading for home.

AUGUST 8 SATURDAY

In Virginia, President Davis rejected an offer by Gen. Robert E. Lee to resign as commander of the Army of Northern Virginia. Lee cited the criticism on his defeat at Gettysburg. He wrote Davis: " . . . in all sincerity, request your excellency to take measures to supply my place." Many cited Lee's general health and depression for his offer to resign.

AUGUST 12 WEDNESDAY

In one of the greater justices of the war, Lincoln refused to give Major Gen. John A. McClernand a new command. McClernand, a political general, had been relieved from command by Grant during the siege of Vicksburg.

AUGUST 17 MONDAY

Admiral Dahlgren renewed the attack on Charleston's defenses, using both ironclads and the Union guns on Morris Island. In all, more than 930 shells were fired at Sumter. Dahlgren's Chief of Staff, Capt. G. W. Rodgers, was killed during the engagement by a shot from Ft. Wagner.

The Chickamauga campaign opened with its first skirmish at Calfkiller Creek, near Sparta, Tenn. Rosecrans moved slowly towards Chattanooga.

AUGUST 19 WEDNESDAY

In New York City the draft was resumed without much difficulty, after the disastrous and deadly riots last month that killed or wounded almost 100 people.

AUGUST 20 THURSDAY

The guns on Morris Island and the blockading fleet were pounding Sumter again, the fourth straight day of bombardment. The mayor of Charleston requested that the Confederate government send the South Carolinian troops in Lee's army back to the state to "defend their native soil."

Rosecrans's 90,000-strong Army of the Cumberland had reached the Tennessee River east of Chattanooga, where Bragg was holed up with 40,000 troops awaiting action.

The interior of Ft. Wagner on Morris Island, S.C., showing the quarters of the Federal garrison

This print depicting William Quantrill's massacre of the citizens of Lawrence, Kans., on August 21, 1863, was published in *Harper's Weekly* shortly thereafter.

AUGUST 21 FRIDAY

Brig. Gen. Q. A. Gilmore on Morris Island demanded the surrender of Charleston or he would continue the bombardment and next time include the city. The Confederates refused to surrender and the firing went on for the fifth straight day.

In one of the more tragic and senseless acts of the war, William C. Quantrill, an outlaw and self-appointed Southern officer, raided Lawrence, Kans., burning the town, looting the stores and people's purses and murdering many of the men in a wanton slaughter that served no useful purpose. Quantrill's raiders murdered about 150 men and boys and destroyed about $1,500,000 worth of property.

In Tennessee, Union troops were close enough to throw artillery shells into Chattanooga. There was skirmishing between the forces in eastern Tennessee near the city.

AUGUST 22 SATURDAY

At about 1:30 that morning a shell landed in the city of Charleston, S.C., terrifying the residents. A total of 16 shells were fired during the morning, 12 filled with "greek fire." Confederate Gen. Pierre G. T. Beauregard, currently in command of the city, sent an angry message to Gillmore, castigating him for firing on innocent civilians. The British and Spanish consuls in the city also sent messages asking that the bombardment be stopped. Gillmore declined.

In Tennessee, Rosecrans's Army of the Cumberland drew closer to Chattanooga as President Davis tried to round up some reinforcements for Bragg.

In Richmond, all of the clerks in the city post office had resigned in a wage dispute with the government. No mail was being delivered, some of which might have been important to the war effort.

AUGUST 24 MONDAY

The Confederate submarine *H. L. Hunley* used a unique approach to torpedo a ship. The sub would dive beneath the ship while towing a floating copper-cylinder torpedo some 200 feet astern. When the submarine was safely under the ship, she would surface and go forward until the torpedo struck the target and exploded.

AUGUST 27 THURSDAY

A previous act of the Confederate Congress decreed that any Union officer who was captured by the Confederacy who had commanded Negro troops would be executed. President Davis declined to order the execution of some of the captives, and, instead, ordered them held indefinitely, without exchange.

SEPTEMBER 1863

THE WAR IN EASTERN TENNESSEE was beginning to warm up considerably. Bragg, in the Chattanooga area, was facing Rosecrans's Army of the Cumberland, currently in eastern Alabama and coming up slowly.

Other than in Charleston, things were fairly quiet. Grant's army was being taken apart by Halleck and scattered to the winds, sent to garrison duty in Louisiana, Mississippi, Tennessee and Kentucky. A good part of the Ninth Corps was sent to Burnside, who now was on his way to the Chattanooga area to lend a little weight to Rosecrans's assault. Meade was sitting quietly near Warrenton, Va., occasionally swatting at pesky guerrillas such as Mosby, who persisted in nibbling at him. The Confederacy lived.

SEPTEMBER 1 TUESDAY

Near Chattanooga, Rosecrans's Army of the Cumberland was crossing the Tennessee River to prepare for the assault on Bragg's army at Chattanooga. Gov. Isham Harris, a governor without a state, was informed by President Davis that reinforcements were being sent to Bragg.

SEPTEMBER 2 WEDNESDAY

Union Gen. Ambrose E. Burnside easily took Knoxville, Tenn., thus blocking any direct communications between Tennessee and Virginia. His presence in

The Army of the Cumberland assembles near Chattanooga, Tenn., with Lookout Mountain on the left.

the area was in support of Rosecrans's operations against Chattanooga.

In Charleston Harbor the guns were almost silent, with the Union troops entrenched only eighty yards from the outer works of Battery Wagner. The Union troops had taken the Confederate rifle pits after a second try, the first being repulsed.

SEPTEMBER 3 THURSDAY

In England there had been much controversy about British shipbuilders providing ships to the Confederacy, an act the United States government felt was a violation of the neutrality which England proclaimed. There were two ironclad rams being constructed at Birkenhead, and Lord Russell finally came down on the side of the Union by ordering the rams to be kept in port.

SEPTEMBER 4 FRIDAY

Rosecrans's Army of the Cumberland was across the Tennessee River and forming for the assault on Bragg. The latter was now faced with Union forces from two directions, Burnside coming from Knoxville.

Gen. Grant, an excellent horseman, was riding in New Orleans when his horse shied and fell on him. His injuries would keep him incapacitated for some time, and on crutches for several weeks.

In New Orleans also, an expedition to capture and hold Sabine Pass, Tex., was getting underway. The Navy would supply the gunboats USS *Clifton*, *Arizona* and *Granite City* with the steamer *Sachem*, all under the command of Acting Volunteer Lt. Amos Johnson. The gunboats, with about 180 Army sharpshooters aboard, would make the assault and drive the defenders from their positions with their guns. Sabine Pass in Federal hands would go far to strengthen the Union position in that area.

It was reported that defection was spreading in North Carolina. In Wilkes County, Gideon Smoot, commander of the insurgents, was reported to have raised the United States flag at the county courthouse.

SEPTEMBER 6 SUNDAY

During the night, Confederate forces secretly abandoned Morris Island by boat. The previous day, the 5th, one hundred of the nine hundred Confederate defenders of Ft. Wagner were killed in the bombardment by shore batteries and naval gunboats. Beauregard, the commander of the Charleston defenses, ordered the evacuation. The Union attackers now had a full view of the city of Charleston.

SEPTEMBER 8 TUESDAY

The operation at Sabine Pass, Tex., was a disaster. The attack was led by the USS *Clifton*, which had her wheel rope shot away and was disabled under the defenders' guns. After having 10 men killed, the captain surrendered the vessel. The *Sachem* was totally disabled by a shot through her boilers. The other gunships recrossed the bar and headed back to New Orleans.

The Chickamauga Campaign opened with fighting at Winston's Gap, Ala., and at Alpine, Ga. In Virginia, Longstreet's corps was moving to the relief of Bragg at Chattanooga.

SEPTEMBER 9 WEDNESDAY

Beginning the night before, an assault by boat was made on Ft. Sumter, led by Commander Stevens. The attack comprised more than 30 boats with some 400 sailors and Marines. The defenders, having recovered a code book from the wreck of USS *Keokuk*, had read the signals and were ready for the attack. More than 100 men were captured, and Ft. Sumter was still safe in Confederate hands.

Outflanked, Gen. Bragg evacuated Chattanooga, Tenn., without a struggle. Rosecrans's Army of the Cumberland immediately occupied the city.

SEPTEMBER 10 THURSDAY

Contact between Rosecrans's and Bragg's armies became more frequent, and the skirmishing heavier.

SEPTEMBER 16 WEDNESDAY

In Georgia, Rosecrans concentrated his troops in the vicinity of Lee and Gordon's Mills, on the Chickamauga Creek, some 12 miles south of Chattanooga.

SEPTEMBER 18 FRIDAY

James Longstreet and his corps from the Army of Northern Virginia arrived at Bragg's location in Georgia early this morning, and Bragg wasted no time. He drove all but three of his divisions across West Chickamauga Creek from Ringgold with a part of Longstreet's corps. Heavy fighting broke out with Rosecrans's cavalry at Pea Vine Ridge, Dyer's Ford, Spring Creek, Stephen's Gap and the bridges at Alexander and Reed.

Going into battle, Rosecrans was outnumbered by about 7,000 men, the balance being Confederates, with the arrival of Longstreet.

At Mobile, the inventor and builder of the submarine *H. L. Hunley*, Mr. Horace L. Hunley himself, wrote Gen. Beauregard at Charleston and requested that the submarine be turned over to his command. The orders were given and Mr. Hunley brought his crew from Mobile, and in a short time was ready for the attack.

Rosecrans and Bragg were unaware of the exact position of the opponent. Thomas was in position on the Union left, guarding the route to Chattanooga. Thomas sent part of his corps up to find the Confederates and the Union forces ran into the dismounted

Confederates advance through the forest toward Union forces at the Battle of Chickamauga, as depicted in this drawing by Alfred Rudolph Waud.

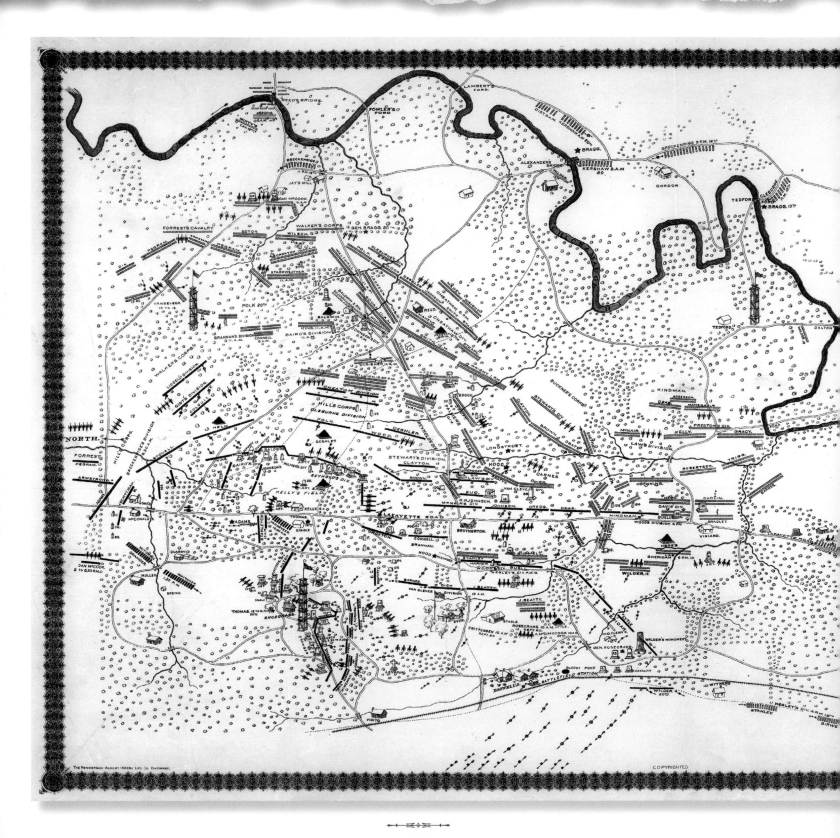

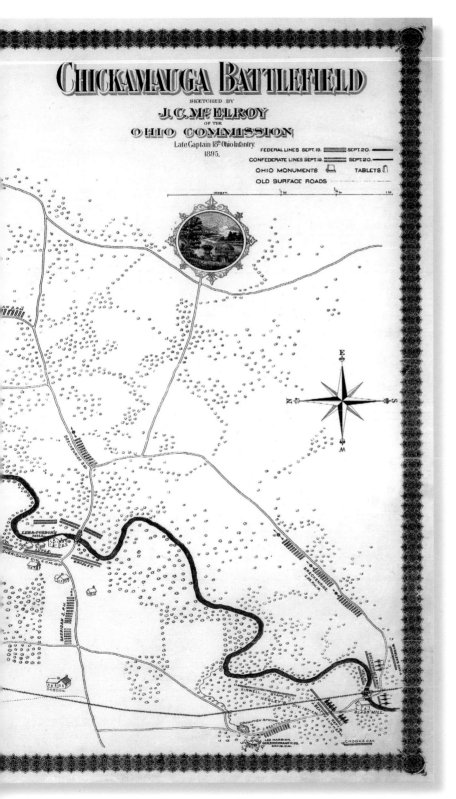

CHICKAMAUGA BATTLEFIELD

SKETCHED BY
J. C. McELROY
OF THE
OHIO COMMISSION
Late Captain 18th Ohio Infantry.
1895.

FEDERAL LINES SEPT. 19. ═══ SEPT. 20. ━━━
CONFEDERATE LINES SEPT. 19. ═══ SEPT. 20. ━━━
OHIO MONUMENTS □ TABLETS ⬠
OLD SURFACE ROADS

cavalry of Nathan Bedford Forrest. By 2 PM the entire three-mile front was engaged. Casualties were heavy on both sides, but at dark the lines were in about the same location.

SEPTEMBER 20 SUNDAY

Bragg, having placed Polk in command of the left flank of the army, and Longstreet the right, ordered an attack for dawn by Polk on the Union right. About noon, Longstreet came up opposite the Federal center and found a hole in the line. Union troops under Thomas J. Wood had been pulled out of the line and shifted to the left, leaving a wide gap that Longstreet immediately filled with Confederates. Thomas held throughout the afternoon, repelling assault upon assault by the Confederates. The "Rock of Chickamauga" earned his nickname this day.

That night, Thomas, under orders, disengaged and withdrew towards Rossville on the way to Chattanooga, where he set up new defensive lines. The casualty rate for both sides was high—about 28 percent of the forces engaged. The Union casualties were 16,170, the Confederate slightly higher at 18,454. Bragg won the battle, but Rosecrans held Chattanooga.

"The Orphan Brigade" had made one last charge towards the end of the day that drove some of Thomas's men back, and the Brigade held the Union line. After playing the role of rear guard on retreats at Shiloh, Baton Rouge, Murfreesboro, and then Jackson, Miss., it felt good for a change. Breckinridge, ever fond of his old Brigade, exulted in its actions.

Jackman, Pvt., "The Orphan Brigade," Battle of Chickamauga, Ga., wrote:

This map of the Chickamauga battlefield was sketched by Joseph C. McElroy of the 18th Ohio Infantry (McElroy later became secretary of the Ohio Chickamauga and Chattanooga National Park Commission) and was published around 1895.

Men and horses were lying so thick over the field one could hardly walk for them. I even saw a large black dog that had been mangled by grape. . . . About 10 o'clock AM. . . Breckinridge [ordered us] to advance in fifteen minutes and adjust his movements to the brigade on the right. . . . When I got to the regiment it was just falling back under a heavy fire having charged three times unsuccessfully. The regiment was greatly reduced—by half at least—Col. G. had been wounded. . . . Gen'l. Helm had received a mortal wound and had to be borne to the hospital on a litter. Col. W., in command of the regiment, had me ride the Gen'l.'s horse back to the hospital. . . .

SEPTEMBER 21 MONDAY

Dawn found Gen. Thomas at Rossville in good defensive positions which he would hold all day, retiring to Chattanooga after dark. Rosecrans had occupied good defensive positions around Chattanooga and with Thomas inside the perimeter, the Union army was safe, at least for the time. Bragg had ordered a new offensive and then cancelled it, missing a chance to severely damage the Union forces.

The defeat had a sobering effect on the North, and the South celebrated. It was the only bright spot this year! Lincoln ordered Burnside to reinforce Rosecrans.

SEPTEMBER 22 TUESDAY

In Washington, Lincoln and his wife, Mary, mourned the death of Confederate Brig. Gen. Ben Hardin Helm, Mary's brother, who was killed at Chickamauga. He commanded the division to which "The Orphan Brigade" belonged.

SEPTEMBER 28 MONDAY

At Chattanooga, Major Generals Alexander McDowell McCook and T. L. Crittenden were relieved of their corps commands and ordered to Indianapolis, where a court of inquiry would be held on the conduct of the Battle of Chickamauga. Gen. Thomas escaped criticism.

SEPTEMBER 30 WEDNESDAY

Barber, Cpl., Co. D, 15th Illinois Volunteer Infantry, Natchez, Miss., wrote:

There were camped here about twenty thousand negroes. Their condition was distressing in the extreme. The small-pox broke out amongst them carrying off as many as one hundred daily. They just rolled in filth and rags, dependent upon the Government for support. A good many earned a little by washing clothes for the soldiers. Most of the able bodied males enlisted and several regiments were formed here. Some of our boys went in as officers of companies.

OCTOBER 1863

AUTUMN. The armies were in camp mostly, with some activity here and there. Bragg, resting at Chickamauga and Lookout Mountain, watched Rosecrans in Chattanooga, doing nothing to follow up his late victory. Burnside was still busy in Knoxville, sitting astride an important rail link to Virginia. Meade, at Culpeper C.H., was being nibbled at by Mosby and still facing Lee, a few miles south at Orange C.H. Both North and South had had abundant crops, so it appeared that food would not be in short supply, but distribution remained a problem in the South.

OCTOBER 2 FRIDAY

Joe Wheeler's cavalry was still spreading havoc behind Rosecrans's lines in eastern Tennessee. At Bridgeport, Ala., just south of Chattanooga on the Tennessee River, Gen. Hooker and 20,000 men arrived, having ridden the railroad for 1,159 miles in seven days. Quite a feat and the first time the trains had been used to transport a Union force that far in so short a time. The only road open to Chattanooga from Bridgeport was the mountainous trail over Walden's Ridge.

OCTOBER 5 MONDAY

Barber, Cpl., Co. D, 15th Illinois Volunteer Infantry, Natchez, Miss., wrote:

Tidings of the bloody battle of Chicamauga now reached us. It came first through rebel sources. There had been a rebel regiment formed from the principal young business men of Natchez which was in the fight and only about thirty escaped unhurt. There was weeping and wailing in the city. These men were the flower of the society here, and

although our foes, we could not but sympathize with their friends in their loss.

OCTOBER 9 FRIDAY

In northern Virginia, Lee was on the move, crossing the Rapidan and moving west, trying to get around Meade's right flank and threaten Washington. Meade, alerted some days before, took immediate action to cover his own flank.

OCTOBER 10 SATURDAY

Lee was trying hard to get around Meade's right flank and behind the Union army, but had no luck. Meade's cavalry was probing heavily trying to find Lee's main force. For once the armies were well matched in strength. Fighting at Russell's Ford, Germanna and Morton's Fords, and other points on the Rapidan.

On October 5, 1863, the USS *New Ironsides*, an ironclad warship depicted in this print by W. H. Rease, was struck by a torpedo attached to a spar on the end of the CSS *David*. The ironclad was only slightly damaged, but the event prompted Union Admiral John Dahlgren to tell Assistant Secretary of the Navy Gustavus Fox: "By all means let us have a quantity of these torpedoes, and thus turn them against the enemy. We can make them faster than they can."

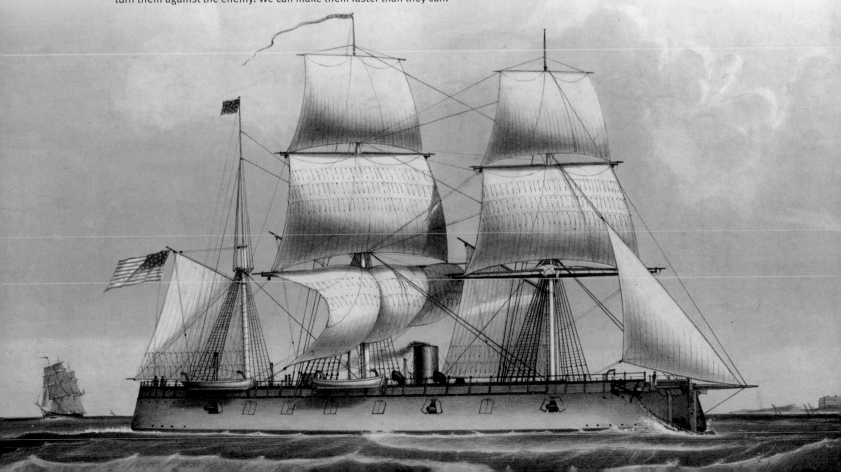

OCTOBER 14 WEDNESDAY

Near Bristoe Station, Va., Lt. Gen. A. P. Hill's Confederates struck Meade's rear guard but not with sufficient strength to dislodge the entrenched Yankees. Meade had time to prepare his lines around Centreville near the old Manassas battlefields. The battle that ensued was fairly matched. Lee found no easy solution and Meade couldn't find a good opening for an attack.

OCTOBER 18 SUNDAY

Grant assumed command of the Union forces from the Mississippi River east to the Cumberland Mountains, replacing several "Department" organizations with a leaner, less top-heavy organization. Rosecrans was relieved of his command at Chattanooga, and Gen. George Thomas was placed in command, with the admonition to hold Chattanooga at all costs.

In northern Virginia, Lee was almost back to his old lines at Orange C.H., with Meade following. There were several brisk fights during the withdrawal, but nothing of any weight.

OCTOBER 20 TUESDAY

JEB Stuart took the last of the Confederate forces back across the Rappahannock River and into Lee's lines at Orange C.H., ending a campaign which had accomplished almost nothing for either North or South. Casualties were about equal—Confederate, 1,381; Union, 1,423.

Maj. Gen. George Henry Thomas (1816–70), United States Army

OCTOBER 24 SATURDAY

In central Tennessee Sherman assumed command of the Army of the Tennessee, replacing Grant.

At Chattanooga, Grant inspected the defenses of the city and the state of the troops. The famous "Cracker Line" was then ordered into effect.

OCTOBER 28 WEDNESDAY

At Bridgeport, Ala., Gen. Joseph Hooker received orders to move his men up the Tennessee River and to secure the crossing at Browns Ferry by cleaning out the Confederates at Raccoon Mountain. Hooker wasted no time, and during the night he was attacked by Longstreet's men. The Union force under Brig. Gen. John W. Geary held, and by 4 AM the Confederates withdrew. The "Cracker Line" was not bothered again for the duration of the campaign.

OCTOBER 29 THURSDAY

The Union troops of Gen. Hooker, in overwhelming numbers, attacked the Confederates on Raccoon Mountain, and the Union thus secured the route for the "Cracker Line" to begin operations.

President Davis approved a request from Brig. Gen. Nathan Bedford Forrest to separate his forces from Bragg's and to go raiding in northern Mississippi and Tennessee. The devil was loose!

OCTOBER 31 SATURDAY

Firing on Ft. Sumter continued today for the third straight day. A total of 2,961 shells were fired at this small dot of landfill in three days, but the Confederate flag still flew.

NOVEMBER 1863

THE ARMIES SETTLED FAIRLY WELL into winter camp along the Rappahannock and Rapidan rivers in Virginia, a time for training and equipment repair. In the west, Grant had relieved the siege of Chattanooga and the "Cracker Line" was in full operation; the Federal troops were eating well again. Bragg, a little crotchety, as usual, was pondering Grant's next move. Ft. Sumter, further reduced to dust, was still defiant. The war ground on.

NOVEMBER 1 SUNDAY

Ft. Sumter was under fire again. Some 780 rounds of artillery and mortar shells would be fired into this crumbling fort, yet the defenders stayed on.

NOVEMBER 2 MONDAY

In Washington, President Lincoln received, and accepted, an invitation to make a "few appropriate remarks" at Gettysburg, Pa., during the dedication of the new National Cemetery.

NOVEMBER 3 TUESDAY

Union guns and mortars sent another 661 shells against the walls of Ft. Sumter.

NOVEMBER 4 WEDNESDAY

In an action quite uncharacteristic of him, Gen. Bragg detached Gen. Longstreet's corps from the Army of Tennessee and sent it against Burnside at Knoxville. The all-important railroad linking Virginia with the west was the goal.

NOVEMBER 6 FRIDAY

In West Virginia, the Confederates defending Droop Mountain were routed by a two-prong advance of Brig. Gen. William W. Averell's Union troops. This was part of a continuing campaign to clear the Confederates from the important rail links to the southwestern part of that state.

NOVEMBER 8 SUNDAY

Around the Rappahannock, Meade's men were not idle. Moving further towards Lee, they skirmished at Warrenton, Brandy Station, Culpeper C.H. and other points.

At Chickamauga, Ga., Major Gen. John Cabell Breckinridge replaced Lt. Gen. Daniel H. Hill as commander of the Second Corps of Bragg's Army of Tennessee. Hill had been relieved of command for his constant carping and back-biting.

NOVEMBER 9 MONDAY

In Washington, President Lincoln, an admirer of the theater, went to see John Wilkes Booth in *Marble Heart.*

NOVEMBER 12 THURSDAY

The Union guns opened again on Ft. Sumter, beginning a four-day bombardment. The target was already a pile of rubble. In Arkansas, pro-Union delegates met to discuss how they could best arrange to get back into the Union.

Confederate sword belonging to Lt. Joseph McLeod Turner, who was killed in action during an engagement with Union forces at Rappahannock, Virginia

At Chattanooga, Grant still waited for Sherman to appear. Grant's problem was really one of morale. The Army of the Cumberland that he inherited from Rosecrans was, he felt, badly demoralized by its defeat at Chickamauga. He also felt that the two corps brought from the Army of the Potomac by Hooker would perform poorly because they had never won a battle. What he wanted was troops that were accustomed to winning and a commander to match them: Sherman and his Fifteenth Corps. The redhead was two days away.

NOVEMBER 14 SATURDAY

Brig. Gen. Nathan Bedford Forrest was assigned an "operational area" of western Tennessee for his raiding parties. At Chattanooga, Sherman arrived after leaving his wagon train at Bridgeport and rushing forward to see Grant. Immediately, Grant, Thomas and Sherman went for a tour of the lines to discuss strategy. What Sherman saw was a huge natural amphitheater running northeast to southwest with the prominence of Missionary Ridge about three miles distant to the northeast. To the southwest was Lookout Mountain, which overlooked Chattanooga. A grand panorama, filled with the tents and camps of the Confederate army.

The town of Gettysburg on the day of President Lincoln's Gettysburg Address on November 19, 1863

NOVEMBER 16 MONDAY

At Campbell's Station, Tenn., Longstreet missed an opportunity to cut off Burnside's line of retreat. Burnside withdrew into Knoxville, which Longstreet immediately besieged. There was other skirmishing and light fighting around Kingston, Tenn.

At Charleston, the fifth day of bombardment continued with 602 more shells being fired at Ft. Sumter.

NOVEMBER 17 TUESDAY

A policy, both North and South, had long existed that permitted soldiers who were wounded to go home to recuperate, providing, of course, they could travel. This served a useful purpose in that it relieved the government of nursing and feeding the wounded.

NOVEMBER 19 THURSDAY

At Gettysburg, Edward Everett, a noted orator of the day, talked for two hours, tracing the history of men at war from the earliest times to the present. Beautifully delivered, as always, when his speech was done, hardly anyone remembered what had been said. This was not because his words were not noteworthy, but because of what followed.

Next on the platform was the tall, lanky President. In a few short moments he delivered one of the most eloquent, moving speeches ever written, and one that has become known throughout the world.

President Abraham Lincoln arrives at Gettysburg, Pa., for the dedication of the Soldiers' National Cemetery on November 19, 1863. He appears, hatless, just left of center in the photograph, with his bodyguard Ward Hill Lamon at his right and Pennsylvania governor Andrew G. Curtin at his left. Lincoln delivered his famous speech about three hours after this picture was taken.

NOVEMBER 20 FRIDAY

Food was ever a problem in Richmond, which had grown from a somewhat sleepy town of less than 40,000 before the war to over 140,000 in about 18 months. Some residents were getting desperate.

At Charleston, the Union gunners fired 1,344 rounds onto Ft. Sumter, killing three men and wounding eleven.

NOVEMBER 21 SATURDAY

At Chattanooga, Sherman was on the move, crossing the Tennessee River at Brown's Ferry and heading northeast to the Confederate right flank around Missionary Ridge. Sherman was to attack the north end of the ridge, Thomas the center. Hooker was to attack the Confederate left flank. There were delays, even more than usual, because of the heavy rains, and the roads were quagmires.

NOVEMBER 22 SUNDAY

At Missionary Ridge, Ga., Gen. Braxton Bragg detached Gen. Simon Bolivar Buckner from Bragg's Army of Tennessee and sent Buckner to Knoxville, Tenn., to support Gen. James Longstreet, who was besieging Union forces under Gen. Ambrose E. Burnside. Bragg was unaware, of course, that a storm of blue was about to descend upon him in the form of Grant's army. As a part of the

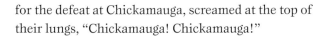

Union buildup, Grant ordered Gen. George Thomas to demonstrate in front of Missionary Ridge the following day.

NOVEMBER 25 WEDNESDAY

In the early dawn light, Sherman's men moved against the north end of Missionary Ridge and Tunnel Hill. Heavy fighting continued until about 2 PM, with little or no progress being made. Grant then sent Thomas with four divisions against the center. The divisions advanced rapidly from the base of the ridge, overwhelming the Confederate line and driving them up the steep slope of the ridge.

Sheridan's division pursued the Confederates, but Hardee's corps held them off and then the Confederates withdrew in the darkness. The battle was over, the siege of Chattanooga was broken, and Bragg's army was intact, but beaten. Grant, with his typical aggressive style, issued orders for a follow-up immediately at first light. The Federal troops, feeling avenged

The Battle of Missionary Ridge is commemorated in this c. 1886 lithograph.

for the defeat at Chickamauga, screamed at the top of their lungs, "Chickamauga! Chickamauga!"

NOVEMBER 26 THURSDAY

The battle for Chattanooga was over. Sherman and Thomas chased Bragg's troops from Chickamauga Station towards Ringgold, Ga., without pause. The Union troops clashed with Pat Cleburne's rear guard near Ringgold and heavy fighting erupted. The Federals finally called a halt, and Bragg had a chance to regroup his army.

At Knoxville, Longstreet was preparing an assault, blissfully unaware that Bragg had been defeated and was withdrawing.

NOVEMBER 28 SATURDAY

Sherman was ordered to send more troops, in addition to those sent with Gen. Granger, to the relief of Burnside. Bragg, feeling like the world had fallen in, wired Richmond, "I deem it due to the cause and to myself to ask for relief from command and investigation into the causes of the defeat." Strangely enough, Bragg was little at fault this time. He was defeated by overzealous Union soldiers who refused to stop at the bottom of Missionary Ridge.

In Virginia, Meade was sending heavy skirmishers against the Confederate positions at Mine Run. The gray line held without too much trouble and it seemed that Meade's offensive was stalled.

At Charleston, the Union guns were still pounding Ft. Sumter and the other harbor defenses.

NOVEMBER 30 MONDAY

Bragg received a telegram from the War Department in Richmond accepting his offer to resign from command. He was directed to turn the army over to Gen. Hardee in the interim. The Army of Tennessee was slowly being pulled together after its near-rout from Missionary Ridge. The troops began to settle in for the winter.

DECEMBER 1863

THE LAST MONTH OF THE YEAR began with fresh victories at Lookout Mountain and Missionary Ridge for the Union and "non-victories" at Charleston and at Mine Run for the Confederacy. Economically, the South was becoming more desperate, distribution of food being of major concern. The grind of war was also taking its toll, North and South. The casualty lists posted attest to the cost of the war in human terms. The major armies were now settled into their winter quarters fairly well and would remain there until spring, with some eruptions. The South had survived another year.

DECEMBER 1 TUESDAY

In Virginia, Major Gen. George G. Meade had decided that he was not going to make it around Lee's flank at Mine Run, so he pulled back across the Rapidan completely and went into winter quarters.

At Knoxville, Longstreet had tried no new major assaults on Burnside's positions, and knowing that more Union troops were on the way, Longstreet prepared to depart.

The bombardment of Ft. Sumter that had begun on November 20th still went on.

In Washington, Confederate spy Belle Boyd, who was ill with typhoid, was released from the Old Capital Prison and was sent to Richmond by flag-of-truce boat, and was told not to come back.

Confederate Gen. Joe Wheeler's cavalry were noted for their raids on the local populace, wherever they were, to obtain rations and mounts. This problem became serious in North Carolina, and the fiery governor of that state, Zebulon B. Vance, wrote to the government in Richmond, "If God Almighty had yet in store another plague for the Egyptians worse than all others, I am sure it must have been a regiment or so of half-armed, half-disciplined Confederate cavalry."

DECEMBER 2 WEDNESDAY

At Knoxville, Longstreet was threatened by a fast-moving Union force coming up on his rear from Chattanooga to relieve the siege.

At Dalton, Ga., Braxton Bragg was leaving the Army of Tennessee, turning the command over to Lt. Gen. William Hardee. Hardee would command only a short time before Gen. Joseph E. Johnston arrived to assume command.

DECEMBER 3 THURSDAY

At Knoxville, Longstreet began moving his troops away from the city, effectively breaking the siege. He moved north and east to Greeneville, Tenn., where he took up winter quarters. Tennessee was now totally occupied by Union forces.

DECEMBER 6 SUNDAY

Gen. Sherman and his staff entered Knoxville, Tenn., officially ending the siege. Parts of his old Fifteenth Corps were close behind and coming up fast.

DECEMBER 7 MONDAY

Capt. John Parker, CSN, devised a plot whereby one John C. Braine, in company with 16 other Confederate sympathizers, were sent from New Brunswick, Canada, to New York, where they acquired weapons and boarded the steamer *Chesapeake*, en route to Portland, Me. When the steamer was off Cape Cod, the Confederates took over the ship, killing the second engineer, and took her to the Bay of Fundy in Nova Scotia, where Parker came aboard. The intent was to refuel the ship and go to Wilmington, slipping by the blockade at that port. The capture of the ship caused great alarm in the Northern ports and the U.S. Navy sent ships out to recapture the *Chesapeake* as soon as possible.

DECEMBER 8 TUESDAY

Messages from both Presidents Lincoln and Davis went to their respective Congresses, Lincoln's reporting success and hope. Davis's was apprehensive.

This photograph of Knoxville and its environs, seen from the south bank of the Tennessee River, was taken shortly after Gen. Longstreet had withdrawn his forces.

Lincoln also offered amnesty with exceptions to those in the South who would take an oath of allegiance.

DECEMBER 11 FRIDAY

Only 220 shells were fired at Ft. Sumter today. One, however, exploded a powder magazine, killing 11 and wounding 41 of the defenders. This would be the last bombardment for the year.

DECEMBER 12 SATURDAY

The United States, until now, had been sending rations to Richmond to feed the 13,000 Union prisoners held there, because the Confederate government did not have the means. This changed today when orders were given in Richmond that no more supplies from the United States should be received by the Federal prisoners.

DECEMBER 14 MONDAY

Gen. Longstreet attacked Union troops at Bean's Station, Tenn., on his way to Greeneville. He drove back the Federals, under the command of Brig. Gen. James M. Shackelford, in a sharp fight. The Federals held for a while, but withdrew further the following day.

DECEMBER 16 WEDNESDAY

It was announced today that Gen. Joseph Eggleston Johnston, CSA, would command the Army of Tennessee, replacing Lt. Gen. William Hardee. Johnston, at Brandon, Miss., left his current command to Lt. Gen. Leonidas Polk.

In Washington, John Buford, who had commanded the cavalry that made the initial contact at Gettysburg, was promoted to Major General, just a few hours before he died of typhoid.

DECEMBER 22 TUESDAY

Capt. Semmes, CSS *Alabama*, moved his base of operations from the East Indies back to the Cape of Good Hope, Africa. He wrote from Singapore:

The enemy's East India and China trade is nearly broken up. Their ships find it impossible to get freights, there being in this port [Singapore] some nineteen sail, almost all of which are laid up for want of employment. . . . The more widely our blows are struck, provided they are struck rapidly, the greater will be the consternation and consequent damage to the enemy.

DECEMBER 25 FRIDAY

Many of the two-year regiments mustered in during 1861 were coming up for reenlistment or discharge. The government, of course, preferred to get the soldier to reenlist because it saved training and provided an instant veteran. The bounty was used as an inducement in most cases, part of which would be paid upon reenlistment, the remainder in installments.

DECEMBER 26 SATURDAY

The CSS *Alabama*, Capt. Semmes, captured and burned the ships *Sonora* and *Highlander*, both in ballast and at anchor in the entrance of the Straits of Malacca. Semmes wrote that one of the ship's masters told him:

Well, Captain Semmes, I have been expecting every day for the last three years to fall in with you, and here I am at last. . . . The fact is, I have had constant visions of the *Alabama*, by night and by day; she has been chasing me in my sleep, and riding me like a night-mare, and now that it is all over, I feel quite relieved.

DECEMBER 31 THURSDAY

In Richmond, the *Examiner* perhaps summed up the totality of the year when it said, "To-day closes the gloomiest year of our struggle."

Matthew Brady's post-war photograph of Gen. James Longstreet, CSA (1821–1904)

1864

... the country mourned the loss of one of its most illustrious defenders, the brave and noble McPherson. When his death became known to the army that he commanded, many brave and war-worn heroes wept like children. . . . It is said that Gen. Grant wept when he heard of his death. . . .

—Corporal Barber, outside Atlanta, July 1864

JANUARY 1864

THE THIRD JANUARY OF THE WAR ended a momentous year and opened one that would prove to be among the bloodiest in our history. Grant had Gen. Joe Johnston stalled at Dalton, Ga., and Meade was watching Lee in Virginia. Economically, the South was in increasingly bad shape. While the blockade runners were getting some material through, many of the ordinary things were gone, or were so costly that only the very rich could afford them. The Confederate currency had depreciated rapidly in 1863, and would worsen in the coming year. The icy wind blowing through the country could be an omen of things to come.

JANUARY 1 FRIDAY

Day, Pvt., Co. B, 25th Massachusetts Volunteer Infantry, Newport News, Va., wrote:

> We have now entered on the last year of our soldier service and are looking forward to the end, and may it not only end our service, but the war as well. . . . About thirty days ago, orders were received from the war department at Washington soliciting re-enlistments. . . . Up to the present time there have been but few enlistments. . . . I shall not re-enlist, and my reasons are, first, I have no desire to monopolize all the patriotism there is, but am willing to give others a chance. My second reason is that after I have served three years, my duty to the country has been performed and my next duty is at home with my family.

PRECEDING PAGES: Maj. Gen. James Birdseye McPherson (1828–64) was killed in the Battle of Atlanta on July 22, 1864, an event depicted in this c. 1888 lithograph. McPherson was the highest ranking Union officer killed in the war. The battle occurred in the middle of Gen. Sherman's Atlanta Campaign, which culminated in the fall of the city around six weeks later.

JANUARY 2 SATURDAY

Secretary of the Navy Gideon Welles proposed to Secretary of War Stanton that a joint Federal effort be made against the defenses of Wilmington, N.C., to close the port. Major Gen. Halleck, the senior general of the Army at this time, vetoed the idea saying that with other campaigns going, the Army could not afford the manpower for this operation.

JANUARY 7 THURSDAY

One of Major Gen. Benjamin F. Butler's brilliant ideas was to send a commercial steamer into Wilmington, N.C., disguised as a blockade runner, and loaded with troops who would then disembark and play havoc with the shipping in the port and be in a position to attack the rear of the forts guarding the port. This was turned down by the Navy when it was found that the entry to the port was too closely checked.

JANUARY 9 SATURDAY

President Davis warned his commanders in Mobile that an attack by Admiral Farragut could be expected soon.

JANUARY 11 MONDAY

In the U.S. Senate, John B. Henderson of Missouri proposed a joint resolution to abolish slavery throughout the country by amendment to the Constitution. This would be the Thirteenth Amendment.

JANUARY 16 SATURDAY

The *Richmond Enquirer* reported that there were 26 ships off Wilmington that:

> . . . guard all the avenues of approach with the most sleepless vigilance. The consequences are that the chances of running the blockade have been greatly lessened, and it is apprehended by some that the day is not far distant when it will be an impossibility for a vessel to get into that port without incurring a hazard almost equivalent to positive loss.

Having secured nearly every seaport on our coast, the Yankees are enabled to keep a large force off Wilmington.

JANUARY 17 SUNDAY

Day, Pvt., Co. B, 25th Massachusetts Volunteer Infantry, Newport News, Va., wrote:

> The balance of the re-enlisted men left for home today, several of the officers going with them. We have now got our ultimatum, either enlist or go into exile. . . .

JANUARY 18 MONDAY

The pro-Union areas of western North Carolina, northwestern Georgia and eastern Tennessee were becoming more vocal in their protests about the South's conscription laws. Evasion was becoming more frequent and open meetings were held to protest the draft.

JANUARY 19 TUESDAY

The South was perfecting another infernal device called a "coal torpedo" to be used against the North.

This device, made of cast iron and filled with powder, was painted to resemble pieces of coal and was to be placed in the coal depots at the ship refueling stations. The torpedo would be put into the firebox of the ship's boiler where it would explode, seriously damaging the ship, if not sinking it. One such device was used at City Point, Va., later in the war.

JANUARY 21 THURSDAY

The "let's all denounce slavery and rejoin the Union" bandwagon was rolling in Tennessee. The pro-Northern faction met at Nashville and proposed a resolution for the abolition of slavery.

JANUARY 23 SATURDAY

One of the major problems with freeing the slaves in the Southern states was what to do with them after emancipation. The problem in the South was having an available labor force that could readily be used as the former slaves were used. A solution to this problem was begun (and would go on for several years) that permitted the former slaves to

The currency of the Confederacy would continue to lose its value throughout 1864. This 100-dollar banknote, dated December 22, 1862, depicts a slave hoeing cotton in the center, John C. Calhoun the prominent South Carolina politician on the left and Columbia (the feminine personification of the Americas) on the right. At the far right, ink from a stamp on the back of the note can be seen. It reads: "Interest Paid to 1st January 1864 at Richmond."

be hired by their former masters at a going wage, based on legal contractual agreements. This solved two problems: the plantation owners got their labor (not necessarily free, but available); and the former slaves got recompense for their labors (not a lot, but it was more than they had before).

JANUARY 27 WEDNESDAY

Cavalry, both North and South, were slowly gaining in efficiency but would never be used like the cavalry of the European armies because of the American terrain. In both cases, the cavalry operated in relatively small, independent bands that relied on the local countryside for survival. Cavalry, generally, was held in low esteem by the infantry.

JANUARY 31 SUNDAY

The month had produced little in the way of "heavy" fighting, the weather being a significant factor. However, the dead from the "light" fighting were just as dead.

The North did not reach a point where those who had paid for substitutes to serve in their stead would be drafted, sufficient manpower being available. In the South, however, the situation was different. By early 1864 the casualties of killed, wounded (those who could not return to the armies) and unexchanged prisoners had mounted considerably, seriously depleting the ranks. Desertion, too, played a role. Many of the Confederates were disheartened and, thinking of their families at home who were in dire straits, left their units, some for a short time, others forever.

∽ FEBRUARY 1864 ∽

In February the Deep South began to come alive. In Florida and southern Georgia, Alabama and Mississippi, the people thought more of gardens and the new year's crops. The armies, too, were awakening. At Chattanooga, Grant had sent Sherman home for a well-earned leave. Grant now sent Sherman to Vicksburg to prepare for the Meridian, Miss., campaign. All remained reasonably quiet in Virginia, neither Lee nor Meade stirring. Economically, the state of the South worsened.

FEBRUARY 1 MONDAY

At Williamsburg, Va., the Union army was still trying to coerce members of the 25th Massachusetts Infantry into reenlisting at the end of their three-year stretch. Legally, they could, and should, be discharged having served their enlistments honorably. The regimental brass, however, had an idea that they should have a show of solidarity, with the entire regiment volunteering to stay for the duration of the war. The resistance from the ranks continued.

FEBRUARY 2 TUESDAY

Major Gen. William T. Sherman was back in Vicksburg after his action at Missionary Ridge, Ga., and was ready to begin his campaign against Meridian, Miss. He requested that a diversionary expedition be undertaken up the Yazoo River to confuse the enemy as to intent, and to draw off enemy troops from his front. Admiral D. D. Porter was more than happy to oblige.

At Morris Island, S.C., Major Gen. Quincy A. Gillmore informed Admiral Dahlgren of his intention to place a force ashore for an assault on Jacksonville, Fla. Gillmore requested assistance for transport and gunboats.

FEBRUARY 3 WEDNESDAY

Sherman marched today with 26,000 men to wreck the railroads of Mississippi and to disrupt the flow of food to the Confederate armies in the east. With him were 7,600 cavalry under Gen. William Sooy Smith and they were late coming up, confirming Sherman's long-held belief that cavalry could not be relied upon. Facing Sherman and Smith were about 20,000 widely scattered Confederate troops under Gen. Leonidas Polk, late of Bragg's Army of Tennes-

Gen. William Sooy Smith (1830–1916) had an illustrious postwar career as a civil engineer, and was awarded the American Centennial Exposition Prize in 1876.

see. Supporting Sherman was an expedition up the Yazoo River to smash things and divert Confederate troops. Part of the troops Sherman would use were at Champion's Hill, on the road to Jackson.

had taken a position just beyond a dwelling house where lived a widow and three small children. She came to the door to see what was going on when a ball struck her, killing her instantly. When our boys got there, they found her form rigid in death. . . . Her little children were clinging frantically to her, not realizing that she was dead. . . .

During the night the rebels received large re-inforcements and they boldly resisted our march on the next day. A sharp, severe fight of fifteen or twenty minutes duration in which a number were killed and wounded on both sides resulted in a total rout of the rebels.

FEBRUARY 4 THURSDAY

Barber, Cpl., Co. D, 15th Illinois Volunteer Infantry, en route to Meridian, Miss., wrote:

The next morning our brigade was in the lead. The cavalry went ahead as skirmishers, but they soon came flying back in disorder. They had met a large force of rebel cavalry and been completely routed. Gen. McPherson ordered Gen. Crocker to send forward his best regiment and deploy them as skirmishers, and the 15th was ordered to perform this duty. . . . We advanced one mile uninterrupted and then came upon a brigade of Wirt Adams' rebel cavalry. . . . Without any delay, we opened fire upon them, which they returned. . . .

Now the order came to advance and we swept across the field in quick time, expecting to meet a withering volley of musketry, but the rebs deemed it prudent to retreat. . . .

We again moved forward and again the rebels retreated. . . . As we advanced, we passed seven dead rebels, thus showing that our fire was not without effect. . . . The rebs

FEBRUARY 5 FRIDAY

Sherman pushed on towards Jackson, Miss., fighting a series of little battles on the way, mainly with Confederate cavalry.

FEBRUARY 6 SATURDAY

The Union force under Sherman left Jackson for Meridian, Miss., about 100 road miles away. Gen. William Sooy Smith had finally left Memphis, Tenn., on his way to support Sherman, but Smith was many miles away and would be of no immediate help.

FEBRUARY 7 SUNDAY

After two days at sea, the Union troops under Brig. Gen. Truman Seymour landed under the guns of Admiral Dahlgren's gunboats at Jacksonville, Fla., and moved inland, capturing several pieces of artillery and a large quantity of cotton awaiting shipment by blockade runners. Little resistance was encountered.

Gen. Pickett, unable to capture New Bern, N.C., was falling back towards Richmond, where an alarm had been given, later proved false, that Gen. Ben Butler's troops were approaching the city from the Peninsula.

Sherman, moving steadily towards Meridian, Miss., skirmished at Brandon, Morton and Satartia, as Polk's Confederate forces fell slowly back.

FEBRUARY 8 MONDAY

Sherman pushed on towards Meridian, Miss., skirmishing at Coldwater Ferry, and maintaining almost constant contact with Polk's cavalry.

FEBRUARY 9 TUESDAY

In one of the most spectacular escapades of the war, Col. Thomas E. Rose of Pennsylvania led 109 Federal officers, including the elusive Col. A. D. Streight who had been captured by Forrest, in an escape through a tunnel out of Libby Prison in Richmond. Eventually, 48 were recaptured, two drowned and the remaining 59, including Col. Streight, made it back to Union lines.

FEBRUARY 14 SUNDAY

The Union troops of Gen. Truman Seymour were divided, and a section of them captured Gainesville, Fla., after a brief skirmish. The main force continued inland.

FEBRUARY 15 MONDAY

After a good night's rest and feeling chipper, Sherman turned 10,000 of his troops loose on Meridian, Miss., where the force proceeded to take apart railroads, warehouses, shops, supply depots, arsenals, offices, cantonments, hotels and nearly everything else in a five-day binge of destruction. The Confederates were worried that Sherman would turn and head for Mobile, Ala., about 150 road miles away. Resistance from Polk's small force was negligible.

Libby Prison in Richmond, Va.—site of a daring escape on February 9, 1864—in a photo taken in April of 1865

FEBRUARY 16 TUESDAY

Sherman's troops continued their binge of destruction in Meridian, while Confederate Gen. Leonidas Polk watched from outside the city.

FEBRUARY 20 SATURDAY

Sherman, having destroyed Meridian, Miss., turned his army back towards Vicksburg, moving at a leisurely pace, destroying the railroad as he went. Once he was clear of Meridian, the Confederates immediately started rebuilding the railroads.

FEBRUARY 22 MONDAY

Jackman, Pvt., "The Orphan Brigade," Dalton, Ga., wrote:

> Just before tattoo I noticed a horse's hoof clattering over the road towards army HdQrs. A courier of course from the front and I remarked that something had "turned up." Sure enough, orders soon came in to be ready to move at a moment's notice and to be prepared for action—to cook two days' rations.

Day, Pvt., Co. B, 25th Massachusetts Volunteer Infantry, Williamsburg, Va., wrote:

> William and Mary College . . . is now a mass of ruins; a company of the 11th Pennsylvania cavalry were the vandals. As this company were returning from a scout, they were fired on with one or two shots from out the college as they were riding past. Instead of surrounding the building and capturing the murderers, they set it on fire and burned it to the ground. . . .

Gen. William Sooy Smith's cavalry was moving towards Memphis, when early this morning Gen. Nathan Bedford Forrest's cavalry made a charge against them at Okolona, Miss. During the fight that turned into a five-mile running battle, a Union Tennessee regiment gave way and was routed. The combat was close, often hand-to-hand, and was one of the few purely cavalry battles fought during the war.

FEBRUARY 24 WEDNESDAY

Braxton Bragg was appointed by Jefferson Davis as Chief of Staff of the Confederate forces. He had lost much of the people's confidence by his defeat at Missionary Ridge, and by his never-ending battles with his generals.

For a special man, the Congress of the United States voted to revive the rank of lieutenant general. Grant would be appointed next month.

FEBRUARY 27 SATURDAY

Federal prisoners of war began filing into a new prison camp near Americus, Ga., today. The camp, named Camp Sumter, would become infamous as Andersonville Prison. Many of the prisoners from Belle Isle in Richmond were transferred there to ease the crowding in Richmond.

Sherman, having completed his Meridian campaign, closed into the Vicksburg area in a somewhat leisurely manner.

∞ MARCH 1864 ∞

SPRING WAS COMING, indeed it had arrived in parts of the South, and the campaigns would begin in earnest. Grant, in Chattanooga, prepared for his offensive against Confederate Joe Johnston; but Grant would soon be called to higher command. Banks, in Louisiana, was organizing the Red River expedition with Admiral Porter. In the North, the fall elections were already on people's minds, and the war had much to do with their feelings; the "peace Democrats" looked to former Gen. McClellan as a candidate. Everywhere the armies stirred and became restive—the winter camps had been long and boring.

MARCH 1 TUESDAY

Major Gen. Ulysses S. Grant was nominated by President Lincoln for promotion to the rank of Lieutenant General.

This 1863 photograph, from *Gardner's Photographic Sketch Book of the Civil War*, shows, from left to right, Maj. Benjamin Chambers Ludlow (1831–98); Col. Ulric Dahlgren (1842–64), standing; Lt. Col. Joseph Dickinson (1830–1904), in straw hat; Count Ferdinand von Zeppelin (1838–1917) and a man whom Gardner identifies as Lt. "Rosencranz, a Swedish officer." Dahlgren was killed on March 2, 1864, in a failed Union raid on the Confederate capital of Richmond.

MARCH 4 FRIDAY

At Vicksburg, Miss., the greater portion of Sherman's men returned from their expedition to Meridian, Miss.

At Washington, Admiral John A. Dahlgren called on the President to try and learn the fate of his son, Col. Ulric Dahlgren, who had been killed on Gen. Kilpatrick's abortive raid on Richmond.

Longstreet was calling for reinforcements from Lee's army to be sent to him as early as possible, citing that he was facing an overwhelming force.

MARCH 5 SATURDAY

Commander John Taylor Wood, CSN, led another daring raid against the Federals, this time at Cherrystone Point, Va. Wood, with some 15 men in open barges, crossed the Chesapeake Bay at night and took the Union telegraph station. Shortly thereafter, two small U.S. Army steamers, the *Aeolus* and *Titan*, stopped at the station, unaware that it was in Confederate hands, and were also quickly taken.

MARCH 8 TUESDAY

At the Willard Hotel in Washington a rather nondescript Major General, accompanied by a small boy, stepped to the desk and asked if a room was available. The clerk, as befitting an employee of the best hotel in town, almost decided to deny the officer a room. However, he asked that the general sign the register and was shocked to see that he had signed "U.S. Grant & Son—Galena, Illinois" in the book. The guests in the lobby of the hotel were dumfounded in seeing this rather small man who had become such a hero. They were more accustomed to the swaggering Joe Hooker and the grand McClellan than to this unassuming general. Lincoln sent word that he was to attend the President in the White House that evening, without informing Grant that this was the day of the President's weekly reception, when anyone who was anyone visited the White House. Grant went the short distance to the White House, and wearing his battered uniform he was

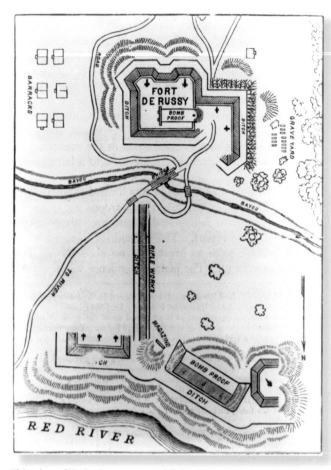

This plan of Ft. De Russy was published in *Harper's Pictorial History of the Civil War* in 1894.

ushered into a hall filled with people dressed "to the nines." Lincoln greeted his guest warmly and asked that Grant stand on a sofa in the East Room so everyone could see him. The crowd cheered and Grant felt embarrassed, as did Lincoln. A feeling of mutual trust was almost immediate.

MARCH 12 SATURDAY

Grant had returned to Washington only long enough to catch a train to Nashville, where he had an appointment with Sherman, soon to be the commander of the western armies. Major Gen. Halleck, at his own request, was relieved as General-in-Chief and named Chief of Staff to Grant; Grant was assigned command of *all* the armies; Sherman was named as Grant's replacement in the west, with McPherson moving to Sherman's vacated billet.

MARCH 14 MONDAY

The combined weight of the naval bombardment and the land assault on Ft. De Russy on the Red River had the desired results, and the fort surrendered. Porter and Sherman's Brig. Gen. Andrew Jackson Smith cooperated beautifully during the action.

The capture of Ft. De Russy, La., on March 14, 1864

MARCH 16 WEDNESDAY

"Devil Forrest" was loose again in western Tennessee on a raid that would last until mid-April.

The Richmond Examiner reported that Gen. Joseph Johnston's report of operations in Mississippi in summer 1863 indicated that the disaster at Vicksburg was caused by Gen. Pemberton's disobedience of orders, Johnston having ordered Pemberton to concentrate his army and give battle before the place was invested, and under no circumstances to allow himself to be besieged, which, of course, would result in disaster. Johnston also said he was about to maneuver in a manner that would probably have resulted in saving a larger proportion of the men, when, to his astonishment, he learned that Pemberton had surrendered! Gen. Joseph Eggleston Johnston's hindsight was always better than his foresight.

MARCH 17 THURSDAY

Grant, now in Nashville, took time to formally assume command of all the armies of the United States and informed everyone that "Headquarters will be in the field, and, until further orders, will be with the Army of the Potomac." Having said that, Grant and Sherman boarded a train for Cincinnati, Ohio, to do their planning in private. Sherman would remember forever after the details of what happened in that room—the plan to skin the Confederacy alive.

MARCH 18 FRIDAY

In Cincinnati, Grant and Sherman were huddled in a hotel room thick with cigar smoke, plotting the destruction of the Confederacy. Sherman officially assumed command of the armies in the west.

MARCH 23 WEDNESDAY

Grant left Cincinnati and returned to Washington, and Sherman headed for Nashville to coordinate his movement into Georgia. The command of the Fifth Corps of the Army of the Potomac shifted from Major Gen. George Sykes to Major Gen. G. K. Warren. Warren was the officer who got the troops to Little Round Top and saved the Union left flank at the Battle of Gettysburg.

Grant and Sherman met in Parlor A of Cincinnati's Burnet House Hotel from March 18 through March 23, 1864. After the war, the Sons of Union Veterans held their meetings in the same room until the building was torn down in 1926.

MARCH 25 FRIDAY

Jackman, Pvt., "The Orphan Brigade," Dalton, Ga., wrote:

> . . . The brigade has gone out to the execution of the sentence of a court martial on one Keen of the 2d Fla. reg't who is to be shot for desertion. This is a murky day. I would hate to be shot on such a day—especially for desertion.

MARCH 26 SATURDAY

By dawn, the Confederate forces which had been attacking Paducah, Ky., were gone, and a silence hung over the defenses.

Grant was back in Virginia and had established his permanent headquarters with the Army of the Potomac at Culpeper C.H. McPherson had taken command of the Army of the Tennessee, reporting to Sherman.

∞ APRIL 1864 ∞

THE LAST THREE WEEKS had been very busy for the newly promoted Lt. Gen. Ulysses S. Grant. Since he stood on the sofa in the White House on March 8 so that everyone could see him, he had moved to the headquarters of Meade's Army of the Potomac—primarily to escape Washington—and had been organizing and consolidating his grasp of the overall situation. He had much to do.

Things began to heat up during April. The inactivity of the late fall and winter came to a flaming end in both the eastern and western theaters of war. Lee, with the Army of Northern Virginia lying quiet in its camps, awaited Grant's first move.

In the west, the Army of Tennessee watched the Federals at Chattanooga and bided their time. Minor skirmishing was going on throughout.

APRIL 1 FRIDAY

Two days ago the Confederates had placed twelve floating torpedoes, each with 70 pounds of powder, in the St. John's River in Florida. The Union army transport *Maple Leaf,* supporting an operation from Palatka to Ft. Gates, struck one of these mines when she returned from a trip upriver to Palatka and was destroyed.

All was fairly quiet in northwest Georgia, where John Jackman and the famed Kentucky "Orphan Brigade" were awaiting developments around Dalton.

APRIL 3 SUNDAY

In western Tennessee, Forrest was raiding near Raleigh. Sumter was being shelled again by mortars.

APRIL 4 MONDAY

Today one tough-minded Major General named Philip Sheridan became the head of the cavalry of the Army of the Potomac. Primarily an infantry commander, Sheridan had seen action in most of the battles in the west and had the full confidence of Grant and a reputation for hard fighting.

APRIL 8 FRIDAY

Gen. Nathaniel Banks had been advancing steadily, with little more than skirmishing, towards Shreveport, La. Now his opponent, Major Gen. Richard Taylor, decided that enough was enough. A full-scale battle was soon going and some of Banks's units withdrew, losing some artillery pieces. Taylor flanked Banks both right and left and the Federals in the middle fled in panic. Finally, the division of Brig. Gen. William H. Emory made a stand that stiffened the Federals' defense, and Taylor's attack petered out. Banks lost a high percentage of his men to capture—about 1,541 out of 12,000.

The United States Senate passed a joint resolution approving the Thirteenth Amendment, which abolished slavery. The vote was 38 to 6.

APRIL 9 SATURDAY

At Culpeper C.H., Va., U. S. Grant issued his famous campaign order to Major Gen. George G. Meade, stating that Lee's army was Meade's objective: "Wherever Lee goes, there you will go also." Grant intended to maintain contact with Lee's army and wear it down.

Giving Banks no respite, Major Gen. Taylor sent his Confederates against the blue defense line drawn up at Pleasant Hill, La., late in the afternoon, gaining some ground, but the Federals counterattacked and drove the Rebels back, ending the engagement. This was supposedly a win for the North, but Banks's not having reached his objective of Shreveport, it was a no-win also.

The Confederates storm Fort Pillow in Henning, Tenn., on April 12, 1864.

APRIL 12 TUESDAY

About 50 miles from Memphis, Tenn., Ft. Pillow had been used for some time to protect a small trading post located nearby. On this night, Gen. Bedford Forrest's troopers struck with about 1,500 men against 557 defenders. The Confederates mounted an all-out assault by midafternoon and the fort was quickly overrun after its commander, Major William F. Bradford, refused to surrender. There was, and still is, more than a century later, controversy over just how many men surrendered and when. Southern accounts say that about 231 Federals were killed and 100 wounded before the surrender. Federal accounts state that the surrender occurred almost immediately without many casualties. Investigations show

that Forrest's men killed nearly 350 of the Union troops at the fort.

APRIL 14 THURSDAY

Since railroads would play a vital role in supplying his army, Sherman had crews trained to build bridges and lay track as fast as Confederate cavalry could tear it up. He sent for the railroad plans for all bridges on the routes and had bridges precut to replace burned ones.

APRIL 17 SUNDAY

In a major change in policy, Lt. Gen. U. S. Grant ordered that no further prisoner exchanges would be permitted until the Confederates balanced Federal releases—in other words, one-for-one. He further directed that "no distinction whatever be made in the exchange between white and colored prisoners." These moves certainly hurt the South more than the North—the South had fewer men to draw upon. Grant's battle of attrition was beginning.

APRIL 18 MONDAY

Gibson, S. J., 103rd Pennsylvania Volunteers, Plymouth, N.C., wrote:

> Last night almost continual skirmishing was kept up. The Rebs seem determined to have Ft. Gray but so far have been repulsed with considerable loss & the loss of 1 piece of Arty. They have so damaged the U.S. *Gunboat Bombshell* that she, after retiring out of action, sunk at her moorings.

APRIL 19 TUESDAY

Gibson, S. J., 103rd Pennsylvania Volunteers, Plymouth, N.C., wrote:

> Morning comes after a night of terror. The Rebs are before us, behind us, and on each side of us. They have carried Ft. Wessell on our right & turned its guns on us. their "RAM" has sunk the G.B. *Southfield* [USS *Southfield*] and driven off our fleet. Now we are "gone up" unless we get reinforcements, but we will die "game." Bombardment continues all day. Work under a galling crossfire all day & at night Co "B" have to go on pickett. The night is made lively by bursting shells and the sharp rattle of musketry.

APRIL 20 WEDNESDAY

Facing an overwhelming Confederate force, and with no protection from the gunboats, the garrison at Plymouth, N.C., surrendered at 10 AM.

APRIL 23 SATURDAY

In Fairfax County, Va., near Hunters Mill, Confederate and Federal patrols clashed in a brief encounter only about 20 miles from the White House.

APRIL 25 MONDAY

Throughout the month Sherman had been stripping his army of "excess baggage." There would be no "company tents" for marching troops and little of other camp comforts. Even his own headquarters was reduced to one wagon for himself, aides, clerks and orderlies. This would really be lean living after the past two years of "bloated" headquarters staff arrangements for most corps, division and regimental staffs.

APRIL 28 THURSDAY

The guns had been periodically bombarding poor Ft. Sumter all month, but not too heavily. That pile of rubble now underwent another seven days of prolonged battering.

APRIL 30 SATURDAY

Personal tragedy struck President Davis and his wife, Varina, when their five-year-old son, Joe Davis, fell from the high veranda at the Confederate White House and was killed.

The Brockenbrough mansion at 1201 East Clay Street in Richmond, Va., built in 1818, served as the White House of the Confederacy and the residence of Jefferson Davis and his family from 1861 through 1865. On April 30, 1864, the Davis's young son Joseph Evan Davis fell from a railing on the east portico and later died. This photograph of the building was taken in 1865.

∞ MAY 1864 ∞

THE SOUTH, expecting action on three fronts—Georgia, Northern Virginia and the Peninsula east of Richmond—waited for the first hammer to strike. Obviously, Grant, now in Virginia, was going to open his summer campaign, but the Confederacy expected much the same from him as from the other Union generals who had faced Robert E. Lee. The economic picture in the South worsened each day. Inflation and currency depreciation had caused near-famine in the larger cities, while the countryside had rations aplenty. Grant and Sherman had made their plans in the hotel room in Cincinnati. The anvil was ready. Which general would swing the first blow?

MAY 1 SUNDAY

In northern Georgia, the contact between Sherman's forces and those of Johnston was picking up. Otherwise it was quiet.

MAY 2 MONDAY

In Richmond, Va., the Second Confederate Congress met for its first session. President Davis held out little hope for foreign recognition but had hopes for a military victory. He spent some time decrying the "barbarism" of the Federal forces against noncombatants. Yesterday, Davis buried his youngest son.

In Louisiana, the lumberjacks of Maine and the Midwest, working at a feverish pace, had nearly completed the dam across the Red River at Alexandria. Admiral Porter hoped the water would rise high enough to get his marooned gunboat fleet over the rapids and safely downriver. The normal depth of seven feet had been reduced to about four feet due to lack of rain upriver, and to the Confederate diversion of the water to other channels. The fate of the entire fleet and Gen. Nathaniel Banks's army hung in the balance.

At the Confederate prison at Andersonville, Ga., a new batch of prisoners of war arrived to join the others in the stockade. Private S. J. Gibson, 103rd Pennsylvania Volunteers, and most of his unit had been captured at Plymouth, N.C., on Wednesday, April 20, 1864. Trains took them to Charleston, S.C., arriving on May 1, and after a brief stop, they were sent on to Andersonville.

MAY 3 TUESDAY

In the area of Brandy Station, Va., Grant notified Meade to move the Army of the Potomac out of winter quarters and to cross the Rapidan River on the morning of the 4th. The new offensive was set to go. In Washington, Lincoln and the Cabinet held long discussions on the events at Ft. Pillow in April, when Negro troops were slain by Forrest's men after the Negroes had surrendered.

The action began to pick up in northern Georgia with skirmishing at Chickamauga Creek, Catoosa Springs and Red Clay, where the two forces came in contact.

Joe Johnston telegraphed to Richmond that scouts in the area of Outawah and Cleveland, Ga., reported that the Federals were beginning to mass their troops for movement.

MAY 4 WEDNESDAY

In the early minutes of this day the long-dormant Army of the Potomac moved across the Rapidan River and headed for the Wilderness crossroads. A long, bloody campaign began that would end with the surrender of Lee's army 48 weeks later. Grant's army had nearly 122,000 present for duty against Lee's 66,000.

On the Peninsula, Major Gen. Ben Butler moved his army, already loaded on transports, towards Richmond.

In Georgia, Sherman prepared to send 98,000 men against Joe Johnston in the area of Dalton, as light skirmishing continued with a brief fight at Varnell's Station.

MAY 5 THURSDAY

At the Wilderness in Virginia, Meade's Army of the Potomac collided with Lee's Army of Northern

Virginia in the tangled wooded area south of the Rapidan. By noon they were locked in full-scale combat. Grant would not commit his forces piecemeal—Lee would have to fight the whole army. At the close of the day, both armies entrenched in their positions and awaited the morrow.

On the James River, where the Appomattox merges, Gen. Ben Butler landed his troops at City Point now Hopewell to begin his movement to Richmond via Petersburg.

MAY 6 FRIDAY

In the Wilderness, the opposing armies awaited daylight to resume fighting. In the early dawn hours the Federals took up the advance and collided heavily with the Rebels. Longstreet made a flank attack that set the Federals back, but temporarily. Late in the afternoon Longstreet tried again, only to be stopped short of the Union lines, and he was severely wounded.

Grant sat and smoked cigars and whittled sticks while receiving reports. At darkness the fighting tapered off slowly. The next question to be settled was in which direction would the Yankees move. Would they recross the river as they had done before, or would they move on towards Richmond? Casualties were heavy for the North—nearly 17,700 killed, wounded, or missing. The Rebels fared better—somewhere around 7,500.

On the James River, within sight of the church spires of Petersburg, Ben Butler's 39,000 troops were opposed by no more than 10,000 Confederates. Butler did some halfhearted scouting and then went into camp. A chance was lost to end the war with one bold stroke.

MAY 7 SATURDAY

Grant would try to dislodge Lee from the woods and get him into the open where the weight of the blue columns could be brought to bear. This army was jubilant; for the first time they were not turning tail and quitting.

Lee realized that Grant was heading for Spotsylvania C.H., and Lee sent cavalry to cut trees to delay the Union advance, while the Confederate general went there and prepared the defenses.

Dalton, Ga., had been the site of Gen. Joseph Johnston's winter camp for the Army of Tennessee. It would now become the initial scene for the Battle for Atlanta. Sherman moved his men out of their camps and lunged for the Rebel lines. The Confederates held a good defensive position on and along a high ridge and they had had all winter to improve it. Now there were few gaps in the line. Sherman's army of nearly 100,000 was facing Johnston's 60,000.

Johnston's position on the high ridge was too strong for a frontal attack, so Sherman sent McPherson around the enemy's left flank, cavalry leading, towards Snake Creek Gap.

MAY 8 SUNDAY

As Major Gen. G. K. Warren's Fifth Corps approached Spotsylvania C.H., they found that Anderson's Confederate corps was there and entrenched. Warren's troops waded into the Rebels, only to find that the Confederates were in strong defensive positions and wouldn't be shaken. Darkness brought an end to the fighting and both sides formed new lines.

MAY 9 MONDAY

Grant and Lee faced off at Spotsylvania C.H. and spent the day sizing each other up and adjusting lines. Burnside moved up closer with his Ninth Corps. Sheridan, drawing Stuart off, began a sixteen-day run around Lee and towards Richmond.

Also at Spotsylvania, Major Gen. John Sedgwick was walking along the line near an artillery unit in full view of the enemy. A rebel sharpshooter placed a bullet through his left eye, killing him instantly.

Jackman, Pvt., "The Orphan Brigade," Rocky-Face, Ga., wrote:

NEW YORK, FRIDAY, MAY 6, 1864.—WITH SUPPLEMENT.

IMPORTANT OPERATIONS IN VIRGINIA.

The Army of the Potomac Across the Rapidan---Scene of the Impending Conflict Between Generals Grant and Lee.

CULPEPPER COURT HOUSE · RICHARDS FORD · BARNETTSFORD · GROVE CHURCH · HARTWOOD CHURCH · POTOMAC · LANDING
CULPEPPER FORD · ELYS FORD · U.S. FORD · SCOTTS · BANKS FORD · FALMOUTH · CREEK · BELLE PLAIN
CEDAR MOUNTAIN · JACOBS MILL FORD · MITCHELLS FORD · FORD · FALMOUTH STATION · KING GEORGE C.H.
MADISON COURT HOUSE · RACCOON FORD · GERMANNA MILLS · LOCUST GROVE · FREDERICKSBURG · STONY POINT · BLUFF POINT
MITCHELLS · RIVER · RAPIDAN · MOUNTAIN R. · MINE RUN · WILDERNESS · CHANCELLORSVILLE · BIRTH PLACE OF WASHINGTON
RAPID'AN · RAPIDAN · ROBERTSONS AVERN · WILDERNESS RUN · MASSAPONAX · RIVER · SKINNERS NECK · RAPPAHANNOCK RIVER
STANHARDSVILLE · CAVES FORD · NEWPORT · MOUNT SWAMP · PORT ROYAL · LIBERTY HILL
ORANGE COURT HOUSE · CORBINS BRIDGE · MARYS BRIDGE · GUNNEYS · VILLEBORO
MADISON · SPOTTSYLVANIA C.H. · SHELLS BRIDGE · RIVER · OLD CHURCH · GUCKLESHELL CREEK
GORDONSVILLE · MELTONS · MT. PLEASANTO · RIVER · THORNBURG · GUINEA S BANCES · PUNANSEND RIVER
LINDSAYS · TREVILLIANS · MAT · RIVER · DOWNERS BRIDGE · BOWLING GREEN · BLACK BURN · OCCODACIA CREEK
BORHAM · LOUISA COURT HOUSE · NORTH ANNA · MILFORD · MATTAPONY
CHARLOTTESVILLE · TOLENSVILLE · VIRGINIA CENTRAL · RIVER · R.R. · PART OF S. RIVER · MILFORD BRIDGE · TAPPAHANN COURT H
TO CHATTANOOGA · FREDERICKSHALL · BUMPRS · OXFORD · CHESTERFIELD · CLARKS V. · BRLINGTON PR.ATAW
YANCEYVILLE · LITTLE · BEAVER DAM · NOELS TURN · DUNKIRK · SEXTONS JUNCTION · WALKERTON
TAYLORS CK. · NEW FOUND CREEK · LITTLE PACES BRIDGE · TAYLORSVILLE · BRANDYWINE · KING WILLIAM C.H.
SHANNON HILL · SOUTH ANNA RIVER · WOODTOWN · HANOVER C.H. · HANOVER STATION · FRAZERS FORD
FLUVANNA C.H. · HADESVILLE · ASHLAND · MONTPELIER · HANOVERTON · PIPING TREE · PAMUNKEY R.
GUM SPRING · NEW CASTLE · PUTNEYS FORD · FISH-HALL
COLUMEM · CANAL · COOCHLAND C.H. · HUNGARY · STONY RUN · WINSTONS BR. · ATLEYS · MECHANICSVILLE · WHITE HOUSE
CARTERSVILLE · JAMES · RIVER · ROCKY BRANCH · SAVAGES · BOTTOMS BR. · TUNSTALS · DISPATCH
ROCKINGHAM C.H. · JEFFERSONVILLE · TAY · RICHMOND · SCUFFLETOWN · MEADOW BR. · MEADOW · FAIR OAKS
TOWER HILL · UNITED STATES ARSENAL · MANCHESTER · ROCKETTS · SEVEN PINES

This headline and map appeared in the *New York Herald* on Friday, May 6, 1864.

∾ THE BATTLE OF THE WILDERNESS ∾
MAY 5 TO 7, 1864

Warren Goss of the 2nd Massachusetts Artillery describes the first day of the Battle of the Wilderness.

The attack was opened by Griffin's division, which at first swept everything in its front. It had simply encountered the van of Ewell's column. . . . The disordered van of Ewell's column re-formed on a wooded hill, and resumed at once the offensive. It so happened that the right of Warren's Corps was at this time uncovered. Wright's division of the Sixth Corps, which should have covered this flank, had not come up, owing to the dense underbrush through which it was compelled to move. On this exposed flank Ewell directed his attack. On Griffin's left was Wadsworth's division. This advanced, but while beating through the dense undergrowth encountered a terrible fire from an unseen enemy. It illustrates the difficulty that beset troops oper-

Alfred R. Waud sketched this depiction of the Battle of the Wilderness, published in the June 4, 1864, issue of *Harper's Weekly*.

This 1887 lithograph depicts the desperate fight near the Orange courthouse during the Battle of the Wilderness, May 6th, 1864.

ating in this tangled region, that there being no other guides, their directions were given to them by the points of the compass. The orders were to advance due west. For some unknown reason Wadsworth advanced northwest, and this brought the fire of the enemy on his flank. Under this terrible flank fire the division broke in disorder. The best way to retreat was for each man to get to the rear, and not stand on the order of his going. The division of Wadsworth finally reformed in the rear and did good service during the fight which followed. . . .

In this abrupt encounter began the Battle of the Wilderness. The opening was not auspicious. Warren had lost three thousand men. The enemy was in force in our front. . . .

Getty had already begun the fight before our arrival. Cheers went up from our sweat-begrimed, dusty veterans, as they came up at about three o'clock and formed in double line of battle in front of the Brock road. The road was very narrow, and densely wooded on both sides. Here we began to construct rifle-pits, by piling up logs and throwing up the soil against them. For this purpose men used their tin drinking-cups, bayonets, and caseknives, as well as the few shovels and picks which accompanied each division on pack-mules. We had not completed our rifle-pits when an order came to move on the enemy.

The scene of savage fighting with the ambushed enemy, which followed, defies description. No one could see the fight fifty feet from him. The roll and crackle of the musketry was something terrible, even to the veterans of many battles. The lines were very near each other, and from the dense under-brush and the tops of the trees came puffs of smoke, the "*ping*" of the bullets, and the yell of the enemy. It was a blind and bloody hunt to the death, in bewildering thickets, rather than a battle.

Among the tangled, darkened woods, the "*ping! ping! ping!*" and the "*pop! pop! pop!*" of the rifles, and the long roll and roar of musketry blending

Wounded soldiers from the Battle of the Wilderness in Fredericksburg, Va.

on our right and left, were terrible. In advancing it was next to impossible to preserve a distinct line, and we were constantly broken into small groups. The underbrush and briars scratched our faces, tore our clothing, and tripped our feet from under us, constantly.

On our left, a few pieces of artillery, stationed on cleared high ground, beat time to the steady roar of musketry. On the Orange plank road, Rickett's battery, or Kirby's, familiar to us in so many battles, was at work with its usual vigor, adding to the uproar.

"We are playing right into these devils' hands! Bushwhacking is the game! There ain't a tree in our front, twenty feet high, but there is a reb up that tree!" said Wad Rider. Two, three, and four times we rushed upon the enemy, but were met by a murderous fire and with heavy loss from concealed enemies. As often as we rushed forward we were compelled to get back. . . .

The uproar of battle continued through the twilight hours. It was eight o'clock before the deadly crackle of musketry died gradually away, and the sad shadows of night, like a pall, fell over the dead in these ensanguined thickets. The groans and cries for water or for help from the wounded gave place to the sounds of the conflict. . . . Thus ended the first day's fighting of the Army of the Potomac under Grant.

After the Battle of the Wilderness, May 5–7, 1864, these nine able-bodied men were the only ones left standing from the 86-man Company I of the 57th Massachusetts Infantry.

Our regiment then clambered up Buzzards Roost and took position. . . . We could see the fields out in front blue with Federals. They now occupied the little ridge we were on the first evening. Sharpshooting commenced on both sides. . . .

MAY 10 TUESDAY

At Spotsylvania C.H., three corps of the Army of the Potomac assaulted the Confederate "mule shoe" positions late in the afternoon, a very heavy attack being made at about 6 PM which temporarily breached the Confederate line; but then the Union forces fell back. Burnside moved closer and entrenched facing Early's corps.

Sheridan and Stuart fought skirmishes along the North Anna River near Beaver Dam Station. Sheridan was now within 20 miles of Richmond, with Custer, commanding one of Sheridan's divisions, tearing up track on the Virginia Central railroad. Stuart took a position between Sheridan and Richmond at a place called Yellow Tavern.

Jackman, Pvt., "The Orphan Brigade," Rocky-Face, Ga., wrote:

Beautiful morning. With the light of day came the sounds of sharpshooters rifles which have been continuously popping all day. . . . Nothing of any interest occurred. . . .

MAY 11

WEDNESDAY

Sheridan's march on Richmond had reached a little crossroads town called Yellow Tavern about six miles north of Richmond when Sheridan was attacked by JEB Stuart's cavalry. In the swirling fight that ensued, a dismounted Federal cavalryman shot Stuart as he rode past, mortally wounding him. He was taken from the field for treatment. When told of the loss of his cavalry leader, Lee stood alone for several minutes in his sorrow and remarked to one of his staff, "I can scarcely think of him without weeping."

At Spotsylvania C.H., Grant and Lee still were in a face-off, awaiting developments. Grant, obviously, had the next move. Lee could not afford to attack the larger army and hope to survive long. He could not stand the casualties.

MAY 12 THURSDAY

At Spotsylvania Court House the Federals charged Lee's prepared lines in wave after wave in one of the costliest battles of the war. The "Bloody Angle" claimed about 6,800 Union and 5,000 Confederate casualties in killed and wounded alone. Another

The Spotsylvania courthouse in 1864

4,000 Confederates were captured. The loss was far greater for the South because of the attrition.

The fabled "Cavalier" JEB Stuart was dead, having succumbed to his wounds received at Yellow Tavern on the 11th. In the concept of death in that century, Stuart was said to have "died well." Richmond went into mourning.

MAY 13 FRIDAY

Grant had failed to break Lee's lines at Spotsylvania C.H. Grant now moved around to his own left with Warren's corps in the lead. Sheridan moved to join Ben Butler's army on the Peninsula. Butler was at Drewry's Bluff wasting time and giving Beauregard time enough to entrench, typical of Butler.

At Resaca, Joe Johnston's army took up positions and awaited Sherman's arrival.

MAY 14 SATURDAY

Sherman arrived at Resaca and immediately ordered probing attacks, especially on the flanks, of Johnston's positions. The main attack would wait.

Jackman, Pvt., "The Orphan Brigade," Battle of Resaca, Ga., wrote:

> Early, ordered further to the left. Just before we fell in, rations of whiskey were issued and some of the boys got so tippsey they could hardly march. . . . [Later], two lines of battle burst out of the woods in front of us and standards up, on the charge. . . . A more vigorous charge was made at the same time on the right of the brigade. . . . The day has passed without our regiment being charged again. Several charges have been made on the right of our brigade and in front of Hinderman during the day. In the evening the roar of musketry to our right was quite loud. We have been kept close by the sharpshooters today having nothing to protect us but our works. The enemy is in the edge of the woods three or four hundred yards off while we lie in an open field. . . . The 4th and 2d regiments have been enfiladed all day by the middle battery and have lost many killed and wounded. At night strengthening our works—worked all night.

MAY 15 SUNDAY

In a battle that would have its anniversary celebrated every year at Virginia Military Institute in Lexington, Va., for more than 125 years, the Confederate army under Major Gen. John C. Breckinridge defeated the Union army under Major Gen. Franz Sigel at New Market, Va. Sigel had about 6,500 troops. Breckinridge had about 5,000 Confederate infantry and a makeshift gathering of everyone he could get his hands on, including 247 students from VMI, who were mostly young boys.

Maj. Gen. Franz Sigel (1824–1902), an immigrant to the U.S. from Germany, was defeated by Confederate Major Gen. John Breckinridge at the Battle of New Market, Va., on May 15, 1864.

On May 21, 1864, Gen. U. S. Grant held a Council of War at Massaponax Church, near Fredericksburg, Va. There, he made the decision to forge ahead with his battle plan, which included the assault on Lee's troops at Cold Harbor, Va. (May 31–June 12, 1864). In this photograph, one of a well-known series by Timothy O'Sullivan taken from the second floor of the church, Grant can be seen, seated at the left end of the bench nearest the tree, writing a dispatch.

When the smoke cleared, Sigel had retreated, suffering about 831 casualties. The Confederate casualties were about 577, including 10 killed and 47 wounded among the cadets.

MAY 16 MONDAY

Sherman's army was still on the move with little contact with the Confederate forces. Heavy rains were making the roads miserable for marching.

In a dense early-morning fog, Beauregard attacked Ben Butler at Drewry's Bluff and nearly did him in. Butler had about 16,000 men, Beauregard about 18,000. Beauregard had audacity, Butler had a bad case of the "slows." Had the characteristics been reversed, Butler could have caused irreparable dam-

age to the Confederacy and could possibly have ended the war by threatening Richmond enough to cause Lee to retreat to defend the city. This was his second blunder— the first was when he failed to take Petersburg on his first movement up the Peninsula. The battle, which accomplished little except killing soldiers, cost the North 4,160 casualties; the South, 2,506. The incompetence of the generals in the North was never demonstrated more clearly than at Drewry's Bluff.

MAY 18 WEDNESDAY

Another attack on the new Confederate lines at Spotsylvania C.H. did little other than create more casualties. Grant moved further south and east.

MAY 19 THURSDAY

Lee, attempting to find out if Grant was moving to his right, ordered Richard Ewell to demonstrate against the Union line at Spotsylvania C.H., which brought on a severe fight which lasted most of the day—again, accomplishing nothing except more casualties. Grant was moving towards the Po River to the southeast. For the several battles which made up the whole of Spotsylvania, the Federals lost about 17,500 out of nearly 110,000 engaged. The South's losses were never accurately recorded but could be estimated roughly at 6,000 from a total engaged of about 50,000. Grant could afford the loss, Lee could not.

MAY 20 FRIDAY

Gen. Nathaniel Banks's army today crossed the Atchafalaya River near Simmesport, La., on a bridge designed by Lt. Col. Bailey, made of steamboats anchored side-by-side. The Red River campaign was closed.

In Georgia, Johnston passed through Cartersville, crossed the Etowah River, and took up strong defensive positions at Allatoona Pass. Schofield's corps followed closely through Cartersville.

In Virginia, Meade was ordered to go to his left and cross the Mattapony River. Lee, onto Grant's movements, began his shift to the right. Butler was still bottled up at Bermuda Hundred.

MAY 24 TUESDAY

On the North Anna River near Hanover Junction, Meade's Sixth Corps moved to the right of the Fifth Corps and held. Hancock's corps, the Second, crossed at the Chesterfield Bridge further east. Burnside's Ninth Corps also crossed the river. The Army of the Potomac was now divided into three parts by the bend in the North Anna River and Lee's protruding line. Sheridan rejoined the army at this time. Lee waited within his position for the axe to fall.

In Georgia, Confederate Gen. Joseph Wheeler and his cavalry were loose in Sherman's rear, attacking wagon trains and creating havoc. Johnston realized that Sherman was around his left flank again and ordered his army towards Dallas via New Hope Church, which was even closer to Atlanta. This would lengthen Sherman's supply line and contract Johnston's, which was based in Atlanta.

The Union Navy came to Ben Butler's rescue when at Wilson's Wharf on the James River, Va., the wooden steamer USS *Dawn*, Acting Lt. Simmons, used naval guns to compel Confederates to desist in their attack on a Union position. Other Union ships also moved in to assist.

MAY 25 WEDNESDAY

At New Hope Church, Ga., in the middle of a fierce thunderstorm, Hooker's corps drove against Hood's corps along Pumpkin Vine Creek. This location, about twenty-six miles north and east of Atlanta, would be the scene of the struggle for Atlanta until about June 4th.

This photograph, taken by Timothy O'Sullivan on May 25, 1864, shows a line of Federal troops occupying the breastworks on the north bank of the North Anna River near Hanover Junction, Va.

MAY 26 THURSDAY

At New Hope Church, Ga., McPherson moved up to the general area of the church as Sherman's advance corps. The entire army moved forward slowly, skirmishing nearly all the time, and the Rebels waited. Both sides entrenched.

MAY 27 FRIDAY

In the vicinity of New Hope Church, Ga., Otis O. Howard's corps attacked the Confederates at Pickett's Mills through heavily wooded country and was repulsed after heavy losses.

MAY 29 SUNDAY

In Virginia, Lee waited at Cold Harbor preparing his lines. Grant was on the way to the next meeting, seeing little opposition.

MAY 30 MONDAY

In Virginia, Grant's and Lee's forces finally met again north of the Chickahominy and not far from Richmond. Grant ordered probing attacks prior to a full-scale assault.

Gen. John Hunt Morgan, in an effort to ease the pressure on Johnston, took Private James Pleasant Gold and several thousand other cavalrymen on a raid into Kentucky.

MAY 31 TUESDAY

Grant, at Cold Harbor, adjusted his lines to get around Lee's right flank, so Lee moved his lines. On May 1, Grant had been north of the Rapidan and Lee had been quietly lying at Orange Court House. In less

Ulysses S. Grant at his headquarters in Cold Harbor, Va., in a c. 1864 photograph.

than thirty days, Grant was outside Richmond and had Lee so heavily engaged that Lee couldn't go anywhere.

In Georgia, Sherman too had moved quite a distance since early May, now knocking on the outside door of Atlanta.

In the North the upcoming Federal elections were being discussed more and more.

JUNE 1864

THIS WAS AN INCREASINGLY ALARMING month for the Confederacy. Attacked on two fronts, Virginia and Georgia, the South's supply problems increased even with the "interior lines" so touted by the military experts. The Southern railroads were wearing down rapidly. Many of the important east–west trunk lines were in the hands of the Union, especially in Tennessee.

Casualty lists lengthened both North and South. The casualty notifications from May were now reaching the homes of the soldiers and the toll in morale was devastating. In Georgia, Gen. Joe Johnston had evacuated Dalton and had fallen back to New Hope Church. Lee, in Virginia, was held by Grant at Cold Harbor. One is reminded of Lincoln's quote, "One holds a leg while the other skins."

JUNE 1 WEDNESDAY

Ghosts seemed to rise over the old Seven Days' battlefields in the vicinity of Cold Harbor as the Union forces arrived to find the Confederates already in possession of the field and digging in rapidly. A sharp fight between the cavalry forces of Sheridan and the infantry of R. H. Anderson's corps livened up the morning. Anderson's troops attacked Sheridan's twice and were thrown back. Action occurred on both flanks of the lines until late afternoon without significant gains for either side.

In Tennessee, Brig. Gen. S. D. Sturgis was about to take a tiger by the tail. He moved out of Memphis with 8,000 cavalry and infantry towards Ripley, Miss., to find and destroy Nathan Bedford Forrest. This was not to be a quiet campaign—or a lucky one.

JUNE 2 THURSDAY

The second day of the Battle of Cold Harbor. Nothing seemed to be working right for Grant on this day. Problems of troop placement, ammunition resupply and a tired army compounded normal situations and caused the delay of the attack until 5 PM. Once again the attack was postponed until morning.

Sherman moved his three armies northeast towards the railroad that linked Atlanta and Chattanooga.

Federal Gen. David Hunter continued his campaign of devastation through the Shenandoah Valley, fighting a skirmish at Covington on the road to Lynchburg. He had some 16,000 men opposing about 8,000 Confederates commanded by Gen. W. E. "Grumble" Jones. The long-awaited Yankees finally arrived in Harrisonburg.

JUNE 3 FRIDAY

At Cold Harbor the fighting opened at 4:30 AM with a charge all along the two armies' entrenchments. The attack was a head-on crash against the Rebel lines, relying on the sheer weight of numbers to breach them. The Federal losses, killed and wounded, were about 7,000 in one hour. Nearly 50,000 troops were in the assault out of a strength

of about 117,000. The South lost about 1,500 from a strength of some 60,000. Within five minutes nearly one-half of the 11th Connecticut Volunteer Regiment was killed or wounded.

JUNE 5 SUNDAY

In the Shenandoah Valley of Virginia, Union Gen. David Hunter moved his forces towards Staunton, forcing the Confederate Military Department of Southwest Virginia to do battle at Piedmont. The Confederate forces, under W. E. "Grumble" Jones, were defeated, Jones was killed and Hunter's troops looted Staunton. The Confederates lost about 1,600 men, 1,000 of whom were taken as prisoners.

At Cold Harbor, Grant petitioned Lee for a truce to remove the wounded and dead. Pending the agreement, both sides withheld their fire as comrades of the wounded recovered them from the field.

JUNE 8 WEDNESDAY

At the Republican Convention in Baltimore, Lincoln was nominated for a second term. Andrew Johnson of Tennessee was named as his running mate, instead of Hannibal Hamlin of Maine.

At Mt. Sterling, Ky., John Hunt Morgan captured the town and its Union garrison. Some of Morgan's

Alfred R. Waud sketched this depiction of the Battle at Cold Harbor, Va., on June 3, 1864.

men robbed the local bank of over $18,000, and Morgan's share of the blame for this was never fully established.

JUNE 10 FRIDAY

In Mississippi, near a little town called Brice's Crossroads, south of Corinth, Gen. Sam D. Sturgis finally found Forrest. In the following fracas, the Federals lost their artillery, over 170 wagons with supplies and over 1,500 prisoners to a much inferior force—Sturgis with 8,000, Forrest with only about 3,500. This particular action was one studied for years afterward as a classic in the use of cavalry. Sturgis fled towards Tennessee.

JUNE 11 SATURDAY

Skirmishing near Pine Mountain continued as Sherman jockeyed for the advantage.

Capt. Raphael Semmes, CSS *Alabama*, arrived at Cherbourg, France, for some badly needed repairs. Lt. Arthur Sinclair, an officer aboard the ship, recorded:

> We have cruised from the day of commission, August 24, 1862, to June 11, 1864, and during this time have visited two-thirds of the globe, experiencing all vicissitudes of climate and hardships attending constant cruising. We have had from first to last two hundred and thirteen officers and men on our payroll, and have lost not one by disease, and but one by accidental death.

This is a remarkable record for a ship of the 19th century when fresh provisions were not always available and scurvy was a constant companion. It showed the great care with which Semmes treated

his crew. In England, the word of *Alabama's* arrival was passed to Capt. Winslow of the USS *Kearsarge*.

JUNE 12 SUNDAY

The Army of the Potomac began its move across the James River in one of the most brilliant moves of the war. Pulling out of Cold Harbor, the troops raced to the previously situated pontoon bridges and were in position near Petersburg within record time. Warren's Corps was left behind to cover Grant's movement and to hold Lee's forces as long as possible.

In Kentucky, Morgan was attacked by the Federals at Cynthiana and was severely beaten. He left the area, driving his captured horses, and moved towards Abingdon, Va., several hundred miles away, arriving there on June 20th.

JUNE 14 TUESDAY

At Pine Mountain the South would lose one of her most stalwart sons this day. Lt. Gen. Leonidas Polk, along with Generals Johnson and Hardee, were watching the Federal movements in front of Pine Mountain when Polk was shot by a Federal cannon. The shot struck him in the chest, killing him instantly. His remains were evacuated from the battle area and sent to Atlanta.

Jackman, Pvt., "The Orphan Brigade," Pine Mountain, Ga., wrote:

> Was wounded a few minutes after making the notes, June 14th, and I did not write any more in my journal for nearly three months. I shall try and give an account of my hospital experience during the time named in a brief manner:

Andrew Johnson (1808–75), a former Senator from Tennessee, was nominated as Lincoln's running mate on June 8, 1864.

. . . I remarked to the Captain that some General and his staff, no doubt, had ridden up to the crest of the hill and the Federal batteries were throwing shells at them. . . . About this time we heard the second shell strike . . . it had struck Lt. Gen. Polk. . . .

Soon after an order came for a report. . . . I was only a few minutes writing the report and . . . suddenly everything got dark and I became unconscious. If I had been sitting erect when the fragment of shell struck me, I never would have known what hurt me. When I came to my senses, Dr. H., our Asst. Surg, and Capt. G. were lifting me up off the ground. I stood on my feet and not feeling any pain I could not imagine what was the matter. The first thought that entered my mind was that my head was gone. I put my hand up to ascertain whether my head was still on my shoulders. I did not hear the piece of shell coming and it was such a quick, sharp lick I did not feel it strike. The fragment probably weighed little more than a pound. It came like a minie ball. After glancing off my head it struck against a rock and bounced and struck Col. C. on the leg but did not hurt him severely. . . .

JUNE 16 THURSDAY

Fighting continued around the Pine Mountain area as both sides adjusted their lines and jockeyed for position.

Brig. Gen. Samuel D. Sturgis (1822–89)—whose son and grandson also served as generals in the U.S. Army—appears in this undated photograph by Matthew Brady. Sturgis was defeated by Nathan Bedford Forrest at Brice's Crossroads on June 10, 1864.

JUNE 19 SUNDAY

The day the Union had waited for so long arrived at last—the CSS *Alabama* had been brought to bay and a naval engagement between her and the USS *Kearsarge* off the coast at Cherbourg, France, would decide the fate of the Confederate raider.

After about one hour and ten minutes of heavy engagement, the *Alabama* was sinking, the enemy's shells having exploded in the side, and between decks, opening large holes through which the sea was rapidly pouring. Semmes hoped to reach the French coast but the water flooded the engine rooms, killing the fires. Semmes hauled his colors and surrendered.

The *Alabama* had captured and sunk 55 United States ships, all unarmed, worth over $4,500,000 and bonded 10 more with a value of $562,000 but this was her first big battle, and she lost. A great raider of ships, and a gallant fighter, her end brought rejoicing to the North. Semmes would return to the South and be promoted to Rear Admiral. Winslow would receive a vote of thanks from Congress and be promoted to Commodore.

JUNE 21 TUESDAY

At Petersburg, Grant and Meade ordered a cavalry raid against the railroads and extended their lines to the left, an action that would continue until the siege was lifted. Grant and Lincoln visited aboard a steamer at City Point, and toured the lines on horseback.

Johnston, in Georgia, was feeling the pressure exerted by Sherman on the Confederate lines. To counteract, Johnston sent Hood from the Confederate right to the left flank of Johnston's line.

JUNE 25 SATURDAY
Things were heating up at Allatoona Pass in Georgia, as the Confederates pressed the Union defenders.

JUNE 27 MONDAY
Sherman's armies of the Cumberland and the Tennessee attacked the Rebel works at Big and Little Kennesaw Mountains in Georgia, with the Army of the Ohio attacking the Confederate left flank. The slaughter of Union troops was one of the worst yet in the west, with nearly 2,000 killed or wounded. The attack failed to break the Rebel lines and many of the troops held on by their fingertips to the ground they had gained. This was a defensive victory for the Confederates, but it was a victory.

JUNE 30 THURSDAY
In all, the month ended with an upbeat note for the North. Grant was holding Lee at Petersburg, Sherman was forcing his way to Atlanta and the war was progressing reasonably well for the North.

BELOW: The battle between the CSS *Alabama* and the USS *Kearsarge*

FACING PAGE: The Battle of Kennesaw Mountain, June 27, 1864

∽ JULY 1864 ∽

Grant now had Lee by the leg and wouldn't let him go. Lee could not leave the entrenchments around Petersburg and do one of his famous "end runs" because he had neither the manpower nor the space. For all practical purposes, Lee's army was useless for offensive operations, and Lee was fully aware of it. In Georgia, Sherman and Johnston were doing the "Georgia reel" or "Southern sidestep." Johnston could not get loose from Sherman's constant pushing. Richmond was in dire straits and the food situation was worsening daily.

JULY 1 FRIDAY

In Washington, the furor over the resignation of Salmon P. Chase, and Lincoln's speedy acceptance of it, finally died down, and Lincoln nominated Senator William Pitt Fessenden of Maine for the Cabinet position. Fessenden had long experience in the Finance Committee in the Senate and took the job reluctantly. Within a year the whole department would improve tremendously.

Barber, Cpl., Co. C, 15th Illinois Volunteer Infantry, near Cartersville, Ga., wrote:

It had now been ascertained that some of the citizens who had professed Union sentiments had been engaged in plots to tear up the railroad, attack foraging parties, etc. and an order was issued to banish all citizens five miles outside our lines, under penalty of having their houses burned if not complying within a certain length of time. Severe as this order may seem, the circumstances justified it.

JULY 3 SUNDAY

The Confederate presence was back at Harpers Ferry when Gen. Jubal Early's Rebel force came down the Valley towards the Potomac. There was skirmishing at Leetown, Martinsburg, etc., as Sigel's Union troops evacuated across the Potomac at Shepherdstown, although Harpers Ferry was still held by the Federals. Washington was getting nervous.

JULY 4 MONDAY

Barber, Cpl., Co. C, 15th Illinois Volunteer Infantry, Kennesaw Mountain, Ga., wrote:

> The glorious Fourth now dawned upon us and we celebrated it as well as circumstances would permit. At the front it was celebrated by the firing of cannon and musketry and the glittering of cold steel. It was no child's play there. . . . After leaving Kennesaw, the rebs made a stand at Chattahoochee River. They were now driven from that into their last stronghold around Atlanta. We were always within hearing of the fighting. At times could see the smoke of battle. . . .

JULY 5 TUESDAY

Gen. Jubal Early decided that Harpers Ferry was too difficult to take for the time being, so he crossed the Potomac at Shepherdstown into Maryland, causing skirmishing at Point of Rocks, Noland's Ferry and other places on the river. Lincoln called for 24,000 militia from New York and Pennsylva-

nia to help defend Washington. Lee believed that if Early put enough pressure on Washington, the Federals at Petersburg would leave to go to the relief of the capital and Lee could possibly escape Grant's hold on his army.

In New York, the *New York Tribune* editor Horace Greeley received a letter alleging that Confederate emissaries were in Canada with authority to negotiate peace. He asked Lincoln to consider investigating this situation.

JULY 6 WEDNESDAY

Near Atlanta, Sherman and Johnston's forces were skirmishing at Nickajack Creek with some action around Allatoona. On the Stono River near Charleston, naval gunfire from the gunboats *Lehigh* and *Montauk* cleared Confederate riflemen out of their firing positions on Morris Island and the gunfire prevented them from building a fortification before the Federal troops could disembark and clear the area. The Federal flotilla returned downriver and the expedition ended on the 9th.

JULY 9 SATURDAY

Major Gen. Lew Wallace had collected some 6,000 Federal troops—many of whom were raw recruits, some troops on leave, and anyone else handy—and faced Jubal Early's nearly 18,000 at Monocacy River between Frederick, Md., and Washington. The Union troops put up a stiff fight but finally broke, losing nearly 2,000 casualties, about 1,200 of whom were captured. Early's force suffered about 700 casualties. The advance of the Confederate army was not stopped, merely delayed by a day.

In Frederick, the Confederates imposed a levy of $200,000 on the city as retribution for the damage done in the Valley previously. The Rebel force continued towards Washington, where panic had set in among the citizens. Grant sent two divisions from the Sixth Corps at City Point, Va., by steamer to the capital.

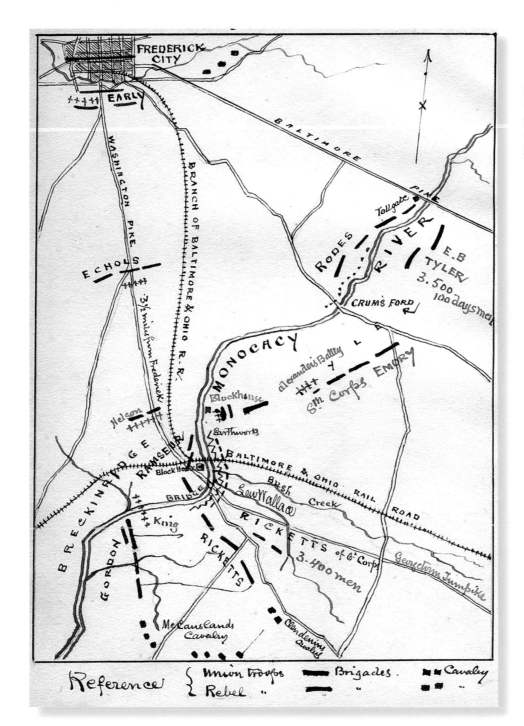

Robert Knox Sneden's map of the battle at the Monocacy River near Frederick, Md., July 9, 1864

JULY 10 SUNDAY

In Georgia, Johnston had his back to Atlanta and Sherman laid his plans to invest the city. At Decatur, Ala., Major Gen. Lovell Harrison Rousseau began a cavalry raid against the railroads operating between Montgomery, Ala., and Columbus, Ga. It would be one of the most successful raids of the war.

JULY 11 MONDAY

Meanwhile, in Washington, on the 6th Street wharves, the steamers carrying the veterans of the Sixth Army Corps, Army of the Potomac, were unloading troops such as the city had never seen. These were not the nattily dressed soldiers normally seen around town. These men were lean, dirty, somewhat ragged, and

A group of Federal officers stands in front of the house that served as headquarters for Confederate Gen. John Bell Hood during the Battle of Atlanta in 1864.

handled their muskets as if they knew exactly what to do with them. These were Grant's veterans of Cold Harbor, the Wilderness and the Chickahominy, and they were not men to be trifled with.

JULY 12 TUESDAY

Early in the morning Jubal Early had second thoughts about assaulting the Washington forts, especially now that some "real" soldiers were there. He started pulling his troops away from Washington, leaving the skirmishers to mask the withdrawal. Major Gen. Wright was given permission to go after the skirmishers. The results were predictable. The firing increased and Lincoln, who had returned to Ft. Stevens, got his first real look at battle casualties immediately after they had been shot.

During the early part of the action, Lincoln had gone up on the parapet and was looking over the top among the twittering and whirring of the minie balls when a young captain named Oliver Wendell Holmes, Jr., yelled at him, "Get down, you damn fool." Lincoln complied and sat with his back to the parapet, safe, but still able to hear the bullets murmuring overhead.

JULY 13 WEDNESDAY

Sherman sent his cavalry around Atlanta to wreck the railroads and generally create havoc while he crossed the Chattahoochee River, preparatory to the advance on the city.

President Davis, still worried over the situation in Atlanta, voiced his concern again to Lee about Johnston's movements and plans.

JULY 14 THURSDAY

Forrest was handed one of his two defeats today when he failed to rout Major Gen. Andrew Jackson

Smith's Federal force at Harrisburg, near Tupelo, Miss. Smith's line repeatedly repulsed the Confederate assaults with heavy Rebel casualties. Of Smith's nearly 14,000 men, only 674 were lost by all causes, while the Confederate losses were about 1,350 out of about 9,500. It was a defeat for the South, but Forrest was not destroyed and was soon roaming the countryside again.

JULY 17 SUNDAY

President Davis, despairing of the loss of Atlanta, had reached a decision that Johnston would have to go. Consequently, he sent a message to Gen. Johnston:

> . . . As you failed to arrest the advance of the enemy to the vicinity of Atlanta, far in the interior of Georgia, and express no confidence that you can defeat or repel him, you are hereby relieved from command. . . .

The command of the Department and Army of Tennessee would go to John Bell Hood.

JULY 20 WEDNESDAY

Hood attacked Maj. Gen. George Thomas north of Atlanta. The attack began three hours late, but was intense for a period of time. Ultimately, it failed, with the Confederates taking dreadful losses. Thomas, with about 20,000, lost about 1,800. Hood, with about the same number of men, suffered losses of nearly 4,800. Nothing had been accomplished except that Hood had fewer men and had no way of replacing them. Sherman still faced him with an overwhelming force on almost three sides of the city, the only openings being to the south and southwest. Hood tried to blame the failure on Hardee, who, he said, was late and did not press the attack. Fruitless attacks and finding scapegoats were two of Hood's best traits.

JULY 22 FRIDAY

The Battle of Atlanta took place amid high temperatures that took a terrific toll on the contestants, both North and South. The Confederate attack failed, with about 3,700 Federal losses from nearly 30,000 engaged. Confederate losses were estimated to be from 7,000 to 10,000, out of about 40,000 engaged. Major Gen. James Birdseye McPherson, USA, was killed, as was Major Gen. W. H. T. Walker, CSA. Hardee, again, was selected by Hood as the scapegoat.

JULY 23 SATURDAY

In the Valley, Gen. Jubal Early had turned on Gen. "Black Dave" Hunter unexpectedly, and Early was coming down the Valley from Strasburg towards Kernstown, just south of Winchester. Major Gen. Crook went out to meet Early at Kernstown.

Gen. James B. McPherson was killed at this spot in the woods outside Atlanta, near the tree with the white sign on it, on July 22, 1864.

Confederate General Jubal Early and his troops burned the town of Chambersburg, Pa., on July 30, 1864, when the townspeople were unable to pay a ransom. This photograph shows the burned-out shell of the Chambersburg courthouse.

In Georgia, the armies of Sherman and Hood were busy tending the wounded and burying the dead after yesterday's fierce fighting. Little skirmishing was going on around Atlanta.

At Memphis, Union Gen. Andrew Jackson Smith and his troops returned after their engagement at Tupelo with Forrest and S. D. Lee.

JULY 27 WEDNESDAY

In Georgia, Sherman was setting up the siege of Atlanta and putting his cavalry to work tearing up track.

In the Shenandoah, Early had ripped up enough track to slow things down and now contemplated recrossing the Potomac and going back into Maryland.

At Petersburg, Hancock's large Second Corps, and Sheridan, with two divisions of cavalry, crossed the James and headed towards Richmond. This was a diversionary tactic to bring pressure on Lee and wear down the Confederate troops.

JULY 28 THURSDAY

North of the James River, Hancock and Sheridan found that Lee had shifted some forces around and the Confederate lines were stronger than the Federals had believed. The expedition petered out and the Federals returned to their lines at Petersburg.

JULY 29 FRIDAY

The Confederates again entered Maryland and the very tip of Pennsylvania. Jubal Early sent John McCausland across the Potomac west of Williamsport near Cave Spring while another cavalry unit demonstrated against Harpers Ferry. Skirmishing was reported at Hagerstown, Md., and Mercersburg, Pa. Panic again stalked the streets of the North.

JULY 30 SATURDAY

For a month, or longer, the men of the 48th Pennsylvania, mostly coal miners, had been digging a tunnel 586 feet long under the siege lines at Petersburg and packed the tunnel with gunpowder. At about 4:45 AM the powder was exploded, creating a hole 170 feet long, nearly 80 feet wide and thirty feet deep in the Confederate entrenchments. About 280 Confederate soldiers died, never knowing what happened to them. The Federal assault began immediately thereafter, and by about 8:30 AM there were nearly 15,000 Union troops in the cratered area. Confederate Gen. Mahone's troops contained the Federals and around 2 PM the Federals pulled back. It cost 4,000 Union killed to about 1,500 Confederates. That did *not* count the wounded or injured.

Jubal Early's Confederates entered Chambersburg, Pa., and demanded $500,000 in currency or $100,000 in gold for ransom not to burn the town. The money was not available, so the town was burned and the Confederates moved towards McConnellsburg.

In Georgia, Sherman's cavalry were fighting all over the place—Macon, Clinton, Newnan and Clear Creek.

JULY 31 SUNDAY

Barber, Cpl., Co. C, 15th Illinois Volunteer Infantry, Kennesaw Mountain, Ga., wrote:

The bloody battle of Peach Tree Creek, before Atlanta, was fought on the 21st and 22d of July. In that battle the country mourned the loss of one of its most illustrious defenders, the brave and noble McPherson. When his death became known to the army that he commanded, many brave and war-worn heroes wept like children. We loved him with a strong, deep love, a love which was born of his kindness to us and the bravery that he displayed on the field. Ohio might well be proud of him. It is said that Gen. Grant wept when he heard of his death. . . . The next day McPherson's body passed through Marietta on its way to his home in Ohio.

AUGUST 1864

GEN. ROBERT E. LEE HAD LOST his mobility. No longer could he rely on movement to surprise the enemy and gain tactical advantage over long distances. Ulysses S. Grant had, in effect, nailed Lee's coattail to Petersburg's fortifications and kept the hammer. In Georgia, Hood was in much the same situation, although he would waste the lives of his men in fruitless attacks believing that he could defeat Sherman's men by sheer force of arms. There was still no light at the end of the tunnel—not yet.

AUGUST 1 MONDAY

Gen. Jubal Early's cavalry under McCausland's command had burned Chambersburg, Pa., and had returned to Hancock, Md.

At City Point, Grant had finally decided that a new commander was needed in the Valley, so he sent the one man in whom he had complete faith to do the job—Major Gen. Philip Sheridan. Sheridan was appointed commander of the Army of the Shenandoah and was sent to Harpers Ferry by the

first train. His task was to rid the Valley of Jubal Early's threat once and for all.

AUGUST 2 TUESDAY

At City Point, Va., the siege of Petersburg went on and on. The buildup of troops, etc., was only a small part of the problem. As always, logistics was the key to success. Grant had developed extensive wharves, warehouses and ammunition dumps at City Point to supply the Army. Huge bakeries were built to bake fresh bread for the troops and an intricate railway system was put in to deliver the supplies and matériel of war to the siege lines. The complex was far more than the South had any capability of providing at any point during the war. Those hated Yankee "mechanics and mudsills" knew how to support a war.

AUGUST 6 SATURDAY

Sherman was trying to cut the railroads south of Atlanta with his advance on Utoy Creek, where heavy fighting flared for the third day. The Federals finally outflanked the Confederate line, forcing the Southerners to fall back.

On the Potomac, Early's men were south of the river again, but things were due to change. Sheridan was coming to the Valley.

AUGUST 8 MONDAY

At 10 AM, the Union flag was flying over Ft. Gaines, Mobile Bay, following the surrender of its garrison by Col. Charles D. Anderson, CSA.

At Atlanta, Gen. John Bell Hood was trying to fix the blame for everything that went wrong on Gen. William Hardee. Hood had problems relating to everyone.

The wharves at City Point, Va., near Petersburg, on August 4, 1864

AUGUST 9 TUESDAY

Ft. Morgan at Mobile Bay had not surrendered, when Forts Powell and Gaines struck their colors. Brig. Gen. Richard L. Page, once a U.S. naval officer and more recently a Commander in the Confederate Navy, refused to surrender Ft. Morgan until he had no means of resistance. The Union army troops in the area prepared for a land assault and the naval ships under Farragut went into position to bombard the fort.

AUGUST 10 WEDNESDAY

The soldiers and sailors stationed in Virginia's Tidewater region were constantly plagued by disease during the summer. The cause of malaria was not then understood. The crews of the ironclads were especially vulnerable to sickness because of the heat inside the iron-covered vessels and the ships' poor ventilation.

AUGUST 13 SATURDAY

At Berryville, in the Shenandoah Valley, fighting erupted between Sheridan's Federals and Early's Rebel forces, as Sheridan moved up the Valley towards Cedar Creek.

AUGUST 15 MONDAY

In the Shenandoah Valley, Sheridan withdrew from Early's front at Cedar Creek, and headed back towards Winchester. For the time being he was giving up his advance until he could get his logistics worked out.

In Georgia, Sherman's force moved slowly to the southeast below Atlanta and the railroads. Fighting flared at Peachtree Road and other points. Joe Wheeler's Confederate cavalry raided the Union supply line on the railroads in Tennessee.

AUGUST 18 THURSDAY

In the Valley, Sheridan moved further north towards the Potomac and Charles Town, W. Va., Gen. Early following towards Bunker Hill.

In the Petersburg lines, Warren's Fifth Corps moved to the left flank of the Federal lines and occupied more than a mile of the railroad going to Weldon, N.C., which was one of the vital supply links for Richmond. Warren, after getting astride the railroad, turned towards Petersburg, fighting his way through densely wooded areas in a heavy rain. Confederate Gen. Henry Heth's division pressured the Federals enough to cause a halt for the night, at least.

In Richmond the sound of the guns could be distinctly heard both from the east and the south but their meaning was unclear.

AUGUST 21 SUNDAY

There were many red faces in Memphis when Gen. Nathan Bedford Forrest and two thousand of his cavalry entered the city in the early-morning hours and nearly captured Federal Generals Hurlbut and Washburn in their beds. The Confederates held the city for a while and then left, going back to the countryside where they could roam freely, having no Federal opposition.

South of Petersburg, Warren still held the Weldon Railroad despite the efforts of A. P. Hill's Confederates to dislodge the Federals. In extreme heat and occasional rain, the Rebels assaulted the Union lines heavily, but were repulsed. The rail link to Petersburg and Richmond was lost, and Lee knew it. In four days the Federals had suffered about 4,500 casualties (mostly captured) out of about 20,000 engaged. Lee's losses were about 1,600 out of 14,000. Grant could afford the loss, Lee couldn't, and things would only get worse. Grant, on the 18th, had again refused to exchange prisoners, believing that such an exchange would help the South in two ways: It would gain them fighting men, and it would relieve them of feeding Union prisoners.

AUGUST 23 TUESDAY

Ft. Morgan, the last bastion at Mobile Bay, surrendered today after two weeks of heavy naval bombardment.

AUGUST 25 THURSDAY

In Georgia, Sherman began his advance to isolate Atlanta completely. He sent his blue columns to cut off the area south and east along the south side of the city towards Jonesborough.

South of Petersburg in the vicinity of Reams' Station, Va., Confederate A. P. Hill again attacked Warren's Fifth Corps with a reinforced corps. About 2,000 Federals were captured, but little else was gained. Hill returned to the Confederate lines, Warren continued tearing up railroad.

AUGUST 27 SATURDAY

At Atlanta, Sherman was nearly ready to cut the final link into the city. Hood had not been able to provide much resistance to Sherman's buildup.

AUGUST 30 TUESDAY

The Democratic Convention meeting in Chicago today named former Major Gen. George B. McClellan as their choice for President, with Thomas H. Seymour, former governor of Connecticut, as Vice-President. The platform was essentially a "peace" platform.

AUGUST 31 WEDNESDAY

George B. McClellan was formally nominated as Democratic Presidential candidate in Chicago, receiving 174 votes, the majority. The Ohio Copperhead, Clement L. Vallandigham, who had been expelled through the Union lines at Murfreesboro, Tenn., was back and attending the convention. He moved that the nomination of McClellan be made unanimous.

This illustration, from an 1864 issue of *Frank Leslie's Illustrated Newspaper*, depicts a particularly rainy moment during the Second Battle of the Weldon Railroad, also known as the Battle of Globe Tavern, August 18–21, 1864. It appeared with the following caption: "Reinforcements to Gen. Warren arriving at the terminus of Grant's railroad near Weldon Road, two miles and a half from the recently captured works."

SEPTEMBER 1864

THE PRESIDENTIAL BALLOT was becoming crowded in the North. Lincoln, McClellan and Fremont were all contesting for the privilege of serving. In the southeast around Atlanta there was little doubt that Sherman would take the city before long. Hood's tactics of constant attack had decimated his own Confederate Army of Tennessee to a mere shadow of what it had been under Joe Johnston. That, plus the infighting between Hood and Hardee, created an unhealthy atmosphere. On the James River, Grant still held Lee immobile, and Grant gave no indication of letting go any time soon. Richmond's food supply was getting lower and prices were getting higher. In the North, abundant crops promised no lack of provisions for the Union Army.

SEPTEMBER 1 THURSDAY

Atlanta was being evacuated and the munitions dumps and railroad yards were blown up by Hood's retreating Confederates. Fires broke out in the area of the explosions and little was done to extinguish them in the hurry to escape. Hood had failed gloriously in his task of holding the largest rail terminal in the South.

The Battle of Jonesborough started about noon, and within a short time the Federals had decimated two Rebel brigades, although other Confederates held their ground. At dark Hardee pulled back to Lovejoy's Station to join with Hood and the remainder of the Army of Tennessee. At the end of the second day of fighting around Jonesborough, the Confederate army was ruined.

SEPTEMBER 2 FRIDAY

From Atlanta, to Chattanooga, to Nashville, to Louisville, to Washington, D.C., the telegraph lines hummed with the message from Sherman to President Lincoln: "Atlanta is ours, and fairly won!" Lincoln could have received no better present at this time. It confirmed his faith in his commanders and showed the doubters in the North that the war could be won.

Lee, feeling the shortage of troops at Petersburg, pressured Jubal Early to return Lee's loaned troops to the Army of Northern Virginia. Lee was also concerned about the diminishing strength of his army due to battle and disease, and the fact that few replacements were arriving.

SEPTEMBER 3 SATURDAY

Sheridan, in the Valley, was moving up the Valley Pike with his now enlarged army. In response to Lee's direction, Early had detached R. H. Anderson's corps from his own army and sent it back to Petersburg. However, en route, Anderson's corps accidentally ran into a corps of Sheridan's army, much to the surprise of both generals. A sharp fight then occurred that caused Early to rethink his decision about sending Anderson back to Lee.

FACING PAGE: Gen. Sherman's order to evacuate Atlanta in September of 1864 led to a frantic rush of citizens to the rail depot. This photograph of the last train to leave the city shows rail cars piled high with personal belongings, and the travelers' wagons abandoned in the yard.

This photograph, taken by George N. Barnard, shows the ruins of the Atlanta train depot, blown up by Gen. Sherman upon his departure from town.

SEPTEMBER 4 SUNDAY

Sherman was in Atlanta and already the civilian authorities were arguing with him about who was responsible for the debris littering the streets, how they could feed the population left in the city and who had control of law and order. Hood, southeast towards Macon, was still collecting his battered units, sorting them out and counting noses.

A round of bombardment on Ft. Sumter lasting 60 days just ended, with 81 casualties on the little island fort after it had received 14,666 rounds of artillery and naval gunfire!

SEPTEMBER 5 MONDAY

Miller, Lt., 1st Ohio Heavy Artillery, eastern Tennessee, wrote:

Special courier arrived early this morning before daylight bringing the news that the detachments under the command of General Gillem had surprised the troops at General John H. Morgan's headquarters, and after a desperate encounter had captured General Morgan and Staff, besides a goodly number of prisoners, but that General Morgan was killed during the fight. The receipt of this important news caused general rejoicing among the citizens of Knoxville, and the stars and stripes could be seen flying over nearly every loyal residence. . . .

SEPTEMBER 7 WEDNESDAY

Sherman took a rather unpopular stand and ordered the evacuation of the city of Atlanta— everyone other than his army was to leave. This included some 1,600 people, comprising about 446 families who left, leaving their possessions and homes in the city. The mayor of Atlanta, Gen. Hood and everyone else who could reach Sherman protested, to no avail. Sherman said he would have enough trouble feeding his own troops and would not feed the civilians. Those who wanted to go south, could go in that direction, all others could go north. He wrote:

If the people raise a howl against my barbarity and cruelty, I will answer that war is war and not popularity-seeking.

SEPTEMBER 8 THURSDAY

At Orange, N.J., Major Gen. George B. McClellan formally accepted the Democratic nomination for President.

SEPTEMBER 11 SUNDAY

At Andersonville prison in Georgia, Private S. J. Gibson, 103rd Pennsylvania Volunteers, among a group of 1,380 prisoners, was packed 60 men to a railway car and sent from the prison as part of a prisoner exchange. The heavily guarded train arrived at Macon at 2 AM the following morning, Augusta, Ga., at 4 PM and finally arrived at Charleston on the morning of September 12.

SEPTEMBER 12 MONDAY

The "Virginia reel" played in the Valley by Sheridan and Early took a rest, much to the dismay of both Lincoln and Grant. Sheridan didn't seem to be able to get things moving.

Sherman continued the evacuation of the civilians from Atlanta amid curses, pleas and threats coming from all sides. No relenting, however, all must go.

SEPTEMBER 13 TUESDAY

In the Valley, skirmishing, however light, showed that the armies of Sheridan and Early were not entirely asleep, as Lincoln was beginning to think. In Georgia, Sherman and Hood were into the third day of a ten-day armistice, and the third day of the evacuation of civilians from Atlanta.

SEPTEMBER 14 WEDNESDAY

In Atlanta the cleanup and clean-out continued. Sherman's troops were restoring the rail link to Chattanooga and the civilians in the city were still evacuating.

This drawing by Alfred R. Waud, to which he gave the legend "Chasing the Rebs through Strasburg" and dated September 19–21, 1864, depicts the Union army under Philip Sheridan pursuing Jubal Early's Confederate troops through Strasburg, Va., at the northern end of the Shenandoah Valley.

SEPTEMBER 16 FRIDAY

At Verona, Miss., Nathan Bedford Forrest started out with about 4,500 cavalry and mounted infantry to operate against Sherman's communications in northern Alabama and middle Tennessee. This particular expedition would last about a month. At Atlanta, the evacuation went on and on.

SEPTEMBER 17 SATURDAY

John Charles Frémont, "Pathfinder," businessman, Major General of Union forces, big spender from the West and, lately, Radical Republican presidential nominee, withdrew his name from the ballot for the November elections. Frémont later said he withdrew to keep the Republicans from splitting the ticket and thereby giving the election to McClellan. Though this was suspect at the time, it may have been true.

Jubal Early, now weakened by the loss of R. H. Anderson's corps, moved down the Valley towards Martinsburg and the Baltimore and Ohio Railroad, which had been repaired after his last track-bending party. Early had about 12,000 men against Sheridan's nearly 40,000.

SEPTEMBER 18 SUNDAY

In the Valley, Early sent a portion of his small force from Bunker Hill north to Martinsburg, where the Confederates drove in the Federal cavalry, and then pulled back to Bunker Hill. Sheridan ordered an advance up the Valley Pike, hoping to catch the separated elements of Early's force.

SEPTEMBER 19 MONDAY

Things were finally moving in the Valley. Sheridan sent his 40,000 troops against Early's 12,000 north of Winchester, Va. The main force of Sheridan's infantry drove up the Valley Pike around Berryville and hit the Confederates hard. Confederate Gen. Robert E. Rodes was mortally wounded during the action that saw the Confederates drive into a gap in the Federal line. The Federals held and drove the Rebels back. The Union cavalry drove Gen. Breckinridge's division from north of the city to a new line east of Winchester. About 4:30, Sheridan ordered another advance, and Early withdrew up the Valley. Federal casualties were 4,000 out of 40,000. Confederate losses were proportionately heavier, 3,921 out of about 12,000. Early retreated with a much-weakened force.

SEPTEMBER 21 WEDNESDAY

In the Valley at Strasburg, Sheridan advanced on Early's fortifications on Fisher's Hill. There was fighting in the town of Strasburg, at Fisher's Hill, and at Front Royal. The fighting at Front Royal was to prevent the Federals from entering Luray Valley. After dark, Sheridan sent Gen. Crook with one of the Federal corps to the right and around the left flank of the Confederates, to a position of attack. The pressure on Early was building.

SEPTEMBER 22 THURSDAY

At Fisher's Hill, Sheridan was poised to attack Early's diminished forces as soon as Crook got into position on Early's left flank. Late in the afternoon, Crook's Federals came boiling over the Rebel entrenchments, taking them in the rear and the flank. The Union troops in front attacked at the same time across the Tumbling Run ravine and up Fisher's Hill. Early lost 1,235 men from his steadily diminishing force.

SEPTEMBER 24 SATURDAY

In the Valley, Sheridan turned to burning crops, barns and anything else usable to the Confederacy, while he slowly advanced up the Valley towards Early. Smoke columns marked the progress of the blue-clad columns as they advanced. Early needed everything, but mostly men, and nothing was in sight.

SEPTEMBER 27 TUESDAY

Sterling Price was still skirmishing around Arca-

dia. At Ft. Davidson, Pilot Knob, Mo., Brig. Gen. Thomas Ewing evacuated the fort after holding Sterling Price off with only 1,200 men. At Centralia, Mo., a small guerrilla force under the command of "Bloody Bill" Anderson, one of the more vicious of the Confederate guerrilla leaders, attacked the town. The force included such notables as George Todd and Frank and Jesse James. Twenty-four unarmed soldiers were murdered at Centralia, and when Federal troops came to rescue the town, they were ambushed, and 116 of them were killed.

SEPTEMBER 30 FRIDAY

Ft. Harrison, north of the James River, and on the Richmond defense line, was now in Union hands and, despite repeated counterattacks by the Confederate troops under Lee, would remain Union. The Confederacy now constructed new works to face Ft. Harrison and these new works were occupied rapidly.

South of Petersburg, Grant sent Meade to extend the Federal line to include the South Side Railroad and the crossings of the Appomattox River. There was considerable fighting and confusion at Peebles' Farm when Confederate General A. P. Hill drove his corps in between the two Federal corps of Warren and Parke. The Union line held and the two Union corps finally joined, causing the Confederates to spread their line a little thinner.

OCTOBER 1864

THE AUTUMN OF THE FOURTH YEAR of the war brought good news for the North when Atlanta fell. The relative quiet along the Petersburg lines was also welcome. No great losses of Union troops had occurred in the Army of the Potomac for several weeks. Sherman seemed to have things in hand, despite the harassment of Forrest and Wheeler. Among the camps, the evenings were getting cooler, the mosquitoes had mostly disappeared and the

Maj. Gen. Philip Henry Sheridan poses with his generals in front of his tent in 1864. From left to right, they are: Henry E. Davies, David McMurtrie Gregg, Sheridan, Wesley Merritt, Alfred Torbert and James H. Wilson.

mornings were very brisk. The troops thought of winter camp.

OCTOBER 2
SUNDAY

At Augusta, Ga., President Davis appointed Gen. P. G. T. Beauregard over the armies of Hood and Taylor in the west. Beauregard was not to interfere with tactical operations, except when he was personally on the field.

OCTOBER 3
MONDAY

Sherman was finally forced to pay some attention to both Hood and Forrest and began to send troops from Atlanta to cope with the problem. Gen. George H. Thomas had been sent to Nashville to organize the defenses in the event that Hood headed in that direction.

President Davis, arriving in Columbia, S.C., made a speech in which he said " . . . I see no chance for Sherman to escape from a defeat or a disgraceful retreat."

Things were fairly quiet both at Petersburg and in the Valley, for a change. Lee's defenders kept diminishing, as they were wounded, killed or taken prisoner. Desertions were on the rise also, as the men slipped through the pickets at night and went to the Union lines.

OCTOBER 4 TUESDAY

Barber, Sgt., Co. C, 15th Illinois Volunteer Infantry, Ackworth, Ga., wrote:

As daylight began to approach and still the enemy remained quiet, Captain Kenyon said that if we were to get a fight out of those rebels, we would have to go out and meet them. . . . We marched boldly up

On October 1, 1864, the British blockade runner *Condor*, with Confederate agent Mrs. Rose O'Neal Greenhow (1817–64) aboard, was run aground by the USS *Niphon* near New Inlet, N.C. Mrs. Greenhow, shown here in a photograph taken after 1855, was carrying dispatches and a bag containing $2,000 in gold around her neck. Fearing capture, she demanded that a boat take her ashore. During the attempt, the boat capsized, drowning her in the surf.

and drove in their light picket and marched up within full view of their camp. They were not yet astir . . . but our vehement attack soon roused them from their repose and some fell before our destructive fire before they had time to form their lines. When they were fully aroused, we saw a large army spread out before us. To oppose this host, we had barely one hundred and fifty men. . . .

I now stole cautiously forward in advance of my men to get a better view of the position. A fierce yell now broke forth and I knew that the rebels were making a charge. . . . A shower of bullets rattled around me, two passing through my clothes. I made a desperate effort and got behind the cover of a house beyond, halted and discharged my gun into the advancing foe and then rejoined my comrades who were already sheltered by our frail defense. . . .

The rebels did not seem disposed to attack us openly while in our fortresses, but they were not idle. They were rapidly surrounding us . . . we saw a long line of troops emerge and a large force of cavalry march in our rear, but more fearful than all, a battery had been placed within easy range of our works and in fifteen minutes could level our defense to the earth, but with a reckless courage, we still fought on. Now was seen a horseman mounted on a white steed advancing towards us, waving a white flag. On the instant, the firing ceased, and we waited anxiously to know our fate. . . the maddening shout rang out that we had been surrendered. I hastened back and found the other boys boiling over with rage at the manner in which they had been sold. A grand nephew of Patrick Henry, of revolutionary fame, bore in the flag of truce, accompanied with a demand for the surrender of the garrison with all stores. He gave three minutes for consideration and if the demand was not complied with, no mercy would be shown except to the sick and wounded. We could do nothing else but surrender. A useless sacrifice of blood would have been the result of a refusal. . . .

The rebel army now began to pour in by the thousand. It was General Loring's division. We were fortunate indeed in falling into that humane officer's hands. . . .

OCTOBER 7 FRIDAY

In a futile attempt to dislodge the bluecoats, Lee ordered an assault on the Union lines along the Darbytown and New Market roads. In Missouri, Sterling Price was in the vicinity of Jefferson City, the capital, skirmishing around the area.

In Georgia, there was fighting at Dallas, as Sherman moved to counter Hood's cutting of the railroad.

OCTOBER 8 SATURDAY

Barber, Sgt., Co. C, 15th Illinois Volunteer Infantry, en route to prison camp, Georgia, wrote:

. . . We indulged in the hope all along that a speedy exchange of prisoners would be made and we would be free soon. Had we known that we were going to Andersonville prison pen, we would not have gone so quietly along. . . .

OCTOBER 10 MONDAY

In the Shenandoah Valley, Sheridan moved to a position straddling the Valley Pike near Cedar Creek and held, awaiting developments. Early was coming down the Valley.

OCTOBER 11 TUESDAY

The elections in the North were showing a strong Republican trend, with gains made in several congressional races and the reelection of Indiana Gov. Oliver P. Morton. Lincoln haunted the War Department telegraph office to get the election returns.

Barber, Sgt., Co. C, 15th Illinois Volunteer Infantry, Andersonville Prison, Ga., wrote:

At 4 o'clock PM the Georgia Hell, which clutched in its iron grasp ten thousand Union soldiers, was seen in the distance. We were marched up to the commandant's headquarters, Captain Wirz, where a rigid search was performed before we were put inside the stockade. This devil in human shape, Wirz. . . .

About sundown we were marched to the outside gate of hell. . . . Its huge doors swung open to admit us and we were in the presence of—I do not know what to call them. It was evident that they were once human beings, but hunger, sickness, exposure and dirt had so transformed them that they more resembled walking skeletons, painted black. . . . Almost the first cry that greeted our ears was "fresh fish," then eager questions as to where we came from, whether there was any prospect of exchange. How eagerly would they watch for the least gleam of

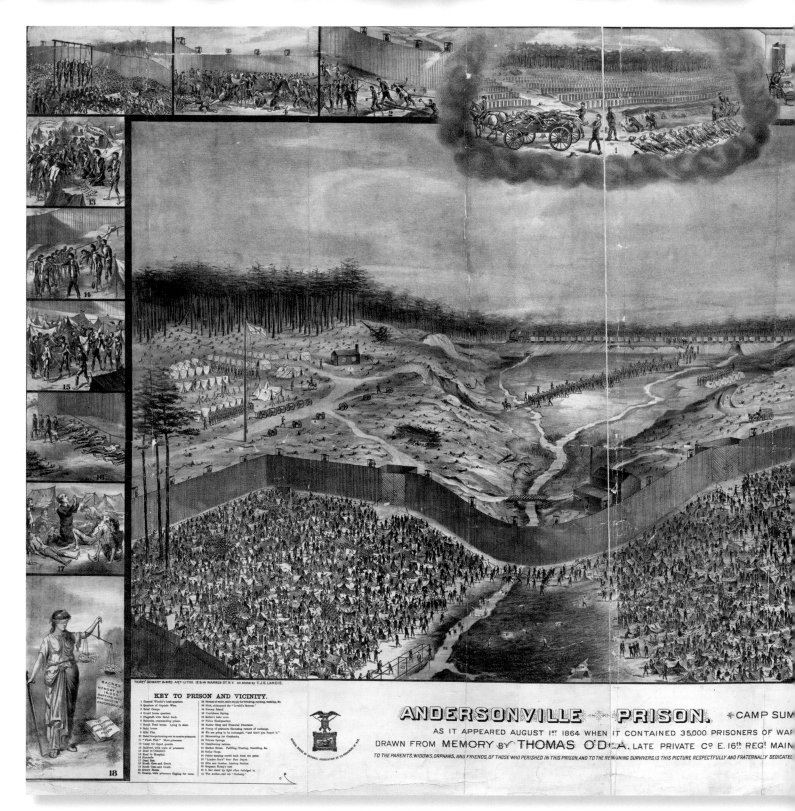

KEY TO PRISON AND VICINITY.

ANDERSONVILLE PRISON. CAMP SUM

AS IT APPEARED AUGUST 1st 1864 WHEN IT CONTAINED 35,000 PRISONERS OF WAR

DRAWN FROM MEMORY BY THOMAS O'DEA, LATE PRIVATE Co E. 16th REGt MAIN

TO THE PARENTS, WIDOWS, ORPHANS, AND FRIENDS, OF THOSE WHO PERISHED IN THIS PRISON, AND TO THE REMAINING SURVIVERS, IS THIS PICTURE RESPECTFULLY AND FRATERNALLY DEDICATED

hope! . . . Such squalid, filthy wretchedness, hunger, disease, nakedness and cold, I never saw before. Thirty-five thousand souls had been crowded into this pen, filling it completely. Poorly clad and worse fed, drinking filth and slime, from one hundred to three hundred of these passed into the gate of the eternal world daily. . . .

OCTOBER 17 MONDAY

At Petersburg, Lt. Gen. James Longstreet returned to the Army of Northern Virginia after recovering from wounds received at the Wilderness in May.

OCTOBER 19 WEDNESDAY

Early this morning, while Sheridan was in Winchester looking at the town's defenses, Jubal Early's Confederates crept through the fog and surprised Sheridan's Eighth and Nineteenth Corps in an attack that sent the Federals flying down the Valley. Wright's Sixth Corps was the next victim of assault, but he held his ground fairly well for a period, falling back in an orderly fashion to north and west of Middletown. Many of the Confederates dallied in the evacuated Union camps to loot the tents and eat the breakfasts still on the cooking fires of the departed Yankees. At this point, Early had most of the artillery and ammunition and much of the equipment of Sheridan's whole force.

Sheridan arrived from Winchester at about 10:30 AM, organized his force again and attacked Early at about 4 in the afternoon. The Union attack was not expected and the troops were out to redeem themselves for running earlier that morning. Sheridan chased Early back to Fisher's Hill, with Confederate losses that reached about 2,900, including Major Gen. Stephen D. Ramseur, out of a force of 18,000. Sheridan had lost nearly 5,700 from a force of about 30,000. While Early was badly beaten, he still had proven that the Confederate Army was a dangerous adversary.

This view of Andersonville Prison—also known as Camp Sumter—portrays the notorious institution as it appeared in August of 1864, when it held as many as 35,000 prisoners. The camp's supervisor, Henry Wirz, was executed in November of 1865 for war crimes.

OCTOBER 20 THURSDAY

Today, Abraham Lincoln proclaimed that the last Thursday in November would be celebrated as Thanksgiving Day. It was to be a national holiday of "Thanksgiving and praise to our beneficent Father who dwelleth in the Heavens."

Barber, Sgt., Co. C, 15th Illinois Volunteer Infantry, Andersonville Prison, Ga., wrote:

> Was on fatigue this morning, filling up old wells. Some of the detail carried out the dead to the dead-house. It is very shocking to human feelings the way the dead are disposed of. They are piled up in a wagon like so much wood, taken to holes dug for them and piled in, with no respect for decency or humanity.

OCTOBER 26 WEDNESDAY

In one of the most daring operations of the war, Lt. William Barker Cushing, USN, and fourteen men went after the ironclad ram CSS *Albemarle*. Cushing had designed, and then had built, two 32-foot steam picket launches, each fitted with a 14-foot spar to which was fitted a torpedo, and each had a 12-pound howitzer mounted in the bow. One of the boats had been lost to the Confederates on the night of October 8, the other was to be used for the raid. The launch left at darkness for the *Albemarle*, but ran aground, and most of the night was spent getting her off and refloated. The attack was postponed until the night of the 27th.

At Decatur, Ala., Hood demonstrated against the Union force holding the town and then proceeded on west. In the west, Pleasanton gave up chasing Price and moved his Federal cavalry to Ft. Scott, Kans., Curtis continuing the pursuit. "Bloody Bill" Anderson was killed in an ambush set by Federal troops.

OCTOBER 27 THURSDAY

In one of the last major actions before troops settled into winter quarters, the Federals took another stab at capturing the South Side Railroad. Two Union corps, Warren's and Hancock's, numbering nearly 17,000, were met by Confederates, at Hatcher's Run, under Heth and Mahone, with Hampton's cavalry thrown in for good measure. As a part of a diversion to the attack at Hatcher's

The operation at Hatcher's Run, Va., on October 27, 1864, was to be the last service with the Army of the Potomac for Gen. Winfield Scott Hancock (1824–86). He was later assigned to Sheridan's former command in the Shenandoah Valley. In 1880, Hancock received the Democratic nomination for president, but was defeated in the election by Republican James Garfield.

Run, the Army of the James skirmished with the Confederates north of Petersburg, towards Richmond at Fair Oaks, and on the Darbytown Road. The Union troops attacked, the Rebels repulsed the attack, and everyone went home to settle in the thirty-five miles of trenches, redoubts, mudholes and louse-ridden hovels for the winter.

∞ NOVEMBER 1864 ∞

THE PRESIDENTIAL ELECTIONS rather than the war seemed to be on everyone's mind at the beginning of the month. However, the two were inseparable. Lincoln's stance was well known—restoration of the Union. McClellan's stand on this issue was not clear in the minds of many people, North and South, since he had never really said what he would do to restore the Union. The soldiers were voting in their units and the ballots were being taken to their home states for counting. Would these war-weary veterans vote Lincoln out of office in the middle of this war?

NOVEMBER 1 TUESDAY

Nathan Bedford Forrest had captured a gunboat (*Undine*) and two transports (*Venus* and *Cheeseman*) on October 30th, and Forrest now went up the Tennessee River, his artillery following along the riverbanks. The goal was Johnsonville, Tenn., where the Union had a depot and a small garrison. Forrest wanted the depot, but he also wanted to get across the river.

NOVEMBER 5 SATURDAY

After a fracas between Nathan Bedford Forrest and the Union garrison at the depot at Johnsonville, Tenn., Forrest left to join Hood, going by way of Corinth, Miss. Forrest estimated that he had caused $6,700,000 worth of damage at the depot.

Barber, Sgt., Co. C, 15th Illinois Volunteer Infantry, Andersonville Prison, Ga., wrote:

Another day has passed and we still remain in this miserable pen, and get rations barely sufficient to sustain life. One year ago this evening, after nearly three years' absence, I crossed the threshold of home. Friends and plenty there surround me. How great a contrast now! . . .

NOVEMBER 7 MONDAY

In Richmond, the Second Session of the Second Congress of the Confederate States of America gathered for its meeting. It would also be its last. The message from President Davis was unduly optimistic in tone, playing down such things as the loss of Atlanta. He also sent a message to Gen. John Bell Hood urging him to beat Sherman, so Hood would have no obstruction on a Confederate march to the Ohio River.

NOVEMBER 8 TUESDAY

Abraham Lincoln was reelected President, and Andrew Johnson elected Vice President, by a 55 percent majority of the popular vote of the people of the United States. Lincoln–Johnson received 212 electoral votes to McClellan's 21. Although the people of the North were not happy with the bloodshed, they were interested in retaining the Union. Interestingly, the soldiers' vote was almost entirely for Lincoln. The war would continue.

NOVEMBER 9 WEDNESDAY

There was much troop movement in Tennessee as the contestants set up the pawns for the next game. There was action at Shoal Creek near Florence, and some skirmishing near Ft. Henry. Gen. George Thomas's army buildup at Nashville was progressing.

At Kingston, Ga., a major decision had been made concerning Sherman's armies. Sherman would now emulate Grant's Vicksburg campaign when Grant crossed the Mississippi and plunged into the interior of Mississippi towards Jackson without long supply trains, living off the land.

First, the army had to be reorganized. The four corps were to be divided into two "wings," the left and right.

Second, there would be no long "trains" in this army. Wagons would be reserved for ammunition and other "essentials," and all comforts were to be left behind. A liberal policy of acquiring draft animals, etc., en route was established, as was a policy for drawing rations from the local populace.

NOVEMBER 10 THURSDAY

In the Valley, Jubal Early's force was now so weak that it had little effect. Early was, however, still there trying.

NOVEMBER 12 SATURDAY

Sherman's army was tearing Atlanta down except for the houses and churches. Sherman's force of 60,000 men and 5,500 artillery was ready to march.

NOVEMBER 13 SUNDAY

In the Valley, Jubal Early's weak force was further weakened when parts of his troops were sent to Richmond to bolster Lee's shrinking army. Although not as famous as Jackson's Valley Campaign, Early's defense of the Valley was better conducted than Jackson's and Early faced a larger Federal force that was more experienced than it was in 1862. Jackson's campaign of 1862, while brilliantly executed, could not compare to the efforts made by Early, who had fought 72 engagements and marched nearly 1,700 miles in a five-month span. The end of this campaign, however, was approaching.

NOVEMBER 14 MONDAY

McClellan, defeated in his race for President, resigned his commission as a Major General. The resignation was readily accepted by Lincoln. Sheri-

Currier & Ives printed this campaign banner for the ultimately victorious Abraham Lincoln–Andrew Johnson Republican presidential campaign in 1864.

dan was promoted to Major General in the Regular Army, ensuring his employment after the war.

NOVEMBER 15 TUESDAY

Sherman's men destroyed what little of value was left in Atlanta, leaving an emotional scar that never healed.

Nichols, Major, USA, Sherman's Hdqtrs., Atlanta, Ga., wrote:

A grand and awful spectacle is presented to the beholder in this beautiful city, now in flames. By order, the chief engineer has destroyed powder and fire in all the store-houses, depot buildings and machine shops. The heaven is one expanse of lurid fire; the air is filled with flying, burning cinders; buildings covering two hundred acres are in ruins or in flames; every instant there is the sharp detonation or the smothered booming sound of exploding shells and powder concealed in the buildings, and then the sparks and flame shoot away up into the black and red roof, scattering cinders far and wide. . . . The city . . . exists no more. . . .

NOVEMBER 18 FRIDAY

Barber, Sgt., Co. C, 15th Illinois Volunteer Infantry, prison camp near Millen, Ga., wrote:

The sick continue to leave daily. About three thousand have left. By paying the doctor a good sum, from twenty to fifty dollars in greenbacks, he will put a person on the sick list, and for this they will get out of prison. Those who are fortunate enough to have money and who are disposed to use it in this manner succeed in getting out, and many of the sick are actually crowded out to give place to those who have bought their freedom. The doctors are making quite a speculating game of it.

DESTRUCTION OF THE DEPOTS, PUBLIC BUILDINGS, AND MANUFACTORIES AT ATLANTA, GEO

November 15, 1864.

NOVEMBER 21 MONDAY

Hood moved with about 30,000 infantry and over 8,000 cavalry, including Forrest's, from Florence, Ala., to Tennessee. Hood's first objective was to get between Schofield at Pulaski and Thomas at Nashville and to try to defeat the Federals piecemeal.

Sherman took on Georgia State Militia at Griswoldville and gave them a severe thumping. There was other fighting along the route of march, but nothing to slow it down.

Barber, Sgt., Co. C, 15th Illinois Volunteer Infantry, Savannah, Ga., wrote:

> All the sick have been removed. Just before dark this evening, very unexpectedly to me, Rollin's name and mine were called, with orders to get ready to march immediately. . . . At three o'clock PM we embarked on board one of our ships and passed entirely out of rebel hands. We had been in their power for forty-seven days.

NOVEMBER 24 THURSDAY

In Tennessee, the footrace to Columbia was won by Schofield's two corps, with Gen. Jacob D. Cox arriving just ahead of the Confederates. Forrest's cavalry, leading Hood's army, was repulsed by the strong Union infantry. Schofield also secured a bridge crossing on the Duck River on the road to Nashville.

NOVEMBER 25 FRIDAY

In New York City rebel arsonists were arrested with incendiary chemical "bombs," and their plot to burn the city was foiled. They had managed to set fire to several hotels and to Barnum's Museum, but all was contained.

NOVEMBER 26 SATURDAY

Sherman moved his wings forward from Sandersville, Ga., slowly waiting until the tail caught up.

These scenes of the November 1864 destruction of Atlanta were published in *Harper's Weekly* the following January.

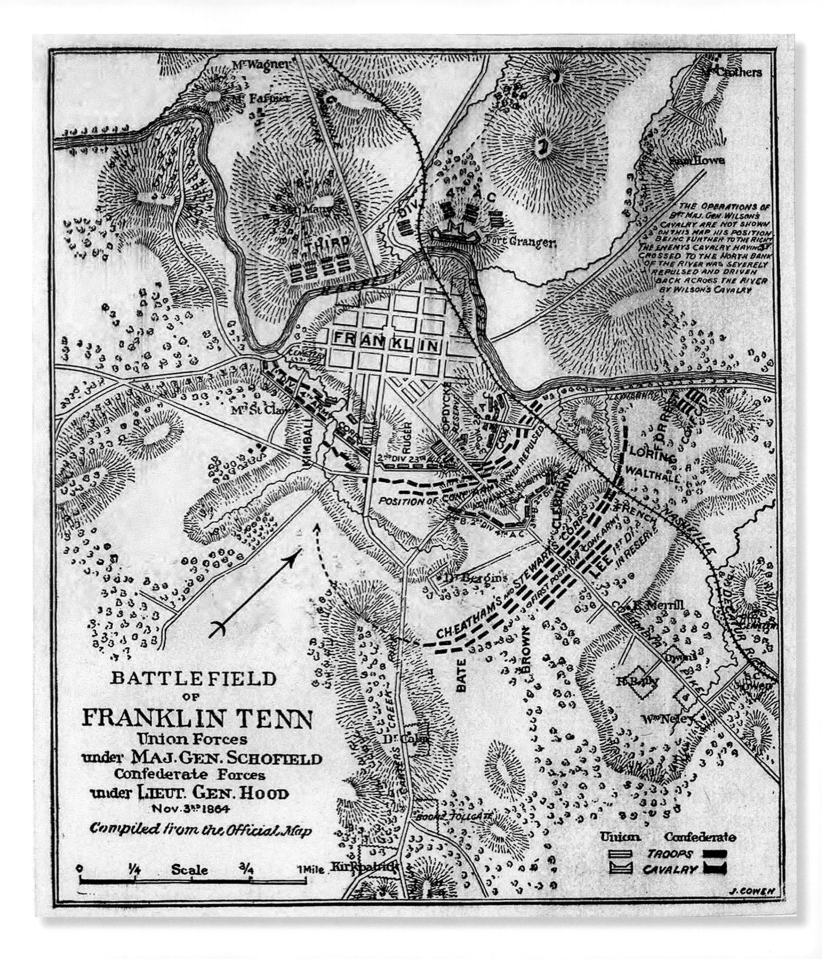

BATTLEFIELD
OF
FRANKLIN TENN
Union Forces
under MAJ. GEN. SCHOFIELD
Confederate Forces
under LIEUT. GEN. HOOD
Nov. 3rd 1864

Compiled from the Official Map

0   ¼   Scale   ¾   1 Mile

THE OPERATIONS OF
BT. MAJ. GEN. WILSON'S
CAVALRY ARE NOT SHOWN
ON THIS MAP. HIS POSITION
BEING FURTHER TO THE RIGHT
THE ENEMY'S CAVALRY HAVING
CROSSED TO THE NORTH BANK
OF THE RIVER WAS SEVERELY
REPULSED AND DRIVEN
BACK ACROSS THE RIVER
BY WILSON'S CAVALRY

Union   Confederate
TROOPS
CAVALRY

J. COWEN

NOVEMBER 27 SUNDAY

Faulty intelligence from the cavalry caused Schofield to move all his men across the Duck River into the trenches dug on the north side at Columbia, Tenn. Schofield believed Hood was across the river and on the Union's flank.

At Waynesborough, Ga., the Federal and Rebel cavalry had a set-to for a couple of days, as Wheeler and Kilpatrick clashed. Sherman was moving again.

NOVEMBER 29 TUESDAY

A near-miracle occurred between Columbia's Duck River crossings and Spring Hill, Tenn. Forrest's cavalry had crossed the Duck River last evening and were skirmishing around Spring Hill by noon. Schofield was still on the Duck River line disengaging his troops and sending them north along the Pike between Columbia and Spring Hill. The Pike was being held open by Gen. David S. Stanley's Union troops. By some quirk, all of Schofield's men went up the Pike without being attacked by Hood's Confederates. The entire Federal force, wagon trains and all, escaped to take positions near Franklin.

Sherman, in an attempt to divert Hardee's attention towards Augusta, had sent Kilpatrick in that direction while Sherman continued his march. The objective was to get across the Ogeechee River on November 30 without major opposition. Kilpatrick was also aiming at the Confederate prison at Millen, Ga., and the possibility of freeing the Union prisoners there.

NOVEMBER 30 WEDNESDAY

Schofield was faced with the problem of repairing bridges to get his wagon trains up to Nashville, so while he waited, he would have to deal with Hood. Hood came swinging up the Pike from Columbia, swung his troops to the left and right, into line of

The Battle of Franklin, Tenn., was fought on November 30, 1864. This map of the battlefield appeared in an 1887 issue of *Century Illustrated* magazine.

battle, and attacked the well-fortified Yankees about 4 PM. The Confederate line came in well, drove the Federals back to the Federals' second prepared line and then pulled back. The casualties for the Rebels were very heavy—nearly 6,300 out of a force of 27,000. Among the casualties were six Confederate generals: States Rights Gist, H. B. Granbury, John Adams, O. F. Strahl and the incomparable Patrick Cleburne. John C. Carter was mortally wounded. The dead generals were all laid on the porch of a local house. Hood also lost 54 regimental commanders killed, wounded or captured. His army was almost decimated. He now had fewer than 18,000 effective infantrymen.

Federal losses were about 2,300 from nearly 27,000 engaged. At night, Schofield pulled his men out of Franklin and headed up the road to Nashville.

∞ DECEMBER 1864 ∞

ALTHOUGH THE PETERSBURG–RICHMOND area was quiet, there was action enough elsewhere. At Nashville, Hood was approaching from the south with his battered army, hoping for a miracle. Sherman was lost in the wilds of Georgia, or so it seemed, since no one had heard from him for a while, and was probably heading for Savannah.

On the political front things were still up in the air. Some were still calling for a negotiated settlement to the war, others opted to pursue it at all costs. In Richmond the picture looked gloomy.

DECEMBER 1 THURSDAY

In Tennessee, Major Gen. Schofield entered the Union lines at Nashville after eluding Hood's forces at Spring Hill, Columbia and Franklin, Tenn. Gen. George H. Thomas had formed his defenses for Nashville in a semicircle, with both flanks resting on the Cumberland River. Hood brought his much-reduced and weary army to the front of Thomas's

This drawing by artist William Waud was made on or around December 2, 1864. It depicts the Thunderbolt Battery, a Confederate defensive fortification along the Savannah River.

defenses to survey the options. Hood could now attack Thomas, or bypass Nashville in a Confederate drive to the Ohio River, leaving Thomas in his rear, a dangerous situation for Hood.

Barber, Sgt., Co. C, 15th Illinois Volunteer Infantry, parole camp, Annapolis, Md., wrote:

> Received two months' pay this afternoon, thirty-six dollars. The officers of this camp labor day and night to get the soldiers' papers straightened out.

DECEMBER 2 FRIDAY

Hood arrived outside the fortifications of Nashville today and began establishing his own lines, conforming to Thomas's. Halleck, in Washington, ordered Thomas out of his defenses to attack Hood. Thomas waited for developments.

Sherman turned his ponderous blue columns from an eastward course towards Augusta to a more southerly direction, pivoting on Millen, Ga., and heading in six columns almost directly south. Until this time, Hardee had no idea of the direction of Sherman's march, except that it seemed towards Augusta. Prior to this, Kilpatrick's cavalry, accompanied by Gen. Davis, had screened Sherman's movements effectively. The advance was now on Savannah, down the peninsula formed by the Savannah and Ogeechee Rivers.

DECEMBER 3 SATURDAY

Hood had now settled his positions around Nashville, sending Forrest's cavalry to probe the Union lines and to attempt a blockade of the river downstream from the city. Federal authorities in Washington pressured Thomas to attack Hood's inferior force. Thomas again awaited developments.

Sherman was in Millen, Ga., with the Seventeenth Corps. Sherman, looking upon the remains of the prisoner-of-war stockade at Millen, told his cavalry commander Judson Kilpatrick to completely destroy the railroads around Millen. The four corps of Sherman's army now began to converge towards Savannah, and Sherman cocked an ear to hear the sound of the sea.

With the increased pressure on Savannah from both Sherman and the blockading fleet, more thought was given to the railroad link from Savannah to Charleston. Capt. W. W. Hunter, CSN, wrote Lt. Joel S. Kennard, CSN, CSS *Macon*:

> The Charleston and Savannah Railway Bridge at the Savannah River is a very important point to defend, and, should it become necessary, endeavor to be in position there to defend it. In order to do so, and also to patrol the Savannah River, watch carefully the state of the river, and do not be caught aground or be cut off from the position at the bridge.

DECEMBER 4 SUNDAY

At Nashville, Thomas still waited to attack Hood, although the Union general was strongly urged to do so by Lincoln and Grant. Hood's cavalry had become aggressive, especially Forrest.

DECEMBER 5 MONDAY

In Tennessee, Hood sent Forrest's cavalry on a demonstration for three days towards Murfreesboro. The cavalry could not capture the town from the Union defenders, so they returned to Nashville.

Sherman, still on the march towards Savannah, wasn't getting much sleep. One of his officers, Major Henry Hitchcock, reported that he often saw Sherman around the camp in the early hours " . . . poking around the camp-fire . . . bare feet in slippers, red flannel drawers . . . woolen shirt, old dressing gown with blue cloth (½ cloak cape)." On the march he would often lay next to the road where the troops were marching and take a cat nap after rising at 3:30 or 4 AM. He never wore boots, always low-cut shoes and only one spur.

DECEMBER 6 TUESDAY

At Nashville, Thomas had received a telegram from an angry Grant directing him to attack Hood at once.

On December 6, 1864, the USS *Neosho* went down the Cumberland River from Nashville to engage Forrest's artillery batteries located at Bell's Mills. In two and one-half hours of engagement, the *Neosho* was struck more than 100 times with no damage to the ship. This drawing of the battle was sketched by Adam Rohe.

George N. Barnard's December 1864 photograph of Fort McAllister, near Savannah, Ga., looking up the Ogeechee River

Grant feared that Hood would slip past Thomas and head for the Ohio River. Thomas replied that he would attack at once without waiting for cavalry remounts.

Nichols, Major, USA, Ogeechee Church, Ga., wrote:

> A significant feature of this campaign, which has not before been mentioned in this diary, received a marked illustration yesterday. Except in a few instances, private residences have not been destroyed by the soldiers, but there has been at least one exception, for an excellent reason. Yesterday we passed the plantation of a Mr. Stubbs. The house, cotton-gin, press, corn-ricks, stables, everything that could burn was in flames, and in the door-yard lay the dead bodies of several bloodhounds, which had been used to track and pull down Negroes and our escaped prisoners. And wherever our army has passed, every thing in the shape of a dog has been killed. The soldiers and officers are determined that no more flying fugitives, white men or Negroes, shall be followed by hounds that come within reach of their powder and ball.

DECEMBER 7 WEDNESDAY

At Nashville, Thomas had still not attacked Hood, and Grant informed Secretary of War Stanton that if Thomas did not attack promptly, Thomas should be removed from command. Forrest was at Murfreesboro engaged in some severe fighting trying to overwhelm the Federal garrison.

Sherman, getting closer to Savannah, was engaged in skirmishing all along his advance, but there were no heavy engagements.

DECEMBER 8 THURSDAY

Sherman could now hear the sea, beckoning like a siren. His soldiers had to contend with "land torpedoes" which had been planted in the roads leading to Savannah. The Union army considered these devices as proper when used around fortifications, etc., because they were something to be expected. Their use on the roads was considered barbaric and "simple murder." Sherman, coming upon a young lieutenant whose foot had been blown off by one such device, went into a rage. Major Gen. Blair had ordered a group of Confederate prisoners to dig up the remaining torpedoes and the prisoners were deadly afraid to do so, understandably. They begged Sherman to interfere and he flatly refused, telling the Confederates that their people had planted them there to assassinate Union troops, rather than fighting them fairly, and they, the prisoners, must remove them; if they were blown up, he didn't care.

DECEMBER 9 FRIDAY

Sherman's march to the sea was almost complete. He was on the outskirts of Savannah! Grant issued an order relieving Gen. Thomas of command at Nashville, replacing him with Schofield. Grant suspended the order when Thomas said that he planned to attack on the 10th, but a heavy storm with freezing rain had made movement impossible. Grant waited.

DECEMBER 10 SATURDAY

There was more action around Petersburg and the Weldon Road as Grant kept the pot boiling.

Sherman was in front of Savannah, and his cavalry was probing the city's defenses. Gen. Hardee, with somewhat fewer than 18,000 men defending the city, had flooded the rice fields of the area, leaving only a few roads available for the approach. Sherman, after a reconnaissance, ordered investigation of Ft. McAllister, south of the city, guarding the Ogeechee River, as the obvious approach to the sea. While rations were not short, forage for the horses and other draft animals was quickly used up, and some source was required.

DECEMBER 11 SUNDAY

Sherman was busy laying siege to Savannah and obtaining a link to the sea, where the Union Navy waited. The Confederates had destroyed the bridge across the Ogeechee River to Ft. McAllister; the bridge had to be rebuilt. Sherman's troops fell to with a will and, using axes to fell trees and parts of dismantled houses, started rebuilding the 1,000-foot bridge.

DECEMBER 12 MONDAY

Sherman was preparing for the assault on Ft. McAllister; the 1,000-foot-long replacement bridge was almost complete.

Rear Admiral John Dahlgren wrote to his friend President Lincoln, reporting news that the country had eagerly awaited. Sherman was at Savannah! Dahlgren wrote:

> I have the great satisfaction of conveying to you information of the arrival of General Sherman near Savannah, with his army in fine spirits. . . . This memorable event must be attended by still more memorable consequences, and I congratulate you most heartily on its occurrence.

Sherman would now use naval ships to resupply his army rather than rely on rail links.

In Tennessee, the weather was still icy, and no movement was possible on the roads. Again, both Grant and Thomas waited.

DECEMBER 13 TUESDAY

The attack on Ft. McAllister was made across the 1,000-foot bridge by the Fifteenth Corps at about 5 PM. Sherman and several officers had climbed atop a rice mill to watch the show. At his elevated platform, Sherman could see the sea; that long-sought goal was there!

As Sherman watched the Fifteenth Corps go into the attack, a man yelled, "A steamboat!" Sure enough, black smokestacks and the Union flag were seen coming upstream on the river. A signal flag on the steamer asked: "Who are you?" Sherman's signalman replied: "Gen. Sherman." The boat then asked: "Is Ft. McAllister taken yet?" Sherman replied: "No, but it will be in a minute."

The link to the sea was open and Savannah was doomed.

At Nashville, the weather was still icy and everyone waited. Grant had ordered Gen. John Logan to Nashville to relieve Thomas if the latter did not attack when the weather cleared.

DECEMBER 14 WEDNESDAY

Gen. George Thomas, in Nashville, decided to attack Hood on the 15th, and so notified Grant.

Sherman spent a busy day visiting the fleet and Major Gen. Foster, commander of the Union Army troops in the area. The message was on its way north that Sherman was safe and on the coast.

DECEMBER 15 THURSDAY

The first day of the Battle of Nashville began when George H. Thomas's blue lines slowly edged their way through heavy fog and, with about 35,000 men, struck Hood's left. Hood's right flank was held in position by more Union forces. The Federal onslaught was almost irresistible, driving the gray-clad veterans more than a mile to the rear, where they held on the Franklin Pike, but barely. The weather was foul, with melting ice. Both lines were adjusted somewhat during the night.

DECEMBER 16 FRIDAY

The second day of the Battle of Nashville was fought today. At 6 o'clock in a morning filled with rain and snow, Thomas's blue-clad troops moved into the assault. The Confederate right was pressed back and then held at the line of its main entrenchments. The Union cavalry got in behind Hood's left flank and the Confederates' rear was threatened. Late in the afternoon the Federals made their main assault and the firing became almost continuous for a time. The Confederate left caved in first, moving back, then the center folded and left the right to play rear guard. Thomas described the action as the Confederates being "hopelessly broken." The Confederate rear guard held off the pursuing Federals until late in the afternoon, when the entire line gave way and the Rebels fled the field. Hood lost most of his artillery and many of his wagons.

Thomas had engaged about 55,000 men and suffered 3,600 casualties, mostly wounded (2,562). Hood's force had a little over 20,000 men, and he lost 4,500 captured and another 1,500 killed and wounded. The Army of Tennessee was an army in name only, having been almost decimated by Hood's actions since he had taken command in Atlanta.

Thomas destroyed the last major threat to Kentucky and the Ohio River, and, in the process, he saved his own career.

DECEMBER 17 SATURDAY

At Savannah, Sherman was demanding that Hardee surrender his troops in Savannah. Hardee demurred, planning evacuation.

This photograph, by George N. Barnard, was taken on December 16, 1864, during the Battle of Nashville. It shows the outer line of Gen. Thomas's Federal forces.

DECEMBER 18 SUNDAY

Sherman waited quietly, resupplying his troops with new uniforms, etc., while Hardee, who had refused Sherman's demand for surrender yesterday, pondered his next move. Sherman wrote Grant that he wanted to drive for Raleigh, N.C., burning and tearing up track all the way, forcing the Confederates to evacuate Richmond. For an example he related the damage done in his march from Atlanta:

> I estimate one hundred million dollars, at least twenty millions of which has inured to our advantage, and the remainder is simple waste and destruction. This may seem a hard species of warfare, but it brings the sad realities of war home to those who have been directly or indirectly instrumental in involving us in its attendant calamities.

DECEMBER 19 MONDAY

The Federal cavalry and infantry were still unable to cross the swollen Rutherford Creek north of Columbia, Tenn., making Hood safe for the time being.

In the Valley, Sheridan, at Grant's order, sent 8,000 cavalrymen under A. T. A. Torbert towards the Virginia Central Railroad and Gordonsville. This resulted in skirmishes at Gordonsville, Madison C.H., Liberty Mills and other points. Torbert returned on the 23rd without having accomplished much.

Sherman's men, waiting for orders, had time to visit the seashore, some for the first time, and to eat their fill of oysters. They ate oyster soup, oyster stew, oysters on the half shell, roasted oysters, fried oysters and roasted goose stuffed with oysters.

DECEMBER 20 TUESDAY

Sherman's demand for surrender to Hardee was coolly refused. Hardee's refusal took some iron,

Confederate General William Joseph Hardee (1815–73) evacuated the city of Savannah, Ga., on December 20, 1864.

since Hardee had only 9,089 men for duty against Sherman's nearly 62,000. Sherman, however, did not want to waste men assaulting the city on the few roads left after Hardee flooded the rice fields. Hardee evacuated Savannah. He left at night on an ingenious bridge of rice-carrying rafts strung across the river, and he headed north. Behind him he left one of the premier cities of the South to the Union and an inventory of 250 cannon and siege guns, plus 40,000 bales of cotton. Little, if any, blood had been shed; there had been only the assault on Ft. McAllister, and one skirmish of any note.

Nichols, Major, USA, Savannah, Ga., wrote:

> . . . The path by which Hardee escaped led through swamps which were previously considered impracticable. The Rebel general obtained knowledge of our movement through his spies, who swarmed in our camp.
>
> It was fortunate that our troops followed so quickly after the evacuation of the city by the enemy, for a mob had gathered in the streets, and were breaking into the stores and houses. They were with difficulty dispersed by the bayonets of our soldiers, and then, once more, order and confidence prevailed throughout the conquered city. . . .

With some sadness, Admiral David G. Farragut, hero of New Orleans and Mobile, hauled down his Admiral's pennant from the mast of the USS *Hartford*, his flagship in both adventures, and turned the ship over to the Navy Yard for repairs. The ship and the man closed their Civil War careers.

DECEMBER 21 WEDNESDAY

Gen. John W. Geary's division of the Twentieth Corps led the march into Savannah, meeting no opposition. Sherman was disappointed that he had not bagged Hardee, but was not sorry for the lives saved in the process.

Thomas's force chasing Hood was plagued by destroyed bridges, swollen streams and increasingly weary troops. It had been almost five days since they left Nashville, and the men had been in the field in rain, snow and slush enough to last them forever.

DECEMBER 22 THURSDAY

Sherman, at the urging of an aide, wrote President Lincoln a telegram to be sent at the first available station:

> I beg to present you as a Christmas gift, the city of Savannah, with one hundred and fifty heavy guns and plenty of ammunition, *also* about twenty-five thousand bales of cotton.

The Federals in pursuit of Hood's beaten Army of Tennessee found part of that army at Columbia, Tenn., and a little skirmishing developed. The weather was still cold and wet.

DECEMBER 23 FRIDAY

The Navy, not to be outdone by the Army's creation of the rank of Lieutenant General, asked that Congress create the rank of Vice Admiral, which would be equivalent to Lieutenant General. Today, Lincoln signed a bill authorizing that rank, and it was conferred on Rear Admiral David G. Farragut; he became the first Vice Admiral in U.S. history, just as he had been the first Rear Admiral.

DECEMBER 24 SATURDAY

Lincoln, at the White House, received Sherman's telegram from Savannah on Christmas Eve. His admiration of, and pride in, that red-headed general knew no bounds. Coming as it did following Thomas's victory at Nashville, it was the best Christmas of the war. Lincoln gave the news to the country as a present. The nation was ecstatic.

Sherman, in Savannah, found that he was besieged by women who wanted protection from those "Yankees." Confederate generals Hardee, Smith and McLaws had left personal letters for Sherman asking his personal interest in the welfare of their families. The wife of Gen. A. P. Stewart, one of Hood's officers, asked Sherman for special assistance, which he gladly granted. A Mrs. Sarah Davenport won Sherman over immediately when she explained that she had three sons in the Union army, three in the Southern forces and a son-in-law serving with Lee.

Sherman followed his usual policy of allowing the ministers of the local churches to pray for Jeff Davis, saying, "Yes, Jeff Davis and the devil both need it." Sherman also maintained the present political officeholders in office without interference, as long as they did nothing to damage the Union's war effort. He also ordered the opening of farmer's marketplaces throughout the city so that the people might find food. All of these things did much to offset the reputation he had developed on his march to the sea.

In Tennessee, the chase after Hood's army was just about to wind down. Hood had been losing men steadily as his retreat continued towards the Tennessee River. Rear Admiral S. P. Lee arrived with gunboats off Chickasaw, Ala., near Muscle Shoals on the Tennessee River, in an attempt to cut off Hood's retreat from Nashville. At Chickasaw, the gunboat USS *Fairy*, Acting Ensign Charles Swendson, destroyed a Confederate fort and magazine but the gunboat couldn't proceed upriver due to low water.

DECEMBER 25 SUNDAY

Hood's beaten Army of Tennessee finally reached the Tennessee River at Bainbridge. There wouldn't be much of a Christmas for these weary men.

Sherman spent Christmas in Savannah, thinking of his family, as did all his men.

DECEMBER 26 MONDAY

John Bell Hood's bone-weary men finally crossed the Tennessee River at Bainbridge, and the Army of Tennessee, for all practical purposes, passed into history. The dream to reach the Ohio River and draw Sherman out of Georgia became a hazy memory, to be remembered as a montage of long, cold marches, colder nights and periods of hellish gunfire.

Lincoln, deeply grateful for the victory at Savannah, wrote Sherman this day and sent the letter with Major Gen. John A. Logan, who was rejoining Sherman:

> MY DEAR GENERAL SHERMAN:
>
> Many, many thanks for your Christmas gift—the capture of Savannah.
>
> When you were about to leave Atlanta for the Atlantic coast, I was *anxious*, if not fearful; but feeling you were the better judge, and remembering that "nothing risked nothing gained," I did not interfere. Now the undertaking being a success, the honor is all yours, for I believe none of us went further than to acquiesce. And taking the work of General Thomas into the count, as it should be taken, it is indeed a great success. . . .
>
> Please make my grateful acknowledgments to your whole army, officers and men.
>
> Yours very truly,
>
> A. LINCOLN.

Logan's arrival brought, for the first time, information on just how close George Thomas had come to ruining his own career. Grant had gone so far as to send Logan to Nashville with orders to relieve Thomas if he did not move against Hood as soon as practical. Logan arrived just as the ice was melting, and Thomas was getting ready to advance through the slush and freezing mud. Thomas did not know that Logan had the power to relieve him, and Logan did not tell him, keeping in the background and letting Thomas win his victory.

There was talk of promoting Sherman to the rank of Lieutenant General, equal to Grant's rank. To this, Sherman responded:

> I will accept no commission that would tend to create a rivalry with Grant. I want him to hold what he has earned and got. I have all the rank I want. I would rather be an engineer of a railroad, than President of the United States. I have commanded a hundred thousand men in battle, and on the march, successfully and without confusion, and that is enough for reputation. Now, I want rest and peace, and they are only to be had through war.

DECEMBER 27 TUESDAY

The remnants of Hood's army entered Mississippi and went into camp. Hood would shortly be relieved of command.

Sherman rested and refitted in Savannah, planning his trip north through the Carolinas.

DECEMBER 30 FRIDAY

At Wilmington, N.C., Admiral David D. Porter was unhappy with Major Gen. Butler's conduct during the attack on Ft. Fisher on Christmas Day, so he wrote his old friend Grant, urging Butler's removal from command and urging that a new assault force be organized. Grant's reply was immediate: "Please hold on where you are for a few days and I will endeavor to be back again with an increased force and without the former commander." Meanwhile, Porter's guns kept up the bombardment of the fort.

DECEMBER 31 SATURDAY

In New York City, the merchants presented a gift of $50,000 in government bonds to the new Vice Admiral David G. Farragut, in appreciation of services rendered his country. This was a nice ending for the year for the hero of New Orleans and Mobile.

The ruined homes of Savannah, Ga., where Gen. Sherman ended his "March to the Sea" in December of 1864

1865

... [I] regard it as my duty to shift from myself the responsibility of any further effusion of blood, by asking of you the surrender of that portion of the C.S. Army known as the Army of Northern Virginia. ...

—Gen. U. S. Grant to Gen. Robert E. Lee, April 7, 1865

THE SOUTH WAS TEETERING on the brink of collapse in this, the beginning of the final year of war. Gone were the bright hopes and dreams of an easy separation from the United States and present were the realities—Tennessee was gone with Hood's defeat at Nashville; Sherman was in Savannah and Atlanta lay in ruins; one serious attempt to close Wilmington had been made and another was sure to come. Peace initiatives were discussed, but nothing happened. Where, or even when, would it end?

JANUARY 1 SUNDAY

After the fiasco on Christmas Day 1864, when Major Gen. Ben Butler's troops had been put ashore to assault Ft. Fisher at Wilmington, and had then been withdrawn immediately with only a halfhearted effort made, Admiral David D. Porter wrote to Grant asking that another expedition be organized but that *another* commander be assigned. Grant immediately replied in the affirmative, and a new expedition was begun. Porter, to support the operation, began issuing orders for 66 warships to assemble off the Wilmington coast with, as he put it, "every shell that can be carried" for shore bombardment.

JANUARY 3
TUESDAY

Grant assigned Major Gen. Alfred H. Terry to command the army element of the assault on Ft. Fisher, the main bastion guarding Wilmington, N.C. In his instructions to Terry, Grant said: "I have served with Admiral Porter and know that you can

rely on his judgment and his nerve to undertake what he proposes. I would, therefore, defer to him as much as is consistent with your own responsibilities." Grant also notified Porter that Terry was coming as the commander of the army troops.

Sherman, in concert with Dahlgren, began moving some of his troops by transport from Savannah, Ga., to Beaufort, S.C., thereby flanking the Confederate troops between the two points.

JANUARY 6 FRIDAY

The passage of the Thirteenth Amendment of the Constitution was a matter of priority for Lincoln in this session of the U.S. Congress. Having failed passage before, this time it had passed the Senate and was before the House of Representatives.

Grant, finally tired of Butler's fumbling and politicking, asked Lincoln to remove Butler from command of the Army of the James. Grant, rightly so, felt that there was no confidence in Butler's ability. Butler's latest failure was on January 2, a failed attempt to build a canal at Trent's Reach near Drewry's Bluff on the James River. Immediately prior to that, he had demanded, by right of seniority, the command of the ill-fated campaign against Ft. Fisher in December 1864. That expedition was completely botched, all due to Butler's incompetence.

JANUARY 7
SATURDAY

Lincoln, who had procrastinated before about Butler's removal from active duty, finally had his fill and, at Grant's request, relieved Butler from the active list,

PRECEDING PAGES: The Soldiers' Cemetery in Alexandria, Va., seen in this c. 1865 photograph, is now called Alexandria National Cemetery. It was one of the original fourteen national cemeteries established in 1862.

ABOVE: Maj. Gen. Alfred Howe Terry (1827–90) attended Yale Law School and served as the clerk of the Superior Court of New Haven County, Ct., before joining the military. He led the Union attack on Ft. Fisher in January of 1865.

This commemorative print honors the joint resolution to abolish slavery in Missouri, which was proposed on January 11, 1864. It features the figures of Liberty (left), Justice (bottom) and Missouri (right). At Justice's feet, a white child holds a document labeled "Natural Philosophy"; a black child holds the "Rights of Man."

and the general would command no more. Controversial from beginning to end, Butler was a prime example of the political generals who permeated the beginning of the war—most of the others were long since gone. Major Gen. E. O. C. Ord was named as Butler's replacement.

JANUARY 9 MONDAY

The spies were active along the Potomac, crossing the river in India-rubber rafts, in the vicinity of Port Tobacco, as Secretary Welles advised Commander F. A. Parker:

These messengers, wear metal buttons, upon the inside of which dispatches are most minutely photographed, not perceptible to the naked eye, but are easily read by the aid of a powerful lens.

JANUARY 11 WEDNESDAY

In Missouri, the Constitutional Convention adopted a resolution abolishing slavery within the state.

Major Gen. Thomas L. Rosser, CSA, led a raid on Beverly, W.Va., that netted him 580 prisoners and tons of rations. Rosser had previously raided in the Cumberland, Md., area.

In Richmond, President Davis was trying, without much luck, to gather all available troops to oppose Sherman's march through the Carolinas.

JANUARY 12 THURSDAY

The largest American fleet ever to be assembled under one command sailed from Beaufort, S.C., up the Atlantic coast towards Wilmington and Ft. Fisher. The army forces under Major Gen. Terry had met with Admiral Porter's fleet, and the assault of Ft. Fisher was set. The armada arrived off the coast, and the Navy prepared for the bombardment, which was to be followed by the landing of 10,000 soldiers, sailors and Marines.

President Davis, still mindful of the problems to be encountered with Sherman's advance, wrote Gen. Richard Taylor in the west that the remnants of Hood's army should be divided between his (Taylor's) command and the command to be named in the east. Troop shortages were plaguing everyone.

JANUARY 13 FRIDAY

Jackman, Pvt., "The Orphan Brigade," Milledgeville, Ga., wrote:

The Judge and I went into Milledgeville this morning. Visited the State House which we found all topsy-turvy. The desks overturned, the archives scattered over the floor—in some places the papers being on the floor a foot deep. This was done by Sherman's men. There are some splendid portraits in the Representative Hall and in the Senate Chamber which are in status quo. The arsenal standing in the State House yard was burned. We also visited the penitentiary which was also burned by Sherman's Army. With the exception of the arsenal and penitentiary and perhaps a little fencing, we could see no further indication of the destruction of property about the town. The railroad depot is in ashes and a bridge across a slough burned. We passed through the cemetery and saw a fine monument to the memory of a Mr. Jordan. The country between here and Macon is not as much torn up as I had expected to see. With the exception of one or two houses, only fences were burned. Griswoldville was the worst served—a large factory for making pistols being destroyed. I saw no dwellings had been burned in the village—that is, no signs of any having been burned, rather. . . .

JANUARY 14 SATURDAY

Federal naval bombardment was pouring 100 shells per minute into Ft. Fisher. The Confederates had suffered 300 casualties and could not bury their dead because of the lethal shrapnel flying around.

The bombardment of Ft. Fisher is depicted in this undated print published by Endicott & Co.

On January 15, 1865, Union forces captured the Confederate stronghold of Ft. Fisher, near Wilmington, N.C.—one of the South's most strategic seaports. Timothy O'Sullivan's photograph shows the area in the fort known as "the pulpit" after its capture.

Only one gun on the land face of the fort was left in a serviceable condition, all the others had been dismounted by the incessant naval gunfire.

Meanwhile, Gen. Terry had prepared defensive works facing his approaches from Wilmington to protect his rear from a possible assault by the 6,000 Rebel troops at Wilmington under Gen. Braxton Bragg. During the day, the CSS *Chickamauga*, based at Wilmington, came down and fired on Terry's Union troops from her position on the Cape Fear River.

JANUARY 15 SUNDAY

After the constant crashing and exploding of shells within the confines of Ft. Fisher, the end of the bombardment at 3 PM must have been a deafening silence. The Confederate gunners, however, manned the guns that were left and began firing on the assault-ing Federals. The naval landing force was the first target available, the Army troops having farther to come, and as the landing party crossed the beach the defenders' fire was point-blank, "ploughing lanes in the ranks." The naval landing force, under the command of Lt. Commander K. Randolph Breese, pressed the attack, with one group headed by Lt. Commander Thomas O. Selfridge reaching the top of the parapet and temporarily breaching the defenses, but it was driven back. Ensign Robley D. Evans—later to become a Rear Admiral with the sobriquet "Fighting Bob"—described the command problem of the assault: "All the officers, in their anxiety to be the first into the fort, had advanced to the heads of the columns, leaving no one to steady the men in behind; and it was in this way we were defeated, by the men breaking from the rear."

The Confederates were cheering upon the repulse of the naval force when they realized that Terry's forces had taken the western end of the fort in strength. A counterattack was immediately launched and hand-to-hand fighting soon ensued. Reinforcements rushing to the western end from other points of the fort now were hit by naval gunfire, firing with pinpoint accuracy and destroying the Confederate columns as they moved. Other ships fired on the riverbank behind the fort to prevent any reinforcements from that direction. Gen. Whiting was mortally wounded during the assault, and command was taken by Major James Reilly after Col. Lamb was hit in the hip by a bullet. Reilly fought doggedly and well but was overwhelmed by the onrushing Union troops and the naval gunfire. He was driven from the fort and surrendered his men later that night.

Union casualties were heavy, nearly 1,000 killed or wounded, to about half that number for the Confederates. Col. Lamb, the gallant defender, said of the assault:

> For the first time in the history of sieges the land defenses of the works were destroyed, not by any act of the besieging army, but by the concentrated fire, direct and enfilading, of an immense fleet poured into them without intermission, until torpedo wires were cut, palisades breached so they actually offered cover for assailants, and the slopes of the work were rendered practicable for assault.

The magnificent cooperation between Terry and Porter signaled the end to the last haven for blockade runners supplying the Confederacy. Admiral Porter wired Secretary Welles, "Fort Fisher is ours."

JANUARY 16 MONDAY

Francis Preston Blair, Sr., had been in Richmond for several days to talk to President Davis informally about peace. While there, Davis gave him a letter for Lincoln. On his return, Blair went to the White House to talk to President Lincoln about his visit with Davis and gave him the letter. The letter spoke of peace negotiations between the *two nations*, not about reunification of the United States. Lincoln turned the offer down. Blair would return to Richmond for more talks, but nothing would come of them.

The Confederate Congress passed a resolution stating that Gen. Robert E. Lee should be given the command of *all* Confederate armies.

At Ft. Fisher, celebrating soldiers, sailors and Marines were firing off their weapons when one shot accidentally set off a powder magazine which exploded, killing about 25, wounding nearly 70, and 13 men were never found.

Near Wilmington, Braxton Bragg ordered the destruction of the remaining forts guarding the port, this despite urgings from President Davis that Bragg attempt to retake Ft. Fisher. With Ft. Fisher lost, the port was effectively closed and there was no need for the Confederates to remain. As the munitions in the forts were blown up and the buildings fired, the Confederate garrisons moved towards Ft. Anderson.

Barber, Sgt., Co. C, 15th Illinois Volunteer Infantry, Governor's Island, New York City, N.Y., wrote:

> Very cold and windy. Heard to-day from the rest of my comrades in rebel prisons by an escaped prisoner belonging to Company D of the regiment. We learned with deep regret that they were suffering horribly, even worse than at Andersonville. Instead of being paroled and sent home as they had been led to believe, they were sent to Florida and were kept moving from place to place, almost naked and nearly starved.

JANUARY 17 TUESDAY

Knowing that the blockade runners, unaware of the capture of Ft. Fisher, would attempt to run in to Wilmington, Admiral Porter ordered the signal lights on the Mound (a towering man-made hill used to hold a flaring light to signal that all was clear in the harbor) ". . . properly trimmed and lighted, as has been the custom with the rebels during the blockade. Have the lights lighted to-night and see that no vessel inside displays a light, and be ready to grab anyone that enters."

JANUARY 18 WEDNESDAY

Francis P. Blair, Sr., was going back to Richmond for further talks with President Davis. Lincoln, on the exit interview, gave Blair a letter to Davis in which he spelled out that he would be willing to talk to anyone about peace as it dealt with "our one common country." Therein lay the problem, Davis insisting that there were "two nations."

JANUARY 19 THURSDAY

Sherman's army was ordered to begin its march north from Savannah and Beaufort, S.C. The army moved in stages, not as one force. The objective was Goldsborough, N.C., on March 15, less than 60 days away.

Lincoln asked Grant if there

Robert Todd Lincoln (1843–1926), seen in this c. 1865 photograph, was the only one of President Lincoln's four sons to survive past his teenage years. He served under Gen. Grant in the Union Army, and later served as the U.S. Secretary of War (1881–85).

was a place in his "military family" for Lincoln's son Robert. Capt. Robert Lincoln was appointed as assistant adjutant general on Grant's staff shortly thereafter.

Gen. Lee, reluctantly, told President Davis that the general would take any assignment given him. However, he felt that if assigned as commander-in-chief, he would not be able to do any good. In essence, it was too late.

JANUARY 20 FRIDAY

The blockade runners *Stag* and *Charlotte*, completely unaware that Ft. Fisher had fallen, and noting the light burning on the Mound, entered the port and anchored near the USS *Malvern*, flagship of Admiral D. D. Porter. They were immediately captured.

JANUARY 22 SUNDAY

Sherman's march along the coast included the areas along the railroad running to Branchville, S.C. Sherman notified Gen. Blair *not to* destroy the railroad, since it would possibly be needed later. Sherman gave all indications of heading towards Charleston.

JANUARY 23 MONDAY

In Richmond, Davis signed an act creating the position of General-in-Chief of Confederate Armies, the position obviously intended for Robert E. Lee.

In Mississippi, Lt. Gen. Richard Taylor assumed command of the remainder of the Army of Tennessee, a motley collection, 17,700 men strong, many sick. John Bell Hood left for Richmond. Whatever men Taylor had, he would send most of them east to Gen. Joe Johnston in the Carolinas to try to stop Sherman. Johnston later reported that due to sickness, desertions, etc., he eventually received only about 5,000. This left Taylor with a large piece of geography and few troops.

JANUARY 24 TUESDAY

The Confederate Congress again offered to exchange

prisoners, and this time Grant accepted. Many Union prisoners who were then suffering in Southern prison camps would shortly be home.

President Lincoln notified Vice President–Elect Andrew Johnson that he shouldn't be late for the inauguration on March 4th.

JANUARY 25 WEDNESDAY

Sherman was notified by Grant that Lee would *not* send any troops from Petersburg to bolster the Confederate forces in the Carolinas. Sherman's armies moved through a flooded countryside, the past four days having been nothing but rain.

Barber, Sgt., Co. C, 15th Illinois Volunteer Infantry, Governor's Island, New York City, N.Y., wrote:

> A petition has been sent to General Sherman, setting forth our grievances and asking for relief, which we have confidence will follow as soon as it reaches him. A copy of the petition was also sent to the *New York Herald* for publication. The language of the petition animadverted in the strongest terms upon the conduct of the government officials upon the island.

JANUARY 26 THURSDAY

Barber, Sgt., Co. C, 15th Illinois Volunteer Infantry, Governor's Island, New York City, N.Y., wrote:

> Very cold to-day. Yesterday a wife came to see her husband who was confined in the Castle with us. She was denied the privilege of seeing him. She could only approach as far as the gate. In his frenzy the outraged husband threw himself over the banister and broke his leg.

JANUARY 27 FRIDAY

Nichols, Major, USA, Pocotaligo, S.C., wrote:

> In the outset of the campaign orders of a general character were issued. All sick, wounded and incompetent soldiers were left behind. Transportation was reduced to the smallest possible space. The amount of hard bread, coffee and salt, the number of wagons for the different headquarters and for each regiment and battery and the size of the supply-train were specified. The number of officers to occupy a tent, and the kind of tent to be used, were also designated. Except for the uses of the adjutant's offices, the wall-tent, which we look back upon with tenderest gratitude, is forbidden, and two officers are permitted to share the "fly" which formerly was stretched over the wall tent. . . .
>
> Wall-tents are not the only luxuries now forbidden. Chairs, camp-cots, trunks and all unnecessary personal baggage are thrown out without exception. No officer is permitted to take with him more horses than the regulations allow, and he is also restricted in the number of his servants. In truth, General Sherman has reduced the army to its simplest and most effective fighting and marching conditions. . . . In all these personal sacrifices General Sherman demands nothing of his soldiers which he does not himself share. His staff is smaller than that of any brigade commander in the army. He has fewer servants and horses than the military regulations allow; his baggage is reduced to the smallest possible limit; he sleeps in a fly-tent like the rest of us, rejecting the effeminacy of a house. . . .

Barber, Sgt., Co. C, 15th Illinois Volunteer Infantry, Governor's Island, New York City, N.Y., wrote:

> Last evening witnessed the perpetration of an outrageous act which came well nigh creating a scene of great confusion and danger. It was no less than an order for a portion of the soldiers to vacate their rooms and go out in the cold so as to give room to

one hundred and fifty rebel prisoners who had arrived that evening. We protested, refused to obey the order and dared them to do their worst. Afterwards the order was rescinded and quiet was restored.

JANUARY 29 SUNDAY

Sherman began to veer away from the coast, towards the interior of South Carolina. Word had reached Sherman that reinforcements were coming from George Thomas's army in Tennessee to him. Few knew that the reinforcements were destined for Wilmington and were already en route.

In the Petersburg lines, the soldiers, blue and gray, huddled against the cold. The major difference was that the Union men were better fed and could stand the cold better.

JANUARY 30 MONDAY

President Lincoln issued passes for the three Confederate Commissioners to enter Union lines at Ft. Monroe, Va. This had been the traditional point of entry for flag-of-truce boats, etc., going between the two opponents.

Sherman turned northwest and headed his avalanche of blue towards Columbia, S.C. This irresistible tide would smash South Carolina, where it had only "touched" Georgia.

Nichols, Major, USA, Army of the Tennessee, S.C., wrote:

During Sherman's march from Savannah back up through the Carolinas in January of 1865, Gen. Oliver O. Howard was ordered to establish Pocotaligo, S.C., as a supply depot for Federal troops. This sketch of Pocotaligo in February of 1865 was created by Theodore Davis.

The actual invasion of South Carolina has begun. . . . The well-known sight of columns of black smoke meets our gaze again; this time houses are burning, and South Carolina has commenced to pay an instalment, long overdue, on her debt to justice and humanity. With the help of God, we will have principal and interest before we leave her borders. There is a terrible gladness in the realization of so many hopes and wishes. This cowardly traitor state, secure from harm, as she thought, in her central position, with hellish haste dragged her Southern sisters into the caldron of secession. Little did she dream that the hated flag would again wave over her soil; but this bright morning a thousand Union banners are floating in the breeze, and the ground trembles beneath the tramp of thousands of brave Northernmen, who know their mission, and will perform it to the end.

JANUARY 31 TUESDAY

At long last, the United States House of Representatives passed the Thirteenth Amendment, abolishing slavery by a vote of 119 to 56. It would be December 18, 1865, before two-thirds of the states approved the Amendment and it would become law.

President Davis proposed, and the Confederate Congress promptly approved, the appointment of Gen. Robert E. Lee as General-in-Chief of *all* Confederate Armies. It was too late to have any effect, most of the armies having melted away.

In Washington, Lincoln directed Secretary of State Seward to go to Ft. Monroe to meet with the "peace" committee from Richmond. The guidelines had not changed. *One* common country, not *two* as Davis had *insisted*.

Sherman continued his march towards Columbia, the smoke still rising from burning buildings, the troops building corduroy roads through the swamps and the movement never stopping. What little resistance they met was out-flanked and brushed aside.

William Henry Seward (1801–72) was Secretary of State from 1861 to 1869. In early 1865, he led a peace delegation from Washington to Ft. Monroe, Va.

❧ FEBRUARY 1865 ❧

EBRUARY'S COLD, WINTRY BREATH was only partially responsible for the chill that settled in the South. Things were not going well for Richmond's government. First Wilmington, and then Charleston fell, the last hope of survival cut by Federal bayonets and naval guns. As Raphael Semmes said: " . . . the anaconda had, at last, wound his fatal folds on us." The blockade was complete.

While things were quiet at Petersburg and in Nashville, Sherman had left Savannah and started north towards Charleston along the coast, only to veer towards Columbia. Carolina was burning!

FEBRUARY 1 WEDNESDAY

Illinois became the first state to ratify the Thirteenth Amendment. Earlier today, Lincoln wired Grant to, "Let nothing which is transpiring change, hinder, or delay your Military movements, or plans," obviously referring to the "peace committee" going to Ft. Monroe from Richmond.

Gen. Slocum, commanding Sherman's left wing, was having a hard time with flooded rivers and streams and getting his troops across the Savannah River at Sister's Ferry, despite the assistance of the Federal Navy. Gen. Howard, Sherman's right wing, encountered burned bridges and felled trees that presented few problems to Sherman's trained engineers and Pioneer battalions. They had plenty of experience with those obstacles before. Progress, though slow, was steady.

Gen. William Hardee had a makeshift group of soldiers to oppose Sherman's legions and, despite calls for help to the local governments, no reinforcements were in sight. The remnants of the Army of

As Sherman's troops marched northward toward Columbia, they passed through McPhersonville, S.C., which they torched on February 1, 1865. This engraving of the event, after a drawing by William Waud, was published in *Harper's Weekly* the following month.

Tennessee were inbound, supposedly, but for the present, nothing. The best Hardee could do was to set his cavalry yapping at the heels and flanks of the blue army.

Sgt. Barber, still recuperating from Andersonville, and free of Governor's Island, sailed for Hilton Head, S.C.

In Richmond, President Davis accepted the resignation of Secretary of War Seddon, with reluctance, and under considerable pressure from the Confederate Congress.

FEBRUARY 2 THURSDAY

President Lincoln left Washington for Hampton Roads, Va., where the three Confederate commissioners had arrived yesterday evening by steamer. Rhode Island and Michigan became the second and third states to ratify the Thirteenth Amendment.

FEBRUARY 3 FRIDAY

At Ft. Monroe, Va., the five men, representing North and South, sat in the salon of the steamer *River Queen* and discussed peace possibilities. Lincoln said that the national authority of the United States *must* be recognized within the rebellious states before anything else could even be considered. There was some talk of a "joint" operation against France in Mexico, but again Lincoln said this would mean recognizing the Confederacy as a separate government, and that this would not be done. Armistice was suggested. Lincoln said this was impossible until Federal authority was reestablished throughout the country. The Southern representatives said that this sounded like unconditional surrender, but Seward demurred, saying that the term had never been used. Lincoln indicated that his terms for reconstruction would be liberal, but he had no control over Congress in this matter. In all, it was a total bust for the Southern commissioners. There would be no peace for the South before surrender.

Maryland, New York and West Virginia ratified the Thirteenth Amendment.

Sherman's Seventeenth Corps cleared the Confederates from Rivers' Bridge by crossing three miles of swamp, water sometimes up to their shoulders, and then outflanking the Rebels. From this point on the Salkehatchie River, the blue columns moved rapidly on towards Columbia.

FEBRUARY 4 SATURDAY

Lt. Commander William Cushing, USS *Monticello*, took a boat expedition on a raid up Little River, S.C., near the North Carolina border. Cushing, the officer who sank the CSS *Albemarle*, was no stranger to small-boat operations. Progressing as far as All Saints Parish, he captured a number of Confederate soldiers and a quantity of cotton. He then placed a guard on that town and remained overnight.

Sherman's whole front was now in motion, headed for Columbia. Slocum's problems getting across the flooded Savannah River had been solved, and he was making good time in the higher, less swampy, terrain. There was skirmishing at several points across the front. The smoke was still rising from the burned houses, barns, etc. President Davis, in Richmond, was discouraged and he placed Beauregard in charge of the defense of the Carolinas.

FEBRUARY 5 SUNDAY

At City Point, Va., Grant sent the Second and Fifth Corps south and west, again extending the line that Lee would have to cover with his dwindling Confederate forces. The objective was the railroads leading south, which supplied the Confederate Army and the Virginia civilians. The action was at Hatcher's Run and the Boydton Plank Road, where the Federals were virtually unopposed.

Sherman was still advancing on Columbia, with part of the Union forces on the road to Millersville and Buford, others on the road to Barnwell. The smoke still rose on the horizon.

Alfred R. Waud's drawing of the Fifth Corps battling the Confederates at Hatcher's Run, Va., in February of 1865

FEBRUARY 6 MONDAY

At Hatcher's Run, south of Petersburg, the Federals ran into some resistance, and in the melee Brig. Gen. John Pegram, CSA, was killed. While the Federals held the Boydton Plank Road with little difficulty, the fighting at Hatcher's Run caused a short retreat for Warren's Fifth Corps when more Confederate troops arrived.

Sherman's columns were fighting for every ford and bridge on the numerous rivers bisecting their march route. The delays were usually neither long nor costly, but they were delays. Fighting took place on the Little Salkehatchie River, at Fishburn's Plantation and near Barnwell, S.C. Most of the Confederates were outflanked, rather than taken head-on.

Major Gen. John Cabell Breckinridge was named Secretary of War in Davis's Cabinet, replacing James A. Seddon. Gen. Robert E. Lee assumed command of all Confederate Armies. Both appointments were too late to do any good.

FEBRUARY 7 TUESDAY

Maine and Kansas approved the Thirteenth Amendment. In Delaware, the Amendment failed by one vote.

At Hatcher's Run, south and west of Petersburg, the Federals dug in to stay, stretching the Confederate lines to nearly 37 miles of fortifications. Lee had only about 46,000 men to man the trenches—not much over 1,000 men per mile—very thin.

FEBRUARY 8 WEDNESDAY

Massachusetts and Pennsylvania ratified the Thirteenth Amendment.

Sherman's advance continued, the blue columns outflanking the Confederate positions, the Confederates withdrawing. In addition to the burning of houses and barns, the railroads were being demolished as the Federal army progressed. Fighting for the fords of the Edisto and South Edisto Rivers continued. An escaped Union prisoner from Florence, S.C., reported that the Union prisoners there were in desperate straits, very low on rations.

285

FEBRUARY 9 THURSDAY

Virginia Unionists approved the Thirteenth Amendment. All was quiet along the Petersburg lines, the troops huddled against the snow and sleet.

In Richmond, Lee took over as General-in-Chief, saying that no major command changes would be made at this time. Lee was fully aware of the manpower problems, so he proposed, and Davis approved, a pardon to deserters who would return to duty within 30 days.

FEBRUARY 10 FRIDAY

Ohio and Missouri ratified the Thirteenth Amendment.

Capt. Raphael Semmes, late of the CSS *Alabama*, was in Richmond, and had been nominated for the rank of Rear Admiral in the Confederate Provisional Navy. He was assigned to command the James River Squadron, replacing Commodore J. K. Mitchell, a step Semmes took most reluctantly, he and Mitchell being old friends.

Barber, Sgt., Co. C, 15th Illinois Volunteer Infantry, Pocotaligo, S.C., wrote:

> The men belonging to the different corps were organized into companies to-day, my squad belonging to Company G, 17th army corps. Six hundred more soldiers arrived to-day. One thousand more are expected this evening. Heard to-day that Sherman had taken Branchville, S.C., and was marching on Columbia, the capital of the State. Yesterday the quartermaster of this post was shot by guerrillas while out a short distance from camp. Six of our men have been found hung and their bodies were outraged and mutilated in the most shameful manner. The country is swarming with guerrillas and cut-throats.

FEBRUARY 11 SATURDAY

Sherman's troops were now in positions between the Confederates on the coast at Charleston and those in Augusta, Ga. In neither place did the South have sufficient men assembled to oppose Union forces successfully. There was fighting in the vicinity of Orangeburg, Aiken and around Johnson's Station. President Davis wired Hardee that if the Confederate army could be gathered around Charleston, the Union army could be defeated—this at a time when Beauregard was counseling evacuation of Charleston to save the army. In South Carolina, the weather remained good, roads dry.

FEBRUARY 13 MONDAY

Sherman's army now approached the Congaree River, S.C., which the troops would cross on the 14th Tuesday. Sherman had severed his supply line to the sea while at Augusta, Ga., and now relied on foraging. The weather remained good and clear. Progress of the columns was marked again by rising columns of black smoke as the troops burned the countryside.

Nichols, Major, USA, Army of the Tennessee, S.C., wrote:

> The magnificent spectacle of a fire in the woods was the striking episode of our march yesterday. The army moved through a tract of hilly country which was thickly clothed with pine forests. Many of the trees were dead, and all had been scraped in order to obtain the resinous substance which formed their fruit and life. Accidently, or otherwise, the dry leaves and pine cones had caught fire, which ignited these trees, and for miles the woods were on fire. It was grand and sometimes awful to see the flames flying over the ground like a frightened steed. As we approached one of these forests, filled with flames and pitch black smoke, it appeared as if we were about to realize the imaginings of childhood, and see dragons and terrible beasts guarding the entrance to some forbidden ground. Wagons, horsemen and foot-soldiers one by

one disappeared into the gloom, to reappear here and there bathed in lurid light. Within, the fire singed our hair and clothes, while our maddened animals dashed hither and thither in an agony of fear. . . .

Gen. William Hardee, commander of the Confederate troops in the area, advanced his preparations to evacuate Charleston and withdrew into North Carolina with the troops from Savannah, and what could be salvaged from Charleston. The Confederate naval ships at Charleston were ordered scuttled and Commodore John R. Tucker, CSN, directed that 300 men and officers go to Wilmington to help defend that city.

FEBRUARY 15 WEDNESDAY

Near Columbia, S.C., on a day that started out cold and rainy and ended with thick fog, there was skirmishing at Lexington, west of the city, and at the Congaree Creek, Savannah Creek and at Bates' Ferry crossing of the Congaree River. Sherman's columns advanced rapidly despite the soggy ground which bogged down wagons and despite the delaying actions of the Confederates. The fog saved many of the mired wagons, since they couldn't be seen by the Confederate gunners manning the artillery.

In a late afternoon action, the Union troops again outflanked the Rebels by wading the river in waist-high water and coming in behind the Confederates,

William Waud inscribed this legend on the back of his drawing, which he created on February 12–13, 1865: "Col. Wells S. Jones's brigade crossing the North Edisto on raft before the pontoons were laid & charging on the enemy's works. The men shown on the left are crossing on a floating foot bridge."

before they knew that they had been flanked. Wade Hampton's cavalry made a charge across an open area that accomplished nothing except to get two of his men killed. Undaunted, this flamboyant Columbian wired President Davis that he had repulsed Sherman at Columbia. For this, Davis promoted Hampton to Lieutenant General.

FEBRUARY 16 THURSDAY

Federal soldiers were within sight of Columbia, S.C., as they arrived on the south bank of the Congaree River, west and southeast of the city. Much movement could be seen in the city, especially Confederate cavalry, probably belonging to Wade Hampton's Legion. The Union artillery fired some shells into the city, probably at the cavalry and at the railroad depot. Beauregard, up from Augusta, left Columbia in the afternoon after notifying Davis that he could not save the city. Cotton bales stored in the city had been fired to prevent their capture by Federal forces.

Lt. Gen. Wade Hampton, CSA (1818–1902), served as South Carolina governor from 1876 to 1879 and as U.S. senator from 1879 to 1891.

Much controversy arose over the shelling of Columbia by the Union; however, investigations showed that no individuals had been killed as a result of the shelling, and that property damage was light.

Near Wilmington, N.C., Ft. Anderson lay on the west bank of the Cape Fear River, midway between the mouth of the river and the city of Wilmington. Ft. Anderson was the prime objective of the Union troops ferried across from Ft. Fisher to Smithville, just down from Ft. Anderson. Major Gen. Schofield's XXIII Corps was readied for the assault and would be supported by naval gunboats.

FEBRUARY 17 FRIDAY

Early in the morning, Major Gen. Jacob D. Cox, part of Schofield's XXIII Corps, advanced 8,000 men north from Smithville towards Ft. Anderson. The Navy, in support, sent the monitor USS *Montauk*, Lt. Commander Edward E. Stone, and four gunboats to bombard the fort, and they silenced the fort's twelve guns. Since he had not been able to get the other monitor back from Admiral Dahlgren at Charleston, Admiral Porter used the same subterfuge he had used on the Mississippi River; he created a bogus monitor using a scow, timber, canvas and paint. The fake monitor, dubbed "Old Bogey" by the sailors, was towed to the head of the bombardment line, where she received much attention from the Confederate gunners.

At Charleston, S.C., the gunboats USS *Pawnee*, *Sonoma*, *Ottawa*, *Winona*, *Potomska*, *Wando*, *J. S. Chambers* and other vessels supported landings of Major Gen. Foster's soldiers at Bulls Bay. This was a diversionary tactic meant to tie down Confederate forces and keep them from Sherman's route of march. Its secondary mission was to put pressure on the city.

During the night, the Confederate defenses at Forts Moultrie, Sumter, Johnson, Beauregard and Castle Pinckney were abandoned, and the Rebel troops marched north to join Lee. The defenses of Charleston were silenced after 567 continuous days of attack. Four Confederate ironclads were scuttled or blown up, the fifth, the CSS *Columbia*, was found run aground and was later salvaged by the Union Navy. Several torpedo boats of the "David" class were also found, one of which was eventually taken to the U.S. Naval Academy and put on display. Several blockade runners were captured in port and several more were lured in by the same trick used at Wilmington—leaving the signal light burning.

Admiral Dahlgren wrote Admiral Porter: "You see by the date of this [February 18] that the Navy's occupation has given this pride of rebeldom to the Union flag, and thus the rebellion is shut out from the ocean and foreign sympathy." Lt. Wilkinson, former commander of the CSS *Tallahassee*, learned of the fall of Charleston while in Nassau, and wrote: "This sad intelligence put an end to all our hopes. . . ." The city that had most symbolized the spirit of the South was in Union hands.

At Columbia, the mayor and a delegation rode out to see Sherman and to surrender the city. As Union troops entered the city, the remnants of Hampton's cavalry departed, leaving cotton bales still smoldering. It has been a bone of contention since as to how the fire had started—evidence points to bales of cotton being fired by Hampton's retreating horsemen; however, many in the city believed that the fire had been set by the Yankees. At any rate, burning bales of cotton were found and thought to have been extinguished. The troops found the liquor supply and were greeted warmly by the freed Union prisoners and the Negro population. Sherman's Provost Guards were soon busy arresting drunken soldiers. Several of the latter held a mock session of the State Legislature in the State House. The colors of the 8th Missouri Volunteers, having been the first to fly at Ft. Donelson, been riddled by Rebel bullets at Shiloh, carried into Vicksburg, flown over Kennesaw Mountain and Ft. McAllister were now hoisted over the state capitol in Columbia.

Sherman set up headquarters in one of the quieter streets of the town and retired. The high winds evidently fanned the flames of the cotton back to life and bits of burning cotton spread over the city like a blanket, starting new fires blocks from the source. Sherman had his Union troops out fighting the fires, but the high winds prevented containment. Wade Hampton's home, one of the finest in Columbia, was burned, along with many others. For more than 100 years the burning of Columbia would be cited by the South as an example of Northern excess during the war.

General Sherman enters Columbia, S.C., on February 17th, 1865.

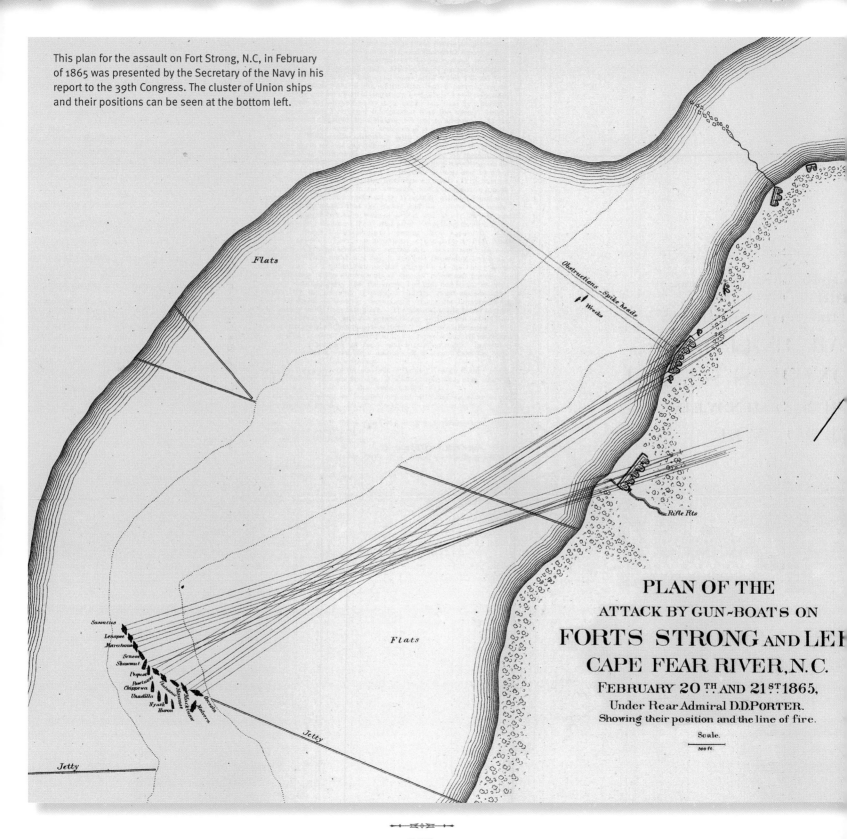

This plan for the assault on Fort Strong, N.C, in February of 1865 was presented by the Secretary of the Navy in his report to the 39th Congress. The cluster of Union ships and their positions can be seen at the bottom left.

Flats

Obstructions - Spike Heads

Wrecks

Rifle Pts

Flats

Sassacus
Lenapee
Maratanza
Seneca
Shawmut
Pequot
Pawtuxet
Chippewa
Unadilla
Tacony
Maumee
Mackinaw
Nyack
Huron
Malvern
Osceola

Jetty

Jetty

PLAN OF THE
ATTACK BY GUN-BOATS ON
FORTS STRONG AND LEE
CAPE FEAR RIVER, N.C.
FEBRUARY 20 TH AND 21 ST 1865,
Under Rear Admiral D.D.PORTER.
Showing their position and the line of fire.

Scale.
500 ft.

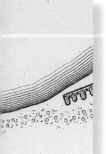

With Charleston empty of defenders and Columbia in flames, this was, indeed, a day of retribution for the North against South Carolina.

FEBRUARY 19 SUNDAY

Nichols, Major, USA, Columbia, S.C., wrote:

. . . Columbia will have bitter cause to remember the visit of Sherman's army. . . . It is not alone in the property that has been destroyed—the buildings, bridges, mills, railroads, material of every description—nor in the loss of the slaves, who, within the last few days, have joined us by hundreds and thousands. . . . It is in the crushing downfall of their inordinate vanity, their arrogant pride, that the rebels will feel the effects of the visit of our army. Their fancied, unapproachable, invincible security has been ruthlessly overthrown. Their boastings, threatenings, and denunciations have passed by us like the idle wind. . . . I know that thousands of South Carolina's sons are in the army of the rebellion; but she has already lost her best blood there. Those who remain have no homes. The Hamptons, Barnwells, Simses, Rhetts, Singletons, Prestons, have no homes. The ancient homesteads where were gathered sacred associations, the heritages of many generations, are swept away. When first these men became traitors, they lost honor. . . .

FEBRUARY 20 MONDAY

At Wilmington, N.C., the Federal boat crews sweeping for torpedoes in the Cape Fear River channels were kept very busy. The Confederates released 200 floating torpedoes during the night, causing much consternation as they floated into the boats clearing the channel, some destroying the small boats, others striking the steamers and doing great damage. Casualties from the torpedoes were slight, but they were worrisome.

Sherman's columns left Columbia, passing through a fertile country for about five miles. They then passed into the area of hills with stunted pines, the sandy soil almost barren. A large train of refugees consisting of several hundred white people followed the army as it left. There were many reasons for the exodus. Some left to escape starvation, some to escape conscription, some to escape persecution. All were a bother to the Union army and they made many demands for protection, provisions, etc., which could not be met. Sherman ordered them expelled from the columns.

FEBRUARY 21 TUESDAY

During the initial landings for the assault on Ft. Anderson, a bogus monitor-type ironclad had been rigged using an old scow, timber, canvas and black paint. This bogus ironclad had been named "Old Bogey" by the sailors who towed her around. Now, with the torpedoes coming downriver, "Old Bogey" was called into service again. She was pushed across the river into the path of the torpedoes. One observer described the action:

Johnny Reb let off his torpedoes without effect on it, and the old thing sailed across the river and grounded in the flank and rear of the enemy's lines on the eastern bank, whereupon they fell back in the night. She now occupies the most advanced position of the line, and Battery Lee has been banging away at her, and probably wondering why she does not answer. Last night after half a day's fighting, the rebs sent down about 50 torpedoes; but although "Old Bogey" took no notice of them, they kept the rest of us pretty lively as long as the ebb tide ran.

FEBRUARY 22 WEDNESDAY

Kentucky rejected the Thirteenth Amendment.

The Confederates evacuated Wilmington, N.C., sending much of the military stores on the railroad towards Richmond. What remained was destroyed.

After the evacuation of Ft. Strong, the Federal gunboats steamed upriver to Wilmington, which was already occupied by Brig. Gen. Terry's troops, Gen. Bragg having evacuated the city. Wilmington had fallen and Admiral Porter wrote Secretary of the Navy Gideon Welles:

> I have the honor to inform you that Wilmington has been evacuated and is in possession of our troops. . . . I had the pleasure of placing the flag on Fort Strong, and at 12 o'clock noon today shall fire a thirty-five guns salute this being the anniversary of Washington's birthday.

It was now official. Gen. Joseph E. Johnston was assigned as commander of all Confederate forces in South Carolina, Georgia, Florida, Tennessee and those concentrating in North Carolina. Gen. Beauregard, in ill health, was told to report to Johnston for orders.

Sherman was skirmishing at Camden and on the Wateree River north of Columbia. The railroads on the route of march were a special target of Sherman's destroyers. The Twentieth Corps reached Rocky Mount, S.C., and waited for the crossing of the Catawba River. Sherman feinted towards Charlotte, N.C., and then aimed his main drive towards Goldsborough and a linkup with Schofield.

FEBRUARY 23 THURSDAY

Things were turning nasty in South Carolina. Not only had heavy rains begun midafternoon, but on the 22nd, two of Sherman's men had been found murdered—their heads crushed by heavy blows. That day, reports of more such findings were circulating. *The Official Records (OR)* cited a report of Gen. Judson Kilpatrick's:

> An infantry lieutenant and seven men murdered yesterday by the Eighth Texas Cavalry after they had surrendered. We found their bodies all together and mutilated, with paper on their breasts, saying

"Death to foragers." Eighteen of my men were killed yesterday and some had their throats cut. . . . I have sent Wheeler word that I intend to hang eighteen of his men, and if the cowardly act is repeated, will burn every house along my line of march. . . . I have a number of prisoners, and shall take a fearful revenge.

Sherman's orders to Major Gen. Otis O. Howard, also cited in the *Official Records*, show his determination to take life for life:

> Now it is clearly our war right to subsist our army on the enemy. . . . I contend if the enemy fails to defend his country we may rightfully appropriate what we want. If our foragers act under mine, yours, or other proper orders they must be protected. I have ordered Kilpatrick to select of his prisoners man for man, shoot them, and leave them by the roadside labeled, so that our enemy will see that for every man he executes he takes the life of one of his own. I want the foragers, however, to be kept within reasonable bounds for the sake of discipline. I will not protect them when they enter dwellings and commit wanton waste. . . . If any of your foragers are murdered, take life for life, leaving a record in each case.

FEBRUARY 25 SATURDAY

Gen. Joseph Eggleston Johnston, at Charlotte, N.C., assumed command of the troops in South Carolina, Georgia and Florida. Upon examination of the troop strength and state, he notified Lee that, in his opinion, his force was entirely too weak to take on Sherman and that it should be consolidated with Bragg's in North Carolina.

FEBRUARY 27 MONDAY

Sherman was still moving through to Fayetteville.

In the Shenandoah Valley, Sheridan was back

with about ten thousand cavalry and was opposed by Jubal Early and two weak Confederate brigades. Grant had directed that the Virginia Central Railroad and the James River Canal be destroyed. Lynchburg was to have its railroads, etc., destroyed, and its military stores burned.

FEBRUARY 28 TUESDAY

Sherman's armies were near the North Carolina line at Rocky Mount and Cheraw, S.C., where skirmishes occurred. Johnston, at Charlotte, was trying to scrape the bottom of the barrel to get a force to oppose Sherman.

∽ MARCH 1865 ∽

THOUGHTS WERE INCREASINGLY of peace and how the reconstruction of the nation would be accomplished. It was obvious that the South was losing the war and that the end could not be far off. The only army of any size was located at Petersburg, and it was tied down by the tenacious and formidable Union Army of the Potomac. Few options were left.

MARCH 1 WEDNESDAY

In the Shenandoah Valley, the thunder of cavalry could be heard again as Sheridan's hard-riding blue-coats pounded up the Valley in pursuit of Jubal Early's two battered brigades. In Washington, news of the passage of the Thirteenth Amendment by Wisconsin was offset by its rejection by New Jersey.

Admiral Dahlgren went back to Georgetown, S.C., up the coast from Charleston, to visit the naval forces at that location and to "inspect" Ft. White, which controlled the bay. Remaining overnight, Dahlgren, in his flagship *Harvest Moon*, was in his cabin awaiting breakfast as the ship sailed for Charleston. The ship struck a torpedo and, in Dahlgren's words:

Suddenly, without warning, came a crashing sound, a heavy shock, the partition between the cabin and wardroom was shattered and driven in toward me, while all loose articles in the cabin flew in different directions. . . . A torpedo had been struck by the poor old *Harvest Moon*, and she was sinking.

Five minutes later the ship was gone. Only one life was lost, and the Admiral had nothing but the uniform he was wearing.

MARCH 2 THURSDAY

Gen. Lee wrote a message to Gen. Grant, proposing a meeting to attempt resolving the present "unhappy difficulties" by a military convention. Grant demurred, saying he had no authority to hold such a conference, there must have been something misunderstood. Dealing with the South in such a manner would, in effect, be a recognition of it as a sovereign military force—a separate nation's military power. This was the same ploy used at the "peace committee" meeting with Lincoln at Hampton Roads, when Confederate Vice President Stephens suggested that the North and South jointly throw Napoleon III out of Mexico.

At Waynesborough, Va., the last battle of any significance in the Valley was fought between Federal cavalry and Confederate infantry. The remnants of Jubal Early's brigades were overwhelmed by a charge of 5,000 cavalry led by Gen. George A. Custer. While Early escaped with his staff, Custer captured 200 wagons, seventeen flags, and well over 1,000 prisoners. The ghosts of Cross Keys, McDowell, Winchester and Kernstown must have cringed. The Valley was lost.

MARCH 3 FRIDAY

The Thirty-Eighth Congress would officially adjourn at 8 AM tomorrow, but tonight much work needed to be done. One major item was the act establishing the Bureau for the Relief of Freedmen

1865

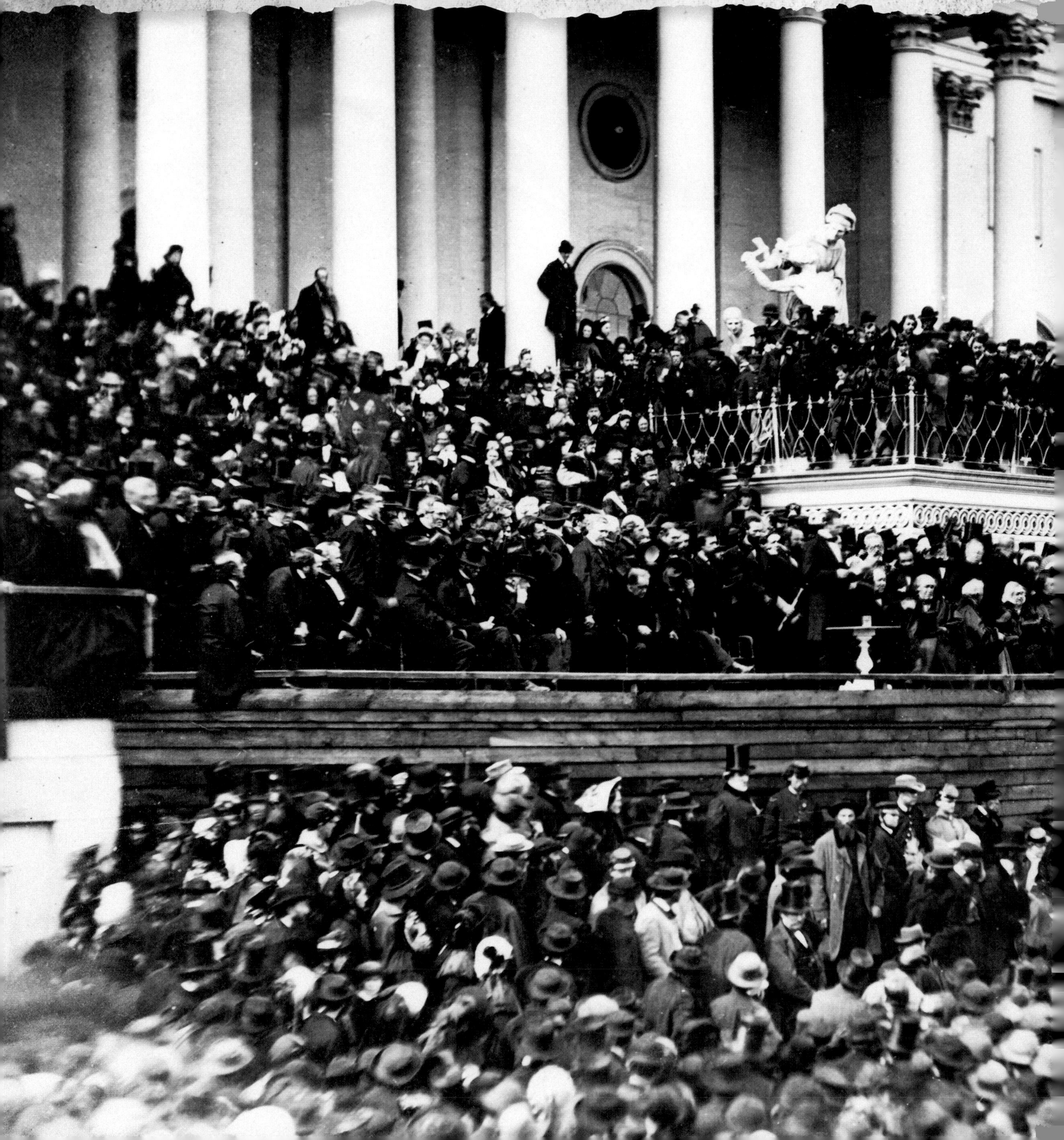

and Refugees—to be known as the Freedman's Bureau. This bureaucratic body would provide the basis for support of the Negro, both economically and politically, for the next 20 years. It would initially provide food, clothing and other assistance. Later, it would be used to build schools, establish secondary learning institutions and provide a political base for Negro elected officials.

The Cape Fear River was the scene of much activity as the Federals worked to clear the Confederate torpedoes and make the river safe for steamers. With Sherman's line of march following the coast towards Wilmington and Goldsborough, N.C., communication routes for supplies would be needed for his large armies.

In the Valley, the guards along the long column of Confederate prisoners from Early's command were attacked several times as they headed north. Sheridan approached Charlottesville, heading back to join Grant with most of the cavalry. Early was inbound to Richmond.

MARCH 4 SATURDAY

It was Inauguration Day in Washington. Vice President Andrew Johnson of Tennessee took the oath of office prior to President Lincoln, as tradition demanded. He had been drinking, and his acceptance speech was slurred and almost incoherent. The feeling of peace was in the air and Lincoln would see it through. The city was in a gayer mood than it had been four years ago, when war was looming on the horizon. Lincoln's inaugural address would be remembered for its brevity and eloquence, especially the closing, which began: "With malice toward none; with charity for all; with firmness in the right, as God gives us to see the right. . . ."

Barber, Sgt., Co. C, 15th Illinois Volunteer Infantry, Pocotaligo, S.C., wrote:

President Lincoln delivering his second inaugural address on March 4, 1865

Cloudy and some rain. Received New York papers yesterday of the 24th of February. It was a rich treat to us. We had been four weeks without seeing any papers from the North. . . . Charleston and Wilmington had fallen, and the dear old flag once more floats over Sumter, in ruins though it be. Sherman's campaign through Georgia to the sea, and through the Carolinas into Virginia, is proving to be one continual series of brilliant successes, on a scale so magnificent that history scarcely furnishes a parallel. . . .

MARCH 5 SUNDAY

Sherman's men were crossing the Pee Dee and moving slowly towards Fayetteville. Schofield was still at Wilmington.

MARCH 6 MONDAY

Sherman's scouts had determined that the Confederate force at Florence, S.C., was too strong for less than a major attack, and Sherman did not want to be sidetracked from Fayetteville. Most of the Federal troops crossed the Pee Dee River and entered North Carolina. At Cheraw, a large explosion killed one man and injured five.

MARCH 7 TUESDAY

Sherman's columns moved north in North Carolina. The roads were finally drying out and progress was good, after several days of constant rain.

The U.S. Congress got the full range of Rear Admiral David Dixon Porter's anger when he addressed that body and scorched the walls with salty comments about Generals Butler and Banks, both of whom he had had the misfortune to serve with. His next stop was City Point to see his old friend Ulysses S. Grant, and to discuss the coming spring campaign.

MARCH 8 WEDNESDAY

Gen. Jacob D. Cox, commanding the buildup at New Bern, was attacked by elements of Braxton Bragg's Confederates coming from Wilmington. During the attack, near Kinston, N.C., some of the Federal troops broke, but the remainder held and fought off the Rebels. Bragg's force was not really strong enough to sustain an attack for long.

MARCH 9 THURSDAY

Vermont ratified the Thirteenth Amendment to the Constitution. Lincoln, in Washington, accepted the resignation of John P. Usher as Secretary of the Interior.

Fighting continued between Bragg's Confederates and Jacob Cox's Federals near Kinston, N.C.

At Monroe's Crossroads, N.C., the cavalry of Wade Hampton and Joe Wheeler attacked the unsuspecting Federals of Judson Kilpatrick and totally surprised them, almost catching Kilpatrick in his bed. Kilpatrick fled, some say without his pants, giving the name to the affair, "The Battle for Kilpatrick's Pants." Kilpatrick rallied his men, counterattacked and severely beat Hampton's Legion.

Sherman's Fifteenth Corps was at Randallsville, N.C. Believing that Schofield was at Wilmington, Sherman sent scouts to make contact. In his memoirs, Sherman wrote:

> I traveled with the Fifteenth Corps and on the 8th of March reached Laurel Hill, N.C. Satisfied that our troops were at Wilmington, I determined to send a message there; I called for my man, Corp. [James] Pike, whom I had rescued [from the prison] at Columbia, and instructed him in disguise to work his way to Cape Fear River, secure a boat, and float down to Wilmington to convey a letter, and to report our approach. I also called on General Howard for another volunteer, and he brought me a very clever young sergeant,

who is now [1875] a commissioned officer in the regular army. Each of these got off during the night by separate routes. . . .

MARCH 10 FRIDAY

In Richmond, Lee proposed putting the legislation on using Negro troops into force immediately. However, the Confederate Congress was still debating it in its House of Representatives.

MARCH 11 SATURDAY

Sherman's armies nearly surrounded the town of Fayetteville, N.C., waiting to go in. Scouts sent in were met with firing from Confederate cavalry, which was soon dispersed, the cavalry leaving town by the bridges over the Cape Fear River. The old U.S. Arsenal at Fayetteville, destination of the rifle-making machinery removed from Harpers Ferry in 1861 by Stonewall Jackson, was occupied and would be destroyed. Sherman's messengers to Schofield had reached Wilmington, and Union boats were on their way upriver to Fayetteville.

In Virginia, Sheridan's cavalry, coming in from defeating Early in the Valley, were outside of Richmond at Goochland Court House, causing a scare in the Confederate capital.

MARCH 12 SUNDAY

Sherman's men fell to with a will to destroy the Arsenal and other military facilities in Fayetteville, N.C., a town of about 3,000 inhabitants. A Confederate steamer had been captured below the city on the Cape Fear River, and this would be loaded with Negroes and refugees, and then sent to Wilmington.

Gen. Grant's cavalry escort was photographed in March of 1865 at City Point, Va. Five buglers stand at the left.

MARCH 13 MONDAY

In Richmond, the Confederate Congress finally passed legislation to use Negro troops in the Southern army. Lee acted promptly on this, and by the end of the month Negro troops were seen in Confederate uniform in Richmond.

Sheridan's cavalry, en route to Grant at Petersburg, skirmished at Beaver Dam Station outside Richmond.

At Fayetteville, N.C., the destruction went on, Sherman's men tearing the place apart while waiting for the supplies to come up from Wilmington. A steamer and two gunboats arrived at the city from Wilmington, carrying a staff officer from Gen. Terry who was critical of Sherman's method of operations—but not to Sherman.

MARCH 15 WEDNESDAY

Sheridan was now at Hanover C.H., heading towards the James River to link up with Grant.

Sherman was again on the move, northeast towards Goldsborough, N.C. Kilpatrick, in front of Slocum's left wing, was skirmishing with Johnston's rear guard units as the Union advance was made. The Confederate Army was now overburdened with generals of all grades, more than were needed for an army three times the size.

MARCH 16 THURSDAY

Slocum, commanding Sherman's left wing, attacked Hardee's force four miles south of Averasborough, N.C., turning Hardee's right flank and causing the Confederate to withdraw. Late in the afternoon, word came to Hardee that Slocum's men were on his left flank, so during the night, in the middle of a storm, Hardee withdrew and marched towards Smithfield. The remainder of Sherman's armies was moving on bottomless roads and through water about two feet deep where the creeks had overflowed. Every crossing, again, was contested by a burned bridge and a small Confederate force that was flanked out of position by Union forces wading the stream, and the whole thing was done over again at the next stream.

MARCH 17 FRIDAY

After the fighting yesterday in front of Slocum, skirmishing continued in front of Sherman's march route as the Union force got closer to Goldsborough. The columns were not quite so long, having closed up during the day yesterday, with the vanguard being slowed by bad roads and the necessity of building bridges.

In the fighting yesterday around Averasborough, Confederate Col. Alfred Rhett, who had commanded Ft. Sumter for a period, was captured by an aide on Gen. Kilpatrick's staff.

Nichols, Major, USA, Army of the Tennessee, Averasborough, N.C., wrote:

> Kilpatrick, who has the advance, ran into a strong body of Rebel infantry this afternoon, and skirmished with them until night came on. He captured several prisoners, among them Colonel Rhett, son of the noted Robert Barnwell Rhett, one of the "first family" names of which South Carolina is so proud. From the conversation of this Rebel colonel, I judge him to be quite as impracticable a person as any of his class. He seemed most troubled about the way in which he was captured. Some of Kilpatrick's fast riders got inside his skirmish line, and one of them, without any sort of regard for the feelings of a South Carolina aristocrat, put a pistol to the colonel's head and informed him in a quiet but very decided manner that if he didn't come along he'd "make a hole through him!" The colonel came; but he is a disgusted man. From what I know of the sentiments of Kilpatrick's men, I make no doubt that they would have had but little

scruple in cutting off one branch of the family tree of the Rhetts if the surrender had not been prompt.

MARCH 18 SATURDAY

The left wing of Sherman's armies, the two corps under Slocum, were just south of Bentonville, N.C., on this warm and clear day. Opposite Slocum was Lt. Gen. Wade Hampton's cavalry, opposing Kilpatrick, whose cavalry was in front of Slocum. Sherman's right wing, commanded by Howard, was south and east of Bentonville, facing Goldsborough. Johnston's 20,000 faced 30,000 Federals and Johnston was going to try and beat the Federal army piecemeal, having no chance at all facing Sherman's full army, including Schofield, of about 100,000. The Battle of Bentonville opened today when Hampton's cavalry began a skirmish with the advance Federal units near Benton's Cross Roads.

Union Gen. Hugh Judson Kilpatrick (1836–81) became active in politics after the war. He served as the U.S. Minister to Chile, and later wrote two plays about his wartime experiences.

MARCH 19 SUNDAY

Sherman, who had been traveling with Slocum on the left wing, left early in the morning for Howard's right wing as the Federals began their advance. As they advanced, they ran head-on into Johnston's prepared positions south of Bentonville, N.C. Slocum pressed his advance, but Johnston wouldn't budge, and by midafternoon Slocum entrenched, not knowing as yet what he faced.

On the Confederate side there was a delay in attacking, and when they did go crashing into the Federal line, the progress was slow. No problems were met with the first Federal line, but Gen. Jefferson C. Davis, USA, rallied his men, who withstood the attack until more units could be brought up. The fighting, which included three separate assaults on the Federal line, lasted until dark, when both sides pulled back and reinforced their positions.

Meanwhile, Sherman, having arrived at Howard's right wing, thought the fight less severe than it was and held Howard's troops in their forward positions. In the evening, couriers from Slocum's headquarters arrived to tell Sherman of the battle and of the current situation.

Sheridan, in Virginia, had reached White House on the Pamunkey River after tearing up the Virginia Central Railroad and the James River Canal. He was almost back in Grant's backyard.

MARCH 20 MONDAY

Early in the morning, the men of Howard's right wing moved towards Bentonville to join the fight against Johnston's Confederate force. The roads were dry and fast, the troops moving easily. Shortly after starting they ran into a body of Confederate cavalry, which delayed them only briefly. As the columns closed up, the cavalry was driven as fast as the infantry could march, until the Federals came up to the main lines and formed to Slocum's right. The battlefield was a quicksand flat that, while no water was showing, had a high water table that made the

ground unable to support artillery or wagons. The ground offered little cover for either force. By late afternoon, Sherman's entire army was facing Johnston and overlapping the Confederate flanks. Things quieted down for the evening.

MARCH 21 TUESDAY

At Bentonville, N.C., Sherman kept the pressure on Johnston's line while Major Gen. J. A. Mower moved around the Confederate left and threatened Mill Creek Bridge, which was on Johnston's retreat line. Some heavy fighting resulted, with the Federal advance being checked. This was the last fighting of the Battle of Bentonville, which was the last major battle of the war in North Carolina. Johnston withdrew, upon getting reports that Schofield had taken Goldsborough. The North lost over 1,500 casualties, mostly wounded; the South, 2,600, mostly prisoners.

MARCH 22 WEDNESDAY

At Bentonville, N.C., skirmishers reported that Johnston's fortifications were abandoned. Sherman ordered that no advance was to be made beyond Mill

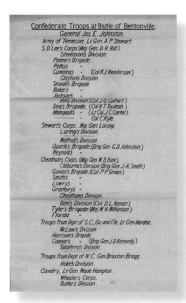
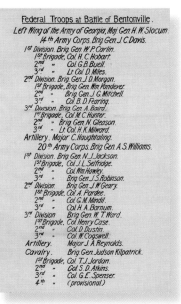

Lists of the Confederate and Federal officers, down to the brigade level, who participated in the Battle of Bentonville.

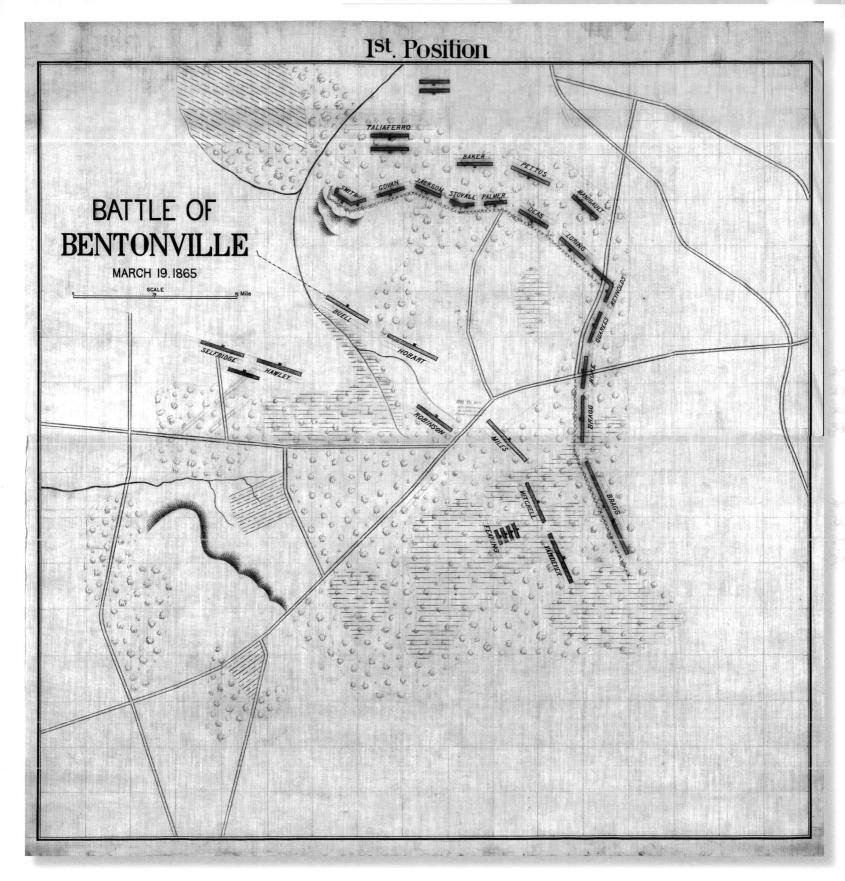

BATTLE OF
BENTONVILLE

MARCH 19. 1865

SCALE
0   ½   ½ Mile

A map of the Battle of Bentonville, N.C., March 19, 1865

Creek below Bentonville until things could be sorted out. After a period of reconnaissance, Sherman ordered Slocum's left wing towards Goldsborough, the right wing to move the next day. The roads were bad and the movement slow.

Schofield was at Goldsborough, and Terry at Cox's Bridge, both prepared to move on Johnston when Sherman gave the word.

MARCH 23 THURSDAY

In North Carolina, Johnston placed his army across the paths to Raleigh and Weldon, both routes Sherman was expected to take. It also put Johnston in position for a linkup with Lee if the Army of Northern Virginia somehow escaped Grant and came to North Carolina.

Sherman joined Schofield and Terry at Goldsborough. The combined armies now totaled more than 100,000 and completely dominated the military situation in the area. Sherman, now linked to his supply line to the sea, would reclothe his army and give them rest before continuing his drive on Johnston and on to Virginia.

Nichols, Major, USA, Sherman's Hdqtrs., Goldsborough, N.C., wrote:

General Schofield is in Goldsboro'. Our army will at once be moved into position in the vicinity of this place to refit for the next campaign; not only to be reclothed, but to gain the repose it needs. Mind, as well as body, requires rest after the fatigues of rapid campaigns like these. These ragged, bareheaded, shoeless, brave, jolly fellows of Sherman's legions, too, want covering for their naked limbs.

Wilson's large cavalry force moved slowly through northern Alabama to meet Nathan B. Forrest.

MARCH 24 FRIDAY

The heavily armed Confederate ironclad CSS *Stonewall*, Capt. T. J. Page, sailed from Ferrol, Spain, after two abortive attempts to leave. She challenged the two wooden Union frigates USS *Niagara* and *Sacramento* under command of Commodore T. T. Craven. Craven explained to Secretary Welles:

At this time the odds in her favor were too great and too certain, in my humble judgment, to admit of the slightest hope of being able to inflict upon her even the most trifling injury, whereas, if we had gone out, the *Niagara* would most undoubtedly have been easily and promptly destroyed. So thoroughly a one-sided combat I did not consider myself called upon to engage in.

Craven would later be court-martialed for not engaging the *Stonewall*. Sitting as President of the Court was Vice Admiral David G. Farragut and sitting as a member of the Court was Commodore John A. Winslow, the destroyer of the CSS *Alabama*. Craven was sentenced to two years suspension on leave pay. Welles, refusing what he called a "paid vacation," restored him to active duty.

In the lines at Petersburg, the Confederates were preparing an attack on Ft. Stedman. If they could break the line there, they could attack City Point, and that attack would require Grant to shorten his lines, which, in turn, would allow Lee to evacuate and join Gen. Joe Johnston in North Carolina. Major Gen. John B. Gordon had been assigned to lead the Confederate force in the attack. The attack, scheduled for tomorrow, would have President Lincoln as an observer. Lincoln arrived at City Point aboard the *River Queen*.

In North Carolina, the refitting of Sherman's ragged troops went along, all the supplies needed having been brought up to Goldsborough by Schofield. The troops, as they entered Goldsborough, presented a somewhat picturesque sight.

MARCH 25 SATURDAY

At three o'clock this morning a group of Confederates appeared at Ft. Stedman, a major Union bastion in the siege lines, and announced themselves as deserters. An hour later, 4 AM, Gen. Gordon threw his troops against the Union strongpoint and completely overwhelmed it, surprising the garrison and the line for nearly a mile. The Confederates swarmed over the defenses, and some selected units headed for City Point. There was not enough weight behind the attack and it faltered, giving the Federals time to regroup and drive the Confederates back to their own lines. The Rebels still held Ft. Stedman. At about 7:30 AM, the Union sent a division against Ft. Stedman, and the Confederates were routed back to their own lines. The Union line was whole again. Grant lost about 1,500 in casualties; Lee, about 4,000, many more than he could spare. The line quieted again.

The expected assault at Mobile Bay got under way, with Gen. Canby coming up to Spanish Fort on the east side of the bay. Brig. Gen. R. L. Gibson's 2,800 men had little hope of holding against Canby's 32,000 without some immediate help—and none was in sight.

Grant and Lincoln were conferring at City Point. Lincoln took the railroad to the Petersburg lines, where he walked over the battlefield at Ft. Stedman.

An 1865 photograph of a bomb-proof shelter at Fort Stedman, near Petersburg, Va.

MARCH 26 SUNDAY

Sheridan's cavalry crossed the James River and headed towards Grant's position at Petersburg. This provided Grant with about 15,000 aggressive cavalry, and an even more aggressive commander. Lincoln was on hand to watch the long lines of blue cavalry cross the river and move on west. Sheridan remained at City Point to confer with Grant on further movements, and Lincoln watched the troops review.

Lee was getting ready to evacuate Petersburg and move west, hoping to join with Johnston in North Carolina.

At Mobile Bay, the Federals began their approach to Spanish Fort, which provoked heavy skirmishing.

MARCH 27 MONDAY

At City Point, Sherman arrived from North Carolina, taking a fast steamer from Wilmington. Admiral Porter also came in from Wilmington for the conference with the President. Upon arrival, both Sherman and Porter called on the President and spent the evening socializing.

MARCH 28 TUESDAY

At City Point, most of the major players in the game were present for a conference. President Lincoln, Generals Grant and Sherman and Admiral D. D. Porter all attended the conference aboard the *River Queen*. Lincoln stressed his desire to bring the war to a speedy close and with as little loss of life as possible. A rather lenient policy was to be followed at the end of hostilities. When the conference closed, Porter sent Sherman back to New Bern, N.C., aboard the fast steamer USS *Bat*. Sherman was to rejoin his troops, which were located only 125 miles straight-line distance from City Point.

In western North Carolina, Stoneman's cavalry was moving slowly down the railroad into the interior of the state, clearing pockets of resistance and meeting many strong Union supporters along the way.

Wilson, in Alabama, had a skirmish at Elyton on his way to Selma and an "appointment" with Forrest.

MARCH 29 WEDNESDAY

Lincoln remained at City Point with Grant, awaiting developments. Sherman returned to North Carolina to begin his drive on Raleigh.

At Petersburg, the Appomattox campaign began with the movement of Grant's army to the southwest and Sheridan's large cavalry force towards Dinwiddie C.H. Lee, trying to defend more than 30 miles of entrenchments, was running out of men for the battles. The whole purpose of the Union movement was to force Lee out of his entrenchments and into the open, where he could be defeated by the larger Union force.

MARCH 31 FRIDAY

As the rain ended southwest of Petersburg, Sheridan put in motion his large force of cavalry and infantry towards Dinwiddie C.H., on the Confederate right flank. Lee had about 10,000 men against more than 50,000 Federals on the western Confederate lines. The Confederates initially drove Sheridan back, but not for long. At night, Pickett realized that Warren's Fifth Corps and Sheridan's mix of cavalry and infantry was too strong for him, so he withdrew to Five Forks. Humphrey's Second Corps repulsed an attack at Hatcher's Run and held without difficulty.

∞ APRIL 1865 ∞

APRIL BEGAN WITH the leafing of the trees in Virginia and the smell of the earth awakening. Deeper in the ravaged South, those remaining in the path of Sherman's "bummers" looked forward to a lean and hungry spring, until a crop could be harvested. Both armies were tired, bloodied and weary of the whole idea of battle. Most of the soldiers only looked forward to the end of the conflict and their return home.

At Mobile, Ala., Major Gen. Canby had Spanish Fort under siege and the city only awaited the sure outcome—surrender. Sherman was back in North Carolina after his visit to City Point, and he was ready to continue the offensive against Johnston's army.

Grant, encouraged by Sheridan's success over the past few days, ordered an all-out assault on Lee's right flank, hoping to smash through Lee's lines.

APRIL 1 SATURDAY

Today, Lee's right flank finally caved in under overwhelming numbers. Grant ordered an assault on the lines for the following morning, and all night the artillery thundered in preparation. Ft. Sedgewick's heavy guns belched forth to sustain its name of "Fort Hell." Lee withdrew from Petersburg during the night.

Jefferson Davis wrote Gen. Lee that the Confederate President had made little progress raising Negro troops and that the distrust in both military and civil circles was embarrassing.

Newspaper accounts:

Petersburg, Va.: It is believed that the enemy is still at Dinwiddie Court House. Thursday afternoon General Fitz Lee attacked and dislodged a division of Sheridan's cavalry from a position it had taken between the plank road and Southside Railroad, and drove the Yankees some distance. . . . Our lines are secure against all attacks of the enemy. On the whole, all goes well with us, and ere long we hope to be able to chronicle a glorious victory for our arms and a crushing defeat to the enemy.

Richmond, Va.: The weather is cool and pleasant. Excited couriers have arrived from off the line of the Southside Railroad and report the Yankees are fighting their way through our lines, and their numbers as so great that we cannot much longer hold Petersburg.

The fall and evacuation of Richmond in April of 1865, as envisioned by Currier & Ives

The numbers of Virginians reported absent from their regiments without leave, will, this morning, exceed fifty thousand. What can this mean? . . . News reaches us tonight that General Pickett has lost control of his troops at Five Forks, and that the Yankees are gradually moving towards Richmond. It seems that our troops have become discouraged and are easily confused. The Yankee assault on Pickett's Division has completely demoralized it, if reports are true.

APRIL 2 SUNDAY

At 4:40 AM, the Federals advanced in a heavy fog against the Petersburg lines. Little resistance was met; in some cases the Confederate battle line sim-

ply vanished. Along the Boydton Plank Road near Hatcher's Run, Lt. Gen. Ambrose Powell Hill, one of Lee's best generals, was killed. Lee notified Davis that "I think it is absolutely necessary that we should abandon our position tonight. . . ." Lee ordered the evacuation of Petersburg and designated Amelia Court House, 40 miles west, as the concentration point for all units.

At 11 PM President Davis and the Cabinet evacuated Richmond, Mrs. Davis and her party having already gone. Richmond became a study in chaos. Many tried to leave the city, jamming the roads and railroad stations, while others decided to stay and face the enemy. Many openly wept in the streets. At the local state prison, inmates overpowered the guards and escaped to begin looting before leaving

THE BATTLE OF FIVE FORKS

APRIL 1, 1865

Gordon McCabe was adjutant to William Pegram, the "boy" colonel of artillery who was killed during the Battle of Five Forks.

April 1st [1865]. Had nothing to eat, so parched some corn taken from the horses' feed. Henry Lee, an old University friend of ours and Ass't Adj't Gen'l Payne's Brigade, afterwards sent us some meat and bread. At 10 o'clk, we put 3 guns, 1 of Ellett's and Early's section, in position in the centre, and Ellett's other 3 on the right commanding a field. Soon afterwards the enemy's cavalry appeared in front of our right at the distance of 800 yds. We could plainly see them and their pennons flying in the wind. We opened at once with our guns. I told one of the gunners to fire on their colours, on which they were forming. He made a splendid shot, bursting a shell just in front of the colours. The whole line fell back into the woods, but their skirmishers occupied the yard of the Gillem House, and we continued to give them an occasional shot. Skirmishing now broke out in the centre and Col. P[egram] and myself rode down to our guns there. The skirmishing was quite heavy, and Col. ordered Lt. Early to dismount, but he wouldn't, so I wouldn't. We fired a few rounds and the skirmishing soon died out. Col. and myself went back to the right, where we expected the attack to be made. We lay down at the foot of a tree, as everything was now quiet, and he soon fell asleep.

The Battle of Five Forks, depicted in this 1880s print by Kurz & Allison, was fought in Dinwiddie County, Va., on April 1, 1865. It pitted Maj. Gen. Sheridan's Union forces against Maj. Gen. Pickett's weakening Confederate army; some call it "the Waterloo of the Confederacy."

Captured Confederate soldiers after the Battle of Five Forks

At about 4½ the enemy attacked him, and we mounted and rode rapidly to the centre. When we reached our guns the enemy were only 30 yds. from them, and the infantry fire terrific beyond anything I have ever seen. We were the only mounted officers at that point. The officers, Lts. Hollis and Early, were as cool as on parade, and the men were serving their guns with a precision and rapidity beyond all praise. Pickett's Divn. were fighting well too. We had not been in the battery very long, when Col. P. riding between Lt. Early's guns reeled out of his saddle, shot through his left arm and left side. He cried out, "Oh, Gordon, I'm mortally wounded, take me off the field." His last order was, "Fire your canister low." I put him on a stretcher, and he took my hand and gave me a message for his mother and sisters. He begged me to remain with him, wh. I intended anyhow to do. When I got him to the ambulance, our skirmishers were falling back, square in our rear, and a line of battle pressing them. We were now completely enveloped, our left having been turned and the enemy in our rear. Our guns were carried within 3 minutes, Lt. Early killed and Lt. Hollis captured and the whole line rolled up.

The rout now became general, with the exception of Corse's Brigade, which had not been heavily engaged. This brigade opened to the right and left and let the rout pass through, and then closed up and came off with their integrity of organization unimpaired. I took Col. in my arms and made the ambulance drive between 2 parallel lines-of-battle of the enemy for 4 or 5 hundred yds. I carried him to Ford's Depot on S.S.R.R. about 10 miles from the field. While in the ambulance we prayed together and he was perfectly resigned to die. At about 10 o'clk we reached Ford's and I obtained a bed for him at Mr. Pegram's. I had given him morphine in small quantities until he was easier, and he soon fell into a doze. The enemy advanced on the place about 12 o'clk, and I was left alone with him. I sent off our sabers, horses, spurs, etc. as I felt sire that we w'd be captured. I shall never forget that night of watching. I could only pray. He breathed heavily through the night, and passed into a stupor. I bound up his wounds as well as I knew how and moistened his lips with water. At about Sunday morning April 2nd, he died as gently as possible.

Brig. Gen. Frederick Winthrop was killed during the Battle of Five Forks.

the city. Confederate Secretary of the Navy Mallory directed that the James River Squadron be blown up and the officers and men be transferred to Gen. Lee's forces, which were evacuating the capital. Mallory left Richmond in the party with President Davis and the Cabinet. Rear Admiral Semmes, CSN, outfitted his men with arms and field equipment, and then had the crews of the CSS *Virginia No. 2*, *Fredericksburg* and *Richmond* burn and sink their ships south of Richmond, near Drewry's Bluff. Semmes then loaded his men aboard wooden ships and returned to Richmond, watching the explosions of the ironclads left at Drewry's Bluff. Upon arriving at Richmond, the wooden ships were fired and set adrift in the James River. The naval crews, lacking transportation west, found a locomotive and several cars which carried them to Danville. Semmes was appointed a Brigadier General in the Confederate Army and given the task of defending Danville, a command he held until Lee's surrender at Appomattox.

At Selma, Ala., the mighty Nathan Bedford Forrest had finally been beaten. This "wizard of the saddle" was finally overcome by superior numbers and a lack of maneuvering space. Forrest and some of his men escaped, leaving the Federals with 2,700 prisoners, 40 guns and a large store of supplies.

APRIL 3 MONDAY

The Confederate government and the army set fire to the business district of Richmond, the bridges, military stores that could not be evacuated and the tobacco warehouses. By the time the Federals arrived the fires were fairly out of control, despite their efforts.

Federal troops entered Richmond. Major Atherton H. Stevens, Jr., of Massachusetts raised the first Union flag over the Capitol building. Major Gen. Godfrey Weitzel accepted the surrender of the city at 8:15 AM at the City Hall. Richmond, although ablaze, was fairly won.

In Petersburg, Union troops entered the city. No mass destruction occurred here, things being quite orderly. President Lincoln, after a conference with Gen. Grant, reviewed the troops passing through the city.

Union newspaper accounts:

Washington, D.C.: The news of the fall of Richmond came upon the Capital shortly after breakfast, and while all were awaiting official bulletins that should announce the renewal of the fighting. It ran from mouth to mouth and from street to street, till within ten minutes the whole town was out, and for a wonder Washington was in a state of old-fashioned excitement such as it has not experienced since the memorable second Bull Run battle. . . .

Boston, Mass.: Bells are pealing, salutes firing and flags flying everywhere, and our citizens are in the highest state of jubilee over the fall of Richmond.

APRIL 4 TUESDAY

Today, escorted by a small naval party of ten men, President Lincoln and Rear Admiral Porter entered Richmond about noon. The President and escort walked to the Confederate White House, where Lincoln toured the former home of Jefferson Davis, taking time to sit at his desk.

Lee retreated towards Amelia Court House, with Sheridan in hot pursuit. Sheridan's cavalry occupied Jetersville on the Danville Railroad south and west of Amelia Court House, thereby blocking the use of the railroad by the Confederates.

President Davis was in Danville on his way south. In Alabama, Tuscaloosa was lost to Brig. Gen. James H. Wilson's cavalry.

Union newspaper accounts:

Washington, D.C.: Mrs. Lincoln received a dispatch from the President to-day, dated as follows: "From Jefferson Davis's late residence at Richmond."

New York City: This morning's *Tribune* contains the following editorial: RICHMOND IS OURS! . . . It might have been ours long ago. It could have been taken with little loss by the tens of thousands whom Gen. Scott persistently held idle and useless around Washington throughout May and June, 1861. It might easily have been taken by McClellan in the spring of 1862, had that illustrious professor of the art How Not To Do It really and zealously tried. It might have been taken, but was not, for God's time had not yet come. At last, that time *has* come, and millions joyfully echo "RICHMOND IS OURS!"

APRIL 5 WEDNESDAY

Lee and the Army of Northern Virginia arrived at Amelia Court House to find that the expected supplies were not there. Sheridan's cavalry was to Lee's front at Jetersville, and the Danville Railroad to Farmville was not usable to bring supplies from Lynchburg. Sheridan, restrained by Meade, waited. In Richmond, Lincoln came back to the city to confer with John A. Campbell and to make a statement that peace was possible only through the reestablishment of Federal authority throughout the South. Lincoln returned to City Point, where he learned that Secretary of State Seward had been injured in a carriage accident that day.

APRIL 6 THURSDAY

Lt. Gen. Richard S. Ewell's entire corps was captured today at the Battle of Saylor's Creek—the last battle between the fabled Army of Northern Virginia and the Army of the Potomac. The last to surrender was the Naval Brigade from Drewry's Bluff, commanded by Commodore John R. Tucker, CSN, who gave his

This photograph of Richmond in April of 1865, taken after it had fallen to Federal forces, shows the Confederate Capitol in the background. A soldier stands in the foreground, near a cannon barrel and cannonballs. The photograph was taken by Andrew J. Russell from the south side of the canal basin.

sword in surrender to Lt. Gen. J. Warren Keifer. Years later, Keifer returned the sword to Tucker.

Union newspaper accounts:

Washington, D.C.: The War Department has been perfectly inundated with applications for passes to visit Richmond, from parties having friends or property there, curiosity seekers and tobacco or cotton speculators. . . .

To-day's City Point boat brought up the band of the Fourteenth Virginia. They numbered twenty-seven pieces, and deserted to us last Sunday. They have been playing "Yankee Doodle," "Star Spangled Banner" and the like in our streets to their own and our citizens' extreme delight.

APRIL 7 FRIDAY

Grant wrote Lee:

The result of the last week must convince you of the hopelessness of further resistance on the part of the Army of Northern Virginia in this struggle. I feel that it is so, and regard it as my duty to shift from myself the responsibility of any further effusion of blood, by asking of you the surrender of that portion of the C. S. Army known as the Army of Northern Virginia.

Lee declined politely, but asked of "the terms you will offer on condition of its [the Army of Northern Virginia] surrender."

APRIL 8 SATURDAY

Spanish Fort and Ft. Alexis, the two key defenders of Mobile, surrendered on this date. The fate of Mobile was sealed.

In Virginia, the road to Lynchburg, passing through Appomattox Court House, was filled with Lee's legions. Trailing closely behind was Meade's Army of the Potomac and the relentless Grant. Sheridan was to the south and in front of Lee,

between him and Lynchburg. Lee refused a general engagement with Meade regardless of the unremitting skirmishing between the two armies. Sheridan had seized the supplies at Appomattox intended for Lee, along with the supply trains from Lynchburg. Grant was at Farmville and received the letter from Lee of the previous day. Grant replied, "Peace being my great desire, there is but one condition I would insist upon, namely that the men and officers surrendered shall be disqualified from taking up arms again against the Government of the United States until properly exchanged." Lee replied later in the afternoon that "I did not intend to propose the surrender of the Army of Northern Virginia, but to ask the terms of your proposition." Lee still indicated a willingness to talk to Grant.

In the evening Lee held a final council of war. It was decided to try a breakthrough to Johnston.

Barber, Sgt., Co. C, 15th Illinois Volunteer Infantry, Pocotaligo, S.C., wrote:

There was a mutiny in the detachment of the 15th corps to-day occasioned by Colonel Henry arresting and tying up hand and foot a soldier belonging to said corps for disobeying orders by firing off his gun without leave. A squad of twenty men marched up to headquarters and the sergeant in command boldly walked up to Colonel Henry and demanded the prisoner's release. Colonel Henry then went to the door and ordered the others to stack arms which they refused to do. Colonel Henry then drew his revolver and told them he would shoot every one unless they obeyed. So the twenty men were cowed by the determined manner of the Colonel. They were all immediately arrested.

Newspaper account:

Richmond, Va.: All the hospitals of Richmond have been taken possession of by the military authorities and are used for the care and comfort equally of the Union and

Confederate sick and wounded. A number of Confederate surgeons left in the city have been paroled to attend to the Confederate sick and wounded. More than half of General Pickett's Division has been brought in or captured, and the country between Richmond and Amelia county is said to be full of Confederate soldiers, nearly all of them Virginians, making their way to their homes. The Castle is used as a receptacle for citizen prisoners, of whom quite a number are gathered there.

APRIL 9 SUNDAY

Generals Lee and Grant met at Appomattox Court House for the purpose of the surrender of the Army of Northern Virginia. After the surrender in the McLean house, Lee returned to his disheartened troops, and Grant notified Washington of his action. Lincoln, returning to Washington from City Point, learned of the surrender that evening when he landed at Washington. The celebration was riotous throughout the North, as the news reached the cities and hamlets that had endured four long years of war.

APRIL 10 MONDAY

At Appomattox Court House, the Union forces, working with their Confederate counterparts, began preparing the lists of troops for parole. Jefferson Davis left Danville, Va., for Greensborough, N.C., by train, hoping to escape the Union

Robert E. Lee surrendered to Ulysses S. Grant on April 9, 1865, at this house in Appomattox, Va. It belonged to grocer Wilmer McLean, a slave owner and retired major in the Virginia militia.

cavalry under Stoneman, which was coming from the west. Sherman's army went on the road again, heading north.

With a saddened heart, Lee prepared his famous General Order No. 9, which disbanded the Army of Northern Virginia, knowing that he had no choice.

Union newspaper account:

Chattanooga, Tenn.: To-day, at ten o'clock, the gratifying news that Lee has surren-

dered was received at General Stedman's headquarters, creating the wildest excitement. As the news spread the men gathered in crowds and rent the air with the most vociferous cheers.

APRIL 11 TUESDAY

Sherman, moving towards Raleigh, N.C., upon entering Smithfield, learned of Lee's surrender. The Union troops cheered themselves hoarse.

Davis arrived at Greensborough, N.C., with his Cabinet, including John Cabell Breckingridge, former Vice President of the United States, and currently Confederate Secretary of War.

This 1867 print by the lithographers Major & Knapp depicts the surrender at Appomattox. Lee, with white hair and a beard, is seated with his hat on his leg. Grant is also seated with his legs crossed. Among the others portrayed in the scene are George Armstrong Custer, second from left; Philip Sheridan, between Lee and Grant; and George Gordon Meade, standing at Grant's left.

In Mobile, the last two forts offering resistance, Forts Tracy and Huger, surrendered.

Union newspaper account:

Appomattox C.H., Va.: Near the Appomattox, and at the point where Sheridan and Wright achieved their brilliant success of Friday, lay the ruins of army wagons, ambulances, forges, caissons, and the *debris* generally of the Rebel army. On the white canvas cover of an army wagon some wag, possibly a good-natured Johnny, had written in glaring capitals, "WE UNS HAVE FOUND THE LAST DITCH." From the scene presented in the

gorge referred to one might very easily believe that it was the long-vaunted "last ditch" of the expiring "Confederacy."

APRIL 12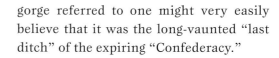

At Appomattox Court House, the formal surrender ceremony took place. Confederate troops marched between two lines of Union troops to lay down their arms and colors. The Federals showed their respect for their former foes, and they watched with a twinge of sadness.

The Mayor of Mobile met the Union military commanders and surrendered the city to prevent it from being destroyed by the ironclad fleet in the bay. The long campaign was over.

At Greensborough, N.C., Davis met with Gen. Joseph E. Johnston and the Confederate Cabinet. Davis indicated that the Union would not negotiate; only full surrender would be allowed. Johnston was authorized to meet with Sherman.

Union newspaper accounts:

Fairfax Station, Va.: Colonel Gamble, commanding the Union forces at this point, received a message from the Rebel General Mosby, in which he says he does not care about Lee's surrender, and that he is determined to fight so long as he has a man left.

Fifth Army Corps, near Appomattox C.H., Va.: General Longstreet's entire corps marched from their camps and formed in line in front of the First Division of this corps and stacked their arms, flags, &c, when they slowly and sorrowfully returned to their camp. It is a sight that cannot be pictured properly to those who have not witnessed it. General Longstreet wore a smile on his face while General Gordon's expression was very different. General Pendleton disliked to give up Lee's artillery, but did so.

Mobile, Ala.: The Stars and Stripes were hoisted on Batteries Porter and Mackintosh at half past ten this morning. The most prominent church steeple also had our flag placed on it at half past two o'clock. General Granger's forces are now in full possession of this city.

APRIL 14 FRIDAY

Today, Major Gen. Robert Anderson, who had surrendered Ft. Sumter on April 14, 1861, raised the same flag that he had lowered on that date over the fort four long, bloody, weary years before.

At 10 PM in Washington, D.C., John Wilkes Booth entered the Presidential box at Ford's Theater and shot Lincoln in the back of the head. Booth leaped to the stage and escaped through the side door of the theater.

APRIL 15 SATURDAY

At 7:22 AM this date President Lincoln died of the wound inflicted to his head. After being shot, he had been carried across the street from the theater to a private home. The national mourning would be deep and lasting. Booth was still at large, having arrived at the home of Dr. Samuel Mudd in rural Maryland. The Cabinet asked Vice President Andrew Johnson to take the oath of office as President.

APRIL 16 SUNDAY

The North went into deep mourning for the fallen President. The North was joined, in most places, by the South. In Washington, Johnson assumed office as President. Mrs. Lincoln was prostrate with grief. Booth arrived at the home of Samuel Cox at Rich Hill in southern Maryland.

Secretary of the Navy Gideon Welles directed that all ships sailing down Chesapeake Bay be searched, as well as all ships leaving any port in the vicinity. All suspicious persons were to be arrested and sent to the Washington Navy Yard for questioning.

APRIL 17 MONDAY

In Washington, the slain President's body was taken to the East Room of the White House, where it would lie in state. Booth and his traveling companion, David Herold, were in the vicinity of Port Tobacco, Md., seeking transportation across the Potomac River.

Jackman, Pvt., "The Orphan Brigade," Washington, Ga., wrote:

On the 17th day of April the "Old Guard" and I took train for Augusta in the morning having in charge several boxes of books, papers, etc. Before starting on our way to Augusta, one of our "telegraph" friends told me that some very bad news had come over the wires, but would not tell me what it was. At 7 o'clock PM we took passenger train for Barnett, 58 miles up towards Atlanta. . . . We got off at Barnett about 2 o'clock at night and slept in a freight car until morning. Barnett is only a station at the junction of the Washington road. We had to lie over until 2 PM the 18th.

Gen'l Hood came down on the train from Washington and took the up train for Atlanta at 12 M. He must of know of Lee's surrender for he looked very "blue." At 2 AM the train left for Washington, and being only 18 miles to run, we soon got there. We immediately went to the building where a detail from our brigade was making saddles. We remained with the detail all the time. . . . I amused myself by writing most of the time. Wrote the first 6 months of my journal from memory and copied from my little memorandum books the notes of each day so far as right after Mar 30th 1862. . . .

The Presidential box at Ford's Theater, where Abraham Lincoln was assassinated by John Wilkes Booth

At last the news came of the surrender of Johnston. We knew then that we had "gone up." One evening the 8th Texas Cavalry—"The Rangers"—came through town making their way west of the Chattahoochee. They "charged" the corn depot at the Court House for forage. They then got the straggling soldiers into a Q.M.'s department and they threw out writing paper, thread, buttons, etc. in the streets by the wagon load. The little negroes and citizens soon had wheel-barrows in the ground to take the plunder home. After the "Rangers" had gone, the Q.M. had a guard to stop the pillage.

Newspaper account:

Army of the Potomac, Burkesville Station, Va.: . . . The announcement of the assassination of Mr. Lincoln and Mr. Seward and his son was received throughout this army with the utmost sorrow. Every man seemed to think it the greatest calamity that could have possibly happened just at this time. . . .

APRIL 18 TUESDAY

Newspaper account:

Raleigh, N.C.: After a two days' conference between Major Gen. Sherman and Major Gen. Joseph E. Johnston, commanding the Rebel forces east of the Mississippi River, with the concurrence of Jefferson Davis, and in the presence and with the advice of Gen. John C. Breckenridge, the whole remaining Rebel army from the Potomac to the Rio Grande has been surrendered to the forces of the United States. . . . Gen. Johnston expresses deep and apparently sincere sorrow and much concern at the assassination of President Lincoln, in which he was joined by each Confederate officer present. Gen. Johnston regards it as the most terrible blow yet inflicted upon the Confederate cause and the Southern people, and seems deeply to deplore the event, coming as it does upon the close of this great struggle.

APRIL 19 WEDNESDAY

Amid tolling bells and the booming of the minute guns in Washington, Lincoln's funeral was held and the body moved in a procession to the Rotunda of the Capitol, where it would be viewed by thousands of mourners.

President Davis's party arrived at Charlotte, N.C., where it would remain until the 26th. Gen. Wade Hampton of South Carolina suggested to Davis that the presidential party move west of the Mississippi and continue the fight. Nothing was done about this.

Newspaper account:

Washington, D.C.: The great and solemn pageant of removing the remains of the Nation's revered and beloved Chief from the White House to the Capitol is closed. Never was such a scene witnessed where each and every one of the vast throng moved in silent sadness, as if bearing the burden of a personal bereavement. . . .

APRIL 20 THURSDAY

Gen. James H. Wilson's cavalry took Macon, Ga. Arkansas ratified the Thirteenth Amendment.

In Washington, the body of the President was prepared for shipment to Illinois, where it would be interred.

APRIL 21 FRIDAY

The President's funeral train left Washington on a circuitous route to Illinois.

Barber, Sgt., Co. C, 15th Illinois Volunteer Infantry, near Goldsboro, N.C., wrote:

Marched at half past five. The news came today that President Lincoln, Secretary Seward and son have been assassinated,

President Lincoln's funeral procession on Pennsylvania Avenue in Washington, D.C., April 19, 1865

David Herold (left) and Lewis Payne Powell (right) were two of the four co-conspirators in the Lincoln assassination plot who were executed in July of 1865. Powell attempted to assassinate Lincoln's Secretary of State, William Seward, and Seward's son, Frederick Seward, the same night that Booth killed the president.

resulting in the President's death and severely wounding the others. And now, while the nation is rejoicing with unspeakable joy at its deliverance, it is suddenly plunged into the deepest sorrow by the most brutal murder of its loved chief.

We are now continually passing paroled men from Lee's army on their way to their homes, or to where their homes were. Many found blackened ruins instead, and kindred and friends gone, they knew not whither. Oh, how much misery treason and rebellion have brought upon our land!

Newspaper account:

Fauquier, Va.: Mosby's Farewell Address: "Soldiers: I have summoned you together for the last time. The vision we have cherished for a free and independent country has vanished, and that country is now the spoil of a conqueror. I disband your organization in preference to surrendering to our enemies. I am no longer your commander. After an association of more than two eventful years, I part from you with a just pride in the fame of your achievements, and grateful recollections of your generous kindness to myself; and now at this moment of bidding you a final adieu, accept the assurance of my unchanging confidence and regard. Farewell."

APRIL 22 SATURDAY

In rural southern Maryland, Booth and Herold crossed the Potomac, headed south. The train carrying Lincoln's body reached Philadelphia, arriving from Harrisburg.

Secretary of the Navy Welles notified the ships in the Potomac that John W. Booth had been seen near Bryantown on April 15, and that all boats were to be searched to obtain his capture.

Barber, Sgt., Co. C, 15th Illinois Volunteer Infantry, near Goldsboro, N.C., wrote:

> Marched at seven AM towards Goldsboro and turned off on the Raleigh road. Went into camp at nine AM to draw rations. To-day I received the startling and sorrowful intelligence that Milton had escaped from prison, been home, returned to the army and been captured by a band of rebel cavalry while out foraging and brutally murdered in company with four of his comrades. One escaped and brought the news to camp. In consequence of this intelligence, my spirits are much depressed to-day. I have a faint hope that the information is incorrect. I will soon know. . . .

APRIL 23 SUNDAY

Secretary Welles ordered the ships on the Mississippi to search all vessels for President Jefferson Davis and his party to prevent their escape west. Rear Admiral S. P. Lee, commander of the Mississippi Squadron, took immediate action to put the search operation into effect.

Newspaper accounts:

> *Vicksburg, Miss.*: Eight thousand Andersonville prisoners are here getting ready to return to their homes.

> *Knoxville, Tenn.*: Among the trophies of Stoneman's expedition are twelve battle flags and banners, one old United States flag found in the house of a loyal citizen of Salisbury. The poisonous pen, where many unfortunate Union prisoners pined their lives away, was burned to the ground. A few Union prisoners were found, skeletons of their former selves. Almost all of them died on the way to Knoxville. They preferred rather to die under the Stars and Stripes than to be left in the loathsome hospitals of Salisbury.

APRIL 24 MONDAY

At Port Conway, Va., Booth and Herold crossed the Rappahannock in their escape from Federal troops. Lincoln's body was now at New York, where it lay in state.

In North Carolina, Grant met Sherman and told him that his (Sherman's) terms given to Johnston were not acceptable to President Johnson. Johnston was to be notified that unless he surrendered unconditionally within 48 hours, hostilities would be resumed.

In Augusta, Ga., Lt. William H. Parker, guardian of the Confederacy archives and treasury, learned that the surrender terms offered to Johnston by Sherman had been rejected by the Federal Government. So, gathering his escort and charges, he departed for Abbeville, S.C., thinking that that would be the most likely place to join President Davis.

The CSS *Webb*, having shaken all pursuers, hoisted the Union flag to half-mast and roared past New Orleans at about midnight going full steam. Federal gunboats fired on her and hit her three times without serious damage. She continued on downriver towards the Gulf.

Newspaper accounts:

> *Selma, Ala.* (from the *Daily Rebel*): The people of the North are now reaping the

President Lincoln's assassin, John Wilkes Booth (1838–65)

riated by tyranny and driven to despair by want, bursts the bonds of law, and a reign of terror and of ruin is established. . . .

Chattanooga, Tenn.: The Atlanta papers know of the assassination of President Lincoln, but make no comment. They deny the surrender of Lee's Army, and say he was all right on the 16th inst.

APRIL 25 TUESDAY

Near Bowling Green, Va., Federal cavalry closed in on Booth and Herold at a farm north of the city.

In North Carolina, Johnston asked Sherman to renew negotiations concerning the fate of the Confederate troops under Johnston's command.

Barber, Sgt., Co. C, 15th Illinois Volunteer Infantry, near Raleigh, N.C., wrote:

> Marched at seven AM. Arrived at Raleigh at twelve M. The corps moved from Raleigh at eight o'clock AM in pursuit of Johnson [General Joseph Johnston]. Hostilities were resumed to-day at seven AM. We rested awhile at Raleigh and then set out to join the corps, which we overtook twelve miles from Raleigh. Then each soldier reported to his proper command. I am now with the mounted squad but have not yet got a horse. I found here about fifty of my old comrades of the 14th and 15th veteran battalion and several boys whom I had left in prison.

APRIL 26 WEDNESDAY

At about 2 AM Federal troops surrounded a tobacco barn located on the Garrett farm north of Bowling Green, Va., where Booth and Herold had taken refuge. The commander of the troops, Lt. Col. Everton Conger, called for their surrender. Booth refused; Herold accepted and left the barn. After a standoff of a few hours, Conger ordered the barn set afire to drive Booth out. While the barn was burning, Sgt. Boston Corbett shot Booth, wounding him mortally.

natural and inevitable harvest of crime growing out of the demoralization incident to a state of war. The last dispatches exhibit a most shocking and horrible state of society. The President and his Prime Minister killed by assassins, and the new President and the Secretary of War murdered by a mob which has obtained and holds possession of the Capital of the Nation. Other cities sacked and a great popular revolution against the rulers impending. While their armies are devastating our land, their own downtrodden populace, infu-

Booth died shortly thereafter, on the porch of the Garrett house.

In North Carolina, Johnston and Sherman met to finalize the surrender of all Confederate forces east of the Mississippi. The terms were the same as those signed by Grant and Lee.

Also in North Carolina, President Davis met with his Cabinet in Charlotte and they agreed to try to escape to west of the Mississippi. The Confederate Attorney General, George Davis, left the presidential party and returned to his home.

APRIL 27 THURSDAY

The body of John Wilkes Booth, the assassin of President Lincoln, and the captured David E. Herold were delivered aboard the USS *Montauk* anchored in the Anacostia River near the Washington Navy Yard. An autopsy was performed on Booth's body and positive identification was made. The corpse was then taken to the Washington Arsenal (present site of Ft. McNair), and there buried in a gun box near the Old Capital Prison. Herold was kept aboard the *Montauk*, along with the other suspected conspirators.

On the Mississippi River another tragedy unfolded. The steamer *Sultana* blew up north of Memphis, killing 1,450 of the 2,000 passengers. All but 50 of the dead were former prisoners of war on their way home. The cause of the explosion was never determined. A sad ending for so many who had endured so much.

APRIL 30 SUNDAY

The Lincoln train reached Indianapolis. The eight conspirators in the Lincoln assassination were transferred by boat to the Old Capital Prison for detention and trial. The old prison building is gone, but the building in which the trial was held still stands and is used for government housing.

Outside Mobile, Federal Gen. Canby met Confederate Gen. Richard Taylor to discuss the surrender of all troops in Alabama and Mississippi.

In North Carolina, Sherman's army was on the march north to Washington, D.C. The government requested 50 bakers each from Baltimore, Philadelphia and New York to help with the rations for the troops expected to arrive shortly.

MAY 1865

IT WAS NOW THREE WEEKS SINCE Lee and Grant met at Appomattox Court House in Virginia to set in motion the disbanding of the Confederate States Army. Much had changed in this short period of time. A new President was at the helm, the smoke had cleared from the battlefields and the troops were on their way home.

MAY 1 MONDAY

In Washington, President Andrew Johnson named nine army officers to head the military tribunal which would sit in judgment on the accused conspirators of the assassination. This was to be a strictly military trial, it having been ruled that the conspirators would not be tried in a civil court.

On the roads of Virginia and North Carolina, long blue lines of Federal troops marched towards Washington and home. The step seemed more sprightly, somehow, heading home.

Newspaper account:

> *Sherman's Troops, Faiport, N.C.*: Another fine day for marching, starting at five in the morning, by three o'clock in the afternoon the troops were in camp at Fairport, having marched twenty-two miles without experiencing more than usual fatigue, owing to the excellence of the roads. . . .

The CSS *Shenandoah*, Lt. Waddell, unaware that the war was over, had ranged to the Bering Sea in search of whalers since leaving Lea Harbor, Ponape, Caroline Islands.

MAY 2 TUESDAY

Newspaper accounts:

Twentieth Army Corps, near Williamston, N.C.: It is painful to be obliged to record the lawless conduct of our soldiers at any time, particularly it is so when that conduct is utterly without extenuation. Despite the stringent orders issued in regard to the peaceable behavior of our troops upon their march to Richmond, some of the soldiers both of the Army of Georgia and the Army of [the] Tennessee have been permitted to straggle from their commands, and have committed depredations upon the inhabitants much to be deplored. It would seem that the roving spirits fostered by army life cannot at once be chastened into a domestic one by the white-winged angel of peace. . . .

Robertson County, Tex.: Brig. Gen. William P. Hardeman's Brigade assembled in mass this evening, and, with General Hardeman in the chair, resolved, among other things, that in spite of the reverses to the cis-Mississippi armies, they would not abandon the struggle until the right of self-government is fully established. . . .

MAY 3 WEDNESDAY

In Illinois, the funeral train carrying President Lincoln had finally reached its destination at Springfield. The country lawyer who had risen to such fame and had suffered so much for the Union was home at last.

This locomotive, named the *Nashville*, was one of twenty engines that pulled Lincoln's funeral train from Washington, D.C., to Springfield, Ill., a distance of 1,666 miles. The *Nashville* served its tour of duty between Cleveland and Columbus, Ohio.

President Davis and his escort crossed the Savannah River and moved to Washington, Ga. Confederate Secretary of State Judah Benjamin resigned his post and left the presidential party, headed for England.

Confederate Secretary of the Navy Mallory resigned from the Confederate cabinet citing the needs of his family. Davis, with regret, accepted the resignation and Mallory departed for LaGrange, Ga., where his family was waiting.

Newspaper account:

Fifth Army Corps, Richmond, Va.: The old pine woods south of Manchester are luminous to-night with the camp fires of the returning veterans of the Fifth Army Corps. To-morrow they will be gratified with their first view of the city for which they so long and so nobly battled. Their first view did I say? No, for in the long column are scores to whom the town will only serve to bring back to memory the long days and longer nights of privation and suffering endured in the former prison dens of the enemy. Following the Fifth will march the Second Corps, both on their way to Alexandria, where they will enjoy for a season the rest and relaxation to which they are so eminently entitled by their arduous service in the field. The battle fields of Cold Harbor, North Anna, Spotsylvania and Fredericksburg will probably be passed on their way to their point of destination.

MAY 4 THURSDAY

Amid much pomp and ceremony, the remains of the sixteenth President of the United States, Abraham Lincoln, were interred at Springfield.

President Davis and his escort continued south through Georgia, seeking a way to escape west.

Newspaper account:

Citronville, Ala:. "Lieutenant General Taylor has this day surrendered to me with the forces under his command, on substantially the same terms as those accepted by General Lee. E. R. S. Canby."

MAY 5 FRIDAY

Sherman's troops continued northward, looking forward to the final Grand Review in Washington. The countryside seemed filled with soldiers moving in all directions. The paroled Rebels were heading home by any means at their disposal, slowly at times, and with sadness.

MAY 6 SATURDAY

The War Department, in accordance with an Executive Order, named Major Gen. David Hunter to head the commission to try the assassination conspirators. Brig. Gen. Joseph Holt was named judge advocate of the commission.

In Georgia, President Davis continued moving south, reaching the town of Sandersville.

Jackman, Pvt., "The Orphan Brigade," Washington, Ga., wrote:

The next evening, May 6th, the brigade came to Washington. As they marched through the streets coming in from one direction, all armed and their flags flying, they passed the 13th Tenn. Federal Cavalry coming from the opposite direction. It looked strange not to see them commence shooting at each other. I worked until ten o'clock at night getting up the proper papers for the regiment to be paroled. The Federal Provost Marshal worked nearly all night paroling us. . . . The next day all the brigade was paroled and we "broke up housekeeping." Each fellow being allowed to wander off as his inclinations led him, with his horse, saddle and bridle.

MAY 7 SUNDAY

Barber, Sgt., Co. C, 15th Illinois Volunteer Infantry, Petersburg, Va., wrote:

Marched at five AM. Moved 12 miles and halted for rest and refreshments. After dinner moved to within two miles of Petersburg and went into camp. For the past day we have been on the tramping and fighting ground of the Potomac army. All along the road is strewed evidence of severe fighting. Our present camping ground is dotted as far as the eye can reach with spots where was camped the vast Army of the Potomac, the brave but unfortunate army which has fought so bravely, suffered so much and accomplished so little. From the Potomac across the Rappahannok to beyond the James River, their bodies lie slumbering in an unbroken sleep, never more to waken to active life, but the cause for which they sacrificed their lives will live and grow, until its splendor eclipses the whole world. . . .

MAY 8 MONDAY

Newspaper account:

Richmond, Va.: Dick Turner, the noted turnkey of Libby Prison, is securely locked up in the most dismal, subterranean dungeon of that place of torture. There is no pity felt for him in Richmond. He is as pale as leprosy, his beard whitening, his deficient teeth ajar and his eyes full of terror. He is now as mean and cringing in his behavior as, in power he was insolent and cruel. When turnkey, he shot men dead with a revolver, who came to the windows for air and light, kicked and knocked down others, and took delight in augmenting the untold miseries of the poor prisoners under his charge. He has heard, in his loathsome cell, that the soldiers have decreed his death so soon as they are fully assured of his identity, and his pleadings for mercy are presented to all who come near him; but he pleads to hearts of stone.

MAY 9 TUESDAY

In an effort to bring Virginia back into the Union as rapidly as possible, President Andrew Johnson recognized Francis H. Pierpont as Governor.

In Arkansas, Brig. Gen. M. Jeff Thompson was considering surrender of his Rebel forces.

In Washington, D.C., at the Old Capital Prison, the trial of the assassination conspirators began.

In Georgia, President Davis met his wife on the Oconee River near Dublin. This was their first meeting since Varina and the children were sent from Richmond before its fall.

MAY 10 WEDNESDAY

Today, President Andrew Johnson officially declared that armed resistance to the Federal Government was at an end.

In Spencer County, Ky., the infamous William Clarke Quantrill was fatally wounded near Taylorsville, and was removed to Louisville for treatment, where he later died. This effectively closed a long and bloody chapter of guerrilla warfare motivated more by criminal than patriotic instincts. The legacy of Quantrill's band of marauders would long haunt the hills of Missouri.

Near Irwinville, Ga., the Fourth Michigan Cavalry surprised the Jefferson Davis party early in the morning and captured the former President and his escort.

MAY 11 THURSDAY

In Arkansas, Brig. Gen. M. Jeff Thompson surrendered the remainder of his force, ending a short but distinguished career.

MAY 16 TUESDAY

Jefferson Davis and the officials of the late Confederate Government, captured at Irwinville, Ga., on May 10, were taken down the Savannah River

This elaborate allegorical print, created by Morris H. Traubel of Philadelphia around 1861, was published in anticipation of the Union victory over the Confederacy.

THE TRIUMPH.

to Port Royal, where they boarded the *William P. Clyde*, Master John L. Kelly, for Hampton Roads, Va. The Clyde was escorted by the USS *Tuscarora*, Commander James M. Frailey, to Virginia.

MAY 17 WEDNESDAY

Major Gen. Philip H. Sheridan was today assigned to command west of the Mississippi and south of the Arkansas rivers—a very large territory. The appointment did not sit too well with some from the South.

MAY 20 SATURDAY

Former Confederate Secretary of the Navy Mallory was arrested at the home of Benjamin H. Hill in LaGrange, Ga. He was charged with "treason and with organizing and setting on foot piratical expeditions." He was sent to Ft. Lafayette in New York, where he remained until his parole in March 1866.

Barber, Sgt., Co. C, 15th Illinois Volunteer Infantry, Alexandria, Va., wrote:

> Went to the city to-day. The streets were crowded with soldiers from both armies. There was a disposition amongst some to blackguard each other. Alexandria is a city

of ten thousand inhabitants and business is very lively, consequent upon so large an army being there. There are over two hundred thousand troops camped in and around it. . . .

MAY 22 MONDAY

President Johnson removed the blockade from most major Southern ports. Former President Davis was imprisoned at Ft. Monroe, Va.

MAY 23 TUESDAY

Today the Army of the Potomac, after four long years of suffering defeat and then final victory over its old adversary, Gen. Robert E. Lee, marched in its last parade down Pennsylvania Avenue in Washington, D.C. The Grand Review, on its first day, contained seemingly endless lines of blue infantry and artillery and a constant clatter of cavalry as that proud army had its last hurrah. For most it was a day of unbounding joy. For others, it seemed that the ghosts of the thousands of fallen sat sadly in the reviewing stands unable to let the moment go without remembrance.

The Grand Review of the Armies took place on May 23 and 24, 1865. This photograph, by Matthew Brady, shows a unit of cavalry passing by the presidential reviewing stand.

Jackman, Pvt., "The Orphan Brigade," en route home, wrote:

At last, about the latter part of May, learning the railroad between Atlanta and Chattanooga was about done, we bade our friends good-bye and in a carriage came to Union Point, 12 miles, to take the cars. At 1 PM the train for Atlanta came along and we "bounced" it. Eight miles above, at Greensburg, our two other companions came aboard. We got to the ruins of Atlanta late at night and slept under a shade tree until morning.

The next day, finding 60 miles or more of the road not completed, we bargained with a Federal, who had two wagons under his charge, going through to Resaca, to take us over the road. We left Atlanta at 1 PM. Atlanta looked desolate having been burned since I had last seen it. We camped at Marietta at night. The town was also in ruins.

The next day we came as far as Acworth. The day after we passed through Cartersville, on the Etowah, and Cassville, which was in complete ruins. In the evening we got to Addairsville and took the train for Dalton. The road had just been finished to A-ville and we came up on the construction train. The employees seemed disposed to show us favor. We bivouacked near the depot at Dalton for the night—got there about 10 o'clock PM. Cold night. Last time I slept on the ground.

The next morning the train, which was flat cars, left for Chattanooga. Got into Chattanooga at noon. Being quite a number of Confeds along, we could not get transportation that day. At night we put up at the Soldier's Home, "Yank" and "Confed" eating out of the same platter and cracking jokes at each other as though they had never met in many a mortal combat.

The next evening we took train for Nashville and by daylight, or a little after the next morning we were in that city.

Barber, Sgt., Co. C, 15th Illinois Volunteer Infantry, Washington, D.C., wrote:

Cleared off pleasant during the night. Moved camp to-day to the south side of the Potomac in full view of the city of Washington. The Capitol towers up majestically above all the other buildings. We can see the White House, War Department, Washington Monument and Smithsonian. . . .

To-day the army of the Potomac was reviewed by Grant, Meade, President, Secretary of War and other high government officials. The army was dressed in its gayest suit. The soldiers appeared splendid, showing the effects of good discipline and good living. Their step was elastic and guided by a strict military gait, quite different from the free step of Sherman's army.

To-morrow Sherman's army appears upon the stage. Thousands of visitors from all parts of the United States are flocking to the Capital to witness these grand reviews, the largest and most brilliant ever known. The interest is enhanced greatly from the fact that the two rival armies are just fresh from the victorious fields. . . .

MAY 24 WEDNESDAY

It was the second, and last, day of the Grand Review in Washington. Today the men who marched six thousand miles and gained fame as Sherman's "Bummers" would have their day. This was a different army from the one that had marched the day before. The Midwesterners, and most were from that area, had a longer stride that seemed to eat the distance. Their formations were less formal and their uniforms were certainly more ragged. But the hit of the parade was the inclusion of goats, sheep,

cattle, chickens, wagons, carts and all the other "equippage" of the "Bummers" that were in the parade. Sherman's men took pride in being a hard-marching, hard-fighting, independent lot.

Sgt. Barber describes his feelings about the Grand Review. He and his comrades of Sherman's Army would today participate in one of the most splendid parades ever held in Washington. Every veteran who marched in this parade never forgot the feeling of pride, patriotism and comradeship that pervaded the air this day.

Barber, Sgt., Co. C, 15th Illinois Volunteer Infantry, Washington, D.C., wrote:

> The eventful 24th of May dawned bright and beautiful. The heart of every veteran in Sherman's Army beat high in anticipation of the events of the day. We could not doubt our success. The eye of our matchless leader was upon us. . . . Our regiments of recruits were divided off into companies of twenty files each, and veterans placed in each company as right and left guide. The remainder of the veterans did not join us. They were too proud to mingle on this occasion with men who had never smelled gunpowder. We only went at the request of our Colonel to act as guides, so as to make the regiment appear as well as possible. Rollin and I were right and left guide in one company.

> Early in the morning the army commenced crossing Long Bridge and moved towards the Capitol grounds, the 14th and 20th Corps in advance. By ten AM we were all massed on the grounds south of the Capitol, and prepared to march in review. At the command to move, seventy-five thousand men in column, with bands playing, drums beating, and colors flying, in exact order and time to

This photograph, also by Matthew Brady, shows the army of Maj. Gen. Henry W. Slocum passing on Pennsylvania Avenue during the Grand Review of the Armies.

the music, marched down Pennsylvania Avenue, saluting our President and commanders as we passed the reviewing stand. For six long hours the steady tramp, tramp, tramp of Sherman's heroes echoed along Pennsylvania Avenue. The shouts of the multitude rent the air. Garlands of flowers were strewed in our pathway, and blessings showered upon us. Though our attire was not as gay as the Potomac Army, yet we excelled them in appearance. We wore the hard, bronzed visage of war incident upon a march of a thousand miles, fighting day after day, bridging rivers, corduroying swamps that before were deemed impassible. I do not wish to detract from the just merits of the Potomac Army, but the press and public bear me out in saying that Sherman's Army bore off the palm. We marched five miles north and went into camp. This is to be our camp while we remain here. . . .

MAY 25 THURSDAY

Newspaper accounts:

> *New Orleans, La.*: Rebel deserters and escaped prisoners of the Thirty-third Iowa Regiment just arrived from Texas, report that the Union prisoners confined at Tyler, Tex., were allowed to escape in large numbers, the guards saying that, when they are all gone, they will have nothing to do, and then can go home. The interior of Texas is in a terribly disorganized condition. A telegraph line is to be constructed from San Antonio to Austin to Matamoras.

> *Boston, Mass.*: The United States gunboat *Tuscarora*, from Fort Monroe, with Alexander H. Stephens and Postmaster Reegan on board, arrived below this port this morning, and anchored in the Narrows. The Rebel party will be lodged in Fort Warren to-day.

MAY 26 FRIDAY

Today in New Orleans Confederate Lt. Gen. Simon Bolivar Buckner, who surrendered Ft. Donelson to Grant in February 1862, met representatives of Major Gen. Canby to surrender the last significant army of the Confederacy. Gen. Jo Shelby, refusing to surrender, would take some of his men and go to Mexico.

MAY 27 SATURDAY

President Johnson ordered that most political prisoners held by military authorities be released.

MAY 29 MONDAY

General amnesty and pardon was granted with a few exceptions by President Johnson to all persons who directly, or indirectly, participated in "the existing rebellion."

Jackman, Pvt., "The Orphan Brigade," home at last, wrote:

> This was May 29th. We were all marched—not under guard—to the Provost Marshal's office and there informed that the Kentuckians could not go home unless first taking the amnesty oath and we were "galvanized." I did not care to wait for government transportation by water, so that evening, at 3 o'clock I took the train for Louisville having to pay my passage and at 7 o'clock at night got off at Bardstown Junction. Rather than wait until the following evening for the train, I immediately started on foot up the railroad and got home about 10 AM the 30th of May, having been absent 3 years, 8 months, and 4 days.

MAY 30 TUESDAY

Barber, Sgt., Co. C, 15th Illinois Volunteer Infantry, Washington, D.C., wrote:

> Warm and pleasant. Went to Washington to-day and visited the Capitol. . . . The most sacred relic I saw was the original Declaration of Independence with the original signatures attached. The marble statue of Tecumseh represented in the agonies of death is splendid. . . . I next visited the Patent Office where equal admiration enchained me. Here are laid up in the archives of the nation many ancient relics of our country. Here Washington's personal and military effects are deposited. . . . Here is Franklin's original printing press and the coat that Jackson wore at the battle of New Orleans . . . a model of all patents ever issued at the Patent Office. . . . I next visited the Treasury and War Department and White House, each of which was full of interest to a stranger. . . . I intend to visit the Smithsonian Institution and Vernon next. The talk is now that we will be sent to Louisville soon and from there to our respective States to be mustered out.

EPILOGUE

I**T WAS DONE**. The South had been defeated, the Union restored, and it was time to go home to other pursuits and to get on with life.

At the camps outside Washington, in neighboring Virginia and Maryland, the last muster rolls of the Union troops who had participated in the Grand Review were prepared by the company 1st Sergeants and attested to by the Commanding Officers. Discharge papers were prepared, accounts settled, and the soldiers began their journey home, for the first time in a long time unencumbered by muskets and cartridge boxes. A cadre remained to complete the housekeeping—compiling the records, preparing them for storage, etc., work that would go on for months.

But the war didn't just end with the Grand Review. Many armed troops were still in the field, and much was to be done to gather these men in and effect their surrender. This epilogue summarizes the final stages of the war.

JUNE 1865

The political prisoners held at various facilities around the country were released and sent home. Some had been incarcerated for up to two years.

The British government officially withdrew belligerency rights from the Confederate government.

In Galveston, Tex., Confederate Gen. E. Kirby Smith officially surrendered, accepting the terms outlined in New Orleans on May 26th. On June 3rd, the Southern naval forces on the Red River officially surrendered.

President Andrew Johnson appointed provisional governors to the various states of the late Confederacy.

On the last day of June, the Lincoln conspirators were found guilty by the military court.

Sgt. Lucius Barber, Co. D, 15th Illinois Volunteer Infantry, had reenlisted for a period of three years on his last reenlistment, believing that he would be discharged at the end of the war.

Barber, since the Grand Review, had been sightseeing in Washington and resting up after his long march from South Carolina. On June 8th, Barber left Washington for Illinois, passing through Harpers Ferry on the Baltimore and Ohio Railroad to Parkersburg, W.Va., where he boarded the steamer *G.R. Gilman* on the 10th. With many stops along the way, he passed Cincinnati on the 12th, and arrived in Louisville with his unit on the 15th. On the 20th he was paid up to date, receiving $369.00.

On the 21st, Barber's unit was on the march again, this time for St. Louis. The reaction to this unexpected event was rather angry:

> Marched at 5 AM. Took the transport *Camilla* for St. Louis. Are just shoving off from shore and slowly dropping down stream. This sudden move still remains a mystery to us. Some think we are going to be mustered out. Some think that we are going to some distant post to do garrison duty. We veterans cannot believe that the government will be guilty of so great an injustice as still keeping us in the service after we have so faithfully performed our part of the contract.

The government, considering that they had at least another year to go on their enlistments, was going to put them to work on the frontier. This was finally disclosed to the troops on June 25th, at which time the reaction became even angrier:

> At St. Louis. Our astonishment and anger knew no bounds when we found out that we were to be sent to the frontier to fight Indians. Our brigade commander, General Stolbrand, was the author of this outrage. The recruits had no reason to complain as they were bound to service one year

The execution of the Lincoln assassination conspirators, July 7, 1865

if their services were required, but we had fulfilled our part with the government to the very letter. Symptoms of mutiny began to manifest itself. A large number of the veterans took French leave, determined not to go. To quiet the tumult, orders were issued to grant furloughs—twenty per cent of all enlisted men, but about ninety per cent were given to the veterans. I obtained a furlough without the asking....

Sgt. Barber went to Pennsylvania to attend a wedding at Titusville, where he arrived on the 29th.

JULY 1865

On a hot and humid summer day, July 7th, the assassination conspirators were hanged at the Old Capital Prison in Washington.

Sgt. Barber, arriving home in Illinois from the wedding in Pennsylvania, found that he and his friend Rollin had received papers from their Company Commander which be useful in getting them mustered out.

On July 24th, Hillery Boss in Illinois wrote a letter to the parents of Julius Allen in North Carolina concerning the death of the Allens' son. Allen, originally from Salisbury, N.C., had been in Asheville, N.C., at the beginning of the war and had walked almost all the way to Illinois to enlist in the Union Army. He had served with the 10th Illinois Cavalry in the western campaigns, but never returned to Illinois. The letter stated that "he got drowned in the Mississippi river. I suppose his body was not recovered. To my knowledge, he was drowned between the 26th of April, 1863 and June 12, 1863."

On the 27th of July, Barber was really no closer to solving the problem of getting mustered out than he had been:

We went to Springfield to see if we could not procure our discharge, but did not succeed. I went to Colonel Oaks, chief mustering officer for the State, and presented my descriptive list, but my furlough ordered me to report back to the regiment and he could do nothing for us. I then went to Adjutant-General Hayne and he told me to go to the commandant of the post and if I could induce him to give me an order for a discharge, I would be all right, but he would not do it, so I had no other resource left but to go back to the regiment or return home. I chose the latter alternative, and in company with five of my comrades, I returned on the evening train. I helped father do his harvesting and then Rollin and I started for the regiment.

SEPTEMBER 1865

At long last, Barber, our final protagonist, was mustered out after many trials and tribulations dealing with the bureaucracy.

September 1: Arrived back at Ft. Leavenworth about the 1st of September, and preparations were immediately made to muster us out. I assisted in making out our company's rolls. I had now been promoted to 3d sergeant.

September 15: We were mustered out about the middle of the month and the next day started for Springfield for our pay and final discharge. Our progress over the Hannibal and St. Joseph railroad was very tedious and slow. There was hardly a mile of track but what had been disturbed by the guerrillas during the way and it was not yet repaired.

September 30: On the 30th day of September we received our final pay and discharge. I had worn the livery of Uncle Sam for four years, five months and twenty-seven days. . . . it is with a thankful heart and intense joy that I lay aside the honorable title of *Soldier* and once more enjoy the proud title of *American Citizen,* a subject of the best and truest government on God's earth. Before leaving for home, in company with several of my comrades, I paid a parting visit to the tomb of Lincoln at Oak Ridge Cemetery. We passed within the enclosure and registered our names beside hundreds of thousands of others who had been there before us. We then went to the grated opening of the sepulcher and took one last lingering look at the narrow resting place where sleeps all that is mortal of Lincoln, whose noble heart and mind had guided us through all the dark and bloody years of our Nation's struggle for existence. . . .

Sgt. Lucius W. Barber recorded the mileage he had traveled during his life in the Union Army. In total it came to an incredible 10,897 miles. Lucius Barber died in Riley, Illinois, on March 12th, 1872, at the age of 32 years and 9 months. He succumbed to consumption, believed to have been contracted while a prisoner at Andersonville.

NOVEMBER 1865

On November 6th, the C.S.S. *Shenandoah*, Lt. Waddell, surrendered to British officials at Liverpool, England. The ship would be stripped of its armament and used as a merchant vessel. At the time it was finally sunk, in 1879, it was owned by the Sultan of Zanzibar.

On November 10th, the infamous Capt. Henry Wirz, former commander of the Andersonville Prison, was hanged after a military-commission trial in Washington.

APRIL 1866

President Johnson officially declared that the war was over and the insurrection was at an end.

For most of our protagonists, the closing of the war wrote a final chapter of a great adventure which would be relived time and time again until, at last, the final bugle sounding "Taps" was played over the last survivor. The mists of memory would gradually cloud the scenes of bloody combat until they were as if in a dream, real, but unreal, in their vivid flashes of remembrance. The old men the veterans were to become would recount their stories to thousands of wide-eyed children for two generations. They would meet in reunions to relive the glory and remember the dead. They are, Blue and Gray, a part of the American heritage forever.

IMAGE CREDITS

INDEX

ABOUT THE AUTHOR

Born in 1929, Robert E. Denney served with the U.S. Marines in China and on Guam. In 1950, he entered the Army, serving in the Korean and Vietnam Wars. He was wounded in action in Korea and was awarded the Silver Star, Bronze Star with "V" device, and Purple Heart. Graduating from the Warrant Officer's Flight Program in 1956 as a helicopter pilot, he went on to become an Assistant Project Officer for the testing of low-level navigation systems for helicopters. For his performance during these tests, he was awarded the Army Commendation Medal. For various actions in Vietnam, he was awarded the Distinguished Flying Cross, Bronze Star (OLC), several Air Medals, and another Purple Heart. On retirement in 1967 as a major in the Signal Corps, Denney pursued his lifelong interest in the Civil War, an avocation he attributed to the influence of a high school history teacher who in the early 1940s, "peppered his American History classes with tales he remembered [from his youth] as told by the veterans, and stories of rural Indiana in the late 1800s."

After his years in the military, Denney earned a Master's degree and became a computer systems consultant. Married with four children and three grandchildren, he passed away in 2002 and is buried in Arlington National Cemetery.